"Don't Shoot, G-Men!"

Also by Michael Newton
and from McFarland

Iceman of Brooklyn: The Mafia Life of Frankie Yale (2021)

Boss of Murder, Inc.: The Criminal Life of Albert Anastasia (2020)

The National States Rights Party: A History (2017)

Unsolved Civil Rights Murder Cases, 1934–1970 (2016)

Hate Crime in America, 1968–2013: A Chronology of Offenses, Legislation and Related Events (2014)

White Robes and Burning Crosses: A History of the Ku Klux Klan from 1866 (2014)

The Texarkana Moonlight Murders: The Unsolved Case of the 1946 Phantom Killer (2013)

The Mafia at Apalachin, 1957 (2012)

Chronology of Organized Crime Worldwide, 6000 B.C.E. to 2010 (2011)

The Ku Klux Klan in Mississippi: A History (2010; paperback 2020)

Mr. Mob: The Life and Crimes of Moe Dalitz (2009)

The Ku Klux Klan: History, Organization, Language, Influence and Activities of America's Most Notorious Secret Society (2007; paperback 2014)

Encyclopedia of Cryptozoology: A Global Guide to Hidden Animals and Their Pursuers (2005; paperback 2014)

The FBI and the KKK: A Critical History (2005; paperback 2009)

The FBI Encyclopedia (2003; paperback 2012)

"Don't Shoot, G-Men!"
The FBI Crime War, 1933–1939

Michael Newton

McFarland & Company, Inc., Publishers
Jefferson, North Carolina

Michael Newton died on September 6, 2021, after completing the manuscript for this book.

ISBN (print) 978-1-4766-8440-6
ISBN (ebook) 978-1-4766-4533-9

LIBRARY OF CONGRESS AND BRITISH LIBRARY
CATALOGUING DATA ARE AVAILABLE

Library of Congress Control Number 2021046203

© 2021 Heather Newton. All rights reserved

No part of this book may be reproduced or transmitted in any form or by any means, electronic or mechanical, including photocopying or recording, or by any information storage and retrieval system, without permission in writing from the publisher.

Front cover: Slayers of the outlaw Wilbur Underhill, Jr., on December 30, 1933; (kneeling, left to right) Ralph Colvin, Jacob "Jelly" Bryce; (standing in foreground, left to right) Paul Hanson, Clarence Hurt, Kelly Deadrick (National Archives)

Printed in the United States of America

McFarland & Company, Inc., Publishers
Box 611, Jefferson, North Carolina 28640
www.mcfarlandpub.com

In memory of
Joseph M. Pinkston
(1931–1996)

My conscience doesn't hurt me. I stole from the bankers. They stole from the people. All we did was help raise the insurance rates.—Harry Pierpont, January 1934

They must be exterminated, and they must be exterminated by us.—J. Edgar Hoover, June 1933

Table of Contents

Author's Note — viii
Acknowledgments — ix
Depression-Era Gangs — 1
Preface — 5

1. "A bureaucratic bastard" — 7
2. Public Enemies — 16
3. "Get 'Em Up! Up!" — 45
4. Cops and Robbers — 65
5. Open Season — 76
6. Trials and Errors — 86
7. Shoot on Sight — 114
8. Wanted Dead — 127
9. Melvin Who? — 163
10. Old Creepy — 187
11. Mopping Up — 200
12. Scorched Earth — 219
13. Redacting History — 234

Chapter Notes — 247
Bibliography — 257
Index — 265

Author's Note

Initially unnamed at its unorthodox creation in July 1908, the future Federal Bureau of Investigation labored under four different names through the next three decades. Attorney General George Wickersham christened it the Bureau of Investigation in March 1909. Successor William Mitchell changed that to the U.S. Bureau of Investigation on July 1, 1932, and Homer Cummings tried again on July 1, 1933, renaming it the Division of Investigation. Its present famous name—inspiring the motto "Fidelity, Bravery, Integrity"—was imposed, also by Cummings, on July 1, 1935, effective at the beginning of Fiscal Year 1936. To spare readers from needless confusion, I follow the example of Bureau publicists, established by Don Whitehead in 1956 and continued thereafter, referring to the agency by its final name throughout the years discussed herein, unless a prior name holds some unique significance to specific events.

Acknowledgments

Thanks to Kiera Parrott, Reviews & Production Director for *Library Journal* and *School Library Journal*, for providing vital information from a review published in 1990, no longer accessible on *LJ*'s website. I also owe gratitude for research on an obscure geographical point to Mike Perkins at the Indianapolis Public Library and to Jeannine Spurgin at Indiana's Plainfield–Guilford Township Public Library. I owe gratitude to Facebook friend Glenn Williams, in the UK, for further information on the same obscure geographic information. Also, thanks to longtime friend and fellow author David Frazier, formerly librarian at Indiana University, who furnished copious research material over the decades when this book was only a dream. Last but never least, thanks again, always, to my wife Heather for her kind assistance in all phases of my research for this work—which she admittedly found slightly more palatable than prior surveys on multiple murder for fun and/or profit.

Depression-Era Gangs

*Indicates members of multiple gangs over time

First Dillinger Gang ("White Caps"), Summer 1933
- John Dillinger*
- Sam Goldstein
- Clifford "Whitey" Mohler*
- William Shaw
- Paul "Lefty" Parker

Second Dillinger Gang, Summer 1933
- John Dillinger*
- Noble "Sam" Claycomb
- George Whitehouse
- Frank Whitehouse
- William Shaw
- Clifford "Whitey" Mohler*
- Fred Brenman

Third Dillinger Gang, September 1933
- John Dillinger*
- Harry Copeland
- John Vinson
- Hilton "Tillie" Cross
- Homer VanMeter*
- Hilton Crouch
- Merritt Longbrake

Fourth Dillinger Gang, 1933
- John Dillinger*
- John "Joseph Burns" Heaps
- James Clark
- Russell "Boobie" Clark
- Walter Detrich
- Joseph Fox
- John "Red" Hamilton
- James Jenkins
- Charles "Fat Charlie" Makley
- Harry "Pete" Pierpont
- Leslie "Big" Homer
- Edward Shouse

Fifth Dillinger Gang, 1933–34
- John Dillinger*
- Homer Van Meter*
- Albert "Pat" Reilly
- Joseph Burns
- Merger with Nelson
- Baby Face Nelson*
- Tommy Carroll
- Harold "Eddie" Green

Nelson Gang, 1933–34
- George "Baby Face" Nelson*
- John Paul Chase
- Jack Perkins
- Jimmy Murray
- John "Fatso" Negri

Barrow Gang, 1930–33

- Clyde Barrow
- Bonnie Parker
- Marvin "Buck" Barrow
- Blanche Barrow
- William "Deacon" Jones
- Raymond Hamilton
- Ralph Fults
- Frank Clause
- Everett Milligan
- Hollis Hale
- Joe Palmer
- Henry "Boodles" Methvin
- Monroe Routon
- Joe Bill Francis
- James Mullin
- S.J. "Baldy" Whatley

Barker-Karpis Gang, 1927–36

- Fred Barker
- Alvin Karpis
- Arthur "Dock" Barker
- Arizona "Ma" Barker
- Jimmy Creighton
- Joe Howard
- William "Lapland Willie" Weaver
- Jimmie Wilson
- Harry "Dutch" Sawyer (né Sandlovich)
- Lawrence "Larry" DeVol
- Jess Doyle
- Bill Weaver
- Harry Campbell
- George Ziegler
- Sam Coker
- Byron Bolton
- Russell "Slim Gray" Gibson
- Thomas Holden
- Francis "Jimmy" Keating
- Bernard "Big Phil" Phillips
- Earl Christman
- Vernon "Verne" Miller
- Volney "Curley" Davis
- Harry Hull
- John "Jack" Peifer
- Charles "Big Fitz" Fitzgerald
- Fred "Shotgun George Ziegler" Goetz
- William Bryan "Byron" Bolton
- Elmer Farmer
- Fred Hunter
- William "Willie" Harrison
- Edmond Bartholmey
- Joe Rich
- Benson "Ben Greyson" Groves

Kelly Gang, 1930–33

- George "Machine Gun" Kelly
- Kathryn Kelly
- Eddie Bentz
- Albert Bates
- Eddie Goll
- Robert "Boss" Shannon
- Armon "Potatoes" Shannon
- Frank "Jelly" Nash
- Thomas Holden
- Francis "Jimmy" Keating

Floyd Gang, 1930–34

- Charles "Pretty Boy" Floyd
- Bob Amos
- Jack Atkins
- James Bradley
- Fred Hildebrand
- William "Bill the Killer" Miller
- George Birdwell
- Adam "Eddie" Richetti

The Bailey-Underhill Gang, 1933–34

- Harvey "Shotgun Tom" Bailey*
- Wilbur "Mad Dog" Underhill

Frank "Jelly" Nash*
Jess Littrell
Bill Shipley
Jim Clark
Sebron "Ed" Davis
Frank Sawyer

The College Kidnappers, 1930–33
Theodore "Handsome Jack" Klutas
Walter Dietrich*
Edward Doll
Russell Hughes
Frank Souder
Gale Swoley
Ernest Rossi
Eddie Wagner
Earl McMahon
Julius "Babe" Jones

"Ozark Mountain Boys"
Walter "Irish O'Maley" Riley
George "Mad Dog" Aye
J. W. Baggett
Harry Obrien Blee
Vivian Chase
Charles Chessen
Lillian Chessen
Russell Cooper
Frank Douglas
Lloyd "Blacky" Doyle
Percy Michael "Dice Box Kid" Fitzgerald
Clem Forrestal
Dewey Gilmore
Daniel "Dapper Dan" Heady
Floyd Henderson
Johnny Langan
Spike Lane
Virgil "Red" Melton
Jackson "Fat Jack" Miller
Michael Musiala
Anna Musiala
Eugene Norvell
George "Mickey" O'Malley
Randol Eugene Norvell
Christ Nicola Oitcho
Fred Reese
Robert Riley
Dave Sherman
George Leonard "Shock" Short
Clarence Sparger
Robert "Major" Taylor
James Traynor
Norma Vaughn

The Brady Gang, 1933–37
Alfred Brady
James Dalhover
Charles Geisking
Clarence Lee Schaffer, Jr.
The Tri-State Gang
Walter Legenza
Robert Mais
Martin Farrell
Anthony "The Stinger" Cugino
Salvatore Serpa
Edward "Cowboy" Wallace
John Zukorsky
Johnny Horn
William "Big Bill" Phillips
Morris Kauffman
John Kendrick
Arthur Misana
Herbert Myers
Roy Willey
Robert Eckert
Joseph Coffey
Edwin Cole

Cretzer-Kyle Gang
Joseph "Dutch" Cretzer
Arnold Kyle

Milton Hartmann
John Herzer

Sankey-Alcorn Gang
Rio Verne Sankey
Gordon Francis Alcorn
Fern Mae Sankey

Elvina Ruth Kohler
Carl Pearce
Ray Robinson
Arthur Youngberg

The Dickson Gang, 1930
Bennie and Stella Dickson

Preface

My fascination with the FBI began at age eight, in October 1959, with Hollywood's release of *The FBI Story*, based on author Don Whitehead's best-selling nonfiction book of the same title. Like the book, it frequently turned history into a puff piece, but I knew no better in those days.

It took the 1960s and '70s to enlighten me, with rapid-fire revelations of illegal FBI activities at odds with basic American principles. Other parts of Bureau history—mythical dismantling of the 1920s Ku Klux Klan, alleged eradication of "all major gangsters" a decade later—remained untouched by journalists, but as more records emerged under the Freedom of Information Act, albeit heavily censored, even those pillars of "common knowledge" crumbled.

"Don't Shoot, G-Men!" is my fifth book published on the FBI since 1981. It aims to correct misrepresentations of the Bureau's "crime war" in the 1930s. While redaction of that record continues to the present day, the truth is now available for all to see.

1

"A bureaucratic bastard"

The FBI was never meant to be.

The Judiciary Act of September 24, 1789, founded America's federal law enforcement system with major restrictions. It established a new Attorney General's office as a one-man part-time job, and while it grew with the bureaucracy it was a toothless watchdog. The U.S. Marshals Service, created simultaneously, served federal courts directly, its officers recipients of patronage from district judges until 1896. The Treasury Department's Secret Service, founded on July 5, 1865, focused on hunting counterfeiters, and would not assume the duty of protecting presidents until 1901. The Justice Department, finally created on July 1, 1870, still lacked its own enforcement arm beyond a small team of "examiners," accountants who reviewed financial transactions of the federal courts. Occasionally, funds were allocated to hire "special agents," usually rented from the Secret Service, to investigate crimes committed on U.S. government reservations. They were efficient but expensive—and resented by Congress when their snooping embarrassed unscrupulous legislators.[1]

There matters rested until December 1906, when President Theodore Roosevelt appointed longtime friend and fellow "progressive" Charles Bonaparte, grandnephew of French emperor Napoleon Bonaparte, as Attorney General. He continued renting Secret Service agents until May 1908, when Congress passed a Sundry Civil Service Bill imposing two-year suspensions on any Treasury agents caught working cases other than counterfeiting. On June 26 Bonaparte ordered creation of a "special agent force" within the DOJ, composed of 34 former Secret Service men and DOJ "examiners." Congress refused to fund the team, but Bonaparte forged ahead, receiving President Roosevelt's approval on July 26, while legislators enjoyed a summer recess, presenting the force as a fait accompli upon their return.[2]

One angry congressman dubbed the team "a bureaucratic bastard," and like other real-life out-of-wedlock offspring, it was born nameless. The unit's command fell to DOJ Chief Examiner Stanley Finch. The squad's initial responsibilities included a mixed bag of antitrust, banking, bankruptcy and neutrality violations, plus interstate shipment of contraband including stolen goods, contraceptives, "obscene" materials, and prizefight films, but that list soon expanded.[3]

George Wickersham succeeded Bonaparte as Attorney General, christening the nameless troop the Bureau of Investigation on March 16, 1909. Chief Examiner Finch won promotion to Chief of the BOI. Privately, Wickersham worried that the BOI "was not yet strong enough to withstand the sometimes corrupting influence of patronage politics on hiring, promotions, and transfers." Even so, its jurisdiction expanded on June 25, 1910, with passage of the White Slave Traffic Act, aka the Mann Act, banning interstate transport of women for "immoral purposes." Ostensibly targeting organized prostitution, the law was soon diverted toward arrests of individual celebrities, often African Americans, traveling with girlfriends or fiancées.[4]

Over the next two years, BOI field offices spread nationwide, employing 300 special agents and as many support employees. A Special Agent in Charge (SAC) led each local office, reporting to Washington headquarters, while individual agents prowled the Mexican border, tracking smugglers and collecting information on Mexico's revolution. On April 30, 1912, Alexander Bielaski, Finch's top aide, succeeded his departing boss as Chief. Before his retirement on February 10, 1919, Finch oversaw a steady increase in Bureau responsibilities.[5]

Those changes arrived with Attorney General Thomas Gregory and America's entry into World War I on April 6, 1917. First came the Selective Service Act on May 18, empowering BOI agents to arrest military draft evaders. Next, on June 15, an Espionage Act sent them after spies and anyone obstructing the war effort. Finally, on May 16, 1918, a Sedition Act imposed sentences five to 20 years for any "disloyal, profane, scurrilous, or abusive language," spreading "contempt" against the U.S. government, its flag or armed forces. Predictably, arrests, trials and imprisonments increased dramatically.[6]

Chief Bielaski retired on February 10, 1919, 23 days before Attorney General Alexander Mitchell Palmer took office, determined to eradicate a rising postwar "Red Scare" by suppressing "radicals." Acting Chief William Allen ran the BOI until June 30, replaced by Director William Flynn, an ex–private investigator hailed by Palmer as "the leading, organizing detective of America ... an anarchist chaser ... the greatest anarchist expert in the United States." On October 28 Congress passed the National Motor Vehicle Theft Act, aka the Dyer Act, sending BOI agents after interstate car thieves (and permitting headquarters to claim credit for autos recovered by local police). Today, even Bureau historians admit that pursuit of hot cars initially lagged while "politics, inexperience, and overreaction got the better of Attorney General Palmer and his department."⁷

Palmer chose young law school graduate John Edgar Hoover, employed at the DOJ since July 26, 1917, as an aide in November 1918, promoted to lead a new General Intelligence Division on August 1, 1919. Under Hoover the GID shadowed countless "disloyal" persons and "hyphenated Americans," infiltrated left-wing organizations, and compiled massive files on America's "enemies," finally warning of a massive plot to overthrow the U.S. government on May 1, 1920. Millions of police and soldiers mobilized to face the threat but nothing happened. That might have doomed a lesser bureaucrat, but Hoover survived, transferring to the BOI with his GID files before Palmer left office.⁸

Meanwhile, America went "dry" for Prohibition in January 1920, while Harry Daugherty, a corrupt member of President Warren Harding's "Ohio Gang," replaced Palmer as Attorney General on March 4, 1921. Daugherty chose former Secret Service agent William Flynn as BOI Director, but his tenure was brief, resigning on August 21 to pursue "a private business matter." One day later, Daugherty replaced him with ex–PI William Burns, who promoted Hoover to his second-in-command as Assistant Director. Under Burns, the Bureau shrank from its 1920 high of 1,127 personnel to around 600 three years later.⁹

Ensuing scandals and Harding's death left the DOJ in disrepute, variously called a "national disgrace" and the "Department of Easy Virtue" for its rampant corruption. FBI historians also acknowledge that the BOI acquired "a growing reputation for politicized investigations" targeting critics of Harding's regime, including various members of Congress. Daugherty retired under fire on April 6, 1924, replaced as Harlan Stone, who found the BOI "filled with men with bad records ... many convicted of crimes ... organization lawless ... many activities without any authority in federal statutes ... agents engaged in many practices which are brutal and tyrannical in the extreme.... I don't know who to trust."¹⁰

On May 10, 1924, Stone chose Hoover as Acting Director, confirmed as full Director by year's end, leading 441 agents and 209 support personnel. Bureau legend claims that Hoover agreed to promotion solely on condition that the BOI should be "divorced from politics," accountable only to the Attorney General. Stone allegedly replied, "I wouldn't give it to you under any other conditions," moving on to a Supreme Court seat in March 1925.¹¹

History would prove that Hoover's scruples were a hollow sham. By 1933 *Collier's* magazine found Hoover using the Bureau as a "personal and political machine." He *did* "clean house" initially, firing 102 agents (including all blacks and women) plus some 260 clerks, but by 1945 the Bureau had ballooned to nearly 5,000 agents. Along the way it changed names thrice more, to the U.S. Bureau of Investigation, then the U.S. Division of Investigation, and finally the FBI.[12]

Fifteen months before the Bureau's "crime war" properly began, news of a kidnapping rocked the world, briefly monopolizing the overused phrase "Crime of the Century" and swiftly increasing the BOI's influence. Around 9:00 p.m. on March 1, 1932, someone snatched 20-month-old Charles Lindbergh, Jr., from a second-story bedroom of his family's mansion in Hopewell, New Jersey. Charles Senior, world-famous for his nonstop flight from New York to Paris in 1927, learned the news with wife Anne from nursemaid Betty Gow. The abductor(s) left a semi-literate note demanding $50,000 ransom and a broken homemade ladder. Local authorities summoned New Jersey State Police under Superintendent Herman Schwarzkopf to investigate. Locating no bloodstains or fingerprints, they focused first on household staffers, suspecting an "inside job" before a second note arrived on March 6, posted from Brooklyn two days earlier, increasing the ransom demand to $70,000. A third note, received on March 8, rejected an intermediary proposed by the Lindberghs, requesting acknowledgment via newspaper classified ad.[13]

That same day, without contacting the Lindberghs, retired Gotham school principal John Condon submitted a notice in the *Bronx Home News*, offering to serve as go-between and pay an additional $1,000 himself. The alleged abductors accepted his offer on March 9. Condon received the $70,000 on March 10 and commenced negotiations using the codename "Jafsie." On the 10th, taxi driver Joseph Perrone delivered a note to Condon, directing him to Woodlawn Cemetery on March 12. There, he met a man who called himself "John," face unseen in darkness, who agreed to furnish an item of Charles Junior's clothing as proof of life. Condon received a baby's sleeping suit with a seventh note on the 16th. An eighth note, five days later, claimed the kidnapping was planned a year in advance. The procession of notes continued, 12 in all, while Betty Gow found the infant's thumb guard on March 29, near an entrance to the Lindbergh estate.[14]

On April 2 Condon met "John" again and gave him $50,000, oddly holding back $21,000. "John" directed searchers to a boat near Martha's Vineyard, Massachusetts, but they found nothing. Condon, meanwhile, told lawmen he was "positive" he could identify "John" if they met again. On May 12, a trucker stopping to relieve himself found a child's partial corpse near Mount Rose, New Jersey, two miles from Hopewell. Despite advanced decomposition and missing pieces, a pathologist "positively identified" the body as "Little Lindy's," dead roughly two months. The child's pediatrician, Dr. Philip Van Ingen, demurred, saying he could not identify the corpse if paid $10 million. Authorities then focused on Violet Sharpe, a servant of Anne Lindbergh's mother, who committed suicide on June 10 with a fourth interrogation pending.[15]

Police in New Jersey and New York City rebuffed initial offers of aid from the BOI, which had no jurisdiction over kidnapping. Agents *did* arrest a former colleague, conman Gaston Means, who swindled well-intentioned meddler Evalyn McClean for $100,000 while posing as an intermediary for Charles Junior's return, sending Means and a cohort to prison for interstate fraud. On June 22, 1932, Congress passed a Federal Kidnapping Act, aka "Lindbergh Law," empowering BOI agents to pursue interstate kidnappers. Fifteen months later, President Franklin Roosevelt granted Hoover's agency central control of federal efforts on the case, collaborating with Treasury's Internal Revenue Service—significant since $40,000 of the ransom had been paid in obsolete gold certificates. That IRS trick would "solve" the crime, after a fashion, but not immediately.[16]

Between new revelations in the case, Director Hoover faced a menace to his job.

Senator Thomas Walsh had helped expose the Ohio Gang's Teapot Dome scandal and BOI agents ransacked his office in reprisal, with those of four colleagues. On February 28, 1933, President-elect Roosevelt announced Walsh as his nominee for Attorney General. That same day, from Florida, Walsh aired his plan "to reorganize the Department of Justice when he assumed office, probably with an almost completely new personnel." Which meant starting at the top.[17]

Walsh's sojourn to the Sunshine State was no coincidence. Widowed in 1917, he had decided to remarry, secretly wedding wealthy Cuban widow Mina Nieves Perez Chaumont de Truffin. On March 2, traveling by train from Florida to Washington for FDR's inauguration, Walsh died suddenly at 73. Rumors swirled: a heart attack, "overexertion" on his honeymoon—or possibly poison. His successor as Attorney General-designate, Homer Cummings, retained Hoover as Director and presided over the six-year "crime war" as one of the BOI's foremost cheerleaders. Old age, coincidence, or something else had saved the day.[18]

Throughout his life, J. Edgar Hoover was obsessed with image. As Director of the BOI he tolerated no embarrassment or challenge to his autocratic rule. Hoover's mantra from day one—perpetuated by Bureau spokespersons today—was a brusque denial that he led a "national police force," feared by Congress from the first time it rebuffed Attorney General Bonaparte's suggestion for a DOJ enforcement arm. The Bureau, by whatever name, was an "investigative agency" and nothing more.[19]

And again, as with his promise of "divorce from politics," it was untrue.

The term "police" derives from the Greek *politea*, meaning government, defined as civil administration.[20] Modern police, identified by badges

Corrupt FBI agent Gaston Means (left), imprisoned for extortion in the Lindbergh kidnapping case, accompanied to court by his wife (National Archives).

and armed (outside of the United Kingdom), not only investigate crimes but apprehend—alive or dead—suspected perpetrators within given jurisdictions. And the FBI does all those things.

By definition, through enforcement of selected federal statutes, it is national in scope, and *international* since 1942, conducting worldwide

1. "A bureaucratic bastard" 13

missions, sometimes clearly violating laws prevailing in the foreign countries where it operates. The Bureau's publicists also insist, up to the present day, that agents "lacked authority" to make arrests or carry guns until the spring of 1934, when new statutes empowered them to wage their all-out "crime war."[21]

Once again, untrue.

No stats are readily available on everyone arrested by the Bureau since its debut in 1908, but certain broad examples give the lie to claims that it was powerless. In 1917 its agents, joined by vigilantes and local police, jailed hundreds of "radical" unionists from the Industrial Workers of the World, often beating them in the process. A year later, nationwide "slacker" raids arrested thousands of alleged draft-dodgers, many of them visibly exempt through age or disability. During 1919 and '20 "Red raids," again bolstered by vigilantes, jailed thousands of suspected "enemy aliens," 249 of whom were deported to Russia, with the great majority released. After a wave of anarchist bombings, Bureau agents seized suspect Andrea Salsedo. A journalist observed them beating him and fled before he could be held in turn, whereupon Salsedo "killed himself" by leaping from a Bureau office window in New York.[22]

Attorney General designate Thomas Walsh, whose sudden death in March 1933 rescued J. Edgar Hoover's career (Library of Congress).

During the coming "crime war," other suspects would be dangled from high windows in Chicago, at least one of them plunging to death below.

The tale of special agents lacking firearms is another myth, amply revealed by Bureau files and veterans. On March 24, 1925, ten months after his appointment as Acting Director, Hoover sent a letter to all SACs nationwide, ordering that confiscated "obscene" matter be stored in each office's gun safe, proving weapons were ready at hand.²³ A memo from 1929 includes this passage:

> Section 11, Firearms: Employees are instructed:
> a. That they are legally entitled to carry firearms for defensive purposes.
> b. That, however, as a matter of policy, they are not to carry the same unless such action is authorized by their Special Agent in Charge.
> c. That they are never to use such firearms except for strictly defensive purposes.
> d. That a supply of firearms is kept in each field office to be issued, when necessary, to the employees by the Special Agent in Charge.²⁴

Further evidence made headlines between June 1933 and April 1934, when Bureau agents engaged in six shootouts with 10 persons slain (see Chapters 3, 5 and 6). A memo dated June 28, 1933, states, "The following equipment is the best which can be obtained for all purposes and should be supplied in appropriate quantities to all field offices," preceding a list of revolvers, Thompson submachine guns and rifles. That same month, Oklahoma City SAC Ralph Colvin appealed to Hoover, writing, "We have only the small light pistols furnished by the Bureau and which are entirely inadequate for the purpose." Records show that Hoover sent Colvin several "Tommy" guns. Another memo, dated July 14/15, 1933, includes a "List Showing Revolvers And Holsters In Bureau Offices And The Number Ordered For Each Office. Total Revolvers In The Bureau: Colts, 174, Smith & Wesson, 40." We also know that

J. Edgar Hoover poses with a Tommy gun for publicity photos. Curiously, the weapon is unloaded, with no magazine in place (Library of Congress).

before year's end, contrary to Hoover's later claims, agents received firearms training at U.S. Army bases and police departments nationwide.²⁵

More breaches in the FBI's disinformation campaign appeared later. In 1955 ex-agent Roy McHenry wrote, "The fact is that long before the passage of the [1934] act, as early as 1917 ... handguns were issued to us by the Bureau," listing various pistols he carried between 1917 and 1920. In 1962 retired agent Mort Davis, active 1917–25, added, "In a state like New York, which had a law requiring those carrying concealed weapons to obtain permits, we were warned by the SAC that we had better apply."²⁶

Clearly, behind the Bureau's smokescreen, agents were armed and ready for battle before congressional "authorization." All they needed was a list of enemies to help them make headlines.

2

Public Enemies

The term "public enemy" dates from 68 CE, when Rome's Senate labeled Emperor Nero a *hostis publicus*, and while applied erratically since then to Vikings, bandits and pirates, it didn't enter general usage in America until April 24, 1930, when Chicago's Crime Commission published its first list of local racketeers with Al Capone ranked No. 1. By 1934 the FBI applied the tag to hunted fugitives, Director Hoover frequently preferring to describe his Bureau's prey as "public rats."[1]

Gangs of the "crime war" era followed in the footsteps of such outlaws as the James-Younger gang, the Dalton brothers, and Bill Doolin's Oklahoma "Wild Bunch," trading cars for horses and modern weapons for Colt Peacemakers. Their most recent example, the bank-robbing gang led by Matthew Kimes and Ray Terrill, sprang from Tulsa in the 1920s, bound by greed and a blood oath to free captured members from jail or die trying. Most were dead or imprisoned by 1927 but one member, Elmer Inman, won parole in time to join the deadly Barker-Karpis gang in 1932.[2]

The coming "crime war's" major players included the following felons, presented in rough alphabetical order.

John Harvey Bailey dropped his first name in the 1920s, bootlegging during Prohibition, later stealing between $1 million and $3 million during a long career as "The Dean of American Bank Robbers," leading some gangs and serving others. Imprisoned in July 1932, he escaped on May 30, 1933, in a prison break where the warden was held hostage.[3]

The *Barker-Karpis gang* began as a family affair and grew over time. Missourians George and Arizona (Clark) Barker produced four sons—Herman, Lloyd, Arthur ("Dock") and Fred—between 1893 and 1901. All turned to crime, worsening after a move to Tulsa, "Ma" doggedly defending them as victims of police harassment, and by the time George left the family in 1924 all four were incarcerated. Though never legally divorced, Ma entered a common-law relationship with unemployed Arthur Dunlop around 1930. By then, son Herman had joined the Kimes-Terrill gang and killed a Kansas policeman on August 29, 1927. Wounded in that shootout, he reportedly killed himself, though Ma called it summary execution.[4]

As brothers Lloyd, Dock and Fred left prison, they brought home ex-convict friends, their gang steadily growing to become the largest and arguably most successful 1930s mob, traveling widely, committing robberies and ransom kidnappings. A jailhouse associate of Fred, Canadian-born Albin Karpavičius Americanized his name to *Alvin Karpis* after his Lithuanian parents moved to Kansas. Friends called him "Ray," while others dubbed him "Old Creepy" after his stare. Blessed with an eidetic memory, strategic brilliance, and a ruthless disposition, Karpis soon rose to co-leadership of the gang with Fred Barker. Years later, FBI headquarters would fabricate a myth of Ma as the gang's autocratic ringleader, but Harvey Bailey scoffed at that, saying, "Mastermind? She couldn't plan breakfast."[5]

Among 40-odd rotating members, the gang included some standouts. One such, *Vernon Miller*, was an Old West throwback, a decorated world war veteran, then a shady lawman in his native South Dakota, convicted of embezzling county funds in April 1923. Paroled 19 months later, he turned to bootlegging, contracted syphilis, and supported a drug habit by working

Albin Karpavičius, aka Alvin Karpis, met Fred Barker in Kansas State Prison (National Archives).

as a freelance hitman, indicted for wounding two Minneapolis policemen in February 1928 (charges dismissed). From there, between contract killings, he joined Harvey Bailey and others in stealing $150,000 ($2.5 million today) from three banks between July 1930 and April 1931. Soon afterward, he joined the Barker-Karpis gang.[6]

Fred Goetz, aka "Shotgun George Ziegler," was stranger yet. Chicago-born, he earned an engineering degree in 1918, flew fighter planes in France, and was discharged as a second lieutenant. Working as a lifeguard in 1922, he raped a seven-year-old girl and jumped bail, committing his first holdup-murder in October 1925. A shift to bootlegging acquainted him with Mob leaders from Kansas City to Chicago, but he continued freelancing, joining a gang that stole $350,000 ($5.9 million today) from a Wisconsin bank in 1929. That February, on his 32nd birthday, he allegedly participated in Chicago's Saint Valentine's Day massacre. From there, joining the Barker-Karpis team was a natural progression.[7]

Russell "Slim Gray" Gibson met the Barker brothers as a youth in Tulsa, as part of their Central Park Gang. In May 1929, with two cohorts, he stole $75,000 from a bank messenger in Oklahoma City, was arrested soon after, but escaped from jail before his trial, then rejoined the Barkers and went on to bigger jobs.[8]

Another Central Park Gang alumnus, *Volney "Curley" Davis* logged his first larceny conviction at 17, in 1919. In August 1921 he joined Dock Barker to burglarize a Tulsa hospital and kill its night watchman, both receiving life terms in separate trials. In November 1932 Davis received a four-month "leave of absence," allegedly in exchange for a $1,500 bribe. Instead of returning on schedule, he reconnected with the Barker-Karpis gang for new depredations.[9]

Harold "Eddie" Green, known for "casing" banks as an expert "jug marker," served his first jail sentence for grand larceny in Minneapolis at 18, in 1916. More arrests followed under various pseudonyms as he drifted from one roving gang to another. A 40-year robbery sentence capped his résumé in November 1922, paroled after five. On January 28, 1933, he joined three cronies to steal $14,500 from a North Kansas City bank messenger, killing one lawman and snatching two more as hostages for their escape, credentials that made him a natural for the Barker-Karpis gang.[10]

Lawrence De Vol, born in Ohio, raised in Tulsa, was another early member of the Central Park Gang who maintained ties with the Barker brothers afterward. At 23, in August 1927, he joined Harvey Bailey and two others to steal $70,000 from an Iowa bank. Six months later the same bandits netted $225,000 from a bank in Ohio. Arrested with Alvin Karpis for burglary in Kansas City, in April 1930, De Vol jumped bail, then killed two Iowa lawmen in June. On November 16, 1930, he robbed a Missouri theater, killing one policeman and wounding another the next day at nearby Kirksville. Christmas found him back in service with the Barker-Karpis gang.[11]

Dr. Joseph Moran, while not a bandit, offered aid and comfort to the gang as its resident medic. His early career paralleled that of Fred Goetz to a point, serving as a lieutenant with the wartime Army Signal Corps before graduating from Boston's Tufts Medical School. Alcoholism sabotaged his career, prompting him to become a "pin artist"—illegal abortionist—for extra income. Imprisoned after one of his patients died in 1928, he lost his license and received a 10-year sentence, paroled in three with aid from Joliet's warden, who also got Moran's medical license restored. Suspected of continuing abortions, Moran served 11 months for parole violation, then established himself with Chicago's underworld, mending bullet wounds, altering infamous faces and removing fingerprints.[12]

Between October 1931 and April 1933 Barker-Karpis gangsters staged 12 raids in seven states, stealing at least $814,000 in cash and securities ($16 million now). Twice they rampaged through small Minnesota towns, ransacking homes and shops for money and weapons, seizing hostages as they fled. In the process, members murdered three lawmen and one bystander. Other victims included loose-lipped Arthur Dunlop, slain in April 1932, and lawyer J. Earl Smith, who'd failed to win acquittal for Harvey Bailey. Gang member Earl Christman suffered fatal wounds in a Nebraska holdup and was planted in an unmarked grave near Kansas City.[13]

None of those events fell under jurisdiction of the FBI.

George Kelly Barnes, aka "Machine Gun Kelly," was the only errant member of a wealthy Memphis family. His troubles began in school, before he dropped out, married in haste, and fathered two children who later claimed he abused them, abandoning them at 19, in 1914. He turned from taxi driving to bootlegging during Prohibition, arrested several times before he received a three-year federal sentence in 1928, for peddling liquor to Native Americans. Jailed again for the same crime in New Mexico, he met and married Kathryn Thorne, née Lera Cleo Brooks, a daughter of outlaws who'd served time for robbery and prostitution. Kathryn saw potential in George, bought him a Tommy gun, and began to train him for life in the criminal "big time." They wed in 1930, in Minneapolis.[14]

That same year, Barnes—now "Kelly"—tried his hand at kidnapping. His first partner in the "snatch racket" was *Bernard "Big Phil" Phillips*, aka "Phil Courtney," a former traffic cop from Chicago or Cicero, Illinois (reports differ), fired for extortion. On their 1930 maiden outing, Phillips accidentally shot and killed the hostage. Later, he invited Kelly along for a second abduction but George wisely declined. That time, Phillips squabbled with his captive over the ransom payment, then released him with orders to bring back the agreed amount. Needless to say, the victim never returned—and to make things worse, Phillips had borrowed Kelly's Cadillac, putting George in the frame as a suspect.[15]

Discouraged from future kidnappings, Phillips turned to bank heists, joining the Barker-Karpis gang, reportedly helping them bag $47,000 from a bank in Fort Scott, Kansas, on June 17, 1932. Somewhere along that road, he also drew suspicion as a "rat," more specifically having "a habit of disappearing when other gangsters were caught" by lawmen. A case in point occurred on July 7, 1932, when FBI agents nabbed Harvey Bailey, Thomas Holden, and Francis Keating on Kansas City's Old Mission Golf Course. Various accounts claim Phillips was supposed to be their fourth but never showed, or that he was "playing one hole behind them" for some unknown reason. In any case, he missed the roundup, while his three friends went to jail. Phillips himself allegedly broke the bad news to other gang members.[16]

From that report—or rumor—grew the tale that Phillips had been executed as a stoolie by gang members still at large. Soon after the golf course fiasco, agents questioned Bernard's girlfriend, one Winnie Williams, recording her allegation that Phillips had been killed with icepicks and buried in a lime pit at some undisclosed rural location. A variation on that theme asserts that Phillips was dispatched in New York City, possibly by Vern Miller and Frank Nash. If the Bureau believed those stories, its trust did not withstand the test of time. Twelve years later, FBI bulletins named Phillips and cohort Harry Loftis as the bandits who robbed a La Crosse, Indiana, bank while four unnamed accomplices waited outside. Inside the bank, Loftis—also wanted for bank heists in Odell, Illinois, and St. Cloud, Minnesota—shot and killed a teller who was standing with his hands raised, leaving both "inside" men charged with murder. Strangely, research for this work found no data available on disposition of their cases.[17]

Kelly also moved on to bank heists, teamed with veterans including Barker-Karpis associates Thomas Holden and Francis Keating, forging trusty passes to help them escape Leavenworth. Kathryn served as his publicist, coining his nickname, and handing out .45 cartridges as souvenirs. Between January 1932 and February 1933 Kelly joined comrades Albert Bates, Eddie Bentz, Eddie Doll, Vern Miller, and others to rob five banks in four states, bagging an estimated $219, 000 ($4.2 million today). After one Minnesota heist, Miller machine-gunned three quarrelsome accomplices, dumping their corpses at White Bear Lake. Kelly's next attempt at kidnapping, with Bates, fell flat in January 1932, when Hoosier industrialist Howard Woolverton's family couldn't raise $50,000, but Kelly and Bates schemed to try again later, with Kathryn's help.[18]

Kelly's most consistent ally, *Albert Bates*, joined the army at 18, in 1911, then deserted and spent 15 months at Leavenworth. He logged his first civilian arrest, for a Nevada burglary, in 1916, sentenced to a term of one to 15 years. Paroled in 1917, he was jailed thrice more on the same charge, in three other states, between 1920 and '27. Released for the last time in July 1930, he joined Kelly for the resultant spree of bank jobs and ransom abductions.[19]

The Texas-based *Barrow gang*, another clique with fluctuating membership, traced its origin to January 1930, when 20-year-old parolee and fugitive Clyde Chestnut (not "Champion," as sometimes claimed) Barrow met 19-year-old Bonnie Louise Parker in Dallas. She was married to a prison inmate but had severed their connection after four months, although they never divorced. Lost to love at first sight, the young couple committed their first joint holdup in March 1932, with Bonnie arrested but never indicted. Elder brother Marvin "Buck" Barrow joined the couple upon leaving prison in March 1933, bringing wife Bennie (called "Blanche"). By that time, Clyde and Bonnie, with various cohorts, were sought by police for an ongoing series of auto thefts, heists and murders.[20]

Another sometime running mate of Clyde and Bonnie, *Ralph Fults*, was Texas-born in 1911. At age 14, police caught him with a suitcase full of stolen goods but Stonewall County's jail couldn't hold him. In the sheriff's absence, attending the county fair, Fults fashioned a key to his cell from an old tobacco can and led a mass escape. Soon recaptured while the other inmates scattered, he was held at Gatesville State School, a reformatory, then escaped once more in April 1927. Two years later, he was convicted of burglary after selling stolen cigarettes to a Greenville grocer, receiving a two-year sentence. He entered Huntsville Prison on June 16, later transferred to Eastham, where he escaped yet again, with two cohorts, in April 1930.[21]

Police in Saint Louis, Missouri, caught Fults burglarizing a hardware store in September 1930, sending him back to Eastham. During his second stay there, Fults met Clyde Barrow, who ignored guards' warnings to shun Ralph as a three-time escapee, and their friendship stuck over time. Paroled in August 1931, Fults helped smuggle hacksaw blades to bandit Raymond Hamilton, facilitating Hamilton's escape from McKinney's lockup on January 27, 1932. He teamed with Hamilton, parolee Clyde Barrow, and Bonnie Parker to rob a Mabank hardware store on March 22, but during their escape Clyde drove their stolen getaway car into a mudhole, where it stalled. Clyde fled on foot with Hamilton, while officers nabbed Fults and Bonnie, resulting in a 10-year sentence for Ralph on May 11, 1932.[22]

Between March 1932 and June 1933, Barrow gang associates committed at least 27 robberies and multiple car thefts across five states. They alternated between raiding banks and local stores, offices, and gas stations. Most of their takes were small, some heists yielding nothing. Published tabulations of their "earnings" from those 16 hectic months comes to $17,420 plus

Bonnie Parker and Clyde Barrow frequently posed for "gag" photos with weapons from their arsenal. This photo was found by police after a Missouri shootout in 1933 (Library of Congress).

"several" diamond rings looted from one shop. Along the way they killed four lawmen, two shopkeepers and one man who caught Clyde stealing his car. Additionally, they kidnapped several police officers and civilians, either to aid in escapes or for personal amusement, releasing all unharmed. On June 10, 1933, Clyde crashed their latest vehicle near Wellington, Texas, leaving Bonnie's legs severely burned. Invading a nearby home for help, one gangster "accidentally" shot a female resident, blowing off her hand with buckshot. Bonnie's burns would hamper movement for the last year of her life.[23]

Gang-hopping *Edward Wilhelm Bentz* spent much of his youth in juvenile detention for burglary, later graduating to armed robbery and safe-cracking, working with headliners Harvey Bailey, George Kelly, Albert Bates, and Lester Gillis. Crime historian William Helmer says Bentz participated in "up to 150" robberies nationwide "without ever being identified" but presents no supporting evidence.

Bonnie Parker also posed once with a cigar, prompting myths that she smoked them regularly, when in fact she favored Camel cigarettes. This photo was also captured by Missouri police in 1933, after a shootout that killed two officers (National Archives).

Bentz and Bailey were prime suspects in the July 1930 robbery or $2.87 million ($44.1 million today) from a Nebraska bank. Authorities also linked him to Kelly and Bates on other bank jobs in Washington ($77,000), Texas and Michigan between July and September 1931 but failed to indict him before he joined Gillis. J. Edgar Hoover once called Bentz "the shrewdest, most resourceful, intelligent and dangerous bank robber in existence."[24]

Kansas native *Fred "Killer" Burke* was born Thomas Camp in 1893, changing his name after he moved to Missouri at 22 and joined Egan's Rats, the dominant gang in St. Louis. Indicted for forgery two years later, he joined the army and fought in France, then returned to serve time for fraud in Michigan. Missouri jurors acquitted him of stealing $38,306 from a railway office in 1923, then he moved to Detroit as a hired gun for the Purple Gang, killing three rival bootleggers in 1927. From there he tried Chicago, becoming one of Al Capone's "American Boys," suspected but never charged in the 1928 murder of New York Mafioso Frankie Yale and 1929's Saint Valentine's Day massacre. Between contract killings he hired out to various bandit gangs, tapping an Indiana bank for $93,000 in October 1929. Two months later, using the alias "Fred Dane," Burke killed a Michigan policeman following a drunken traffic accident. In September 1930 he helped steal $18,000 from a New Jersey bank. Police finally captured him in Missouri, on March 26, 1931, resulting in a Michigan life sentence. Police reports conflict as to whether two submachine guns found in Burke's arsenal played roles in the Yale and Saint Valentine's Day murders.[25]

Irvin Carl Chapman, nicknamed "Charlie" for a perceived resemblance to comic Charlie Chaplin, personified other victims of the Great Depression who turned to crime, albeit on a much more lethal, sweeping scale. Born on his parents' farm outside Philadelphia, Mississippi, in December 1898, he moved to Arkansas in his twenties, becoming "an influential and respected member of society, operating a road contracting business, and was looked upon as a leading citizen of the community." At 30 he expanded his business to Florida, but the Wall Street crash of 1929 left him "practically penniless," owing $26,000. On April 30, 1931, he logged his first arrest in South Florida, for hijacking and carrying concealed weapons. One day later, in Miami, police charged him with "assault to kidnap," then released him on bond. He promptly fled to New Jersey, jailed there on August 31 for highway robbery, but jurors acquitted him in October. Leery of the Northeast, he made a beeline southward, robbing his first bank in Louisiana. Oklahoma lawmen captured him on July 2, 1932, leading to conviction and a nine- to 14-year sentence. While awaiting transfer to Angola's state prison, Chapman and inmate Charles O'Keith sawed through bars at the Caddo Parish jail, used a rope of torn mattress covers to descend eight floors, stole a car and fled Louisiana. On February 21, 1933, federal grand jurors indicted Chapman for violating the Dyer Act. Little Rock police caught and jailed him in El Dorado, then released him on $6,000 bond 18 days later. He fled once more, missing his trial on June 7, and resuming life as a fugitive.[26]

Rare female gangster *Vivian Davis Chase* first drew attention from police when husband George Chase was shot by Ella Keller in Kansas City, in December 1923. Keller told authorities that George, Vivian, and others attacked her when she threatened to report their recent robberies, forcing her to fire in self-defense. Arresting officers found Vivian wearing six unexplained diamond rings but ultimately filed no charges. She surfaced next in February 1926, jailed with three others for a brawl in Wichita. Four months later she was present when two Kansas companions died in a shootout with deputies hunting them for a May 1926 bank holdup. Once again, Vivian was arrested, then released without prosecution. June 1932 saw her arrested with two male companions for the $1,500 robbery of a North Kansas City bank. Held on $50,000 bond, she sawed through the bars of her cell and escaped using a rope of knotted bed sheets, disappearing from the public record for a time.[27]

The *College Kidnappers* derived their name from leader Theodore "Handsome Jack" Klutas, who attended the University of Illinois in 1923, as "John Edward Klutas," then left without obtaining a degree. Other members included Walter Dietrich, Edward Doll, Russell Hughes, Julius "Babe" Jones, Frank Souder, Gale Swolley and Eddie Wagner. One source mentions "12 or more members" but names no others. The same source refers to "at least nine abduction cases in which the victims paid from $10,000 to $150,000 for their release" but identifies only five.[28]

The gang started small, with an Iowa car theft by Klutas and Dietrich in June 1930. Pursued by lawmen, Klutas killed two officers and escaped, while Dietrich was imprisoned for bank robbery six months later. The group then turned to snatching racketeers for ransom, trusting that their victims wouldn't call police. Identified targets include bookie John Lynch ($50,000), gambler William Urban ($100,000), bootlegger James Ward ($45,000), and interstate conman Albert "The Alabama Kid" Blair (payment unknown). Others are described simply as three Illinois gamblers ($10,000 each) and two from Iowa ($8,000 each). The best-known victim, gambler James Hackett, was abducted twice, but reports conflict over the ransoms paid: $150,00 or $225,000 total, versus $75,000 the first time and nothing the second.[29]

Inevitably, the gang crossed Chicago boss Al Capone, with uncertain results. Conflicting authors say Scarface warned Eddie Doll or Babe Jones to lay off his men, whereupon Klutas either murdered Doll as a "weakling" or tried to kill Jones, prompting his confession to police in self-defense. Author Anthony Breuer adds an unverifiable twist, claiming that Doll actually worked with George Kelly and Albert Bates to plan kidnappings before FBI agents seized him in March 1933. That muddle remains unresolved.[30]

John Herbert Dillinger was the "crime war's" undisputed star, described in one account as the 1930s underworld's "matinee idol." Indianapolis-born in 1903, cursed with "a bewildering personality," he engaged in fights and petty theft before quitting school to work in a machine shop. Concerned, his father moved the family to rural Mooresville in 1921 but it didn't help. Arrested for car theft in 1922, Dillinger joined the navy a year later but fared no better, deserting in Boston and receiving a dishonorable discharge. Back in Mooresville, he married in April 1924 but couldn't hold a job. With cohort Edward Singleton he robbed a local grocer and both were soon arrested. Singleton pled innocent at trial, receiving a sentence of two to 14 years. Dillinger, on his father's advice, pled guilty without an attorney, expecting probation, but received a 10- to 20-year sentence, seething with bitterness toward everyone except himself.³¹

Dillinger's first stop was Indiana Reformatory in Pendleton, where he reportedly told guards, "I will be the meanest bastard you ever saw when I get out of here." His intake physical revealed gonorrhea, requiring painful treatment. His wife surprised him by filing for divorce (her second) in 1928, granted in 1931. Meanwhile, he was distracted by new friends who would become his mentors for a more successful life of crime.³² They included—

John Dillinger, primary headliner of the FBI's "crime war" during 1933 and 1934 (Library of Congress).

Harry "Pete" Pierpont, born in Muncie during 1902. Pierpont first entered the reformatory in 1922, convicted of auto theft and battery with intent to kill. The superintendent deemed him "as wild as a March hare" in 1923, yet he was paroled the following year, to organize a bank-robbing gang with cohorts William Behrens, Everett Bridgewater, George Frazer, Robert Morse, Earl Northern, Thaddeus Skeer, and Marion "Red" Smith. Between November 1924 and March 1925 they looted five banks and a hardware store (for guns). Caught and convicted in May 1925, Pierpont returned to the reformatory that month for a term of 10 to 20 years, already plotting to escape. His friends inside, soon to be joined by Dillinger, included *Russell "Boobie" Clark, Charles "Fat Charlie" Makley* and *John "Red" Hamilton*.³³

Hoosier native Clark, born in 1898, received a dishonorable discharge from the Marine Corps in 1919, then joined partner Ralston "Blackie" Linton to rob speakeasies during Prohibition. Suspected of an Illinois murder and two Indiana kidnappings by 1926, he wasn't charged with those crimes but confessed a roadhouse robbery in 1927, receiving a 20-year term that December. Inside, he studied heists with jailed experts when not engaged in organizing inmate strikes. His nickname was prison slang for a joker, which assisted him in making friends.[34]

Ohio-born in 1899, Makley (pronounced "make-lee") quit school in eighth grade to commit petty thefts, bootleg liquor, and later rob banks, while marrying a brother's ex-wife. After multiple arrests in Michigan and Missouri, he logged his first conviction for a Wichita bank job in July 1924, paroled in May 1928. Days later he hit an Indiana bank, was convicted and sent back inside by June 25. Despite his criminal career, when free he posed as a successful entrepreneur, listing his profession on inmate records as "salesman."[35]

Canadian Hamilton, born 1899, was cut from rougher cloth. His hair explained the "Red" nickname; a childhood sledding accident that maimed his right hand added the sobriquet "Three-Finger Jack." In May 1927 jurors convicted him of robbing an Indiana gas station with sidekick Ray Lawrence, whereupon Hamilton received a 25-year sentence.[36]

The odd man out among Dillinger's new pals was *Homer Van Meter*, another Hoosier, born in 1905. Like Russell Clark, he was a joker, but his humor had a cutting edge that riled Harry Pierpont, making them lifelong enemies while Dillinger befriended both. First jailed as a teen for drunk and disorderly conduct, Homer served 51 days for larceny in 1923, then returned to prison for an Illinois car theft in January 1924. Paroled in December, he joined an ex-cellmate to rob passengers aboard an Indiana train in March 1925, drawing a 10- to 21-year sentence. In July 1925, his rule-breaking earned a transfer to Michigan City's state prison. Six months later, transported to Chicago as a defense witness for an innocent suspect in the train heist, Homer briefly escaped custody. Police found him panhandling change on the street. Soon afterward, he staged another breakout attempt with cellmate Charles Stewart, spending two months in solitary confinement.[37]

Reformatory administrators transferred Pierpont, Makley, Clark and Hamilton to Michigan City in July 1929. Dillinger waited two years, then requested a transfer, explaining that state prison had a first-class baseball team.[38] Upon arrival, he did join the team, while also making more friends. Those included—

Joseph Burns, né John Heaps, leader of a holdup team dubbed the "Culver Bandits," with accomplices Joseph Byers, Art "Abe Silver" Silbert and Peter Fox, aka "Charles Penders."[39]

James "Oklahoma Jack" Clark, a protégé of Herman "Baron" Lamm who helped Lamm's gang steal $15,567 from an Indiana bank in December 1930, then survived the gang's last shootout with police and vigilantes days later, in Illinois.[40]

Walter Dietrich, associated with the "College Kidnappers" before he

Friends and future accomplices from Indiana's Michigan City prison. Top row (left to right): John Dillinger, Harry "Pete" Pierpont; Second row (left to right): Charles Makley, Edward Shouse; Third row (left to right): Homer Van Meter, James "Oklahoma Jack" Clark; Bottom row (left to right): John "Red" Hamilton, Russell "Boobie" Clark (National Archives).

joined Lamm's gang, also lived to face conviction after the Illinois shootout in December 1930. He received a life sentence at Michigan City in January 1931, where records misspelled his name as "Detrich," listing his profession as "plumber."[41]

Joseph Fox, an alumnus of the gang once led by Frank Badgely, other members including Ed and Russell Clark, Charles Hovious, and Martin O'Leary.[42]

Dillinger played ball at Michigan City, but the real game by summer 1932 was plotting a mass escape. Pierpont's girl on the outside, Mary Kinder, offered to help since her brother, Earl Northern, was on the list of intended escapees. A brothel madam Pierpont knew in Kokomo also pitched in with timely aid, while Pierpont supplied a list of banks ripe for looting if the break-out succeeded. Dillinger's father, meanwhile, had collected 188 signatures on a petition supporting John's parole, duly granted on May 22, 1933.[43]

Pierpont excluded enemy Van Meter from the plot, but Homer didn't need the help. Once out of solitary, he became a seeming model prisoner. Michigan City's director of research questioned the turnaround, writing, "This fellow is a criminal of the most dangerous type. Moral sense is perverted and he has no intention of following anything but a life of crime. He is a murderer at heart and if society is to be safeguarded, his type must be confined throughout their natural lives." The chaplain disagreed, telling administrators, "Van Meter is ready to prove that he is no longer the man who got off on such a bad start." The parole board took that advice, releasing Homer three days before Dillinger.[44]

Back on the street, Dillinger formed a gang nicknamed the "White Caps," for their distinctive headgear, with cronies Sam Goldstein, Clifford Mohler, Paul Parker, and William Shaw. On June 10 Dillinger and two others took $10,600 from a bank in Ohio, rebounding hours later to rob a drugstore in Indianapolis before dropping out of sight.[45]

Seven hundred miles southwest of Indianapolis, Oklahoma spawned another gangland headliner. *Charles Arthur Floyd* was Georgia-born in 1904 but his family moved to Akin when he was seven, settling a half-hour's drive from the rugged Cookson Hills, an historic hideout for fugitive bandits. Nicknamed "Choc" after his fondness for Choctaw beer, he would later be dubbed as "Pretty Boy" under disputed circumstances. Floyd logged his first arrest at 18, for stealing $3.50 from a post office, married in 1924, and received his first prison term in 1925 for an $11,929 Missouri robbery. Wife Ruby filed for divorce in January 1929, two months before his parole, and Floyd returned at once to crime, arrested thrice more between March and May, with two cases dismissed, serving 60 days for vagrancy in Colorado.[46]

And along the way, he became a killer.

On March 8, 1930, police in Akron, Ohio, charged Floyd (as "Frank Mitchell") with killing a patrolman during a robbery, then released him in time for another arrest at Toledo, in May. Sylvania jurors convicted him of bank robbery in November 1930, imposing a 12- to 15-year sentence, but Floyd escaped and made for Kansas City, meeting future girlfriend Beulah

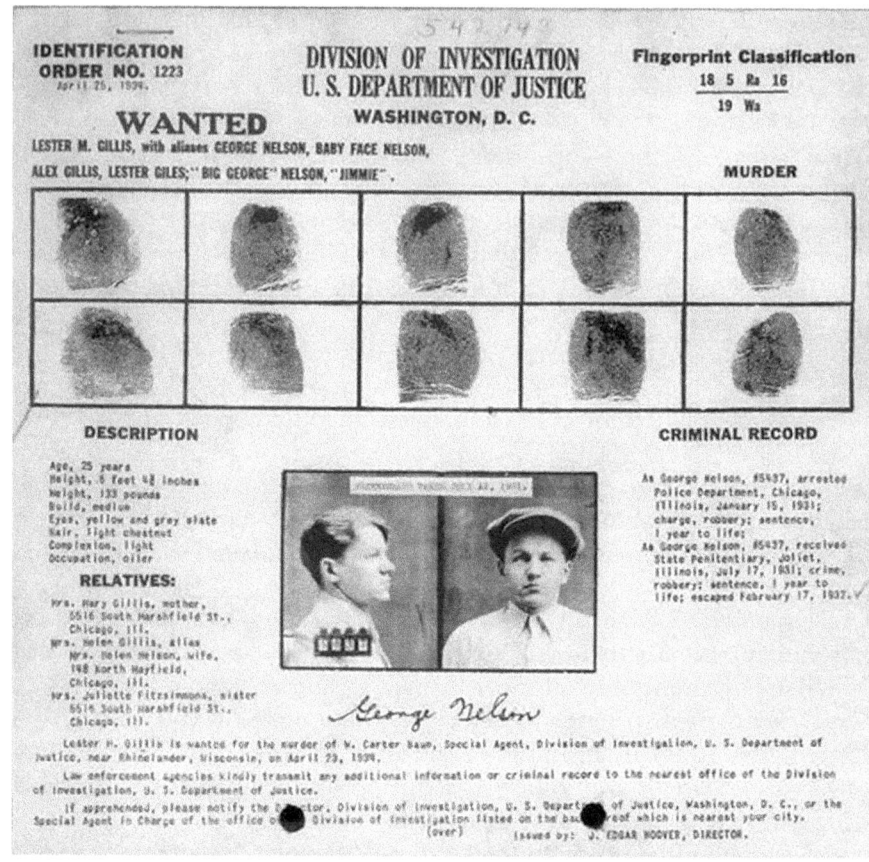

Federal "WANTED" poster for George "Baby Face" Nelson (National Archives).

Baird. Local officers suspected him of killing bootleggers Wallace and William Ash, sons of his landlady, in March 1930, but filed no charges. One month later, members of his gang killed a patrolman in Bowling Green, Ohio. July saw him kill Prohibition agent Curtis Burke during a Kansas City liquor raid. In April 1932 he murdered sheriff-turned-bounty hunter Ervin Kelley, who tried to arrest him in Bixby, Oklahoma.[47]

Between March 1925 and mid–June 1933 Floyd, with various accomplices, robbed at least 12 banks in four states, fleeing with an estimated $38,205 ($715,000 today). Blamed for several other heists in which he took no part, Floyd allegedly tossed money from his fleeing getaway car in one case, while burning mortgages in others, actions that evoked Depression-era public sympathy and earned him another nickname: "Robin Hood of the Cookson Hills." Whether or not such incidents occurred, in fact, remains a subject of debate.[48]

Floyd worked with various accomplices throughout his criminal career. Best-known associates included—

Aussie Elliott, an Oklahoma native born in 1914, convicted of bank robbery at 18, who escaped from McAlester's state prison in August 1932. He reportedly joined Floyd for two heists, in August 1932 and January 1933, bagging a total of $5,530.[49]

William "Billy the Killer" Miller, Ohio-born in 1906, who slew his brother at 19 in a brawl over a woman. Jurors acquitted him of murder on grounds that he'd "suffered enough," but his course was set. Charged with multiple Ohio and Michigan bank jobs in August 1932, he escaped to Oklahoma and teamed up with Floyd in March 1931. He began dating Beulah Baird's sister, Rose Ash, allegedly joining Floyd to kill her husband and his brother in Kansas City. He robbed at least two banks with Floyd during March and April 1931, fleeing with $5,262, before police spotted them in Bowling Green, Ohio, on April 16. Officers killed Miller in the shootout, while Floyd slew one patrolman and escaped.[50]

George William Birdwell, a Sooner native born in 1894, one of Floyd's more notorious associates. Author Myron Quimby credits Birdwell with 10 murders and "countless" holdups from the 1920s onward but provides little supporting evidence before March 1931, when he joined Floyd and William Miller for a $3,000 Oklahoma bank raid. Between August 1931 and January 1932 Floyd and Birdwell struck seven more times, netting $14,291. Tulsa police traced the fugitives to a local address in February, but the duo escaped after wounding an officer. During March and April they robbed two more banks of $1,100, shooting their way out of another police trap in June. November 1932 found the pair, with Aussie Elliott, robbing another bank of $2,350. Soon afterward, Floyd and Birdwell parted company over "Bird's" plan to rob a bank in all-black Boley, Oklahoma. Birdwell proceeded with cronies George Glass and C.C. Patterson on November 23— ironically the first day of local bird-hunting season—and were ambushed by locals stocking up on ammunition at a local hardware store. Birdwell and Glass died in the shootout while Patterson, gravely wounded, survived to serve time in prison.[51]

Adam "Eddie" Richetti, Floyd's most notorious accomplice, was a Texan born in 1909, moving to Oklahoma with his family at age three. An alcoholic by 14, he logged his first arrest for robbery in Indiana, two days after his 19th birthday. Drawing a sentence of one to 10 years at Pendleton Reformatory, he secured parole in October 1930, robbing his first Oklahoma bank in 1932. During the chaotic getaway, police killed accomplice Fred Hamner, wounding and capturing Richetti, with brothers L.C. and W.A. Smalley. Convicted and sentenced to prison on April 5, Richetti posted a $15,000 appellate bond four months later and skipped town, surfacing in

January 1933 to raid another bank with Aussie Elliott and Edgar Dunbar. He teamed with Floyd thereafter, still drinking heavily and keeping company with Rose Ash, sister of Floyd's lover.[52]

Chicago native *Lester Joseph Gillis,* born to Belgian immigrants in 1908, preferred to call himself "George Nelson" or "Big George," although he stood only five feet four inches tall. His youthful appearance earned him the hated nickname "Baby Face Nelson," while gangland friends often called him "Jimmy." His criminal career apparently began by accident on July 4, 1921, when he shot a friend in the face with a found pistol. That cost him a year in juvenile detention, followed by an 18-month sentence for car theft in 1922, succeeded by an identical charge in May 1924. In 1928, while working at a gas station staffed by teenage tire thieves, he met and married salesgirl Helen Wawrzyniak, remaining devoted to her for the rest of his life. Their two children were less fortunate, farmed out to relatives when their parents became fugitives.[53]

In January 1930 Nelson joined (or led) a gang of home-invading "tape bandits," so called for their method of binding victims while they ransacked mansions, stealing $98,000 worth of jewelry ($1.5 million today) in four months. They tried bank robbery in April and October ($8,600), then switched to roadhouse stickups in November 1930, resulting in shootouts that left four persons dead and three wounded. Also in November the gang botched one bank heist and scored $4,000 from another. Police caught Gillis in January 1931, resulting in a July conviction and sentence of one year to life. Returned for a second robbery trial, he received another 20-year term

Lester Gillis, aka "George 'Baby Face' Nelson" (National Archives).

for bank robbery in February 1932, then escaped from guards while returning to Joliet two days later, using a pistol slipped to him by an unnamed relative.[54]

Contacts in Chicago's Touhy Gang helped Gillis flee to Reno, Nevada, where he made new underworld connections, serving as a guard on bootleg liquor shipments between Reno and northern California. While in Reno with Helen, he met bandits Alvin Karpis and Eddie Bentz, among others. Visiting Indiana in May, he also met Homer Van Meter and accompanied future Dillinger gang members to San Antonio, purchasing customized weapons.[55]

Before joining Dillinger's fifth and final crew, Gillis's most frequent accomplices were *John Paul Chase* and *Joseph Ray Negri*, both of whom he met on trips from Reno into northern California. Chase, a San Francisco native born in 1901, quit school after fifth grade to work on a ranch, then in railway machine shops, before he drifted into rum-running. He worked with Gillis as a guard on bootleg liquor trucks and Gillis often introduced Chase as his "half-brother." Some accounts claim he served as getaway driver for Gillis on a Reno contract murder, later following his comrade to rob banks in the Midwest.[56]

Negri, another Frisco native, born in 1905 and raised on the city's Barbary Coast, bore the nickname "Fatso" for his bulk. From rolling drunks at nine, he moved to stripping cars and running crooked dice games in his teens, graduating to armed robbery at 20. Confined to San Quentin Prison in 1925, he emerged four years later, briefly going "straight" as a cabbie, then switched to driving trucks for bootlegger Joe Parente, an employer of Gillis. By 1932 he'd teamed with Gillis and Chase, trailing them eastward to crack the "big time."[57]

A third cohort of Gillis, *Thomas Leonard Carroll*, born 1900 in rural Montana, was a world war veteran and boxer, jailed by Nebraska police in 1920 "for investigation," then discharged. More arrests followed, including a February 1922 theft conviction and five-year sentence (paroled in March 1923), with four charges filed, then dropped, by police in Missouri and Oklahoma between November 1924 and September 1926. Indiana jurors convicted him of possessing burglar's tools in January 1927, but he was free again by April, nabbed with a stolen car and sentenced to five years in Leavenworth under the Dyer Act. Paroled in October 1931, he remained at large until another arrest with burglar's tools on May 17, 1933—but again the charge was dismissed. Soon afterward, he teamed with Gillis and company, rushing headlong into trouble that would ultimately claim his life.[58]

German native *Herman Karl "Baron" Lamm* is sometimes called "the father of modern bank robbery." Born in 1890, he joined the Prussian Army but was cashiered for cheating at cards. He immigrated to America in 1914 and applied his military skills to robbery, meticulously planning every aspect of a heist in what became known as the "Lamm technique," surveilling bank security, mapping approaches and escape routes (nicknamed "cat roads") in advance, leaving nothing to fate. Arrested by Utah police in 1917, he served a short prison term, then emerged more committed than ever to honing his methods. Employing full-scale mockups of prospective targets, he assigned team members to serve as lookouts, getaway drivers, lobby men (sometimes dubbed "tigers") and vault men, timing raids to the minute. Credited with unspecified "dozens" of holdups after his Utah parole, Lamm and his men reportedly stole more than $1 million ($15.4 million today) by 1930.[59]

Lamm's system failed him on December 16, 1930, in Clinton, Iowa. As raiders fled the Citizens State Bank with $15,567, an armed local barber rushed their getaway car, causing driver W.H. Hunter to make a sharp U-turn and crash. Lamm's gang stole another vehicle, unaware that its owner had installed a speed regulator to stop his aged father from driving recklessly. Two more vehicles failed them in turn, one low on fuel, the other with a leaky radiator. Surrounded in Slidell, Illinois, by 200 officers and vigilantes, Lamm and septuagenarian G.W. "Dad" Landy committed suicide. The posse captured Walter Dietrich and James Clark, both later sentenced to life in Indiana, where they met John Dillinger and taught him Lamm's methods.[60]

Edna "Rabbit" Murray, born Martha Stanley in Kansas during 1898, was the "crime war's" quintessential "gun moll." Married twice in her teens and twice divorced, she bore son Preston Paden in 1917. Three years later, she moved to Kansas City, settling with sister Doris and her husband, fugitive Emory Connell. She soon wed Connell's crime partner, jewel thief "Diamond Joe" Sullivan, but he was charged with murder in 1923, executed the following year. Next she married bandit Jack Murray and joined him for holdups, famously smooching victim H.H. Southward in an incident that saw her dubbed "The Kissing Bandit." Arrested together in October 1925, the duo drew matching 25-year sentences, but Murray escaped from prison in May 1927, earning the nickname "Rabbit." She remained at large until captured in Chicago on September 10, 1931, then staged two more escapes in November 1931 and December 1932. In Chicago, she reunited with former acquaintance Volney Davis, also a fugitive, and they soon teamed with the Barker-Karpis gang for more illicit adventures.[61]

Some authors call *Frank "Jelly" Nash* "the most successful bank robber in U.S. history," participating in some 200 holdups with various cohorts, while others dispute that title. The source of his nickname is also contested, either a shortening of "Jellybean"—referring to his stylish youthful grooming—or a reference to the blasting compound used for cracking safes.

2. Public Enemies

Though born in Indiana, Nash spent much of his early life in Arkansas and Oklahoma, where his father owned a hotel chain, describing Hobart, Oklahoma, as his hometown. After working in his dad's hotels, Nash served in the army from 1904 to 1907, then turned to crime. In 1913 Oklahoma jurors convicted him of robbing a store and killing accomplice Nollie "Humpy" Wortman to avoid splitting the $1,000 take, resulting in a life sentence. Five years later Nash persuaded McAlester's warden that he wished to reenter the army and fight overseas. Authorities reduced his sentence to 10 years, releasing him into uniform on August 16, 1918. Some sources claim he saw action in France, at Belleau Wood, but that battle ended on June 26. A few Allied offensives still remained, but no records exist of Nash seeing action before war's end on November 11.[62]

Returning stateside, Nash received a 25-year sentence for burglary with explosives in 1920, becoming a prison trustee and seeing his sentence reduced to five years, released in December 1922. He promptly joined a bandit gang led by Oklahoman Ethan Allen Spencer, helping rob the Katy Limited mail train in August 1923. He fled to Mexico, wedding a local woman and allegedly backdating their marriage certificate to give himself an alibi for the train heist. Lured back across the border in early 1924, Nash was convicted in March, with three accomplices, for robbing the train and assaulting a postal custodian. Their sentence: 25 years each at Leavenworth. Chosen as the deputy warden's chef and handyman in 1930, Nash was sent outside prison walls for an errand on October 19 and fled to Chicago, where he met barmaid Frances Luce. On December 11, 1931, he aided George Kelly and Thomas Holden in freeing lifers Charles Berta, Stanley Brown, George Curtis, Grover Durrill, William Green, Earl Thayer, and Tom Underwood from Leavenworth, smuggling guns and dynamite inside before they kidnapped Warden Thomas White and fled. Three died in a subsequent shootout, four more were recaptured by December 13.[63]

Before that breakout, in July 1930, Nash had joined Holden, Kelly, Francis Keating, Vern Miller, Harvey Bailey, Eddie Bentz, Lawrence De Vol and others on a Midwestern bank-robbing spree. Following a $70,000 Minnesota heist on July 19, Miller killed accomplices Frank "Weinie" Coleman, Mike Rusick and Samuel "Jew Sammy" Stein. During September and October, more raids netted the gang $2,852,000 ($44 million today). After the final raid in Wisconsin, bandits Charles Harmon and Frank Weber murdered hostage James Kraft, then paid with their lives for that breach of discipline. In July 1932 FBI agents caught Bailey, Holden, and Keating golfing in Kansas City. By the time Bailey escaped again, in May 1933, Nash had settled in Hot Springs, Arkansas, wedding Frances Luce and adopting the surname "Moore" while he planned new holdups, sheltered by corrupt police.[64]

Another Missouri-based gang, dating back to the 1920s, was variously known as the "*Ozark Mountain Boys*" or the "*Irish O'Malley Gang*." Conflicting accounts name two alternate leaders, perhaps collaborating over time. One, George Leonard "Shock" Short, was the brother of politician Dewey Jackson Short, who served in Congress from 1929 to 1957, with a two-term hiatus during 1931–35. The other, popularly called "Irish O'Malley," appears in press reports as Walter Riley, Leo O'Malley, and Walter Holland, the latter surname apparently borrowed from a foster father. Born in Galena, Missouri, Shock Short's early path to notoriety remains obscure. Riley, St. Louis–born in 1898, joined the National Guard in 1916, then deserted the following year and fled to Canada, joining that nation's army. He claimed foreign service during the world war, but his record's only highlight is a sentence to the brig, offense uncertain, capped by a bad conduct discharge in October 1919.[65]

Returning home in time for Prohibition, Riley joined Egan's Rats, robbing a railway express messenger of $17,423.65 in June 1921, at Granite City, Illinois. Police nabbed him the same day, with accomplices Clem Forrestal, Robert Riley (no apparent relation), and James Traynor, adding charges for a $5,000 diamond theft. All posted bail, then skipped, though Forrestal and Traynor were later convicted. In December 1921, with cohorts George "Mad Dog" Aye and George "Mickey" O'Malley, Riley stole $31,000 in cash and bonds from a bank at Panama, Illinois, wounding a bystander they mistook for a policeman. Several days later, they tapped another Illinois bank for $15,000, but Nebraska officers jailed Riley for vagrancy in January 1922, extraditing him for trial in Illinois.[66]

Further details of that case are unavailable today, but Riley was free again by May 18, 1932, when he joined accomplice Jackson Miller to steal $2,000 from a bank in Avilla, Missouri, taking cashier Ivy Russell as a hostage during their escape. Over the next three years, the gang roamed through five states, allegedly committing "dozens" of bank heists and at least one headline-grabbing ransom abduction before lawmen began connecting the dots and hunting them down. Rumors persist to this day of loot stashed in various tunnels throughout Missouri, but none of it has been uncovered yet.[67]

Canadians *Rio Verne Sankey* and *Gordon Francis Alcorn*, born in 1890 and 1905 respectively, met while working on the Canadian Pacific Railway, which Alcorn's father served as a section manager. (One source, claiming Sankey was born in Iowa during 1901, is mistaken). Tiring of labor on the rails, Sankey ran a casino in 1930 and shuttled bootleg liquor into the U.S., traveling as far south as Denver. Next, he tried farming but failed, rejoining Alcorn to rob banks in Saskatchewan and South Dakota. After killing bank manager P.B. Holbrook during a Canadian holdup, the pair rethought their plans and turned to ransom kidnapping.[68]

Enlisting various accomplices, the pair abducted socialite Haskell Bohn from Saint Paul, Minnesota, on June 30, 1932. They demanded $35,000 from Bohn's father, a local refrigerator magnate, but finally settled for $12,000, releasing him unharmed. Next, in Denver, they snatched Charles Boettcher II—son of a self-made millionaire from Germany—leaving his wife with a strange note, filled with misspelled words, the victim's name left blank, demanding $60,000. (Authorities later determined that Sankey and Alcorn had complied a list of 30 Denver targets, winnowed to five, but forgot to update their note before grabbing Boettcher.) Held at Sankey's South Dakota ranch, Boettcher was liberated when the cash came through. The haphazard affair led to indictment of Sankey and Alcorn on April 6, 1933, but they remained elusive. Alcorn married widow Angeline Christopherson in Chicago on May 9, under the name "Walter Thomas," while FBI agents searched nationwide for the kidnappers.[69]

Roger "The Terrible" Touhy was an atypical gangster, born in 1898, one of six brothers sired by a Chicago policeman, five of whom turned outlaw during Prohibition, dominating northwestern Cook County, warring against rival Al Capone. Police killed James Touhy, Jr., during a 1917 robbery, while rival gunmen finished brothers John in 1927 and Joseph in 1929. Roger, the youngest, quit school after eighth grade then tried to go "straight" as a telegrapher, oilfield worker, union organizer, and a navy seaman during World War I. He married in 1923, drove cabs and formed a trucking firm, but Prohibition's profits proved irresistible, augmented from illicit gambling. By 1926 his gang earned $1 million yearly ($14.5 million today) and Capone's jealousy turned violent. Revenue agents imprisoned Capone in 1931, but the war dragged on without him, led by Frank Nitto and Paul Ricca.[70]

Touhy's foremost ally in that struggle was *Basil Hugh Banghart*, called "The Owl" for his protruding eyes, a Michigan native born in 1900, reputedly possessing a 107 IQ. Unlike Touhy, Banghart finished high school and one year of college before turning to crime, allegedly stealing more than 100 cars around Detroit before his first arrest in January 1926 (settled with probation). That April, Ohio FBI agents jailed him in for Dyer Act violations, resulting in a two-year sentence in Atlanta's federal prison. Banghart escaped with other cons in January 1927, absconding to Montana, where he formed another car-theft ring. October 1928 saw him captured in Pennsylvania, charged with another Dyer Act violation, but he escaped from Philadelphia's federal building. Traced two weeks later, still in Philly, Banghart had shaved his moustache, dyed his hair, and donned spectacles.[71]

Returned to Atlanta, he completed his sentence in February 1930, transferred to Tennessee for trial on his latest federal charge. Another escape bid in Knoxville failed, as did a plea for mercy from his judge, who imposed a two-year sentence. Released again in January 1932, Banghart was jailed in Detroit two months later as a robbery suspect. Police there extradited him to Indiana, for trial on a 1927 armed robbery charge. Boasting that South Bend's jail couldn't hold him, he blinded a deputy with pepper, seized keys and a machine gun, shooting his way to freedom. At his next stop, Chicago, Basil enlisted with the Touhy gang as a triggerman, bombing a Nitto nightclub in February 1933.[72]

Missouri native *Wilber Underhill, Jr.*, appeared more often in print as "Mad Dog" or "The Tri-State Terror," after his propensity for violence. Born in 1901, the middle of seven children, his three elder brothers all turned to crime but without achieving Wilber's notoriety. George drew a life sentence for murder in 1913, while Wilber began displaying a "wild streak" his mother blamed on a childhood accident that "didn't leave him quite right." Around the same time, Wilber changed his given name's spelling to "Wilbur," considering it "more manly." His first arrest, for burglarizing a neighbor's home in 1918, earned him a four-year sentence. Released in 1922, he made news as Joplin's "Lovers Lane Bandit, caught and sentenced to another five years."[73]

Free again in 1926, he teamed with Ike "Skeet" Adams to rob a drugstore in Okmulgee, Oklahoma, killing a teenage customer. Captured in January 1927, the duo escaped with inmates Red Gann and Duff Kennedy. Police traced Adams to Lamar, Missouri, on February 9, killed by Barton County's sheriff when he tried another escape. One day later, Underhill robbed a Picher, Oklahoma, theater of $52, but was accosted by a constable, seizing the lawman's gun and slaying a deputized civilian. Caught on March 20 in Panama, Oklahoma, Underhill received a life term for his latest murder on June 3, 1927.[74]

After multiple attempts to flee McAlester's state prison, Wilbur succeeded on July 14, 1931. On the 26th he bought a car in Cherryvale, Kansas, then stole $300 from a local theater. Next, he enlisted nephew Frank Underhill to rob $14.68 from a Wichita filling station. Fleeing that scene, Wilbur collided with another vehicle, had his towed to a garage, and booked a hotel room. Patrolman Merle Colver arrived next day, on a round of local hostelries, and Underhill shot him three times, killing him. Escaping on foot, he traded shots with other officers, a two-year-old boy slain in the crossfire, before a neck wound dropped Wilbur and he was jailed. Another life sentence followed, this one at Lansing's state prison. Frank Underhill, discharged without trial, abandoned the underworld life. At Lansing, Wilbur met Harvey Bailey and other inmates, joining in plans for a mass breakout.[75]

2. Public Enemies

Kansas State Prison at Lansing, scene of a mass escape by "public enemies" on May 30, 1933 (author's collection).

Most crimes committed by early 1930s "public enemies," aside from kidnapping and interstate car theft, fell outside the FBI's jurisdiction—which did not ensure a hands-off attitude.

One case that *was* within the Bureau's purview, the unsolved Lindbergh kidnapping, showed early hopeful signs of breaking on May 2, 1933, when New York's Federal Reserve Bank discovered 297 gold certificates on May 1, totaling $2,980. Treasury agents checked records, identifying the depositor as "J.J. Faulkner," allegedly residing on West 149th Street in Manhattan. Meanwhile, examination of the ransom notes found graphologists "virtually unanimous" in claiming one hand wrote them all, a person "of German nationality" based on various misspellings such as "boad" for "boat." Dr. Condon still described "cemetery John" as Scandinavian, claiming he could spot the ransom negotiator on sight, but had no luck with piles of mugshots. The FBI, largely frozen out of the case by state and local police, transcribed Condon's alleged conversations with "John," recording them on phonograph records for which Condon imitated the suspect's accent. Today, Bureau historians still claim that "in this manner the nationality, education, mentality, and character of the kidnapper were more clearly defined and permanently preserved for future use," though in fact it captured nothing but "Jafsie's" dubious acting skill.[76]

Another angle of attack involved "wood experts" examining the crude ladder found in Hopewell. Police found no fingerprints, nor could any Lindbergh neighbors or local woodworkers identify the homemade relic. One such "expert," Arthur Koehler from the U.S. Forest Service, dismantled the ladder, allegedly identified the mismatched bits of lumber used, and studied the patterns of nail holes. According to the Bureau, he made field trips and struck out at various factories, but his opinions, still debated, "later played a critical role in the trial of the kidnapper."[77]

Twelve hundred miles to the west, in Kansas, convicts at Lansing state prison celebrated Decoration Day—now Memorial Day—with a baseball game, tied 2–2 in the sixth inning when 11 inmates staged a daring escape. Unknown to guards, Frank Nash had smuggled four pistols into the prison, inside a bale of sisal used for making whiskbrooms. Thus armed, the convicts seized three hostages—Warden Kirk Prather and two guards—and fled in a stolen car, some speeding south toward Oklahoma's Cookson Hills, while others scattered to the winds. Two headline fugitives, Harvey Bailey and Wilbur Underhill, drove southward to Oklahoma's Cookson Hills, leaving their hostages with $5 bus fare back to Lansing after Bailey stopped Wilbur from killing the trio for pleasure.[78]

Even so, the break was not without violence. Bailey suffered a leg wound while stealing a backup car from prison farm superintendent W.W. Woodson, and Patrolman Otto Durkee died in Chetopa, Kansas, when he caught the fugitives stealing a spare tire for their getaway vehicle on May 31. From there, the escapees dispersed, launching a Midwestern crime wave.[79] Others who escaped with Bailey and Underhill included—

Lewis Bechtel, serving 10 to 31 years for bank robbery. He was recaptured on June 2, at a farm near Dripping Springs, Oklahoma, showing "no fight" when deputies found him dining with the farmer and his wife.[80]

Robert "Big Bob" Brady, Oklahoma-born in 1904, was first arrested for larceny in Kansas at 15. Forgery sent him to prison in 1922, armed robbery in 1925. Released in 1931, he joined Clarence "Buck" Adams to steal $5,300 from a Sooner bank that September. Captured at Carlsbad Caverns on the 26th, he was deposited in Amarillo and tried a jailbreak, suffering a near-fatal head wound. Surgery saved his life but left him with defective vision. He escaped from McAlester in July 1932 and launched another crime wave, robbing a Missouri bank and a Kansas auto dealership. On October 1, with Frank Philpot, he hit a New Mexico bank. Four states wanted him at the time of his capture in Des Moines, on December 20, but Kansas won the toss and sentenced him to life.[81]

Kenneth Conn, alias "Lewis Thagard," born 1910, was sentenced to life for murder in May 1931.[82]

Oklahoman *Edward "The Fox" Davis*, born in 1900, joined the army at 17 but was prematurely discharged for undisclosed reasons in January 1918.

Over the next year he committed minor robberies while riding the rails with cohorts Earl Berry and Oscar Steelman, earning a two-year prison term in 1920. Released in 1922, he was next jailed in Kansas with a concealed weapon (charge dismissed with orders to leave town). In January 1923 he burglarized an oilman's home with Bill Sheppard, stealing $2,475 in cash and jewelry, but police tracked their footsteps through fresh snow and both pled guilty at arrest, receiving 10 years each at McAlester. Paroled again in 1928, suffering a painful ear infection, Davis turned more violent. In April 1931, with accomplices Jack Alfred and John Schrimsher, he killed one officer and wounded another before return fire disabled their getaway car. Texas lawmen captured Davis, living with his wife as "Paul Joiner," all three gunmen receiving life sentences in August 1931. Davis escaped from McAlester with two other convicts in May 1932 and turned to bank robbery, joining veteran bandits Jim Clark and Frank Sawyer. Captured in Arkansas on June 17, all three were charged with a Kansas robbery and auto theft, each sentenced to long terms at Lansing.[83]

Clifford Dopson, sentenced for larceny in Cherokee County, was a last-minute "tagalong" to the escape. Once free, he teamed with fugitive Harold Harris, making for Texas and the Mexican border.[84]

Alvie "Sonny" Payton, born in 1910, was an auto mechanic gone bad, drawing a 20- to 100-year sentence for bank robbery in October 1930.[85]

Oklahoma native *James Franklin "Frank" Sawyer*, born in 1899, learned nothing from his strict Baptist parents, turning to crime as a teenager, robbing the first of "countless" banks in 1917–18 with cronies Jeff Davis, Bud Maxwell, and Henry Wells. In 1920 he killed fellow bandit John Moore in a quarrel over cards. Sawyer received a life sentence but escaped from McAlester in 1922, suspected (but not charged) with joining Frank Nash and others to steal $20,000 from a mail train in August 1923. One month later, he was allegedly "in the area" when an Oklahoma posse including "Ed Robinson, federal man" killed gang leader Al Spencer near Bartlesville. Arrested and returned to McAlester in 1924, he escaped from a prison work party in February 1930 and resumed his holdup career. Sawyer robbed a Missouri bank in May 1932, then was caught with Jim Clark and Ed Davis after a bungled heist in Fort Scott, Kansas, all returned to Lansing as escapees.[86]

Harold Wesley Harris, imprisoned as "Billie Woods," was another "tagalong" escapee, serving five to 15 years for a bank job in Ford County.[87]

A sweeping manhunt, excluding the FBI, initially yielded meager results. Two days after Lewis Becthel's capture, on June 4, Frank Sawyer surfaced in Caddo County, Oklahoma. Menaced by a posse, he used County Clerk Bob Goodfellow as a human shield, leaving him with a police bullet in his groin, then snatched Goodfellow's sister Lois, with her car, demanding that she flee the scene. Instead, she crashed into a ditch, allowing officers to swarm and disarm Sawyer, returning him to custody. On June 10 Customs agents spotted escapees Dopson and Woods near San Angelo, Texas, arresting both without incident. Their scattered compatriots remained at large.[88]

Gangsters cannot operate without support from various accomplices providing shelter and weapons. In the 1930s there was no shortage of either.

One reliable hideout was a Missouri farm owned by *Herbert Allen "Deafy" Farmer* and his wife Esther. Born in 1891, frequently arrested as a juvenile, Herbert met the Barker boys around 1910 and stayed in touch thereafter, FBI reports claiming Ma's sons "were practically raised by Herb Farmer's mother." Slapped with a five-year Oklahoma sentence for assault with intent to kill, Farmer emerged on parole to marry and purchase a farm southwest of Joplin, hosting fugitives including the Barkers, Harvey Bailey, Frank Nash, Wilbur Underhill, and others. Police ignored the Farmers until mid–1933, the year a Bureau report called Deafy "a very dangerous man, a killer, his favorite weapon being the knife."[89]

When the Farmers lacked spare room, fugitives were always welcome in Saint Paul, Minnesota, initially corrupted by Police Chief John O'Connor's "layover agreement" dating from 1900, under which felons could purchase immunity with cash and a vow to abstain from any local crimes. Bagmen William "Reddy" Griffin and "Dapper" Dan Hogan collected bribes at the Hotel Savoy, earning Saint Paul a 1920s reputation as a "poison spot of crime." Local author Steve Thayer opened his 1988 best-seller, *Saint Mudd*, with the observation "In Saint Paul gangsters can fuck in the streets," and while not literally true, he captured the city's renegade spirit.[90]

In 1930 control of the city passed to Chief Thomas "Big Tom" Brown, born in 1895. Beginning his police career with the "Purity Squad," assigned to close brothels, casinos, and speakeasies, he prospered under the "O'Connor system." Arrested in 1926 for stealing confiscated liquor, Brown won reinstatement when his case was dropped for "lack of evidence." Mobster Leon Gleckman engineered Brown's appointment as chief four years later, corruption expanding as Brown's Kidnapping Squad shifted from tolerance of gangsters to active collusion in planning abductions. Demoted to detective lieutenant by Mayor William Mahoney for collaborating with the Barker-Karpis gang, Brown kept his badge, accepted a $1,000 contribution from Homer Van Meter for an unsuccessful county sheriff's race, and continued aiding felons until 1935.[91]

Bandits need weapons, and America suffers no shortage of firearms. Aside from standard pistols, rifles and shotguns, the world war introduced portable automatic weapons that were soon adopted by felons and lawmen alike. One, the .45-caliber Thompson submachine gun or "Tommy gun," entered service with Chicago's bootleggers in 1926 and quickly took the underworld by storm. Another, the Browning Automatic Rifle (BAR) fired .30–06 Springfield rifle cartridges and was particularly favored by the Barrow gang. A "civilian" version, the Colt Monitor, found its way to various police departments and to gangsters including Lester Gillis.[92]

Both weapons were available without restriction until 1934, but criminals often required discretionary sales, along with various customized weapons. In that pursuit, they patronized specific gunsmiths in Chicago and Texas.

Chicago's premiere gangland armorers were *Louis Scaramuzzo, Oswald Von Lengerke,* and *Peter Von Frantzius.* Scaramuzzo ran a shop on South Halstead Street, later moving to Blue Island Avenue, described by Chief of Detectives William Shoemaker as a "gun mechanic" for West Side mobs including Al Capone and the Genna brothers. Rival Von Lengerke operated from a shop on South Wabash, selling 50 Tommy guns within an eight-year period. A middleman between Scaramuzzo and Von Frantzius was Alex Korecek, owner of a hardware store. Police raided Scaramuzzo's second shop in November 1931, seizing bootleg booze and several guns with their serial numbers removed. Scaramuzzo denied the latter offense but jurors convicted him in February 1932, resulting in a one-year sentence and $300 fine. An appellate court reversed that verdict and he never spent a day in jail.[93]

Von Frantzius first sold mail-order guns from his parents' home, then opened a shop on Diversey Parkway, selling Tommy guns for $175 to $200 apiece, magazines for $4.72, and obliterating serial numbers for $2. Disputed police reports claim that one of his Thompsons killed Frankie Yale in 1928, paired with another for the 1929 Saint Valentine's Day massacre, but he was never charged in either case.[94]

Far to the south, in San Antonio, Russian-born *Hyman Saul Lebman* provided a more extensive service, not only furnishing automatic weapons but customizing others, commonly adding Tommy-gun foregrips to rifles and shotguns, converting semiautomatic rifles to full-auto fire. His most famous production, called "baby machine guns"—favored by Lester Gillis, Roger Touhy, and John Dillinger—added foregrips and extended magazines to standard Colt semiautomatic pistols, while converting them to full-auto fire for close-range shootouts. Unlike Von Frantzius, Lebman faced conviction under a state law banning machine guns, convicted and sentenced to a five-year term, but he successfully appealed that verdict and never entered prison.[95]

Two days before the Bureau's "crime war" formally began, a series of events occurred that would change everything for Hoover, his agents, and the underworld.

On June 15 FBI agents Francis Joseph Lackey and Frank Smith learned that Frank Nash was living under protection of corrupt police in Hot Springs, Arkansas. With Police Chief Otto Reed of McAlester, Oklahoma, they traveled to Hot Springs and heard that Nash, with other fugitives, frequented a cigar store owned by gangland fixer Richard Galatas. On the 16th they surprised Nash and arrested him, whisking their quarry off toward Little Rock. Twice en route they were stopped by police roadblocks, at Benton and near the capital city, but refused to surrender their prisoner. After the second stop, Nash prophetically muttered, "I hope we make it out of this state alive."[96]

Texas gunsmith Hyman Lebman's customized "baby machine gun," popular with various bandits (author's collection).

Also on June 15, in Saint Paul, members of the Barker-Karpis gang, acting in collaboration with Tom Brown's Kidnapping Squad, abducted William Hamm, Jr., president of Hamm's Brewing Company. The gang drove Hamm to Illinois after demanding $100,000 ransom and collected their payoff on the 17th, providing a cut to police.[97]

On June 16, between Hamm's abduction and release, with Frank Nash and his escorts on the road, President Roosevelt signed legislation creating the Federal Deposit Insurance Corporation (FDIC), designed to help depositors at U.S.–insured banks. The initial plan, increased over time, insured deposits up to $2,500 ($49,000 today), easing the burden on depositors if banks were robbed. Within a year, it would open the door for FBI investigation of holdups at FDIC–insured banks.[98]

That same afternoon, Charles Floyd and Adam Richetti kidnapped Polk County Sheriff William Killingsworth from Bolivar, Missouri, driving him toward Kansas City in his brother's stolen car. In Clinton, the outlaws switched cars and abducted the second vehicle's owner, releasing both hostages at nightfall in Lee's Summit, 22 miles from Kansas City. Thus unburdened, they proceeded to lose themselves in the Show Me State's largest city, unaware that they would soon be blamed for mass murder and the "crime war's" beginning.[99]

3

"Get 'Em Up! Up!"

Every war has a precipitating incident. The FBI's long-running "war on crime" in the United States began by accident.

Frank Nash's June 16 arrest galvanized lawmen and gangsters alike. FBI agents Lackey and Smith, with Chief Reed, drove their prisoner to Fort Smith, Arkansas, hustling Nash aboard a Missouri Pacific train bound for Kansas City at 8:30 p.m. Before embarking, one of them phoned SAC Reed Vetterli, arranging for an escort to greet them at Kansas City's Union Station when their train arrived at 7:15 the next morning. Someone from their party also spoke to an Associated Press reporter, airing details of their plan, which hit newsstands shortly after midnight in the *Kansas City Star*'s morning edition. Vetterli, in turn, advised his second-in-command, Agent Monte Spear, of the quartet's impending arrival, saying Agent Raymond Caffrey would lead the escort detail, adding that he expected no trouble since Caffrey "had done a lot of work on the Nash case."[1]

Despite that misplaced optimism, Vetterli also sought reinforcements from the Kansas City Police Department. Given the department's pervasive corruption, including 60-odd officers burdened by criminal records, that choice might seem unwise, but by all accounts the two detectives ordered to assist—Frank Hermanson and William "Red" Grooms—were honest cops, normally working the downtown burglary detail. A superior officer told them to take the department's "Hot Shot" car, equipped with two Tommy guns for use in emergencies. Sometime during the night of June 16, persons unknown removed the submachine guns, leaving Grooms and Hermanson with no weapons except their .38 revolvers.[2]

Meanwhile, friends of Jelly Nash—and possibly some others worried over the illicit knowledge he possessed—were busily consulting one another over phone lines that connected Hot Springs and Fort Smith to Joplin, Kansas City, and other mobbed-up communities. Hot Springs Chief of Detectives Herbert "Dutch" Akers conferred with Richard Galatas, owner of the smoke shop where Nash was arrested, then reached out to corrupt counterparts in Little Rock and Fort Smith, reporting that businessman

"George Miller"—Nash's alias—had been kidnapped by unknown gunmen. Galatas rendezvoused with Frances Nash, Jelly's wife, and more phone calls ensued, some reaching Herbert Farmer near Joplin, others alerting tavern owner Frank Mulloy and Louis "Doc" Stacci in Kansas City. Jelly's escorts badged their way past two bogus roadblocks before Galatas and Frances Nash reached Joplin, around the same time husband Frank and his captors entrained at Fort Smith. At 10:17 p.m. Esther Farmer phoned Vern Miller's home in KC and spoke to girlfriend Vivian Mathias, arranging for Miller to stage a morning rescue at Kansas City's Union Station.[3]

All sources agree that the Missouri Pacific train arrived on time. Agent Lackey left Nash in a stateroom, covered by Frank Smith and Otto Reed, while Lackey stepped onto the loading platform, looking for his party's backup officers. Agents Vetterli and Caffrey were on hand, having arrived in Caffrey's private four-door Chevrolet sedan. Detectives Grooms and Hermanson, also present, had found their Hot Shot's submachine guns missing as they left headquarters but decided to report it later, after they returned. Those five surveyed the station's parking lot, saw nothing that alarmed them, and returned to fetch their prisoner, with lawmen Smith and Reed, from the stateroom.[4]

The party left, with Nash in handcuffs and surrounded by his escorts. One witness in the depot mistook Jelly Nash for Charles Floyd, whose mugshot had graced the front pages of Saturday's newspapers. Others noted Reed and Lackey armed with shotguns, Reed's a vintage Winchester Model 1897 in 16-gauge, Lackey's a 12-gauge pump-action borrowed from the Bureau's Oklahoma City office. Reed also wore a revolver on his hip. No onlookers noted the .38s carried concealed by Caffrey, Grooms, Hermanson or Smith (the latter backed up by a hidden .45). Of the seven lawmen present, only Vetterli was unarmed.[5]

Various diagrams of Union Station and its parking lot appear in books and articles detailing what ensued within the next few moments. Few agree with one another, FBI historians claiming that Caffrey's 1931 or '32 Chevrolet with Nebraska plates stood "directly in front of the east entrance of Union Station," while other reports place it 60 to 175 feet from that portal, across a driveway. One account puts the KCPD Hot Shot vehicle "alongside" Caffrey's car without specifying which side, while others have it facing Caffrey's car from the opposite direction. All agree that to the right of Caffrey's Chevy, facing in the same direction, sat a green Plymouth, 1926 or '29 model, owned by Mrs. Parnie Miller (or "Millikan," in one account). As the lawmen and their prisoner approached, Miller and her mother were inside the depot, waiting to greet a passenger on arrival.[6]

Wedging six men and their weapons into Caffrey's car posed problems. Caffrey unlocked the Chevy's right-hand doors, whereupon Nash moved to sit in the rear. Agent Lackey stopped him, telling Nash to sit up front, "so we can all keep an eye on you." Jelly complied, sliding across the Chevrolet's front seat, coming to rest behind its steering wheel. Lackey then emulated Nash, sliding across the backseat to a point directly behind him, with Agent Smith to Lackey's right, and Chief Reed to Smith's right at the end of the bench seat. Caffrey circled around the Chevy's front end, intending to drive. Reed Vetterli's written report to Washington read, "The two Kansas City detectives were on the right side of Caffrey's car, walking toward their own car which was parked in front of us. I was on the right side of the car waiting for the men to load and for Nash to move over to the middle of the front seat so that I could enter the right front door and ride to the outside of him, *Both Reed and I leaned our shotguns against the right side of the car*, and I was going to pick them up and carry them into the car when I got in" (emphasis added). Modern FBI historians amend that claim, writing that "Vetterli stood with Officers Hermanson and Grooms at the right side near the front of the car."[7]

Then, suddenly, it all went wrong.

Most sources agree that a man's voice shouted, "Put 'em up! Up, up!" but from that point onward, chaos reigns in print, as it did in the depot's parking lot.

The aftermath of Kansas City's Union Station Massacre, which claimed five lives on June 17, 1933. The shot-up cars belong to Agent Raymond Caffrey (right) and Parnie Miller (left). Kansas City detective William Grooms and Frank Hermanson lie where they fell between the vehicles (Library of Congress).

In the Chevy's backseat, Agents Lackey and Smith both turned to their right, looking past the green Plymouth parked beside them. FBI historians online say Lackey saw two men emerge, both armed, "at least one of them" holding a Tommy gun. Smith allegedly saw only one man, covering the Chevy with a submachine gun. A contradictory FBI version places "an individual crouched behind" the Plymouth's radiator, some 15 feet distant, as the same voice or another called out, "Let 'em have it!" Detectives Grooms and Hermanson "immediately fell to the ground," both slain "almost instantly." Standing with them, Agent Vetterli suffered a wound to his left arm, either dropping and scrambling around the Chevy's left side to join Caffrey or "crouched and sprinted for the safety of the station." One report has Nash shouting, "Be careful or you'll hit me, too!" seconds before "bullets from the hoodlums' guns" killed him and Chief Reed. Agent Caffrey, having reached the left side of his car, received a fatal head wound and collapsed. In the Chevy's backseat, Agent Smith dropped down and played dead, while Lackey—shot at least three times from behind—slumped over near him. A conflicting version has Nash slain first, "the back of his head blown off" by Reed's .38, before the Chief was shot twice in his skull.[8]

The shooting ended swiftly. Various reporters peg the firefight's length somewhere between 30 seconds and "less than 100." Accounts of what came next pose yet another mystery. Surviving agents Smith and Lackey, hunched down in the Chevrolet's backseat, both claimed to hear a man's voice say, "They're all dead. Let's get out of here!" One version says Reed Vetterli heard the same comment, but that claim negates reports that he'd run to hide in the depot. Another source says "at least two of the gunmen rushed to the lawmen's car" before one shared the news. Strangest of all, the Bureau's website—insisting that only three shooters were present—claims "the three gunmen" all looked inside Caffrey's car before one of them spoke, but in that case, who was he warning?[9]

Nothing remained, at any rate, but for the murderers to flee the scene, and once again, reports are hopelessly confused. Some observers said a REO sedan—short for REO Motor Car Company, founded by Robert E. Olds in 1905—was first to flee the depot's parking lot, speeding west along 24th Street. Others missed that vehicle entirely, but saw a dark-colored Chevrolet, possibly green, retreating from the crime scene. Patrolman Myron "Mike" Fanning emerged from the depot in time to see a husky man running for that Chevrolet and fired at him, reporting that his target nearly fell but stumbled on and reached the car and leapt inside. The Chevy fled west from the depot's parking lot, but others noted deviations in its route of travel.[10]

Mrs. J.E. Goodling hailed a traffic cop at 39th and Main, reporting, "I was walking south on the west side of Main Street when this car, going at least 60 miles an hour, turned right off Main at 38th and almost ran me over. It turned the corner on two wheels and I didn't think the driver could make it without wrecking the car. He kept control, though, and roared off west on 38th toward Broadway." Streetcar conductor Robert Woods was more precise, reporting, "At 7:23 Saturday morning I had stopped my car at 31st and Main St. to discharge passengers. I saw a dark coach or sedan, fairly new, maybe a Chevrolet, turn the corner from West 31st Street and turn right on Main. It was going at a high rate of speed, and it turned so fast it burned tire marks on the street." From there, he watched the speeder turn left onto Broadway, following the elusive REO's path toward Kansas City's southern quarter.[11]

No full roster of witnesses from Union Station exists, due in part to J. Edgar Hoover's

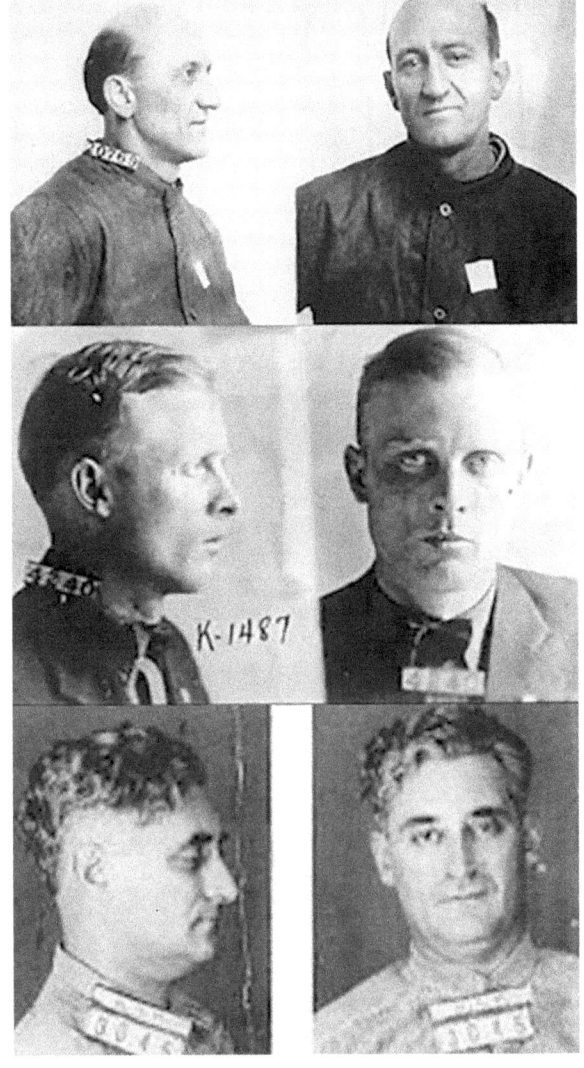

Known or suspected massacre participants. Top: Frank "Jelly" Nash, slain either accidentally or deliberately (stories differ) in federal custody; Middle: Vernon Miller, the only gunman ever positively linked to the Union Station ambush. Bottom: Harvey Bailey, "The Dean of American Bank Robbers," named by multiple witnesses as a Union Station gunman (National Archives).

bias against statements from "colored people," understood and mimicked by his agents. As for agents at the scene, all trained observers, Ray Caffrey died en route to a local hospital, while survivors Lackey, Smith and Vetterli offered divergent accounts.[12]

Joe Lackey's first report to headquarters, referring to himself in the third-person, said, "Agent saw these men through the window glass on the windshield of the Plymouth, which was none too clean, and therefore a clear view could not be obtained by agent. Agent did not at any time see but two of the attackers, but judged from the shooting, there were at least four and possibly more men shooting, as the shots were coming from nearly all directions. Agent got such a hurried glance at these two men and this glance was through a none too clean window and windshield of the Plymouth, that he is not sure he could identify either of these men nor is he positive that he could identify the voice of the man who commented that Nash was dead." Shot three times, he also gave a statement to the *Kansas City Star* from his hospital bed, declaring, "Bullets poured into the car from every direction, front, sides and the rear of the car. It all happened in a flash. We never had a chance to defend ourselves. But I remember that it flashed through over me that this was the thing we had been fearful would happen. I remember saying to myself, 'Here they are.'" One account has Lackey hospitalized until July 8, finally discharged but "still unable to walk" with two or three slugs near his spine.[13]

Frank Smith, the only agent left unscathed, adopted a similar style in his statement to Hoover. "At the first volley," he wrote, "the writer dropped his head down below the front seat as if shot and remained in that position until the firing ceased. While the writer observed by a glance a man behind the machine gun pointed and shooting in his direction, he was unable to obtain any kind of a description of him and was unable to see anyone else who did the shooting." As with Joe Lackey, Smith's testimony would change radically two years later, delivered under oath in a Kansas City courtroom.[14]

Reed Vetterli's account to Hoover was the only statement that identified a suspect. "I saw but one man, who was operating the machine gun from my right," he said. After viewing many mugshots, Smith declared, "I am convinced that the man who first opened fire from our right, with a machine gun, is Bob Brady." That put Lansing's fugitives, all friends of Nash, in line as suspects, but like Smith and Lackey, Vetterli would later change his testimony to identify another public enemy entirely.[15]

Civilian witnesses at Union Station were equally confused, none more so than Lottie West, a 51-year-old employee of the Travelers Aid Society (now Travelers Aid International).[16] In fact, she told so many different stories of the massacre that it's impossible to say if she saw anything at all.

First and foremost, West was the only witness who reported seeing Pretty Boy Floyd at the depot on June 17, although it took two days for her to make that revelation. First, she told authorities that a strange man she did not recognize entered the depot, approached her as if to ask a question, then "turned and walked away" without speaking. After scanning mugshots, West could identify no one on Saturday, but the mental fog lifted two days later, in the office of Sheriff Thomas Bash. There, she "immediately" fingered Floyd's photo, embellishing her tale to say that he was seated at her desk when she arrived for work at 7:00 a.m. Agent William Trainor reported that ID to Washington, noting that other depot employees contradicted West, insisting that the man behind her desk was fellow worker Harry Blanchard. One unnamed fed dubbed her second story "very good," while the *Kansas City Journal-Post* noted that West was shown a different photo of Floyd on June 19 than she had viewed two days earlier. Worse yet, on June 17 she described only two gunmen, later adding a third. One, she claimed was about 40, an "older type of man" and "elderly ... rather swarthy and seemed to have a growth of beard, dressed in a dark suit and felt hat." His companion was "younger," but West "could not give a clear description" of him.[17]

After her dubious Floyd sighting in the depot, West allegedly stepped outside to help six Benedictine nuns in full habit hail a taxi when the shooting started. As with Pretty Boy, no other station witness saw the nuns or Lottie West, standing in plain view and obvious danger while others around them ran for cover. In that statement, she reported two men firing machine guns, while a third used two pistols, one a "blue gun," the other "nickel-plated." In yet another version, Lottie told the *Journal-Post*, "I ran to the door in time to see two carloads of machine-gunners drive away." The reporter added, "She said she saw the faces of several of them." West also "believed" that Ray Caffrey shot Nash before he—Caffrey—was killed in turn. Embroidering her story further, she later claimed that Vern Miller fired his Tommy gun while crouched behind her own Oakland sedan. The half-dozen nuns remain unidentified today.[18]

As for her distance from the carnage, and the odds that she saw anything at all, West initially claimed that she stood "within 30 feet" of the gunmen, while the *Kansas City Star* doubled that estimate and other witnesses insisted that she never left the depot till the shooting stopped. Author L.R. Kirchner—Agent Caffrey's second cousin—personally measured the distance from the FBI death car to Union Station's recessed doorway, reporting that West must have been at least 75 feet from the shooters, perhaps as much as 100. Cabbie Alva Parman placed West *inside* the doorway, roughly 110 feet from the bloodletting. In 1993 yet another of West's many statements surfaced, claiming one shooter "was carrying one of those guns with a cylinder on top of it [sic]. He started shooting right at two of the officers. Nobody said anything. There wasn't a sound. He just started shooting." That claim, of course, refutes the testimony of all three surviving agents who reported hearing one or more of their attackers speak.[19]

Concerning Agent Caffrey's final moments, more confusion reigns. West claimed that he shot Jelly Nash before he was gunned down. Other witnesses allegedly saw Caffrey fall, then rise again to fire at his assailants, not at Nash, before he finally collapsed. To this day, FBI historians insist that Caffrey never drew his pistol, found still in its holster and unfired when he arrived dead at the hospital.[20]

Another civilian witness, Samuel Link, was more clear-headed than West but posed worse problems for the FBI's eventual "solution" of the massacre. A self-described "local manufacturer" in June 1933, Link was previously a Kansas City deputy constable during 1926–27. In that capacity, he'd gone to serve attachment papers on a female resident of Brooklyn Street and "was confronted with Harvey Bailey, then using the name of 'Morris' Bailey, alias Morris [sic], and I had an encounter at this time by virtue of which fact I have a very vivid memory of him." On massacre morning, entering the depot's parking lot, Link was about to park beside a green REO sedan, standing along a curb outside the depot, when the REO's driver told him to move on, clearing his path to an adjacent driveway. Seconds later, Link "heard a voice say, 'Duck, you blankety-blank, duck!' So I looked up and saw a man coming out of the left side of the REO sedan. I recognized him as Harvey Bailey, the notorious criminal." Bailey lost his hat while exiting the REO, Link reported, exposing his shock of red hair, then raised a submachine gun to his shoulder and "fired into the officers." Link's story never altered, but the FBI later decided to ignore it as it sought alternate suspects.[21]

Margaret Turner, one of the few black witnesses whose statement Bureau agents deemed "reliable," drove to Union Station with friend Walt Berry on the night of June 16 to meet a train arriving from Mexico, Missouri, but it was late, prompting them to wait in their car. As time passed, she saw two vehicles—a black Chevrolet and a green REO—occupied by several men and one woman wearing a white dress, cruising the parking lot, the Chevy making stops at the depot every 45 minutes on the quarter-hour. At each stop, one or more of the passengers briefly entered, then returned to their car. Turner identified one of those men as Reed Vetterli, but investigators deemed that "impossible." The REO, for its part, parked within 10 to 15 feet of Margaret's car for three hours straight, giving her ample time to identify its occupants as Harvey Bailey and Wilbur Underhill. Each time the Chevy passed the REO, she recalled, "the drivers acknowledged one another." When the shooting finally started, Turner and Berry were inside the station, ducking lead and flying glass.[22]

Another witness, depot porter J.D. "Red" Jameson, told Agent J.R. Calhoun that a man closely resembling Bailey's mugshot—oddly, walking with a cane—accosted him moments before the Missouri Pacific arrived, saying that "he and some friends would like to go down to the platform and pick up an invalid who was arriving on the train." Jameson referred him to the stationmaster for the platform's number and the stranger moved on, but Jameson later glimpsed the same man from the depot's sidewalk, firing a Tommy gun at Ray Caffrey's car, "and he later ran around the rear of the car and fired again."[23]

Concerning Harvey Bailey as a suspect in the massacre, Oklahoma City SAC Ralph Colvin cited "an absolutely reliable source" that Nash had arranged the Lansing breakout in May, thus incurring a debt from Bailey and his fellow fugitives. "I have no doubt," Colvin added, "that the shooting was done by the Lansing escapees and I don't believe that Pretty Boy Floyd had anything to do with it."[24]

Taxi drivers were another fruitful source of information, although none apparently attempted to identify the gunmen. One told the *Star* that two assassins fled after the shooting in "a 1930 or 1931 REO sedan or a sport model coach, kind of light, pea green color." One of those passengers, described as five foot eight, around 200 pounds, with "a brown face," wearing a panama hat and dark-colored suit, "carried two automatic weapons" (presumably meaning pistols, rather than Tommy guns awkwardly fired one-handed). That gunman's companion seemed older, age 40 to 45, and was smaller, with a lighter complexion. A second cabbie told the *Journal-Post* of seeing one gunman "come behind the government car and start firing into the back end of the car. He first fired high up, then he crouched and fired low into the car." Without advancing an ID, his statement echoed that of witness Samuel Link.[25]

More telling testimony came from Yellow Taxi driver Harry Orr, who watched the slaughter from close range. Referring to the law enforcement escort team, Orr said, "As they got across and some of them got in the car, I saw one man with what looked like a shotgun, and he was trying to fire it." As we shall discover, although Orr was unacquainted with the lawmen, his remarks confirmed Joe Lackey's statement of events before the ambush team cut loose.[26]

After nine decades and counting, confusion still surrounds the actual number of gunmen involved in the ambush. Various witnesses told reporters they'd seen four, five, six, or seven shooters, while Reed Vetterli's 1949 obituary in the *Salt Lake Tribune* claimed that he was "severely wounded"— the FBI says "nipped" on his left arm—by "10 machine gun bandits." The first page of the Bureau's hefty file described the killers as "unknown parties believed four altho [sic] definite number unknown," adding "license number of shooting car obtained."[27]

Today, no source disputes Vern Miller as the hit team's leader, while no witness aside from Lottie West ever identified his backup with a Tommy gun as Charles Floyd. Dismissing her shaky ID of "Pretty Boy," who else comprised the firing squad?

Harvey Bailey ran a close second to Miller, based on statements from Harry Link and Red Jameson. Soon after the slaughter, J. Edgar Hoover ordered longtime San Antonio SAC Gus Jones to take over the case as "head investigator," adding another vote to Bailey's column. On June 20 Hoover dictated a memo of his latest phone conversation with Jones, saying, "Mr. Jones stated that there is no doubt that the shooting was done by…. Harvey Bailey, Wilbur Underhill, Ed Davis and Bob Brady, all Lansing escapees, with the addition of Jim Clark … but that he does not believe that 'Pretty Boy' Floyd had anything to do with it." Arriving in KC, Jones told his subordinates, "As of right now, Harve Bailey is at the top of my list of suspects." Agent Raymond Suran, a critic of Jones, said, "Gus wouldn't even consider anything else. He knew it was Harvey Bailey and that was that." Suran rejected Bailey on grounds that he was not a contract killer, but he *was* a well-known friend of Jelly Nash, the man who had allegedly planned Lansing's mass escape just 18 days before the Union Station massacre. Jones subsequently returned to his post in Texas, serving there until 1941, while FBI headquarters claimed his Lansing theory "had not held up."[28]

A dark horse suspect, named by Melvin Purvis in those days when he was still Director Hoover's favored pen pal, was Fred Goetz, a gun for hire and sometime member of the Barker-Karpis gang, but Goetz remained at large and was not questioned by the feds before underworld enemies killed him in March 1934. No evidence today connects him to the Union Station crime.[29]

While Hoover's agents scoured the countryside for suspects, Kansas City law enforcement took a more ambivalent approach. On one hand, Chief of Detectives Tom Higgins told journalists, "a net of guns and steel had been placed around the city. We expect to have them in our custody at any hour now. They simply can't get out of Kansas City." On the sly, meanwhile, Director of Police Eugene Reppert instructed his subordinates, "This is not a police matter. Hands off. Have nothing to do with it." After dining with Reppert and Higgins the night of the slayings, City Manager Henry "Judge" McElroy announced, "It has been definitely established that no Kansas City gangster had anything to do with the shooting at the Union Station this morning."[30]

Established by whom? Based on what evidence? Most Missourians were well aware of Kansas City PD's rampant corruption, including control by Tom Pendergast's political machine and its lucrative collaboration with

KC Mafia boss John Lazia. That aside, nagging suspicion persists that some unnamed police official played a more direct role in the massacre.

Specifically, those doubts were spawned by disappearance of one or two machine guns (reports differ) from the department's Hot Shot car during the night of June 16, 1933. That theft not only left Detectives Grooms and Hermanson without their heavy weapons for the Nash transfer on Saturday, but some observers still suspect the Tommy guns may have been used against them at Union Station the next morning. When asked about the theft, one department spokesmen called it a "bureaucratic foul-up," while another said, "We don't know. It's just one of those things." Even today, divergent sources disagree as to whether the weapons ever turned up. One Internet source claims the guns "would surface a few hours later," while author L.R. Kirchner writes that they "were never recovered." Indicted conspirator Michael "Jimmy Needles" LaCapra, spinning convoluted tales to spare himself from major prison time, told Bureau agents that the Tommy guns were stashed at John Lazia's headquarters in the North Side Democratic Club, from whence they disappeared to parts unknown. All we can say with certainty, at this remove, is that the Tommy guns were never test-fired to discover whether one or both played any part in Union Station's bloodletting.[31]

The FBI had no jurisdiction to enter the case in June 1933, but legal niceties meant little to Washington. Attorney General Cummings told the nation, "The gauntlet has been thrown down. The murder of a Department of Justice agent is an open challenge to the government of this nation. The entire department has been ordered to assist in this case." Director Hoover charged into the fray immediately, firing off a memo to Reed Vetterli which read, "Confirming my several telephonic conversations with you today, it is my desire that every effort and resource of this Bureau be utilized to bring about the apprehension of the parties responsible.... I cannot too strongly emphasize the imperative necessity of concentrating upon this matter, without any let-up in the same until the parties are taken...." The last three words of that sentence, overstruck with x's on Helen Gandy's typewriter but still legible on photocopies, read "dead or alive." A month into the manhunt, Hoover told a Washington convention of the International Association of Chiefs of Police, "Those who participated in this cold-blooded murder will be hunted down. Sooner or later, the penalty which is their due will be paid." Privately, he told his troops, "They must be exterminated, and they must be exterminated by us, and to this we dedicate ourselves."[32]

One lead never pursued on the record rated a headline from the *Journal-Post* on June 20, trumpeting "Second Nash Ambush Plot Uncovered." According to the paper, unnamed DOJ agents had revealed that "a motor carload of gangsters seen along the highway leading to Leavenworth early Saturday afternoon was a second group determined to prevent his return to the federal penitentiary." Neither those gangsters nor the Bureau's source of information were identified, much less how Hoover's men determined their intentions without grilling them. Before long, the manhunt would narrow its scope to three fugitives, excluding all others. L.R. Kirchner's tabulation of the Bureau's Union Station file notes 13,786 items gathered between the massacre's date and Charles Floyd's slaying in October 1934. Of those, 17 percent—2,360 letters and memos—traveled between Hoover's desk and Gus Jones in the field, all but 127 of them dated between June 17 and September 1, 1933, all leading nowhere if the Bureau's final verdict is believed. In fact, Kirchner estimates that statements from "roughly one-third" of all witnesses present on June 17 were ignored by agents increasingly focused at Hoover's direction on a three-man hit team.[33]

While deliberately discounting various eyewitnesses—including nearly all the "colored" ones—agents made sweeping use of wiretaps without warrants. The previous year, Hoover had claimed the Bureau only listened in on phone calls while pursuing kidnappers, "white slavers," or potential threats to "national security," but after Kansas City Washington expanded its web of eavesdroppers, with mixed results. One particular target was the "safe" ranch run for fugitives near Joplin, by Herb and Esther Farmer. Years later, Agent Hal Bray recalled moving into a cabin near the Farmers' place, with his wife and children, to monitor a wiretap on their rural party line. "We sat there for two weeks," he said, "and we didn't hear a thing. I know it was so hot we stripped to our underwear and sat in lawn chairs with all the windows open, but we got nothing." The reason was simple: Herb and Esther had embarked on a vacation, lying low until July 7, when they returned to face arrest by Joplin police.[34]

One oddity contained within the Bureau's Kansas City file was Hoover's unexpected acknowledgment of organized crime in America. From the date of his appointment as director until 1957, when state police raided a Mafia convention in Apalachin, New York, Hoover stubbornly denied existence of a Mob or Syndicate, much less a "Maffia" (the common Bureau misspelling). While acknowledging proliferation of "hoodlums" at large, Hoover dismissed them as problems for local police. As late as 1953, two years after epic revelations by the televised Kefauver Committee, Hoover formed a team within the Bureau "to determine and document the nonexistence or organized crime." Even so, the massacre file contains repeated references to a "national crime operation" led chiefly by Italians, represented in KC by John Lazia.[35]

Some within the Bureau found their efforts to solve the Union Station case hampered by FBI mythology. We noted the fable of unarmed G-men in Chapter 1, and ex–Agent Ray Suran was still pushing that fabrication after he retired in 1955, insisting, "We had only one pistol in the office. They [Caffrey and Vetterli] both couldn't have been carrying it. And I'm sure they weren't carrying shotguns." In fact, we know Frank Smith had two pistols and Caffrey had one, as did Joe Lackey. And Lackey, in addition to Chief Reed, *was* carrying a shotgun, for a total of two at the scene. It may be said, therefore, that Suran lied by omission of Lackey in his blanket statement about nonexistent scatterguns, although his motive may soon be revealed. Agent Vetterli also admitted that the team carried two shotguns but claimed they had been propped against the side of Caffrey's car and played no part in the shootout—another lie, as we shall see.[36]

As for Joe Lackey, his report to headquarters said, "Agent had his shotgun pointed toward the floor, and the muzzle of the gun being between agent and the [left] side panel. In endeavoring to cock this gun to fire, it jammed, and to the best of agent's recollection, he was unable to get it unjammed during the proceedings.... The writer is thoroughly familiar with shotguns and is positive that the gun carried by Chief of Police Reed was 12-gauge. The writer was sitting within two feet of Chief of Police Reed in the rear seat at the time that this shooting took place and has always been firmly of the opinion that no shots were fired by Chief of Police Reed and certainly that no shots were fired from a shotgun by Chief of Police Reed."[37]

In the Great Depression, as today, some felons corresponded with police or journalists by mail, though missives from the underworld during the 1930s were more likely to protest their innocence of certain crimes than to mock lawmen or inflame the public, as with "Son of Sam" in 1970s New York.

On June 30, 1933, Charles Floyd addressed a postcard to Kansas City police from Springfield, Missouri. It read: "Dear Sirs—I—Charles Floyd—want it made known that I did not participate in the massacre of officers at Kansas City." An inked thumbprint below Floyd's signature convinced the brass that the postcard was genuine, if not truthful—as if they even cared.[38]

Denials are one thing, but alibis are another. Around the same time Floyd was writing to protest his innocence, a longer letter reached KCPD. It read, in part:

> This is to certify that we, the undersigned, of lawful age, make the following statements of facts of our own free will and accord, and submit fingerprints as a testimonial of the affiants' identity. It is apparent that the Oklahoma officers have been misled to believe that certain innocent parties (some of whom are now being detained in jail) are guilty of participating in the robbery of the Black Rock, Arkansas, Bank on June 16, 1933, at about 8:45 a.m. o'clock. We the undersigned are the perpetrators of the robbery.[39]

That letter did not mention Union Station, but its gist was obvious. Those who signed it with their fingerprints appended—Lansing fugitives Harvey Bailey, Bob Brady, Jim Clark, Ed Davis, and Wilbur Underhill—offered specifics on the robbery, including details of the currency, coins, and money orders stolen, with a complaint about the bank's manager exaggerating their haul for insurance purposes. They also described a botched getaway, forcing them to abandon the car they'd stolen while fleeing Lansing in May, forced thereafter to hike all day through woodlands on June 16, finally hitching a ride to Batesville, Alabama, after sundown. Ironically, the letter rebounded to Bailey's detriment when Charles Appel, head of the FBI's new laboratory, identified the bandits' typewriter as the same one used to generate Charles Urschel's ransom notes.[40]

While local lawmen worked the press, FBI agents got a boost from Earl Smith and his wife, nosy neighbors of Vern Miller and girlfriend Vi Mathias on Edgevale Road in Kansas City. The Smiths had observed the reclusive couple for six weeks, noting visits by "curious looking characters" in cars bearing out-of-state plates, but when they finally spoke to Agent George Harvey and three colleagues on June 22 the G-men seemed blasé. Mrs. Smith phoned again on the 26th, reporting that a moving van was cleaning out the suspect domicile, but another six days passed before agents sought access from Miller's landlord. They found the house a hollow shell, but in its basement they located a two-gallon milk can half-filled with roofing nails, favored by outlaws for flattening patrol car tires during getaways. The attic yielded bloody rags, a syringe, dusty beer bottles, and marks on the floor where beds had been dragged. Even then, it was June 29 before Agent John Brennan checked the house for fingerprints, a talent derived from his father who'd pioneered fingerprinting for the St. Louis Police Department.[41]

The bloody rags recalled testimony of one gunman possibly wounded outside Union Station on June 17, but they were relatively useless in that era, 30 years before scientists James Watson and Francis Crick mapped out the double-helix structure of DNA at England's Cambridge University. In 1933 police could only match blood samples by type—A, B, AB, and O, each with positive and negative subtypes—but no trace could identify specific individuals. As an example, some 45 percent of U.S. residents have Type O blood, either positive or negative, roughly 156,000 persons nationwide in 1933.[42]

Ballistics might have cracked the Union Station case, but once again, the FBI was mired in bad luck, obfuscation, and ineptitude. Considering the Bureau's final, incorrect solution to the crime—three shooters, two with Tommy guns, one with a brace of automatic pistols—the crime scene should have been strewn with cartridge casings. If the FBI was wrong, and there were gunmen it declined to name, from four up to the *Salt Lake Tribune*'s ten—that castoff brass should have been scattered everywhere. And yet....

Various sales brochures for Thompson submachine guns, firing .45 caliber rounds identical to those used in the U.S. military's standard automatic pistols, claim that the weapon fired at a variable full-automatic rate of 800 to 1,500 shots per minute. Scaling back that awesome firepower, four magazines were commercially available: "stick" magazines holding 20 or 30 rounds each, and "drums" containing 50 or 100 rounds apiece. At those rates and capacities, two Tommy guns should have littered the depot's parking lot with anywhere from 40 to 200 brass casings.[43]

If so, where did they go?

One answer lies with herd mentality, the morbid gawkers—thousands or them—who converged upon the depot as news bulletins announced the massacre. They posed beside Ray Caffrey's bullet-riddled Chevrolet and the adjacent shot-up Plymouth in the only two "official" crime scene photos, snapped not by police but rather by Ray Hense, a staff photographer serving the *Kansas City Star*. A sea of others, all anonymous, surround the vehicles and stretch back to the depot, doubtless grabbing any gruesome souvenir they could before authorities arrived to push them back.[44]

Beyond that incalculable looting or evidence, FBI reports note nine bullet holes in the rear of Caffrey's car, with no enumeration for other hits to the Chevy's front or sides. Other shots struck Parnie Miller's Plymouth, shattering its windshield and the driver's window, puncturing its sun visor. Still more blew out Union Station's windows and scarred its façade, leaving pockmarks still visible decades later. Of those struck by gunfire, Reed Vetterli was "nipped" on one arm by a bullet never recovered. Chief Reed suffered two head wounds, one .45-caliber, the other from a .38. Joe Lackey, shot three times in the back, carried two slugs with him to his dying day in 1974. Frank Nash, Ray Caffrey and Detective Hermanson all died from head wounds—two for Jelly, one each from front and back. Detective Grooms expired with two .45-caliber slugs in his chest.[45]

Some cartridges and projectiles found at the scene contradicted official statements. Joe Lackey had insisted that the escort party only carried 12-gauge shotguns and that neither one was fired during the massacre, yet two expended 16-gauge shells were recovered, one on the rear floorboard of Caffrey's Chevrolet, the other outside, on the Chevy's running board. Chief Reed also carried spare unfired 16-gauge rounds in his pocket.[46]

Merle Gill, a self-taught "ballistician," lived in Kansas City but served many law enforcement agencies on a contracted case-by-case basis, including the FBI's KC field office, testifying in hundreds of court cases. For months after the Union Station killings, he tried to match weapons captured from various Midwestern gangsters to the depot massacre, including guns seized from the Barrow gang after shootouts near Platte City, Missouri, and Dexfield Park, Iowa, but all in vain. Sixteen months elapsed before he wrote to Bureau headquarters on November 19, 1934, with a copy mailed to the *Journal-Post*. "Until yesterday," Gill wrote, "I was unaware that Chief Reed had a 16-gauge shotgun with him when he was killed." He had accepted Agent Lackey's statement that both shotguns carried by the team were 12-gauge models, although an addendum to his letter called that judgment into question. In fact, Gill wrote, "The next day after the shooting we opened up an unexploded 16-gauge case in the Justice [FBI] office and found three ball bearings in place of the regular buckshot"—identical to projectiles that killed victims Hermanson and Caffrey. Coming close to the truth, Gill speculated that Reed had fired twice from the Chevy's backseat, one blast striking Nash from behind and slaying Caffrey, the second killing Hermanson.[47]

J. Edgar Hoover had already soured on Gill by then, writing a "personal and confidential" letter on March 20, 1934, that read in part, "I deplore the use of private detectives or of experts upon government work. Our K.C. office should never have gone along in this set-up without getting our approval." After Gill went public with his findings nine months later, Hoover penned a memo reading, "Well it serves us right for ever having dealt with Gill. I always opposed it and never approved the turning over of the evidence to Gill."[48]

That said, the Bureau's final version of the massacre—a relatively simple three-man job—prevailed in court two years after the depot ambush and remains an article of faith with FBI historians today.

Despite assurances from Washington that G-men solved the Union Station case, naming the sole participants as Vern Miller, Charles Floyd, and Adam Richetti, serious doubts remain. Former U.S. Attorney Maurice Milligan, writing in his 1948 memoir *Missouri Waltz*, said, "The FBI agents were puzzled. They could produce no evidence which would link Floyd and Richetti to Miller. Their activities had been entirely separate. Their trails had not even crossed. Moreover, there was not one bit of evidence to show that Floyd and Richetti had participated in the Union Station Massacre." Within three days of the slayings, Agent Gus Jones told Hoover that Floyd was not involved, but Hoover dismissed his concerns.[49]

After Milligan, the next challenge to Hoover's version of events in Kansas City came from author L.L. Edge in 1981. Rather than adding other gunmen to the mix, Edge dropped Adam Richetti from the list and made the massacre a two-man job, committed by Vern Miller and Charles Floyd. In that scenario, Patrolman Fanning arrived on the scene to find Lottie West pointing toward a stocky gunman, shouting, "Shoot the fat man!" Fanning tried, perhaps wounding his target, then observed three men escaping in a dark coupe. At that same moment, Agent Vetterli—unarmed in all reports—allegedly stood up and fired at the getaway car with one of the mythical leaning shotguns, rather than running for the depot as described by multiple witnesses. Edge claims that Vetterli and Fanning put four bullets in the trunk of Miller's car, an observation unconfirmed today. He also questions Fanning's glimpse of three men in the car, writing, "What he actually saw was Miller, Floyd, and Miller's coat flying over the seat." From Union Station, Miller drove back home to Edgevale Road and hauled Adam Richetti out of bed, where he was sleeping off a day and night of drinking. While dramatically portrayed, that version of events lacks any factual support today.[50]

Next up to challenge the FBI's version was L.R. Kirchner, deviating wildly from Edge's trimmed-down account of the murders to suggest multiple firing squads at Union Station, perhaps with disparate motives. Declaring that "two separate teams were involved," Kirchner opined that the bullet holes in Caffrey's car and damage to the depot's façade "confirm the three shooting parties, or two groups." One team, allegedly, intended to free Nash from custody, the other being sent to silence him from sharing inside knowledge of the Pendergast-Lazia alliance. One team, dispatched by Lazia, included Miller, brothers Homer and Maurice Denning, plus William "Solly" Weissman. Unknown to the first group, Harvey Bailey led a team of Lansing fugitives intent on liberating Nash. Miller and Maurice Denning wielded Tommy guns, while Weissman was the stocky man with two Colt automatics, and Homer Denning served as their wheelman. Kirchner says both Miller and Weissman were "slightly wounded" before escaping. The Lansing group, armed with shotguns and pistols (despite reports of Bailey wielding a Tommy gun), purportedly fired from behind Caffrey's car. In Kirchner's scenario, Reed Vetterli, though slightly wounded, seized one of the shotguns he described as being left outside the Chevrolet, firing "a couple of blasts" at Miller's getaway car. Kirchner rejects accounts of Caffrey shooting Nash, insisting that the necessary angle of his shots was incorrect.[51]

For all his evident sincerity, Kirchner's theory proceeds from two serious errors. First, after acknowledging one newspaper report that claimed Nash was killed by a shotgun blast from the Chevrolet's backseat, he dismisses that prospect, preferring to accept Reed Vetterli's statement that both shotguns remained outside the car, confidently stating, "There were no shotguns in the car with the officers (regardless of their statements). They were leaning against the fender of the motorcar at the time of the attacks." Worse yet is his reliance on the word of ex-convict James

Henry "Blackie" Audett to identify three members of Vern Miller's hit team.[52]

A Canadian native, Audett dictated his alleged life story to Gene Lowall, special investigator for Denver's district attorney, in 1953, published the following year with the title *Rap Sheet*. Among other adventures, Blackie claimed he'd seen action with the Canadian Expeditionary Force in World War I, performing heroic deeds in France and suffering a head wound that required insertion of a metal plate. Later, he claimed credit for a $560,000 train robbery ($8.7 million today), various daring jailbreaks, and intimate association with most of the Depression Era's infamous banditti. In *Rap Sheet*, Audett claimed that 1933 kidnap victim Mary McElroy, daughter of Kansas City's corrupt city manager, had invited him to join her at Union Station and "watch the show" as outlaws liberated Jelly Nash. Audett, and he alone, named Vern Miller's companions as the Denning brothers and Solly Weissman, clearing Charles Floyd—another purported close friend of Blackie's—from any involvement in the massacre.[53]

Alas, hardly a word of Audett's published tale proved verifiable. Author Edward Butts, researching a book on Canadian outlaws, found no record of Blackie's military service, no decorations or head wound, no epic train heist—little at all, in fact, except for some minor arrests that ranked him as a "small-time hood" with a gift for gab. More to the point, Butts unearthed records proving that Audett could not have watched the Union Station massacre, since he was jailed elsewhere when it occurred. The title of his chapter in the Butts anthology—"Liar, Liar"—says it all, but would not stop at least one other author from regurgitating Audett's fantasies two decades after *Rap Sheet* passed out of print and into used-bookstores.[54]

Robert Unger, a Pulitzer Prize winner and professor emeritus at the University of Missouri–Kansas City, came closest to the final truth in 1997 with a theory of the massacre supported by ballistic evidence and eyewitness accounts. His version of events hinges on a particular firearm and the ever-changing stories of G-men who managed to survive the incident.

Specifically, he documents that Chief Reed's favored weapon, both for hunting wild game and intimidating outlaws, was a 16-gauge Winchester Model 1897 pump-action shotgun, fed by a five-round tubular magazine beneath its barrel. For law enforcement work, Reed hand-loaded shells with three steel ball bearings apiece. American troops first used the Model 1897 to combat Moro tribesmen during the Philippine Insurrection of 1899–1902 and later carried it to France, where it was dubbed "the trench gun," prompting diplomatic complaints from German soldiers who feared its awesome close-range firepower.[55]

The Winchester's prime selling point for troops and lawmen—also a potential cause of grievous accidents—was the absence of a safety lever found on most other shotguns and rifles. To make the Model 1897 "safe," a user had to place its external hammer on half-cock, thus disengaging the trigger. Conversely, the gun was capable of "slam-firing" in combat if a shooter held its trigger down and pumped the slide action, discharging one round after another in rapid fire until the magazine emptied.[56] It was a tricky proposition, even in the most expert of hands, and doubly perilous for novices.

At Union Station, Unger theorizes, Agent Lackey inadvertently swapped scatterguns with Otto Reed, picking up Reed's 16-gauge, with which he had no previous experience, while Reed carried the 12-gauge borrowed from the Bureau's Oklahoma City office. Later, in the backseat of Ray Caffrey's car, when Lackey glimpsed gunmen approaching, he fumbled with the unfamiliar gun and accidentally discharged two rounds. The first nearly decapitated Jelly Nash, spraying windshield glass *outward*, across the Chevy's hood, while one of its three ball bearings also struck Agent Caffrey in the head and killed him. (The deadly pellet later "fell out of his brain" at autopsy.) The second inadvertent shot cut down Detective Hermanson, whose postmortem report attributes cause of death to a shotgun blast striking above his left ear, exiting through the back of his skull. No ball bearings remained in Hermanson's corpse, but they flew on to strike Parnie Miller's Plymouth next-door, one scarring its left-front window post, with another projectile dropping to the floorboard by the driver's seat. Those blasts surprised the ambush party, Unger says, and prompted them to open fire.[57]

As for the official Bureau story, Unger writes, "Lackey lied. Knowingly and with intent, he lied to Hoover about the shotguns, just as he would lie again and again in the months ahead." He also lied about being "thoroughly familiar with shotguns"—at least where Chief Reed's was concerned—and about handing 12-gauge shells to Reed while they were seated in Ray Caffrey's car. Agents Reed Vetterli and Gus Jones clearly recognized those lies, as both were present when Merle Gill opened one of the 16-gauge shells from Reed's pocket on June 20, yet neither G-man—nor any other from the KC office—reported that fact to Hoover. Soon after the murders, Vetterli personally returned the Winchester to Reed's family in Oklahoma, where it remained a treasured heirloom well into the 1990s. Subsequently, after reading Gill's report and fuming over its submission to the press, Hoover dispatched an agent to Reed's home, where he examined and test-fired the Winchester, confirming Chief Reed's custom loads for stopping outlaws in their tracks. From that point onward, Hoover and his inner circle actively participated in the cover-up of Lackey's fatal error.[58]

As for Reed's two lethal head wounds, one was inflicted by a .45 slug, fired either from a Tommy gun or automatic pistol, while the other was a .38 caliber projectile. Since no witnesses described the ambush party carrying revolvers, Merle Gill speculated that Patrolman Fanning may have shot Reed accidentally, while firing at the "fat man" wielding a machine gun. Unger disagrees, deeming it "more likely" that the .38 was fired from the south or southwest, when Detective Grooms reacted to the shotgun blasts from Caffrey's vehicle, before two submachine-gun bullets dropped Grooms in his tracks, falling beside Detective Hermanson.[59]

From that point onward, Unger theorized, Hoover and his agents in the field collaborated in a cover-up to spare the Bureau from embarrassment, buttressed by Lottie West, "a well-intentioned police wanna-be trying hard to please," whose various statements were "so contrived and contradictory as to be useless." Adam Richetti's lone fingerprint, allegedly recovered from a beer bottle in Vern Miller's attic, was "at best highly suspicious and at worst a Bureau fake. Hoover's version of the truth surrounding the print is, in a word, unbelievable." Final confirmation comes from William Becker, special counsel to the Missouri Insurance Department from 1936 to 1944, counsel to Governor Lloyd Stark in the Pendergast investigation of 1938–39, and a U.S. district judge in Kansas City from September 1961 until his death in February 1992. In later life, Judge Becker recalled a conversation with an unnamed G-man concerning the Union Station massacre. That source told Becker, "Our agent sitting in the backseat pulled the trigger on Nash and that started it. The machine-gunners didn't shoot first. Our guy panicked."[60]

The bottom line: of five men killed at Union Station, Agent Lackey almost certainly shot three by accident. A fourth, Chief Reed, may also have been slain by "friendly fire." Persons unknown wounded Agents Lackey and Vetterli, while William Hermanson remains the only victim definitely killed by members of the ambush party.

In the slaughter's aftermath, Frank Nash's sister, Alice Long, claimed his remains and buried him at Linwood Cemetery in Paragould Arkansas. The funeral attracted many strangers, whom locals assumed to be visiting gangsters.[61]

Maurice Denning, a depot gunman only in Blackie Audett's fervid imagination, was arrested for bootlegging at Council Bluffs, Iowa, in 1933. He pled guilty on October 20 and received a 60-day jail term. In August 1934 he organized a bank-robbing "Ghost Gang" with cohorts Francis Harper, Earl Keeling, Thomas Limerick, Ralph Morrison, and William Pabst, staging various Midwestern raids before Nebraska police captured Morrison in July 1936, resulting in an 18-year sentence. G-men hunted Denning in vain, finally dropping his name from their list of wanted fugitives in 1960s, assuming that he must be dead.[62]

4

Cops and Robbers

While America reeled from the Missouri massacre, and FBI headquarters scrambled to conceal its agent's role in touching off mayhem, manipulating sparse evidence, various gangs went on about their crimes.

John Dillinger robbed his first bank in New Carlisle, Ohio, on June 21, escaping with $10,000, then regressed from that success to briefly teaming with wannabe teenage gangster Earl Shaw, raiding a thread mill in Monticello, Indiana, on the 24th and an Indianapolis sandwich shop five days later. Unimpressed, he ditched Shaw shortly before the teen's jealous wife betrayed him to police over an extramarital affair.[1]

Two weeks after skipping bail in Eldorado, Arkansas, Irvin Chapman joined accomplices on June 21 to steal $25,000 in cash and bonds from a Camden bank, 30 miles north. Witnesses identified him as a builder of local highways before his bankruptcy, launching a 15-month manhunt by Ouachita County Sheriff Arthur Ellis.[2]

On June 23 Buck Barrow and William "Deacon" Jones robbed a store in Fayetteville, Arkansas, and fled toward Alma on Highway 71, colliding with another car. Alma Town Marshal Henry Humphrey and Crawford County Deputy Sheriff Ansel Salyers stopped at the accident scene, seeing Barrow and Jones exit their vehicle with guns. Buck killed Humphrey, while Jones wounded Salyers, fleeing in the lawmen's car. Parting shots from Salyers severed two of Jones's fingertips.[3]

On July 1, the Capone mob initiated a conspiracy to save cohort John "Jake the Barber" Factor from extradition to England, while eliminating members of the Touhy gang. Factor's son Jerome had been kidnapped in April, ransomed for $25,000 by unidentified persons, and while John called for revenge, he was indicted overseas for swindling British investors out of $7 million or $8 million (reports differ). Before his deportation, John "disappeared," then returned home 12 days later, spinning tales of abduction and abuse. Capone mobsters hired Touhy gangsters Basil Banghart and Charles "Ice Wagon" Connors to pose as bagmen, collecting the alleged ransom with an offer to let them keep it if they made the snatch "look real."

William "Deacon" Jones joined the Barrow gang in multiple holdups and murders, also posing for snapshots while on the run. Some newspaper captions of this photo showing Jones in 1933 misidentify him as Clyde's brother Marvin "Buck" Barrow (National Archives).

On July 17, Touhy and three associates—Eddie "Chicken" McFadden, Gustav "Gloomy Gus" Schaefer and William "Wee Willie" Sharkey—crashed their car near Elkhorn, Wisconsin. Police found weapons in the vehicle, including one of Hyman Lebman's "baby machine guns." While detained for investigation, the four drew attention from Chicago FBI agent Melvin

Purvis and Cook County's prosecutor, all soon indicted for kidnapping victims William Hamm, Jr., and Jake Factor.[4]

On July 3, Lansing fugitives including Harvey Bailey, Bob Brady, Jim Clark, and Wilbur Underhill looted $11,000 from a Clinton, Oklahoma, bank. Two days later, Underhill alone robbed a bank in Concordia, Kansas.[5]

Still floundering after Union Station, FBI agents and sheriff's deputies raided the Kansas City home of mobster Frank "Fritz" Mulloy, arresting fugitive Capone associate James "Fur" Sammons, sought for fur and payroll robbery charges in Chicago, Baltimore, and Philadelphia. (Unconnected to the massacre, he posted $20,000 bond on the 18th and fled again.) On the 7th, Herb and Esther Farmer returned to their farm from a 20-day vacation, discovering a phone bill listing suspicious calls from June 16. Herb called Joplin Police Chief Ed Portley, who arrested the couple. Frances Nash joined them in jail on the 11th. Upon learning that Agent Vetterli's men had not searched Farmer's ranch, Director Hoover demanded an explanation. Director for Investigations Harold "Pop" Nathan, tried to help, claiming Vetterli assumed there was "ample time" with the occupants in jail. Hoover wrote back, saying, "This is absurd," and ordered an immediate search—which found no useful evidence.[6]

After her 1932 jailbreak, Vivian Chase fled to St. Louis and joined "Irish O'Malley's" gang to kidnap 77-year-old banker August Luer on July 10, 1933. Driven to an Illinois farm and kept in a dank subbasement, Luer was freed after 123 hours. Conflicting reports claimed no ransom was paid, or that the abductors settled for 10 percent of their $100,000 demand. FBI agents announced "solution" of the case on July 19, arresting gang members Frank Douglass, Percy "Dice Box Kid" Fitzgerald, Michael and Anna Musiala, Randol Norvell, and Norma Vaughn, but Chase and O'Malley eluded the dragnet.[7]

Lansing escapees Kenneth Conn and Alvis Payton tried to rob an Altamont, Kansas, bank on July 14, seizing bank vice president A.H. McCarty's wife as a hostage, but the heist went disastrously wrong. Teller Isaac McCarty—son of A.H.—fired on the bandits, slaying Conn instantly and wounding Payton, who survived, blinded, despite early reports that he was "expected to die." After a scolding for risking his mother's life, Isaac McCarty received a $500 reward.[8]

Three days later, John Dillinger robbed a Daleville, Indiana, bank with comrades Harry Copeland and Hilton Crouch, escaping with $3,500. To celebrate, on July 30 Dillinger visited Chicago's Century of Progress World's Fair with Mary Longnaker, sister of cellmate Jim Jenkins at Michigan City. Longnaker later described Dillinger asking policemen to snap the couple's photo and posing beside smiling officers.[9]

On July 18, the Barrow gang booked rooms at the Red Crown Tourist

Court, south of Platte City, Missouri. Owner Neal Houser became suspicious when they paid with coins, then backed their cars into a garage, "gangster-style," and taped newspapers over their windows. Houser alerted police, who arrived with an armored car and steel shields on the night of the 19th. Gunfire followed a call for surrender, and the gang escaped, but at a cost. Buck Barrow suffered a mortal head wound, while shattered glass gashed both of Blanche's eyes. Hiding out at an abandoned amusement park near Dexter, Iowa, the fugitives dug a grave and awaited Buck's death, but locals spotted them on July 24, springing another ambush. Buck absorbed six more bullets, while Blanche was captured at his side. Clyde, Bonnie, and W.D. Jones escaped on foot, all wounded, and commandeered a passing car. Buck died in Perry, Iowa, on the 29th, from pneumonia after surgery. Blanche, permanently blinded in her left eye, was convicted of attempted murder for the Platte City shootout, sentenced to 10 years in prison.[10]

George Kelly and Albert Bates tried another kidnapping on July 22, taking wealthy oilman Charles Urschel and a friend, Walter Jarrett, from Urschel's Oklahoma City home at gunpoint. After identifying their primary target, the abductors released Jarrett and drove Urschel to a Texas ranch owned by Kathryn Kelly's parents. There, Kelly and Bates compelled Urschel to write his own ransom note, including precise details for delivery of $200,000 ransom ($3.9 million today) in $20 bills. The note reached John Catlett, a Tulsa colleague of Urschel's, on the 26th, and delivery was accomplished at Kansas City's LaSalle Hotel on July 30, resulting in Urschel's release the following day. Bates and the Kellys separated after collecting their booty, Bates heading west, while George and Katheryn made their way toward Memphis.[11]

Although blindfolded during most of his captivity, Urschel proved to be a dangerous "earwitness." From the moment he was trundled into Kelly's car, until he made it home, he memorized sounds—noises from the car in transit, multiple voices at the ranch, sounds of rain and airplanes passing overhead—and furtive glimpses of his wristwatch gave him times for the rainstorm and fly-overs. While confined, Urschel also deliberately left his fingerprints on any handy surfaces, facilitating future identification of the kidnappers' hideout. Painstaking comparison of weather reports and daily flight schedules within a 600-mile radius of Oklahoma City, coupled with timely tips from Texas lawmen, led Bureau agents toward Wise County, Texas, and the ranch owned by Kathryn's mother and stepfather, Ora and Robert Shannon.[12]

August was another hectic month as the fledgling "crime war" gained momentum.

On August 4 John Dillinger robbed a bank in Montpelier, Indiana,

4. Cops and Robbers

with partners Copeland and Crouch, bagging $6,700. Ten days later the same trio scored $6,000 from a bank in Bluffton, Ohio. Tracking their moves with interest was Captain Matthew Leach of the Indiana State Police, founded in April 1933. A 38-year-old world war veteran who believed in using psychology to foil felons, Leach impressed Governor Paul McNutt sufficiently that McNutt often called Leach directly to consult on open cases, bypassing his boss, Superintendent Albert Feeney. That created animosity toward Leach within the ISP, exacerbated when J. Edgar Hoover took umbrage toward Leach and his small force of 42 officers outshining federal agents in pursuit of Dillinger. Over time, Leach also received taunting calls from Dillinger himself, who'd learned of Leach's stammering when nervous, calling up to ask, "How are you, you stuttering bastard?"[13]

Lansing fugitives Bailey, Brady, Clark, and Underhill raided a bank in Kingfisher, Oklahoma, on August 9, escaping with $11,000, Ed Davis serving as their getaway driver. They planned another heist in Brainerd, Minnesota, but Bailey made a last-minute diversion to lie low at the Shannon ranch in Paradise, Texas.[14]

On August 8 Chicago's FBI field office announced a "breakthrough" in the Union Station massacre investigation. While Vern Miller remained at large, a *New York Times* headline reported, "Federal officers say they know [the] identity of other gunmen" who failed to liberate Frank Nash. The only one in custody that day was roadhouse operator Louis "Doc" Stacci, named as "the man who plotted the scheme." As for the rest—a haphazard laundry list of suspects including most of the Bailey-Underhill gang—the feds, according to a subsequent alternative "solution" to the case, were wrong across the board.[15]

On August 10 FBI agents and Texas lawmen raided the Shannon ranch at Paradise, arresting Kathryn Kelly's mother, stepfather, and brother, Armon "Potatoes" Shannon, as conspirators in Charles Urschel's abduction. At the same time, they caught Harvey Bailey literally napping, relieving him of $1,000 cash, $700 of that a loan from George Kelly consisting of Urschel ransom funds. Thus, in addition to charges of escape from Lansing and suspicion of participation in the Kansas City massacre, Bailey also faced false charges of violating the Lindbergh Law. A search of the Shannon spread revealed various items described and fingered by Urschel: a water bucket and tin cup, items of furniture, and so on. Urschel toured the farm under guard and quickly confirmed it as the site of his confinement. Two days after the Texas raid, agents bagged Albert Bates in Denver, carrying $660 from the ransom payoff. Almost as an afterthought, trucker Sam Frederick was jailed for passing ransom bills through banks in Minneapolis and Fargo, North Dakota. On August 23, the Kellys, Shannons and Bates were indicted on kidnapping charges, but agents still couldn't locate ringleaders

George or Kathryn. They *did* arrest more alleged money-passers, including Minneapolis crime boss Isadore "Kid Cann" Blumenfeld and four associates: Edward "Barney" Berman, Sam Kronick, Sam Kozberg, and Clifford Skelly.[16]

Despite his eventual rejection of evidence suggesting Bailey's participation in the Kansas City massacre, J. Edgar Hoover did not abandon that theory immediately. Nine days after Bailey's Texas capture, Hoover told Pop Nathan, "I want Bailey tried for the massacre immediately. I want a commitment from the local prosecutors now. If there's any doubt about it, tell Keenan to call me." Joseph Keenan, special assistant to Attorney General Cummings, was Hoover's superior at Justice, not subject to his whims. When he and Missouri prosecutors ignored Hoover's demand, the Director warned his subordinates, "I have been somewhat disturbed since receiving telephonic advice from Mr. Keenan, at Kansas City, that while he felt the state would secure a conviction in the Bailey case, at the same time he thought that some further investigation should be conducted in so far as the identification is concerned. I wish that you would promptly advise me in what respect the investigation is lacking and as to what was overlooked by the agents." On September 13 a federal grand jury indicted Bailey, Bob Brady, Lou Conner, Herb and Esther Farmer, Frank Mulloy, Doc Stacci, and Wilbur Underhill on charges of obstructing justice in Kansas City, the only federal charge available before new laws were passed nine months later. Meanwhile, Hoover sought new suspects who could be safely "exterminated"—or perhaps framed—for the massacre, regardless of the shaky evidence against them.[17]

In Chicago, the double frame-up of Roger Touhy and three cohorts proceeded on August 12, with their erroneous indictment for the Barker-Karpis gang's abduction of William Hamm, Jr. Five days later, Basil Banghart and Ice Wagon Connor went to collect the fake ransom payoff for Jake Factor outside Chicago, driving into an ambush by 250 FBI agents and local police, supported by 62 squad cars, 10 machine guns, and two airplanes carrying aerial bombs. Adding insult to injury, the bag alleged to hold $50,000 contained only $500.[18]

One day after that trap closed in Illinois, Lester Gillis struck a bank in Grand Haven, Michigan, accompanied by Tommy Carroll, Eddie Green, Homer Van Meter, and local outlaw Eddie Doyle. Police nabbed Doyle, the rest escaping with $30,000. Bentz took his share and decamped to Portland, Maine, where he purchased a home and founded Ultra Products, a toy company. Traveling widely as Ultra's president and general sales manager, he compiled a list of banks as sources of additional revenue should his legit business fail.[19]

On August 24, Indiana's State Clemency Commission considered

Harry Pierpont's parole bid, based on a contention that Pierpont possessed a strong character as a "leader and not a follower." The board agreed, but only to a point, rejecting the application after noting Pierpont's two prior convictions, plus 10 punishments and two reprimands for misbehavior in prison.[20] Unfazed, "Pete" went back to planning a mass escape with his cohorts.

Barrow gang survivors spent six weeks recuperating after their brush with annihilation, ranging from Minnesota west to Colorado, then southeast to Mississippi. FBI files claim Clyde and Jones burglarized a National Guard armory at Plattville, Illinois, on August 20, stealing three BARs, several pistols, and a quantity of ammunition, but recent investigation proves that report incorrect. The Bureau's grossly inaccurate memos actually refer to weapons recovered from the Red Crown Tourist Court in July, noting that serial numbers matched those of guns reported stolen from an armory in Enid, Oklahoma, on July 7, 1933, and from "Company E, 129th Infantry, Illinois National Guard" on April 19, 1933, at nonexistent "Flattsville, Illinois." Meanwhile, agents tracked the gang for Dyer Act violations, never coming close to an arrest.[21]

The case against Harvey Bailey as a Union Station massacre gunman weakened on August 29. Witness Samuel Link's description of Bailey firing a machine gun at lawmen on June 17 appeared to collapse with a report from Chicago SAC Melvin Purvis that Link also "claims he was with Teddy Roosevelt in South America and has personally met all the crowned heads of Europe." Link's business associates called him "mentally deficient" and "a very erratic person [who] made many statements which could not be relied upon." Still, Bureau headquarters continued citing Link as its "star witness" for another two months.[22]

On August 30, the Barker-Karpis gang robbed a bank in South Saint Paul, Minnesota, stealing $30,000, killing one policeman and crippling another for life. Big Tom Brown got his usual cut of the spoils, but the gang's raid sounded a death knell for Saint Paul's lucrative "layover system."[23]

Bad luck for the Barkers continued on September 6, when FBI technicians reported finding fingerprints from Alvin Karpis, Dock Barker, and other gang members on Hamm ransom notes. That discovery should have scuttled the false case against Roger Touhy and friends, but their prosecution forged ahead regardless. On September 22, the gang robbed two Chicago bank messengers, killing one policemen after crashing their getaway car. Erroneous reports blamed that crime on Charles Floyd, George Kelly, and Vern Miller.[24]

The Barrow gang, still several states ahead of Bureau manhunters, allegedly visited family in West Dallas on September 7, but W.D. Jones later told a different story, claiming they were in Clarksdale, Mississippi, that night, when he absconded in a newly-stolen car, fleeing to his mother's home in Houston.[25]

Trouble continued for the Touhy gang on September 8, when rival syndicate gunmen killed member James Tribble. Meanwhile, prosecutors pressed their spurious case in the Hamm kidnapping, fully aware of Barker-Karpis gang responsibility.[26]

Trial of six defendants for the August Luer kidnapping convened in Edwardsville, Illinois, on September 11. Randol Norvell claimed he had been "forced" into the plot, but jurors ignored him, convicting all six on the 30th. They handed life prison terms to Lillian Chessen, Percy Fitzgerald, and Norvell, while Charles Chessen and Christ Oitcho drew five years apiece. Prosecutors had called for death sentences, but jurors balked at the prospect of executing a woman.[27]

On September 13, a federal grand jury indicted 11 conspiracy "suspects" in the Kansas City massacre, including both guilty defendants and those already known to be innocent. Their number included Harvey Bailey, Bob Brady, Lou Conner, Herb and Esther Farmer, Richard Galatas, Vern Miller, Fritz Mulloy, Frances Nash, Doc Stacci and Wilbur Underhill. Galatas eluded lawmen for nine days, until the 22nd.[28]

On September 6, the trio of Dillinger, Copeland and Crouch made their biggest score yet, taking $24,000 ($473,000 today) from an Indianapolis bank. Sixteen days later, police watching Mary Longnaker's rooming house in Dayton, Ohio, caught Dillinger there, looking over photos of himself with policemen at Chicago's World's Fair. (Some reports claim Longnaker betrayed him.) Officers seized a pistol and a crude diagram of Michigan City's prison marked with X's, but Dillinger refused to explain it. September 23 found him lodged in the Allen County jail at Lima.[29]

Charles Floyd and Adam Richetti met the Baird sisters, Beulah (née Juanita) and Rose, in Toledo, Ohio, on September 21, moving on from there to hide in Buffalo, New York. They rented an apartment as "Mr. and Mrs. George Sanders" (Floyd and Beulah), rooming with "Mr. and Mrs. Ed Brennan" (Richetti and Juanita), keeping a low profile but ingratiating themselves by passing out candy to neighborhood children.[30]

On September 24, three men stole $1,000 from a bank in Stuttgart, Arkansas. Their leader, brandishing a Tommy gun, announced, "I'm Machine Gun Kelly! You've read about me!" but witnesses identified him from mugshots as Wilbur Underhill. The bandits fled with hostages, later released unharmed, and eluded police.[31]

On September 4 Harvey Bailey escaped from the Dallas County jail, using smuggled hacksaw blades and a pistol, but officers caught him before nightfall, in Ardmore, Oklahoma. That same Labor Day, Kathryn Kelly picked up three homeless hitchhikers—Luther Arnold, his wife Hilda, and their daughter Geraldine—near Hillsboro, Texas, and drove them to Cleburne, where she bought them dinner and paid for their motel room. Next day, she bought clothes for the women and confessed her identity, gave Luther $50, and sent him to Fort Worth with questions for her attorney, then on to Oklahoma City, to observe the pending Urschel trial. Meanwhile, Kathryn "borrowed" daughter Geraldine Arnold as cover while driving to Chicago with husband George. They stopped en route to bury $73,250 of their ransom money on a Texas farm owned by Kathryn's uncle, Cassey Coleman.[32]

On September 19 Charles Urschel received a letter at home, threatening mayhem if Kathryn's parents went to prison. "It is up to you," the message warned. "If the Shannons are convicted, you can get another rich wife in hell, because that will be the only place you can use one. Adios, smart one. Your worst enemy, Geo. R. Kelly. I will put my fingerprints below so you can't say some crank wrote this." The prints matched, but authorities believed that Kathryn wrote the letter, a judgment confirmed by an independent graphologist. The point remains disputed since Kathryn was not allowed to call her own expert at trial.[33]

In Chicago, the Kellys found themselves unwelcome among fellow outlaws. Joseph Bergl, a mechanic friend of George who customized cars for bandits and mobsters, gave them a vehicle, $200 and a bottle of whiskey before warning them to move on and lie low. The couple fled to Memphis on September 21, but heat followed. On the 22nd, Barker-Karpis gangsters used one of Bergl's "special" cars for a Chicago holdup, police grilling Bergl until he pointed manhunters toward Memphis. There, George Kelly had dispatched ex–brother-in-law Langford Ramsey and Geraldine Arnold to Texas, hoping to retrieve their hidden cash from Cass Coleman. Upon arrival, Ramsey found FBI agents watching the farm, wired Kelly that "the deal fell through," and put Geraldine aboard a train to meet her parents in Oklahoma City. Agents waited for her there and she regaled them with the details of her recent travels with the Kellys.[34]

On September 26, Memphis police descended on a house Kelly had rented. FBI agents Ralph Colvin, James Perkins and William Rorer, Sr., accompanied the cops, but contrary to legend, took no part in the arrest. Detective Sergeant William Raney and Officer Seth Waterson entered the house on Rayner Street, armed with shotguns, and caught George emerging from the bathroom in pajamas, whereupon he surrendered while remarking, "I've been waiting for you all night." Kathryn, hungover from a night of drinking, lay on a nearby bed. Claims that Kelly cowered in the face of stalwart feds, crying, "Don't shoot, G-men!" were fabricated for the press, another case of Bureau agents claiming credit for the work of local officers.[35]

In custody, Kelly allegedly boasted, "I'll be out of this in no time. Let's see them keep me." Kathryn tried another angle, waiving extradition and contending that her relatives had been coerced into guarding Urschel, a fable her parents and brother repeated, claiming they had lived in fear of George. Reversing their personal history, Kathryn told Memphis police, "I'm glad we are both arrested because I am not guilty and I can prove it. I'll be rid of him and that bunch. I don't want to say anything about that guy Kelly, but he got me into this terrible mess and I don't want to have anything more to do with him." G-men raided Cass Coleman's ranch on the 27th, retrieving the ransom and jailing Coleman, with cohort Langford Ramsey, under the Lindbergh Law.[36]

On the same day George and Kathryn were arrested, September 26, Dillinger's plan to liberate his friends from Michigan City paid off. Using smuggled pistols as at Lansing, 10 Dillinger cronies broke out of Michigan City's state prison. Those on the lam included Joseph Burns, James Clark, Russell Clark (no relation), Walter Dietrich, James Fox, John Hamilton, James Jenkins, Charles Makley, Harry Pierpont, and Edward Shouse. Locking Warden Louis Kunkel and several guards in a vault, beating others and shooting one clerk in the stomach, the fugitives split up. One group—Burns, Dietrich, Fox, and James Clark—met Harrison County Sheriff Charles Neel in the parking lot, fresh from

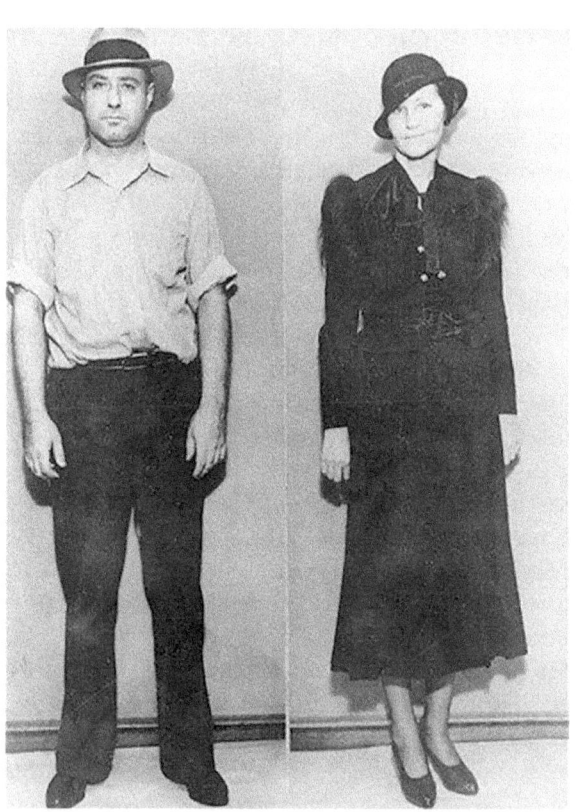

George and Kathryn Kelly following their arrest by Memphis police (not FBI agents) on September 26, 1933. Contrary to Bureau mythology, Kelly never spoke the words, "Don't shoot, G-men!" (National Archives).

John Dillinger engineered a mass escape of friends from Indiana's State Prison at Michigan City on September 26, 1933 (author's collection).

dropping off a prisoner, taking Neel and his car on a run toward Chicago. The others crossed a street to seize hostages Herbert Van Valkenberg, his wife, and a female friend, with their car, from a gas station, racing toward Indianapolis. After various highway mishaps, James Clark was the first to be recaptured, found wandering on foot near Hammond, Indiana, on the 28th, returned to prison and facing new charges. Two days later, townspeople in Beanblossom, 217 miles southwest of Michigan City, killed James Jenkins in a shootout that left one of their own slightly wounded.[37]

After splitting from the Bailey-Underhill gang in August, Ed Davis launched a solo bank-robbing spree across Texas, collecting enough loot by late September to move west, settling in Los Angeles, where he "went straight" until the cash ran low again.[38]

5

Open Season

By early autumn 1933 a de facto state of war existed in America, unknown for 15 years. This time, the enemy was neither "Hun" nor Ottoman, but a subculture of civilian rogues obsessed with profit at all costs. Worse yet, they did not haunt the robber barons' Wall Street enclave, but roamed aimlessly across the heartland, wolves who might strike anywhere at any time.

Befitting a first victory for "law and order," nine airplanes in convoy brought the Kellys into Oklahoma City on October 1. On arrival, fearing a repeat of Kansas City, one FBI agent kept a Tommy gun trained on George while another covered the crowd. Charles Urschel and his wife were at the airport, with U.S. Attorney Herbert Hyde, identifying George as one of his July abductors. Ten cars rushed the prisoners to Oklahoma County's jail, facing trial before Judge Edward Vaught on October 9.[1]

The day before George and Kathryn deplaned in OKC, September 30, Judge Vaught convicted seven defendants—Harvey Bailey, Albert Bates, the Shannons, Edward Berman and Clifford Skelly—under the Lindbergh Law, while acquitting Isidore Blumenfeld with cohorts Sam Kronick and Sam Kozberg. On October 7, Vaught sentenced Bailey, Bates, Robert and Ora Shannon to life imprisonment. Berman and Kelly got five years apiece, while Armon Shannon received 10 years suspended "conditional upon his future good conduct."[2]

George and Kathryn were present for those pronouncements, arriving in a 10-car motorcade. During the sentencing, Kathryn "stared at the judge icily," then burst into tears. Leaving court, George warned Charles Urschel, "You'll get yours yet, you bastard," drawing a finger across his throat. On October 8, Bailey and Bates were transported to Leavenworth. Judge Vaught gave Robert Shannon 60 days to settle his affairs, then granted Ora 10 days to dispose of her personal property.[3]

More drama ensued on the 9th, when the Kellys arrived in court under guard. Spying her father, James Brooks, in the lobby, Kathryn tried to embrace him. Agent James "Doc" White pushed her away, whereupon

5. Open Season

Federal agents escort George Kelly (in handcuffs) to court in Oklahoma City (Library of Congress).

she slapped his face. George lunged at White and was pistol-whipped in turn, facing the judge with a bloody lump on his head. Their trial was brief, a mere two days, including prosecution testimony from the Urschels, John Catlett, and Kathryn's grandmother, arriving in a wheelchair. On day two, an unchallenged graphologist named Kathryn as author of the ransom note, while Hilda Arnold described the Kellys "virtually kidnapping" her daughter after she, Hilda, granted permission for "a little ride" without her. Hilda described Kathryn's hatred of Charles Urschel, alleging that "Mrs. Kelly said they ought to have killed the son of a bitch and then she wished she could do it herself." Geraldine Arnold, already counting her share of a $12,000 reward for capturing the Kellys, claimed she had somehow overheard George threatening to kill Judge Vaught. Kathryn, testifying on the 11th, denied any role in the kidnapping, asserting that she "begged" George not to kill Urschel once she found out the victim was confined inside a shed. Unimpressed, Vaught convicted both defendants on October 12 and sentenced them to life. While awaiting transfer to prison, Kathryn told reporters she still loved George, adding, "He told me he will break out [at] Christmas and get me out. He always does as he says he will."

George seemed equally confident, quipping, "Don't worry about me going stir crazy. I won't be there long."[4]

The final acts played out in Texas and Tennessee. On October 4, Dallas grand jurors indicted Will Casey and Cassey Coleman for harboring the Kellys, adding a second charge against Coleman for helping conceal the ransom money. Coleman pled guilty on the 17th, receiving a 366-day prison term. Casey took his chances with a jury and lost, drawing a two-year sentence. In Jackson, Tennessee, Langford Ramsey and J.C. Tichenor faced charges of conspiracy and harboring fugitives for concealing the Kellys in Memphis. Convicted on October 21, the defendants received matching 30-month sentences.[5]

John Dillinger's newly-freed friends needed traveling funds in order to liberate their benefactor. On October 3 they stole $14,000 from a bank in Charles Makley's hometown, St. Mary's, Ohio. Nine days later, while Copeland, Hamilton and Shouse stood guard outside, Clark, Makley and Pierpont entered Lima's jail, posing as officers sent to transport Dillinger back to Michigan City for parole violation. When Sheriff Jesse Sarber asked for their credentials, they shot and pistol-whipped him, inflicting mortal wounds. Next stop: Leipsic, Ohio, Pierpont's hometown, to celebrate his birthday on the 13th. Preparing for future raids, the gang struck Auburn, Indiana's police station on the 14th, stealing one Tommy gun, a rifle and shotgun, six pistols, three bulletproof vests and 1,245 rounds of ammunition. A week later, in Peru, Indiana, they repeated that feat, escaping with two Thompsons, two shotguns, two rifles, four pistols, and six more bulletproof vests.[6]

Thus prepared, they resumed looting banks, bagging $75,000 (or $78,000, reports differ) from a raid in Greencastle, Indiana, on October 23. Three days later, Governor McNutt, panicked by press reports of a "Terror Gang" at large, called out the National Guard in Indianapolis, patrolling with armored cars and machine guns, all in vain. Matt Leach took a different approach, sensing that Pierpont was the gang's true leader, spreading tales of the "Dillinger gang" to sow internal dissension, but Pierpont blithely ignored it. October was also the month when Dillinger met Mary Evelyn "Billie" Frechette, a self-described "half French and half Indian" divorcee who would spend the next seven months as his de facto wife.[7]

The Lansing fugitives had mixed luck in October. With Bailey already in jail, Wilbur Underhill took nominal control for a $3,000 bank heist in Baxter Springs, Kansas, on October 6. That same day, police surprised Bob Brady and Jim Clark following a $5,000 holdup in Frederick, Oklahoma, stopping them in Tucumcari, New Mexico, and wounding Brady three times. Reporters predicted Brady's death, but he survived and returned to

Kathryn and George Kelly receive matching life sentences on October 12, 1933, for the Charles Urschel kidnapping (National Archives).

prison. Before his transfer back to Lansing, Reed Vetterli visited Brady's hospital room, failing to identify him as a Kansas City shooter from June.[8]

On October 23, with the Terror Gang busy in Indiana, Lester Gillis took $32,000 from a bank in Brainerd, Minnesota, aided by cohorts Tommy Carroll, John Chase, Charles Fisher and Homer Van Meter, Gillis spraying the street with machine-gun fire as they fled. Afterward, Gillis, wife Helen and Carroll fled to San Antonio, lying low and visiting gangland gunsmith Hyman Lebman.[9]

G-men kept spinning their wheels on the Kansas City massacre case in October. Vern Miller hid out in New Jersey, acquiring false ID as "Frederick J. Glaubach," a traveling optician, complete with a valise of sample spectacles with aid from Alan "Al Silvers" Silverman, a member of powerful bootlegger Abner "Longy" Zwillman's mob. In the meantime, agents grilled Vern's girlfriend, Vivian Mathias, finally coercing her into betraying Miller if he came to see her in Chicago. Despite staking out Vi's apartment, the Bureau missed Miller on Halloween, losing him after a shootout, but they jailed Mathias instead and procured her confession to harboring a fugitive, along with coerced testimony falsely identifying Charles Floyd and Adam Richetti as Miller's accomplices at Union Station. Henceforth, no other suspects in the slaughter would be seriously scrutinized. Unknown to agents at the time, word spread that Miller had murdered a New Jersey aide of Zwillman's, earning the national syndicate's wrath.[10]

The "crime war" heated up during November, though events reflected poorly on the FBI.

On November 2 Wilbur Underhill joined Ford Bradshaw and others to steal $13,000 from a bank in Okmulgee, Oklahoma. Five days later, Bradshaw, Jim Benge and Newton Clanton took $11,238 from another bank in Henryetta—falsely blamed on Charles Floyd, George Birdwell and Aussie Elliott. On the 18th Underhill celebrated by appearing at the Coalgate courthouse, applying under his own name for a license to wed Hazel Jarrett Hudson, a sister of the outlaw Jarrett brothers. One day later, Wilbur's gang hit a bank in Frankfort, Kentucky, to finance the honeymoon. Despite a total lack of jurisdiction, FBI Director Hoover assigned Agent Ralph Colvin to join local lawmen pursuing Underhill.[11]

While that went on, the College Kidnappers began unraveling. On November 9 headlines announced that federal and state authorities had jailed "12 or more" gang members and were busily rounding up its "last remnants." Only three suspects were named—Julius "Babe" Jones, Frank Souder, and Gale Swolley—allegedly recruited from the Sheldon brothers' bootlegging gang in southern Illinois and Egan's Rats in St. Louis, their list of potential victims including Chicago Mayor Edward Kelly. On the 11th, prisoner Jones offered a unique defense, claiming *he* had been snatched, paying a $2,000 ransom, and that police only arrested him when he tried to put another kidnapper "on the spot" as retaliation. One day later, alleged gang member Russell Hughes died in a shootout with Peoria detectives, wounding two lawmen before he expired. That same day, Chicago officers pressed their search for Jack Klutas, lately accused of abducting department store heir Brooke Hart from San Jose, California, and killing him on June 9 after ransom negotiations broke down. That charge, at least, proved incorrect. Police nabbed the actual slayers, two Golden State residents, on November 17, and a lynch mob killed them 10 days later, after Governor James Rolph, Jr., promised pardons to their executioners. Meanwhile, on the 24th, a Peoria grand jury indicted "John" Klutas for counterfeiting "many thousands" of $5 bills with named accomplices including businessman Rex Howard, ex–State Highway engineer George Milligan, plus Chicagoans Frank Lauer, Howard Minnima, and Leo Trant.[12]

Halting progress of a sort continued in the Union Station case through November. On the 6th, New York authorities arraigned Abraham Chait and Herman Borenstein for helping Vern Miller obtain a false driver's license, while alleged cohort Alan Silverman remained at large, his wife denying knowledge of his whereabouts. Two weeks later, officers in Somers, Connecticut, found Silverman hogtied, beaten, and strangled to death, his nude body draped with a robe. G-men questioned "Miller acquaintance" Louis "Lepke" Buchalter, a Gotham racketeer and co-chief of "Murder, Inc." with Albert Anastasia, regarding rumors that Miller "might be bumped off within 30 days" by Syndicate killers. Lepke replied, "Let me look into that," but never called back. One day later, Vivian Mathias and Bobbie Moore pled guilty to federal charges of harboring Miller, receiving identical one-year sentences. Later that same Wednesday, a motorist spied Miller's corpse in a roadside ditch outside Detroit. Like Silverman before him, Miller had been beaten and strangled, left naked but draped in a cheap auto robe. Theories on his murder, still unsolved, abound, including revenge for killing a member of Longy Zwillman's gang, payback for the bungled liberation of Frank Nash, and belated vengeance for the Fox Lake massacre of June 1, 1930, when unidentified machine-gunners shot five Irish Chicago gangsters, partying in Lake County, leaving three dead and two wounded.[13]

Whoever killed Vern Miller, his execution left G-men with only two surviving suspects in the Kansas City massacre, but neither could be found.

November also saw federal prosecution of the Touhy gang for William Hamm, Jr.'s kidnapping collapse. Alleged bagmen Basil Banghart and Charles Connors knew better than to seek revenge on the Capone mob for their bungled frame-up, fleeing all the way to Charlotte, North Carolina, where they stole $105,000 from a U.S. Mail truck on November 15.[14] Despite full knowledge of the Barker-Karpis gang's responsibility, G-men sought confessions from Touhy and his codefendants with brutal "third-degree" tactics, describe in Touhy's 1959 memoir.

The government took us in chains from Elkhorn to the County Jail at Milwaukee. Weeks of hell followed. We were maximum-security prisoners, in separate cells. No visitors; no consultations with lawyers; no visits by families; no radio broadcasts; no newspapers.

I went into the jail in excellent physical shape. When I came out, I was 25 pounds lighter, three vertebrae in my upper spine were fractured and seven of my teeth had been knocked out. Part of the FBI's rehabilitation-of-prisoners system, I supposed. All of the men who gave me the treatment were strangers to me.

They questioned me day and night, abused me, beat me up and demanded that I confess the Hamm kidnapping. Never was I allowed to rest for more than half an hour. If I was asleep when a team of interrogators arrived at my cell, they would slug me around and bang me against the wall. I trained myself to sleep for 20 minutes and be on my feet for the questioners.

I couldn't have confessed if I had wanted to. I didn't know what Hamm looked like, how the ransom was paid, where he was held, or anything else. Neither did McFadden, Schaefer or Sharkey. But that seemingly made no difference.[15]

Despite those efforts, jurors saw through the sham and acquitted all four defendants on November 28, 1933. That didn't mean their ordeal was finished, however. Jake Factor had identified Touhy as his abductor on July 22, at a "secret" lineup that nonetheless made headlines. Freed on one fake kidnapping charge, the prisoners would face trial on another in the new year.[16]

John Dillinger contracted ringworm while confined at Lima. On November 15 he sought treatment from dermatologist Dr. Charles Eye in Chicago, escaping with Billie Frechette from police when informer Arthur McGinnis reported his appointment. Four days later, Chicago police nabbed Harry Copeland, returning him to Michigan City. On the 20th, Dillinger, Pierpont, Makley, Russell Clark, Red Hamilton and Leslie Homer stole $27,000 from a bank in Racine, Wisconsin, wounding a teller and a policeman as they escaped. Police rebounded on the 24th, arresting Leslie Homer in the Windy City.[17]

Lawmen also hounded the Barrow gang through November, capturing W.D. Jones in Dallas without incident on the 16th. Two days later, Jones told police a story blaming Clyde and others for all murders committed during his tenure with the gang, exonerating himself. On the 22nd, Clyde and Bonnie planned a rendezvous with relatives near Sowers, Texas, but informers tipped off Dallas County Sheriff Robert "Smoot" Schmidt. With Deputies Robert Alcorn and Ted Hinton, Schmidt lay in wait for the fugitives, armed with a BAR and two Tommy guns. As the lovers approached, their would-be slayers blazed away, nearly catching kinfolk in the crossfire, but only a single bullet drew blood, drilling one of Clyde's legs and one of Bonnie's. Abandoning their vehicle, they stopped a local attorney, stole his car, and later dumped it in Oklahoma. On November 28, a Dallas grand jury belatedly indicted both fugitives for killing Tarrant County Deputy Malcolm Davis in January 1933. Following the ambush, as a reward for Jones's confessions, Schmidt agreed to charge Jones only as an accessory to the Davis slaying, thus avoiding possible execution for other murders.[18]

December brought no respite for imprisoned members of the Touhy gang. Although acquitted of kidnapping William Hamm, Jr., they remained in custody based on Jake Factor's false identification of his nonexistent abductors. Worn down by incessant torture, William Sharkey killed himself in Saint Paul's jail on December 1. Three days later, Chicago officers formally arrested survivors Touhy, McFadden, and Schaefer, returning them to the Windy City for trial.[19]

That same Monday, Babe Jones of the College Kidnappers pled guilty in Chicago to abducting gambler James Hackett. Despite his history of spinning phony stories for detectives, prosecutors announced that Jones would testify against his codefendants. Jack Klutas remained at large despite sweeping dragnets.[20]

After collecting firearms in San Antonio, Lester Gillis, his wife, and Tommy Carroll shared Thanksgiving dinner with Hyman Lebman's family, enjoying the Texas weather. On December 9, an informer tipped local police to the presence of "high-powered gangsters" in their city, whereupon Detectives Al Hartman and Howard Perrin began a manhunt. On the 11th they spotted Carroll and gunfire erupted, killing Perrin and wounding Hartman. Carroll escaped to Minneapolis, where he had another run-in with authorities on the 15th, that time fleeing barefoot, abandoning three guns and $16,000 cash to make his getaway. Gillis and his wife next surfaced in San Francisco, renewing contact with John Paul Chase and planning more holdups.[21]

Not to be outdone by Indiana State Police, Chicago PD organized a dedicated "Dillinger Squad" in December 1933. Their prey was close at hand but reining in the gang proved problematic. On the 13th, gang members chiseled through the wall of a bank vault to empty 96 safety deposit boxes. Officially, they stole $8,700, while rumors of unreported cash and jewelry taken topped $50,000. One day later, Red Hamilton killed Sergeant William Shanley at a commercial garage, then escaped. On the 20th, officers captured Ed Shouse in Paris, Illinois, and returned him to Michigan City. Hilton Crouch was next to fall, on the 23rd, facing 20 years in prison for one of his holdups committed with Dillinger.[22]

Reports of gangland romance vary widely in December. One account claims Dillinger and Billie Frechette visited John's father—John Wilson

Dillinger—in Mooresville, enjoying quiet time together, while another source claims Dillinger and Billie quarreled, whereupon he beat her, "threw her out," and sent her home to the Wisconsin Indian reservation where she was born. An alternate story claims Dillinger and Frechette decamped for Florida, trailed by other gang members in the face of official heat and mobster Frank Nitto's wrath over Red Hamilton's latest murder. Most versions agree that the gang regrouped in Daytona Beach around December 19, accompanied by "molls" Mary Kinder (for Pierpont), Mary's sister Margaret (with Makley), and Opal Long (with Russell Clark). They remained in Florida till New Year's Eve, when tipsy Dillinger entertained them by firing a Tommy gun at the rising full moon.[23]

On December 21, Bonnie and Clyde allegedly robbed a private citizen in Shreveport, Louisiana, and eluded pursuers.[24]

Wilbur Underhill continued raiding in December. On the 11th, with Jack "Tom" Lloyd, Elmer Inman, and Ralph "Raymond" Roe, he tried to burglarize a bank in Harrah, Oklahoma, but weak floorboards collapsed, dropping the safe into a basement. Rebounding on the 12th, Underhill, Lloyd, and Roe stole $4,000 from a bank in Coalgate. On December 26 lawmen finally traced Underhill, his bride, Ralph Roe, and Roe's girlfriend Eva Mae Nichols to a small rented cottage in Shawnee. They gathered in force, with known posse members including Shawnee Night Chief Frank Bryant; Oklahoma County deputy sheriffs John Adams, Bill Eads, George Kerr, and Don Stone; plus Oklahoma City detectives Clarence Hurt, Jacob "Jelly" Bryce, and Mickey Ryan. Also present were seven G-men: Ralph Colvin, Tyler Birch, Kelly Deadrick, J.M. Edgar, George Franklin, Paul Hanson, and Union Station survivor Frank Smith. At least three agents—Birch, Edgar, and Franklin—carried shotguns, while Colvin had a Tommy gun. Despite a lack of jurisdiction, some reports call Agents Colvin and Smith the posse's leaders.[25]

Surrounding the bungalow before dawn on December 30, lawmen called for its occupants to surrender. Colvin later wrote that Underhill, dressed only in long underwear, moved "as if to pick up his guns," whereupon Colvin and the others poured bullets and tear gas into the house. Accounts of the battle differ, but it seems that lawmen firing through the house from front and back did most of the shooting. Wilbur escaped, barefoot, armed with a pistol, while Eva Nichols suffered fatal wounds. Ralph Roe, hit twice, surrendered and was taken into custody with Hazel Underhill. Her husband covered 16 blocks, finally cornered and disarmed inside a hardware store. Fatally wounded, he staunchly denied participating in the Kansas City massacre with Harvey Bailey. Confined to McAlester's prison hospital, Underhill died on January 6, his last words recorded as "Tell the boys I'm coming home."[26]

5. Open Season

Slayers of Wilbur Underhill, December 30, 1933. Standing (left to right): Paul Hanson, Clarence Hurt, Kelly Deadrick; Kneeling (left to right): Ralph Colvin, Jacob "Jelly" Bryce (National Archives).

Ford Bradshaw didn't wait for Underhill to die before he led a gang through Vian, Oklahoma, on New Year's Eve, shooting up the town's jail, a restaurant and hardware store in reprisal. Soon after the Shawnee shootout, Clarence Hurt applied to join the FBI and was quickly accepted, joining Director Hoover's growing team of "gunfighters."[27]

6

Trials and Errors

J. Edgar Hoover opened the new year in fury toward his Kansas City office for its lack of progress on the Union Station massacre. A memo from Assistant Director Hugh Clegg advised:

> This morning I telephoned Acting Agent in Charge M.C. Spear, at Kansas City, and told him that the Division was very much displeased with the reported lack of vigor in the Kansas City massacre case; that it appeared that they had let this case fall by the wayside and it was being handled intermittently by any one of a number of agents and it was not being pursued vigorously toward a logical conclusion.[1]

More specifically, only two agents were working the case full-time, and one of those, new recruit A.C. "Gyp" Farland, had questioned Leavenworth prison inmates, convincing himself that Vern Miller's "two" accomplices were Fred Barker and Alvin Karpis. Clegg's memo noted that there "had arisen some friction with the handling of the case," adding, "I informed Spear that various theories that they might develop had no bearing on the case; that it was not the policy of the Division to get into disputes over theories; that we were seeking the facts, whatever they might be, and that he should not tolerate any friction in his office."[2]

Hoover's hand-scrawled reply fumed, "This must stop *at once*. See that a sharp letter be sent to K.C. re. such bickering. It must stop *at once*."[3]

The director's prescription for progress focused on heightened "third-degree" tactics, as already experienced by Roger Touhy and his codefendants. According to Kansas City suspect Dick Galatas, Bureau methods included denial of sleep for five straight days, while he was held incommunicado from attorneys in a private residence, unable even to lie down during that time; denial of food while manacled to a straight-backed chair; interrogation lasting hours on end, including physical assaults, death threats from agents brandishing pistols; advice including "You haven't any rights till we finish with you," "We're going to get your story one way or another," and "You could be found dead on the street and all we would have to say is that you tried to run." When Galatas finally started talking, he claimed his words were altered by G-men to suit themselves before he signed off in agreement.[4]

In short, the Bureau cared no more for truth or constitutional protection of a suspect's rights than did most other law enforcement agencies nationwide.

While Hoover's agents broke the law, achieving little from their efforts, Illinois police wrapped up the College Kidnappers with no help from the feds. After Babe Jones's guilty plea, accomplices Souder and Swolley saw their trial dates set for January 8 and 15th, but leader Theodore Klutas didn't last that long. On January 6 officers surprised Handsome Jack in Bellwood, a Cook County village 13 miles west of Chicago's downtown Loop, at a house across the street from Bellwood Police Chief Henry Eggebrecht's home. Klutas allegedly reached for a weapon and died in a blaze of gunfire, while companions Adolphe Anzone and Paul Stroud surrendered. Next morning, "victims of a dozen kidnappings and extortion plots" filed past Klutas's slab at Chicago's morgue, reportedly identifying him as their tormentor. On the same day Klutas died, police raiders surprised late gang addition Walter Dietrich during his morning shave, returning him to Michigan City's lockup on the 10th. Anzone and cohort Earl McMahon remained in custody, unable to raise $50,000 bond apiece. Souder and Swolley, both swiftly convicted, received matching life sentences on January 24, with victim James Hackett on hand to observe their denouement.[5]

Oklahoma police nabbed parolee Elmer Inman on January 7, one day after cohort Wilbur Underhill's death, at a gas station in Bowlegs. Injured while resisting, he was shuttled back to McAlester's lockup. Girlfriend Lena Nichols faced charges of harboring a fugitive.[6]

Around the same time, FBI headquarters created a new Chicago-based "Flying Squad" to pursue "public enemies" across state lines. Its leader, Agent Samuel Cowley, was Idaho-born in 1899, son of a polygamist who sat on the Mormon Quorum of Twelve Apostles. Samuel attended Utah State Agricultural College before graduating with honors from George Washington University Law School in spring of 1929 and joined the Bureau that April. Director Hoover ignored Cowley's family background, although "plural marriage" was and is today illegal, promoting Cowley to Inspector in 1932. His primary qualification, in publicity-hungry Hoover's eyes, was spelled out in Cowley's personnel file, where the Director called Samuel "the sort of man who never could be found in the limelight, and his excellence was his intelligent persistence and his thoroughness at doing what ought to be done."[7]

At the other end of field experience, the Flying Squad—operating independently of Chicago Special Agent in Charge Melvin Purvis—included rookie agent Thomas McDade, hired in 1934 and gone by '38, perhaps worn out by his experience hunting desperate fugitives. Others on the squad included Herman Hollis (hired in 1927), Daniel "Sully" Sullivan (1932), and Charles Campbell (1934). By May, the team would welcome an influx of local policemen, Hoover's "gunfighters," added specifically to keep the Director's vow of "extermination."[8]

The Flying Squad's primary targets were members of the Dillinger gang, but the Bureau always seemed to be a day late and a dollar short. Illinois police caught Walter Dietrich on January 6, while Daytona Beach officers allegedly pursued gang members in vain on the 14th. That report is probably in error, since the bandits surfaced one day later in East Chicago, Indiana, 1,126 miles northwest of Daytona. There, they stole $20,000 from a local bank, escaping after a shootout that left Red Hamilton with five wounds, while Officer William O'Malley lay dead. Chicago police found their bloody, bullet-scarred getaway car on the 17th but could not locate the fugitives.[9]

Controversy still surrounds the East Chicago raid. While Dillinger would be charged with O'Malley's murder, Mary Kinder later said that Dillinger missed the holdup, naming its participants as Harry Pierpont, Hamilton, Homer Van Meter, and an associate of Lester Gillis named in various accounts as Tommy Carroll, John Paul Chase, or Eddie Green. We know that Dillinger visited his father in Mooresville, arriving in the predawn hours of January 17 with Russell Clark, Charles Makley, and Opal Long. All but Dillinger left that morning, headed for Tucson, Arizona, while John stayed with his father overnight. In conversation with his father—and to his dying day—Dillinger denied O'Malley's murder.[10]

On Thursday, the 18th, Dillinger drove to Chicago, checked up on Hamilton's condition and collected a gambling debt from Red, paid in loot from East Chicago. Afterward, he met Billie Frechette and headed for St. Louis, making another stop at Mooresville to repeat his denial of involvement in the East Chicago raid. On the 19th he and Billie attended an auto show at the St. Louis Municipal Auditorium. Billie's Boston bull terrier, a gift from Dillinger, briefly escaped, caught by a policeman who returned it to the couple, unaware of Dillinger's identity.[11]

The gang's luck soured in Arizona. On Monday, the 22nd, fire broke out at Tucson's Congress Hotel, where guests Clark and Makley, registered under pseudonyms, paid firefighters $50 to rescue their belongings, including baggage heavily laden with weapons, then moved to a house on North Second Avenue. Next morning, while Harry Pierpont and Mary Kinder rented a Tucson tourist cabin, a fireman recognized Clark's mugshot in a detective magazine and tipped local police. Dillinger and Billie Frechette reached Tucson on the 24th, after scouting escape routes to Mexico. On the

6. Trials and Errors

Dillinger gang members in court after their 1934 roundup in Tucson, Arizona; seated (left to right): Russell Clark, Charles Makley, Harry Pierpont, John Dillinger, Evelyn Frechette, and Mary Kinder (National Archives).

25th, officers caught Makley at a downtown radio shop, then bagged Clark and Long at their rented house. Before day's end, Pierpont and Kinder were stopped and arrested on South Sixth Street, trying to leave town, while cops made a clean sweep on North Second Avenue, catching Dillinger and Frechette.[12]

On the 26th, Pima County Justice of the Peace C.V. Budlong set bond at $100,000 for all of those arrested except Billie, who could not post her $5,000 bail. Matt Leach flew from Indiana with extradition papers for Dillinger, charging him with the O'Malley homicide. On the night of January 29, Dillinger began a six-stop flight to Chicago's Midway Airport, where a 13-car caravan bristling with weapons delivered him to Lake County, Indiana's "escape-proof" jail at Crown Point. Attorney Louis Piquett and investigator Arthur O'Leary tried to visit Dillinger on the 31st but were illegally denied access to Piquett's client, returning to Chicago.[13]

Piquett was what many people in those days might call "a character." From bartending, he plunged into Chicago Democratic politics and studied law in night school. By 1915 he was chief clerk for Chicago's city prosecutor, elevated to the prosecutor's post during the 1920s by another "character," Mob-allied Mayor William "Big Bill" Thompson. Grand jurors indicted Piquett for corruption in 1923, but the case fell through, Chicago-style. That summer he entered private practice, successfully defending a purveyor of then-illegal prize fight films. Eight years later he failed to win acquittal for Capone triggerman Leo Vincent Brothers in the death of *Chicago Tribune* reporter Jake Lingle. When finally allowed to meet his latest client, Piquett convinced Lake County to permit Dillinger's appearance in court without chains or armed guards. Meanwhile, Dillinger seemed to enjoy himself at Crown Point, joking with reporters, mugging for their cameras with one arm on prosecutor Robert Estill's shoulder as if they were old friends. Estill and Sheriff Lillian Holley both smiled as Dillinger vowed to escape from their lockup.[14]

Roger Touhy and his surviving codefendants faced trial for Jake Factor's mythical abduction on January 15. Despite the FBI's best efforts at a frameup, prosecution witnesses fumbled their scripted lines, caught in one lie after another. Midway through the inquisition, one juror stopped reporting for duty, while a second admitted perjuring himself during pretrial voir dire. Judge Michael Feinberg reluctantly declared a mistrial on February 2, preparing to start over.[15]

On January 16 Clyde Barrow and Bonnie Parker teamed with cohorts Floyd Hamilton and Jimmy Mullins to orchestrate a breakout from the Eastham prison farm near Huntsville, Texas, liberating inmates Raymond Hamilton (Floyd's brother), Henry Methvin, William Hilton Bybee and Joe Palmer. Palmer seized a weapon, fatally wounding Major Joe Crowson, who died on the 27th. Officers recaptured Bybee on January 30, while the others remained at large, presumably enjoying bad publicity that swamped Texas Department of Corrections Chief Lee Simmons. Simmons, in turn, issued a "shoot-to-kill" order on Barrow and Parker, along with their new gang members.[16]

Ray Hamilton was not the best fit for the Barrow gang. Born in 1913, in an Oklahoma tent encampment, he grew up in Dallas but returned to Oklahoma as a felon, killing Stringtown Undersheriff Eugene Moore in August 1932. In January 1934 he was serving 266 years for murder, auto theft and armed robbery. Soon after the escape, he met 19-year-old Mary O'Dare, wife of a bank robber locked up for 99 years. Bonnie and Clyde disliked O'Dare, calling her a "washerwomen," prostitute and gold-digger, her presence with the gang a nagging irritant that boyfriend Raymond would soon exacerbate.[17]

Louisiana-born in 1912, escapee Henry Methvin is sometimes described as the "final" or "last" Barrow gang member. In September 1930 he slashed an oilfield worker's throat in Victoria County, Texas, and stole

6. Trials and Errors

John Dillinger (right) poses with Lake County, Indiana, District Attorney Robert Estill at the Crown Point jail, for a photo that doomed Estill's political career (Library of Congress).

the man's car. The victim survived, while Methvin, arrested two hours later, received a 12-year prison term. Like William Jones before him, he would later blame others for most crimes committed while he traveled with Bonnie and Clyde.[18]

To hunt the fugitives, Chief Sullivan hired 49-year-old Francis Augustus Hamer, a retired Texas Ranger with an awesome Old West reputation. Hamer nabbed his first felon, a horse thief, as a civilian in 1905 and joined the Rangers a year later. He lasted until 1908, then held jobs as City Marshal of Navasota, a Houston "special investigator" (1911–14), and a Harris County deputy sheriff. Rejoining the Rangers in 1915, he soon switched again to become a "range detective" for the Southwestern Cattle Raisers Association. Hamer killed the first of a reputed 53 criminals in 1917, then joined the U.S. Treasury Department's Prohibition Unit in 1920, finally rejoining the Rangers as a Senior Captain in 1921. Before retiring in 1932, Hamer allegedly rescued 15 persons from lynch mobs and suffered 17 gunshot wounds in various showdowns. He blamed his exit on the election of Governor Miriam "Ma" Ferguson, saying, "When they elected a woman governor, I quit," but the Rangers' commander kept Hamer listed as an active-duty Senior Captain. While neither Chief Sullivan nor Hamer had any legal authority outside Texas, on February 10, 1934, Hamer accepted a commission to pursue the Barrow gang wherever their trail led. From that day on, Hamer stayed on their track, living out of his car for the next 15 weeks, typically a town or two behind his prey, relentless to the bitter end.[19]

Meanwhile, frustrated in its search for the Lindbergh kidnappers, angry at playing second-fiddle to state and local police, FBI headquarters cabled its New York City office on January 17, ordering agents to contact all Gotham banks, requesting "an extremely close watch" for any ransom gold certificates. Another eight months would elapse before the first break in that case.[20]

On the same day that the Lindbergh memo reached New York, January 17, the Barker-Karpis gang kidnapped Edward Bremer, owner of Saint Paul's Schmidt Brewery and president of the Bremer Bank, which counted mobsters Leon Gleckman and Harry "Dutch" Sawyer among its depositors. The brewery had survived Prohibition's 14 years by switching to soft drinks and "near beer," simultaneously pumping alcoholic beer through underground tunnels to Sawyer's Green Lantern speakeasy. Bremer's abductors demanded and received $200,000 ransom—double the Hamm kidnap payoff—slipping the usual cut to Tom Brown's aptly-named Kidnap Squad. The snatch terrified other wealthy Saint Paul residents, and the gang made matters worse by wounding Northwest Airways Company employee M.C. McCord, mistaking him for a lawman. Bremer could not identify his abductors, but G-men subsequently lifted Dock Barker's fingerprints from a gasoline can left at the ransom drop site.[21]

Recaptured fugitives Bob Brady and Jim Clark staged their second escape from Lansing on January 19, accompanied by five other inmates from a kitchen work detail. Brady and Clark separated on the outside, Clark joining Frank Delmar to carjack schoolteacher Louis Dresser, making their way to Oklahoma, where Clark's girlfriend Goldie Johnson waited with a getaway car. Dresser, released unharmed, was so distressed by the experience that he misidentified Johnson as Bonnie Parker. Undersheriff Harvey Lininger and Deputy Ed Schlotman traced Brady to a farm near Paola, Kansas, on January 22. Brady threatened them with a shotgun but it misfired, prompting the officers to kill him.[22]

G-men mistakenly thought they'd solved the Lindbergh case on January 31, when they joined Chicago officers to nab Verne Sankey at a Windy City barbershop. Soon afterward, raiders arrested Helen Mattern, who shared Sankey's apartment, then released her when she claimed to know the fugitive only as "W. E. Clark." Headlines blared: "Lindy Confession Sought; Kidnaper Gets 'Third Degree' for Lindy Clues; Crack U.S. Agents

Work Relays, Grill 'America's Public Enemy Number 1.'" When Saint Paul Police Chief Thomas Dahill and D.A. M.F. Kinkead arrived to extradite Sankey for the Haskell Bonn abduction, Chicago SAC Melvin Purvis told them "that the government is not yet through questioning Sankey and until then he will not consider extradition requests"—a pronouncement far outside his legal authority. From Washington, Director Hoover echoed Purvis, saying Sankey "will be considered as a suspect in the Lindbergh baby kidnaping until he is eliminated definitely." D.A. Kinkead stoked the flames of supposition, declaring his belief that Sankey not only kidnapped Charles Lindbergh, Jr., but also planned to snatch sports figures Jack Dempsey and Babe Ruth.[23]

The Bureau faced more embarrassment when reporters learned that three Chicago detectives, "assigned to the case under Mr. Purvis," had traced Sankey on November 9, 1933, but refrained from arresting him in hopes he would lead them to cohort Gordon Alcorn. Meanwhile, authorities in Minnesota and Colorado squabbled over who would try Sankey first, for the Bonn or Boettcher kidnappings, if Purvis ever released him.[24]

South Dakota authorities outmaneuvered G-men on February 1, dragging Alcorn from a trolley in Sioux Falls and rushing him to the state penitentiary, where he sat—and was presumably interrogated—"under special Federal guard." News swiftly came that he would plead guilty in the Boettcher case, a crime also freely confessed by Sankey. Sankey cheated justice on February 8, hanging himself in his cell with two cravats his jailers carelessly failed to confiscate when he was caged. One day later, Alcorn pled guilty in the Boettcher case and received a life sentence. *Time* magazine, behind the curve, chortled that "a one-man necktie party" had closed two major cases, but declined to mention that G-men were still no closer to the murderer of Little Lindy.[25]

While suicide and a confession closed two of the Bureau's pending files, the frameup of Roger Touhy, Albert Kator and Gus Schaefer forged ahead in Chicago. The second trial began on February 1, with prosecutors seeking executions for the crime that never happened. Defense attorney William Stewart challenged the state's flimsy case, telling jurors, "Factor stands alone in the giving of direct evidence, and he is not to be believed." The panel agreed, failing to reach a verdict, but authorities—either foolishly gullible or corrupt and malicious—scheduled yet another trial to start on February 13.[26]

In the interim, authorities traced Basil Banghart to a Baltimore apartment, arresting him on February 10. He joined Touhy and company for their third trial on the Factor case, and that time, flagrant perjury carried the day, resulting in conviction of all defendants on February 22. Roger

Touhy filed the first in an eight-year string of appeals that depleted his bootlegger's fortune with all pleas denied. In Chicago, the FBI celebrated its "triumph."[27]

That hollow victory, handed to the Bureau by the Capone gang, prolonged a romance of sorts between Director Hoover and his Windy City SAC, Melvin Purvis, Jr. A South Carolina native, born to a family of wealthy tobacco farmers in 1903, Purvis set his sights on federal service after graduating from law school. His first attempt brought rejection from the State Department, whereupon he applied to the FBI in December 1926, exerting influence through friendly Senator Coleman Blease. Despite Hoover's 1924 pledge to shun political pressure and "hacks," Assistant Director Harold "Pop" Nathan approved the application on January 22, 1927, and Hoover hired Purvis one week later, assigning him to the Bureau's Atlanta field office. From there, he served in Oklahoma City, Cincinnati, and Birmingham, finally named as Chicago's Special Agent in Charge on October 25, 1932.[28]

Along the way, Hoover became enamored of Purvis, relentlessly pressing friendship upon him in a series of letters preserved in FBI files. Analysts differ on whether this amounted to simple camaraderie or "a homosexual courtship" on Hoover's part, but the correspondence clearly reveal Hoover's unaccustomed fawning admiration for Purvis. In February 1931 Hoover began addressing Purvis on paper as "Dear Melvin," insisting that Purvis respond by calling the Director "Jayee" or "Ed."[29] One year later, after Purvis sent Hoover a press clipping with a group photo including Purvis, Hoover replied:

> I do wish that in the future when you send something of this kind to me, if your picture appears in it, that you be kind enough to cut it out and not send the photo along with it for it has disrupted my office this morning. My secretary [Helen Gandy] has been floating around in the air, so to speak, and has been saying how "SWEET" you look. I don't expect to get any work out of her today. It is a crime what effect you have upon the fair sex.[30]

In July 1932, returning to the subject of Gandy's alleged infatuation, Hoover advised Purvis to "embark upon the matrimonial sea.... Consequently, I think you owe it not only to yourself and the lady but it would be of great assistance to the efficiency of my office to get straightened out and straightened out as early as possible."[31]

Purvis would not marry until 1938. Meanwhile, on August 4 Hoover wrote:

> The last report from the battle front, ... following the baseball game of yesterday, is that the front office was further disgraced publicly and I personally have been humiliated and embarrassed and I know that you will feel crushed at the

news in view of the relation pending between you and my secretary. The facts are that Mr. Keith [Memphis SAC John Keith], otherwise known as the Dean or Sir John of Ivanwold, had precipitated upon his lap at the initiation of my secretary one Helen Gandy and so overwhelmed was the chauffeur of the car … that he drove around the Ellipse twice, not being able to find the outlet; the chauffeur having lived in Washington all his life. During this episode John Keith kept saying sweet nothings to one Helen inspired by her actions and the event has now resulted in much speculation as to whether Sir John of Ivanwold will be challenged to a duel by one Melvin of Birmingham. I am informed that this so-called "snaking" in the car continued all the way to the city.[32]

As October 1932's FBI Halloween Ball approached, Hoover continued his locker-room bid at matchmaking, writing, "Following our talk I told Miss Gandy you said you would be here with bells on and she said she can hardly wait until that time. Incidentally the ball is to be a masquerade affair and Miss Gandy has promised she will wear a cellophane gown. You can look forward to seeing all of Miss Gandy." Four days prior to the ball, Hoover promoted "Dear Melvin" to top G-man in Chicago.[33]

On February 9, 1934, Lansing fugitive Jim Clark and partner Frank Delmar raided a bank in Goodland, Kansas. They escaped with $2,000, but not before a policeman, hiding beneath his patrol car, shot Clark in both feet, sidelining the bandit for three months' recuperation.[34]

That same day, John Dillinger faced arraignment for Officer O'Malley's murder in Indiana. Louis Piquett requested four months' postponement for preparation, whereupon Judge William Murray split the difference, scheduling trial for March 12. Prosecutor Robert Estill asked Murray to lodge Dillinger at Michigan City's prison for safekeeping, but Murray denied the request. On the 14th, in Ohio, Clark, Makley and Pierpont went on trial for Sheriff Sarber's murder, while authorities released Mary Kinder. Billie Frechette visited Dillinger at Crown Point on the 26th, posing as his wife.[35]

On February 13, Kansas City SAC Edward Conroy wrote to Hoover, belatedly announcing discovery of latent fingerprints at the home of massacre suspect Frank Mulloy in June 1933, closing almost plaintively, "And by the way, will the Bureau try to match the prints against those of 81 suspects on the attached list?" Furious, Hoover cabled back: "Refer your letter February 13th with which transmitted evidence apparently available since June. Desire full immediate explanation Air Mail why this latent evidence not immediately transmitted upon discovery to Division and where held in interim. Also desire detailed statement your desires for analysis and purposes such analysis."[36]

Conroy groveled, claiming the delay was caused by "numerous special agents" invading Kansas City on "special assignment" after the massacre, thus creating chaos. On March 14, after another month's delay, Washington identified one of the various prints as belonging to former Oklahoma prison inmate Adam Richetti, instantly shifting the Bureau's focus away from gunmen allegedly seen in action by Union Stations witnesses eight months earlier. As to when or why Richetti might have entered Mulloy's home (as opposed to Vern Miller's), no one could say.[37]

February brought a new Bureau push on the Lindbergh case, all 31 field offices nationwide receiving full lists of ransom bill serial numbers. In Gotham alone, G-men distributed copies of that pamphlet to each employee handling currency in banks, clearinghouses, grocery stores in certain selected communities, insurance companies, gasoline filling stations, airports, department stores, post offices, and telegraph companies. A few bills had already been passed in New Jersey and New York, but sparse details of those transactions failed to reveal any suspects.[38]

On the night of February 19 Clyde Barrow, Ray Hamilton, and Henry Methvin stole guns and ammo from a National Guard armory in Ranger, Texas, using the new hardware to loot $4,138 from a bank at Lancaster, 122 miles farther west. Frank Hamer, in pursuit, recruited three lawmen to help him: ex–Ranger Benjamin "Maney" Gault; Sheriff Henderson Jordan of Bienville Parish, Louisiana; and Dallas County Deputy Sheriff Bob Alcorn, who had missed Bonnie and Clyde in a 1933 ambush near Sowers, Texas. The FBI, while maintaining an open file on the gang, played no active role in the search.[39]

Ripples from the Urschel kidnapping continued on February 22, when grand jurors in Fort Worth, Texas, indicted Louise Magness for harboring fugitives George and Kathryn Kelly.[40]

Focus of the Barrow-Parker search shifted from Texas to Louisiana on March 1, 1934, when Clyde and Bonnie drove Henry Methvin to meet his father—Ivan "Ivy" Methvin—near Gibsland. After that get-together, Ivan contacted Sheriff Jordan, seeking potential remedies for Henry's escalating legal problems. Meanwhile, Clyde exiled Ray Hamilton and Mary O'Dare after he caught them stealing loot from the gang's traveling funds. In peripheral news, recaptured Eastham fugitive Hilton Bybee, described as a "desperado and lifetime convict," escaped from Houston County's jail at Crockett, with inmate Cecil Lewis, on March 23. Fleeing in the jailer's car, the duo drove to Lake Worth, relieving a stranger of his car and cash, then rolled on toward Jacksboro, where they stole 68 pistols from a National Guard armory on March 28.[41]

On March 3, Ford Bradshaw ran out of luck and time in Ardmore, Oklahoma. Cornered by Deputy Sheriff William Harper, Bradshaw reached for a gun and died with his boots on, in classic frontier outlaw style.[42]

On the same day Bradshaw died, John Dillinger escaped from Crown

Point's jail with accused murderer Herbert Youngblood, slipping past National Guard troops outside in machine-gun emplacements and fleeing in Sheriff Holley's personal auto. Legend has it that he carved a "gun" from wood and blackened it with shoe polish, then seized real weapons from the jail's arsenal before departing. Alternate versions claim that Louis Piquet bribed jailers to facilitate the breakout, or—as Piquet later wrote—that investigator Art O'Leary smuggled a real pistol into Crown Point on his own initiative. Whatever the case, Dillinger was free again and reams of bad publicity deluged Indiana authorities.[43]

Lawmen found Sheriff Holley's car in Chicago, on March 5, while Dillinger hid with Billie Frechette at a Minneapolis apartment. On the 6th, Dillinger stole $49,500 from a bank in Sioux Falls, South Dakota, accompanied by Tommy Carroll, Eddie Green, Lester Gillis, and Homer Van Meter. Departing, one of the bandits wounded Patrolman Hale Keith. A day later, G-men started tracking Dillinger for violation of the Dyer Act, driving Sheriff Holley's stolen car across the Indiana-Illinois state line.[44]

On March 13, Dillinger and his Sioux Falls companions, plus Red Grant, looted $52,344 from a bank in Mason City, Iowa. A wild melee erupted as they fled, involving police and local civilians, leaving Dillinger, Hamilton, and bystander R.H. James with bullet wounds. The next day, Dillinger and Hamilton sought medical treatment from Dr. Nels Mortensen in Saint Paul. That same Wednesday, March 14, police spotted Herbert Youngblood—who had split from Dillinger after their great escape—in Port Huron, Michigan. A shootout erupted, killing Youngblood and Saint Clair County Undersheriff Charles Cavanaugh.[45]

In Chicago, on the 16th, Dillinger and Billie Frechette sought an audience with Louis Piquett to discuss Billie's divorce from her imprisoned husband, enabling her to wed Dillinger. Piquett was unavailable, but Art O'Leary took the message (and may have received a payoff for the Crown Point escape). Dillinger and Billie discussed the problem again with O'Leary, two days later, then Billie traveled to Mooresville alone, delivering cash and Dillinger's purported wooden gun to John's father. On the 20th, Dillinger and Billie rented a Saint Paul apartment as "Mr. and Mrs. Carl Hellman." On Thursday, the 22nd, Lester Gillis arrived in Reno with his wife and John Chase, going to ground. Dillinger drove to Leipsic, Ohio, two days later, visiting Harry Pierpont's mother, discussing plans for another prison escape, leaving cash for the attorney representing gang members Clark, Makley and Pierpont. The payoff didn't help, as Makley and Pierpont received death sentences on the 24th, with Clark sentenced to life. The trio entered Ohio's state prison at Columbus on the 27th.[46]

Undaunted, Dillinger, Billie, Red Hamilton, his "moll" Pat Cherrington, and her sister, Opal Long, partied through the night at Dillinger's

Saint Paul apartment on March 30. The morning after, tipped off by a suspicious caretaker, G-men Rufus Coulter and Rosser "Rusty" Nalls approached the "Hellman" apartment with local Detective Henry Cummings, surprising Dillinger, Frechette, and Homer Van Meter after their night of revelry. All three escaped, Van Meter in a passing coal truck, while Dillinger—hit in the leg by a bullet—drove to Eddie Green's apartment, and from there to visit Dr. Clayton May in Minneapolis. Dillinger, convalescing, remained with Dr. May and his nurse, Augusta Salt, until April 4.⁴⁷

The purported wooden gun used by John Dillinger to escape from Crown Point, Indiana's, jail on March 3, 1934, resulting in his first federal charge for driving Sheriff Lillian Holley's stolen car across state lines. Skeptics claim an employee of Dillinger's lawyer smuggled a real pistol into the jail. The wooden gun was later housed at Indiana's John Dillinger Museum (author's collection).

While John Dillinger remained at large in March 1934, authorities began stalking a newer group, sometimes called "the Dillingers of the East," more commonly known as the Tri-State Gang for its focus of operations in Pennsylvania, Maryland, and Virginia. Leader Walter Legenza was a Polish immigrant, born in 1894. Faithful comrade Robert Howard Mais, 12 years younger, helped ride herd on 16 accomplices, shifting over time. The gang started hijacking Virginia cigarette trucks in 1933, then hoped to make a "big score" with a Federal Reserve truck in Richmond, on March 8, 1934. Expecting a fabulous shipment of cash and gold, Legenza, Mais, and two others stopped a mail truck by mistake and Legenza murdered driver E.M. Hubard, although Hubard offered no resistance. They fled with 11 sacks, which contained nothing but 25,000 worthless canceled checks, and landed on the FBI's WANTED list for their trouble, since the holdup involved U.S. Mail.⁴⁸

In Illinois, the Factor kidnapping frameup continued. Police found fake bagman Charles Connors murdered at Willow Springs on March 13, the same day Chicago jurors convicted Basil Banghart of his role in the mythical abduction. Ike Costner took the witness stand against him, falsely claiming he and Banghart had been hired to aid with the kidnapping, and

6. Trials and Errors 99

jurors chose to believe him. Two months later, a North Carolina court rightly convicted Banghart and Costner for their Charlotte mail train robbery, but Tarheel State jailers were forced to wait while The Owl returned to serve 99 years in Illinois for a crime that never happened.[49]

When the FBI's Scientific Crime Detection Laboratory officially opened in Washington, on November 24, 1932, Director Hoover called it "cutting edge." It was, in fact, a one-room operation with a single full-time employee, Agent Charles Appel, laboring with a borrowed microscope and a pseudo-scientific device called a "helixometer," purportedly used to examine gun barrels, but "actually more for show than function." Soon overwhelmed by demands from the spreading "crime war," Hoover skimped on vital resources and left Appel to find private, mercenary "experts" in various fields.[50]

One such was Merle Gill, a "ballistics pioneer" living in Kansas City, working freelance for any law enforcement agency that met his price. At Appel's request, Gill took charge of the Kansas City massacre's scientific aspects nearly from day one in June 1933, subsequently testing weapons abandoned by the Barrow gang in July and determining they played no role in the slaughter. By March 1934, the Bureau had nothing but garbled descriptions of gunmen, the coerced "admissions" of Vivian Mathias, and a stray beer-bottle fingerprint from Adam Richetti—irrelevant to the shootings—that suggested any killer but Vern Miller. Reviewing projectiles and cartridge cases gleaned from Union Station, Gill reported to Appel that "Pretty Boy Floyd had absolutely nothing to do with the massacre." In Washington, fledgling Inspector Quinn Tamm warned Hoover that "it would be difficult to later convince anybody of the facts" should Richetti and Floyd be killed before indictment and trial. "If the public knows about it," he went on, "and these people are knocked off, this will be a solution to the case."[51]

To serve that end, however, they must be "knocked off" by G-men.

Furious, Hoover replied to Tamm with his previously quoted memo claiming that he "deplored" the use of private experts, more specifically claiming that he "never approved the turning over of the evidence to Gill." That belated objection, of course, was merely whitewash. Hoover closely supervised every aspect of the massacre investigation. If he had "opposed" and "deplored" Gill's employment, he would have cut it short and chastised Agent Appel.[52]

On March 20, 1934, time ran out for Barker-Karpis gangster Fred Goetz, a participant in the January Bremer kidnapping. Standing outside the padlocked Minerva restaurant in Cicero, Illinois, Goetz fell prey to drive-by gunmen wielding shotguns, blasting him four times. On his corpse, police found a $1,000 bill, membership cards for various clubs bearing variations of his name, and six slender steel blades concealed inside his belt, presumably meant to facilitate future jailbreaks. Two theories of his murder, still unsolved, involve Goetz's loose lips, either boasting of involvement with the Barker crew or of participation in the 1929 Saint Valentine's Day massacre.[53]

Lester Gillis continued his rampage in March, although years would pass before G-men linked him to his latest crimes. On March 4, an unidentified gunman killed local resident Theodore Kidder in Saint Louis Park, a Minneapolis suburb. An ammunition salesman for the National Lead Company, Kidder was driving home when two men in fedoras stopped his car on Brookside Avenue, one emerging to say, "Come over here, Ted, we want to talk to you." After brief conversation, the unknown man shot Kidder 17 times with a .32-caliber pistol. Early speculation claimed Kidder was slain for informing on perpetrators of a local 1933 post office robbery, but no supporting evidence emerged. In 2003 author Bryan Burrough cited interviews with ex–FBI agents, claiming G-men traced the murder car's California license plate to one "James Rogers," a Gillis alias. In that scenario, Kidder innocently cut Lester's car off in traffic, prompting an outburst of homicidal road rage—but in that case, how would he know his victim's name?[54]

Following the Mason City bank heist, Gillis, his wife, and John Chase fled to Reno, Nevada, seeking shelter with their former Mob-connected employers, William Graham and Jim McKay. Both racketeers were then fighting a federal mail fraud charge, and FBI headquarters claimed, years later, that Gillis and Chase aided their friends by kidnapping and killing key prosecution witness Roy Frisch, a former Reno city councilman, last seen walking home from a movie theater on March 22. Although the victim's corpse was never found, memos allege that he was shot, his body dismembered, then dumped in an abandoned mine shaft.[55]

California police caught up with Michigan City escapee Ed Davis in March, raiding his apartment and arresting him on charges that included six counts of robbery, three counts of burglary, and two counts of kidnapping. Prior convictions on similar charges left him indicted as a habitual criminal, convicted on all counts and sentenced to life at Folsom State Prison on June 22.[56]

Easter fell on April 1 in 1934 and brought grim news to Texas. That Sunday, the Barrow gang, including Ray Hamilton and Henry Methvin, were idling outside Grapevine when Texas Highway Patrol officers Holloway Murphy and Edward Wheeler approached on motorcycles, then parked and proceeded on foot. Within seconds, both patrolmen were dead, under circumstances still disputed.[57]

Various locals claimed to be long-distance eyewitnesses to the murders, but their tales were contradictory, twisted and elaborated further by the press, until reality caught up and most accounts were finally discredited. Farmer William Schieffer described Bonnie Parker standing over Murphy, laughing as she shot him, while his "head bounced like a rubber ball" on asphalt. A parallel story, wholly false, claimed that investigators found a cigar at the scene "bearing tiny teeth marks"—a reference to a spoof snapshot from April 1933, recovered after the Joplin shootout, in which Bonnie posed with a cigar and pistol. (In fact, she chain-smoked Camel cigarettes, but never stogies.) As anger roiled, Governor Ferguson posted $500 bounties on Bonnie and Clyde, while Highway Patrol Chief Louis Phares offered $1,000 for "the dead bodies of the Grapevine slayers," nothing for live capture. The *Dallas Journal* ran an editorial cartoon of an electric chair with the caption "Reserved for Clyde and Bonnie."[58]

Over time, the lies began to fade, though some are still repeated and portrayed in films today. Mabel Giggal, out for a Sunday drive with her husband, saw an unidentified man standing over the Grapevine victims but glimpsed no woman. Clyde Barrow, speaking to relatives afterward, claimed that when the officers approached he told Henry Methvin, "Let's take 'em"—his usual phrase for a kidnapping joyride—but that Methvin misunderstood and opened fire instead, while Bonnie dozed in their auto's backseat. Later, in custody, Methvin admitted firing the first shot, followed by Clyde, adding that Bonnie woke and approached the patrolmen attempting to "help" them but did no shooting. Barrow confused matters further, penning a letter to authorities that named Hamilton as the killer.[59]

By then, truth hardly mattered.

Five days after the Easter murders, the gang killed again, near Commerce, Oklahoma. Encountering two lawmen on the highway, Clyde and Methvin gunned down Constable William Calvin Campbell, then disarmed Chief of Police Percy Boyd and drove him into Kansas, where they released him unharmed. Boyd could not identify Methvin, so murder warrants named Clyde, Bonnie, and a "John Doe." Police captured Hamilton on April 25, after his expulsion from the gang with Mary O'Dare. Five days later, Eastham fugitive Joe Palmer reconnected with the team, helping steal $2,800 from a bank in Kansas.[60]

From Washington, on April 3, Director Hoover wrote once more to Melvin Purvis in Chicago, his tone still sweetness and light.

Dear Melvin:

I received the Tru-Vue and films, bombs, magic tricks and your sassy note. What did the Tru-Vue and films cost? I asked you to get them for me and I intend to pay for them. The films were both educational and uplifting but I thought they would include a series on "A Night in a Moorish Harem" or was it a "Turkish Harem." Nevertheless it was some night and I am still looking forward to you producing a set. Of course, my interest is solely as a censor or as chairman of the Moral Uplift Squad.

The bombs are the best yet. I have already caused Miss Gandy to jump two feet and that is something considering the fact that she is now in the heavyweight class. That damned magic trick had me almost "nuts" trying to figure out how it was done. I probably will take it apart to find out.

The cartoon is swell. Can you get me the original from the magazine? I have started to collect some cartoons particularly pertinent to our work and I would like to add this for it tells a real story.

Well, son, keep a stiff upper lip and get Dillinger for me and the world is yours.

Sincerely and affectionately,
Jayee[61]

Purvis couldn't get Dillinger, but G-men Bill "Red" Gross and Edward Notesteen traced Eddie Green to Saint Paul on the same day Hoover penned his note to Chicago. Armed with Tommy guns they descended upon the apartment Green shared with wife Bessie, staking it out from the home of talkative neighbor Leona Goodman. Notesteen's report to headquarters stated that he telephoned Inspector William Rorer, Sr., and asked Rorer what to do if Green approached, whereupon Rorer replied, "If [Mrs. Goodman] says that's the man, kill him."[62]

Green was unarmed when he came home, but the agents followed orders, blasting him from ambush, later claiming Green "assumed a threatening attitude ... accompanied by menacing gestures." They failed to kill him outright, though, as Green survived for eight days at Aucker Hospital, often raving incoherently, recovering enough at times to spill information the Bureau did not yet possess. He revealed the Barker-Karpis gang's existence and supplied the address of a Dillinger safe house, though Dillinger was gone when agents arrived. Bessie Green, charged with harboring her husband, confirmed Barker-Karpis guilt in the Bremer kidnapping, naming various gang members and their girlfriends. The FBI, previously ignorant of the gang's existence, swiftly obtained indictments of all concerned under the Lindbergh Law.[63]

While Green gasped out his final revelations, agents focused on Adam Richetti as their third Union Station suspect. Rumors linked Richetti to Charles Floyd, and G-men tapped the phones of relatives ranging from Texas and Oklahoma to Ohio, but they eavesdropped in vain. A virtual family outcast, Richetti wasted no time chatting with his kin over long-distance lines.[64]

Eddie Green's summary execution prompted another Mooresville visit by Dillinger and Billie Frechette on April 4. Two days later, Dillinger and half-brother Hubert touched base with Harry Pierpont's kin in Ohio, still floating nebulous plans for Harry's escape. On the 6th, John and Hubert Dillinger wrecked a car in Noblesville, Indiana. The next day, John and Billie paid cash for a new auto in Indianapolis, listing Hubert's address as their own. Lawmen raided that house and Mary Kinder's, but Dillinger and Billie were already back in Mooresville. Despite surveillance on the family's farm, Dillinger slipped past watchers and returned to Chicago. There, on April 9, Melvin Purvis and other agents captured Frechette on North State Street. Dillinger, observing from a car nearby, slipped through the dragnet unnoticed. Four days later, Dillinger and Homer Van Meter stole two pistols and four bulletproof vests from Warsaw, Indiana's police station. On the 14th, the duo asked for lodgings at the Evening Star Tourist Camp in Cedar Rapids, Iowa. Owner Frank Cargin explained that the camp wasn't open for business, but on the 17th he found one cabin broken into, apparently occupied for at least two nights.[65]

On Tuesday, the 17th, Dillinger and Red Hamilton visited Hamilton's sister in Sault Ste. Marie, Michigan. Wednesday saw Dr. Clayton May and nurse Augusta Salt arraigned for harboring Dillinger in March, held in lieu of $50,000 bond each. The 19th found Dillinger and Van Meter huddled with Tommy Carroll, Lester and Helen Gillis, Marie Conforti and Jean Delaney, plus small-time gangster Albert "Pat" Reilly from Chicago, at the Crystal Ballroom in Fox River Grove, Illinois. Owner Louis Cernocky had many underworld contacts, frequently hosting fugitives in his private dining room. Over dinner, someone in the party recommended cooling off at the Little Bohemia lodge in Northern Wisconsin, usually short of guests in spring. By dessert, the gang had agreed to depart next morning for the 338-mile road trip.[66]

The Badger State was a popular vacation spot for gangsters from the dawn of Prohibition until midway through the Great Depression, many of them hailing from Chicago. Al Capone had a fortified home on a lake near Hayward, where hydroplanes delivered Canadian whisky. His subordinates patronized brothels and speakeasies in Hurley, while Roger Touhy shot fish with a Tommy gun at Minocqua before his kidnapping arrests. Nan LaPorte ran her brother's bootleg booze downstate from Manitowish, and there met Emil Wanatka. Married, Emil and Nan ran Chicago's Little Bohemia bar, "a favorite of underworld figures," and took the name with them in 1929, when they returned to Nan's hometown and opened a tourist resort on Star Lake.[67]

Van Meter, Reilly, and Marie Conforti reached the lodge at 1:00 p.m. on April 20th, followed by the rest around 5:30. Most took rooms on the building's second floor, while Gillis, Carroll and their wives occupied an adjacent cabin. Emil Wanatka allegedly failed to recognize any of them, but when a porter complained about their gun-laden luggage, Emil snapped,

"Shut up and mind your own business!" Some sources claim that Gillis brought Wanatka a letter from Louis Cernocky, urging Emil to "take good care of my friends." Others say Wanatka recognized the fugitives immediately, but welcomed their money, let his son play catch with them, and joined them for a bout of target shooting.[68]

On April 21 Pat Reilly drove to Saint Paul with Pat Cherrington, sent to collect $4,000 that Harry Sawyer owed to Van Meter. Sawyer allegedly directed Reilly to cohort Harry Gannon, but he was roaring drunk and Reilly settled for $1,000 owed to Homer by a local bootlegger, Phil Clarrity. Meanwhile, Nan Wanatka grew suspicious of her guests and contacted her sister Helen, operator of another local resort with husband Phil Voss. Lloyd LaPorte, Emil's brother-in-law, shared Nan's suspicion, while Gillis, in turn, began to have doubts about Nan Wanatka, voicing his hunch with the gang.[69]

The stage was set for betrayal, but stories of how that occurred remain garbled and disputed after nearly 90 years. One version claims that Emil Wanatka belatedly recognized Dillinger from newspaper photos and told Nan, then confronted Dillinger, who told him not to be afraid. Another says Emil alerted Harry Voss and drove with him to Rhinelander, informing Oneida County's sheriff, who in turn phoned Chicago's FBI office. Yet another states that Voss alone summoned G-men, drawing a map of Little Bohemia with some significant omissions. A fourth scenario claims Nan Wanatka visited her brother, George LaPorte, and spilled the beans, unaware that she'd been followed by Lester Gillis. That story blames LaPorte for summoning the FBI.[70]

In any case, Melvin Purvis learned of the gang's whereabouts on April 22 and prepared to stage a raid, forgetting Hoover's lie that the Bureau "lacked authority" to make arrests or carry guns. Purvis chartered two planes from Chicago to the Rhinelander-Oneida County Airport, taking 11 G-men with him, while nine others made the trip by car. Simultaneously, Hoover ordered Assistant Director Hugh Clegg to lead an airborne team from Saint Paul, assuming overall command of the assault. The aircrafts landed by 6:00 p.m. and G-men studied the crude map of Little Bohemia, unaware that it omitted Emil Wanatka's two watchdogs, a ditch, and a barbed wire fence on site.[71]

As night fell, Hoover's city boys drove 48 miles northward from Rhinelander to Little Bohemia, some agents clinging to their auto's running boards. Upon arrival, they began to filter through the woods, heavily armed—and everything went suddenly, disastrously wrong. Some agents ran into the fence and were delayed, others fell into the ditch, while Emil's watchdogs raised a clamor from the lodge's yard, forewarning occupants. Two lodge employees stepped out to investigate the hubbub, as three

6. Trials and Errors

Melvin Purvis (in white) with unidentified G-men outside Little Bohemia Lodge the morning after their disastrous raid, April 23, 1934 (National Archives).

customers departed from the lounge and piled into a single car. Those men included John Hoffman, a gas salesman from nearby Mercer, and two workers from a local Civilian Conservation Corps camp, elderly cook John Morris and young laborer Eugene Boisenau.[72]

Purvis and Clegg, forewarned of five gangsters residing at the lodge, mistook those innocent civilians for bandits in flight. One or both agents in charge ordered their men to stop the vehicle by shooting out its tires. In the resultant fusillade, riddling the car with gunfire, Boisenau died instantly, while Hoffman and Morris each suffered multiple wounds. That barrage alerted Dillinger's gang, who returned fire from the lodge's upstairs windows and the nearby cabin, then fled into the night, leaving their women behind. Reilly and Cherrington, just then returning to the lodge, reversed direction and took off at top speed, running on one rim when their car suffered a blowout. G-men outside, pouring bullets and buckshot into the lodge, failed to notice their quarries escaping.[73]

So far, the raid was a disaster, although agents seized three "molls" and a small arsenal, together with Jean Compton's puppy, named Rex. No fugitives remained, nor any sign that even one of them had suffered injury.[74]

And worse still lay in store.

Purvis and Clegg dispersed their men to prowl the local roads in borrowed cars, hoping to apprehend their prey. By then, Dillinger, Hamilton, and Van Meter had reached the home of elderly E.J. Mitchell and his wife, one mile from Little Bohemia. Unable to start Mitchell's pickup truck, they stole a car from next-door neighbors and sped off toward Saint Paul with three hostages, all freed unharmed on arrival.[75]

About that same time, Tommy Carroll emerged from the woods and hiked to Manitowish Waters, stealing a car outside the Northern Lights Resort. His goal was Mercer, but he lost his way and wound up on a dead-end logging road.[76]

Gillis, meanwhile, reached the home of another elderly couple, Mr. and Mrs. G.W. Lang. Brandishing one of Hyman Lebman's "baby machine guns," he made the couple drive him toward Highway 51, not knowing that G-men had gathered there, at Henry Voss's lodge. The Lang car died en route, outside the home of telephone exchange operator Alvin Koerner. Koerner, who'd been handling urgent phone calls since the raid began, saw Gillis and his hostages approaching, summoning G-men from Voss's place. Moments later, George La Porte arrived at Koerner's home with Emil Wanatka and two bartenders from Little Bohemia. Selecting La Porte and Wanatka as hostages, Gillis prodded them into Emil's car, but it refused to start, further enraging Baby Face.[77]

Just then, another vehicle arrived, driven by Agent Jay Newman, a 27-year-old Mormon lay preacher. Beside him sat Agent Willis Carter Baum, 29, and local policeman Carl Christensen, in uniform less than one month. Gillis ordered all three from their car at gunpoint, then opened fire, killing Baum and Christensen, wounding Newman eight times. In the confusion, Koerner retreated to his home and locked himself inside, while Wanatka ran back toward Little Bohemia. Gillis escaped in La Porte's car, under fire from Newman, and escaped. Back at Little Bohemia, Wanatka broke the news to Purvis and Clegg, gasping, "All your men are dead at Koerner's."[78]

The news could scarcely have been worse: three dead, including two lawmen and an innocent bystander; two more lawmen and two innocents wounded; six fugitives at large; three women tear-gassed and arrested on a minor charge of "harboring" their menfolk. Journalists flayed the Bureau in print, and even comic Will Rogers piled on, telling delighted audiences, "Well they had Dillinger surrounded and were all ready to shoot him when he came out, but another bunch of folks came out ahead, so they shot them instead. Dillinger is going to get in accidentally with some innocent bystanders sometime, then he will get shot."[79]

And the bloodshed was not finished yet.

On Monday, April 23, en route to Saint Paul, Dillinger, Hamilton, and

Van Meter crashed through a police roadblock near Hastings, Minnesota. Officers fired on their car, one bullet drilling Red Hamilton's back. The trio reached Chicago, seeking underworld help, but Frank Nitto refused. Next, they tried Dr. Joseph Moran. He likewise declined, but passed them on to Volney Davis and Edna Murray, at their home in Aurora, Illinois. Hampton survived until the 27th, then was buried at a gravel pit near Oswego, allegedly with Dock Barker assisting his sendoff. Months passed before G-men learned of the clandestine funeral. Alternate rumors, spread by Hamilton's friends and a cousin, claimed that he survived and made it home to Canada. That bubble burst at last in August 1935, when police found his unmarked grave and matched his teeth to prison dental records.[80]

Near month's end, Louis Piquett contacted longtime friend Dr. Wilhelm Loeser. Loeser had practiced medicine in Chicago from 1904 to 1931, when feds convicted him of violating the Harrison Narcotics Tax Act. A judge sentenced him to three years at Leavenworth but Loeser won early parole with Piquett's aid in December 1932. In April 1934, Loeser agreed to alter Dillinger's face and remove his fingerprints with a caustic soda solution. The price: $5,000 ($97,000 today), with Loeser, Piquett and Art O'Leary splitting $4,400, while anesthetist Dr. Harold Cassidy pocketed $600. After the surgery, scheduled for late May, Dillinger would convalesce at the home of another Piquett crony, 67-year-old James "Cabaret" Probasco.[81]

Unaware of those maneuvers, Director Hoover tried to salvage his Bureau's damaged reputation. While he had placed Hugh Clegg in charge of the Wisconsin raid, Melvin Purvis was better known to journalists and bore most of the heat, offering his resignation, which Hoover declined to accept. Citizens clamored for Purvis's dismissal, but an April 25 memo from headquarters seemed to support him. It read, in part: "Mr. Purvis was greatly disturbed and wanted to assure me that he would be in perfect accord with any action I might desire to take affecting him personally. I explained to him that while we are receiving criticism from many sources we are still assured of 100 percent cooperation from the Attorney General.... I impressed upon Mr. Purvis that I wanted less raiding and more confidential informants."[82]

Attorney General Cummings told journalists, "If we had had an armored car up there in Wisconsin, our men could have driven right up to the house where Dillinger was. The terrible tragedy would not have happened." President Roosevelt also weighed in, on one of his radio "fireside chats," urging Congress to pass the Attorney General's sweeping Twelve Point Crime Program.[83]

April closed with an echo of the Kelly-Urschel case. On the 30th, Louise Magness pled guilty to harboring the Kellys and received a 366-day sentence at the Federal Industrial Institution for Women in Alderson, West Virginia.[84]

As a direct result of Little Bohemia, the FBI recruited more "gunfighters" into its ranks for the eradication of bandits. Three, lured into Bureau service from the Oklahoma City Police Department, were Jacob "Jelly" Bryce, Charles "Jerry" Campbell, and Clarence Hurt. Hurt had first applied in 1925, rejected for lacking a college education, but such niceties no longer troubled headquarters. Charles Winstead—a G-man since 1926, who had failed in several attempts to bag Bonnie and Clyde—left Dallas in May to join Oklahoma's finest in pursuit of the Dillinger gang.[85]

Their quarry, meanwhile, remained elusive.

On May 2, Chicago police found Dillinger's bloodstained Wisconsin getaway car. That same afternoon, Billie Frechette pled not guilty to harboring Dillinger, held in lieu of $60,000 bond. On Thursday, May 3, Dillinger, Carroll, and Van Meter stole $17,000 from a bank in Fostoria, Ohio, leaving Police Chief Frank Culp wounded by a burst from Homer's Tommy gun. Two days later, Bessie Green, Eddie's widow, received a 15-month sentence for harboring Dillinger. On May 10, Dillinger visited Fred Hancock's Indianapolis gas station, where Hancock worked with Hubert Dillinger. The fugitive gave Hancock $1,200 in four envelopes: $500 for Dillinger's father, $500 for Hancock's mother Audrey, plus $100 each for Fred and Hubert. On Tuesday, May 15, Billie Frechette, Dr. Clayton May, and August Salt faced trial in Saint Paul before Judge Gunnar Nordbye, charged with harboring Dillinger. Jurors convicted Frechette and May one week later, while acquitting Salt.[86]

Awaiting plastic surgery, Dillinger and Van Meter divided their time between a woodland cabin near East Chicago and a red panel truck that kept them mobile, avoiding the "heat." On May 24, East Chicago patrolmen Francis Mulvihill and Martin O'Brien stopped the truck and Van Meter blazed away with his Thompson, killing both officers. One day later, on Wednesday the 25th, Marie Conforti, Jean Crompton, and Helen Gillis pled guilty to harboring Homer Van Meter, Tommy Carroll, and Baby Face Nelson, each receiving 366-day sentences followed by 18 months' probation. All received early release and soon broke probation to rejoin their men in hiding.[87]

Motivated largely by Dillinger's headlines and the FBI's Wisconsin debacle, on May 5 the House of Representatives passed multiple acts from the Roosevelt administration's anti-gangster agenda, and the Senate followed suit on May 18. None of those laws had any immediate effect on syndicated crime, deeply entrenched nationwide since Prohibition's advent, but they applied directly to the stock in trade of roving outlaw gangs.

One penalized the killing, obstruction, or intimidation of any federal law enforcement officer during performance of his duty, imposing a $5,000 fine, three years in prison, or both. Use of a deadly weapon doubled the fine and increased prison time to 10 years. Crossing state lines to avoid prosecution or giving testimony carried a $5,000 fine and/or an unspecified term of imprisonment. Federal prison employees who aided inmates' escape faced a maximum 10-year sentence. Robbery of any Federal Reserve bank carried fines of $1,000 to $10,000 per incident, with prison terms ranging from five to 25 years. Murder resulting from such holdups might result in execution at a federal court's discretion. An amendment to the Lindbergh Law added potential execution in cases where kidnap victims were "harmed," with said injury left undefined, ranging from minor bruises to murder. More laws still remained to be passed, but the first surge greased the skids of Hoover's "crime war," ensuring that federal fugitives found no succor in crossing state boundaries.[88]

One day after those statutes passed Congress and moved on to FDR's desk, on May 19, federal grand jurors in Wisconsin indicted Dillinger, Tommy Carroll, and Homer Van Meter for "harboring" each other on the lam. The charge was trivial, but at that moment, Hoover and the FBI were not particular. Soon afterward, Jean Crompton was released from prison and reunited with Carroll, setting off for Tommy's home state of Idaho. On Sunday, the 27th, Dillinger moved into James Probasco's Chicago home, awaiting surgery to change his face and fingerprints. Drs. Loeser and Cassidy arrived the next day, escorted by Art O'Leary, to begin the slow, often painful procedures, lasting until May 31. The surgery included removal of several moles from Dillinger's forehead, plus minor alterations to his nose, chin, and cheeks. Although Loeser was sometimes called "a magician with a knife," his work allegedly left Dillinger dissatisfied and barely changed.[89]

Modern Bureau historians claim that "the FBI and local law enforcement authorities in Louisiana and Texas concentrated on apprehending Bonnie and Clyde, whom they strongly believed to be in the area." In fact, G-men never came close to the killer couple, leaving the search to Frank Hamer, Maney Gault, and their contacts at county sheriffs' departments. Focus on the Lone Star and Bayou States was elementary, since Clyde and Bonnie hailed from Texas and returned there frequently, while sidekick Henry Methvin kept in close touch with his father Ivan in Bienville Parish.[90]

On Monday, May 21, the gang partied with Ivan and other Methvin relatives at Black Lake, between Creston and Campti in Natchitoches Parish. That same day, in Texas, Eastham escapee and former gang associate Hilton Bybee was indicted, with cohort Clarence Lewis, for their Jacksboro armory holdup in March. While they awaited trial and ultimate conviction, Hamer and Gault approached Ivan Methvin—or he approached

Slayers of Clyde Barrow and Bonnie Parker, May 23, 1934. Standing (left to right): Prentiss Oakley, Ted Hinton, Bob Alcorn, "Manney" Gault. Kneeling (left to right): Frank Hamer, Henderson Jordan (author's collection).

them, accounts differ—and struck a bargain to finish Bonnie and Clyde. Ivan sought to spare Henry from execution on Texas murder charges, and the lawmen agreed on condition that Ivan put their other quarries "on the spot."[91]

Somehow, Ivan warned Henry not to join Bonnie and Clyde when they returned to Louisiana the next time, on May 23. Staked out as bait along Louisiana State Road 154, feigning car trouble, Ivan Methvin waited for the couple to appear. Concealed by roadside trees, Hamer and Gault lay in wait with posse members Bob Alcorn, Ted Hinton, Henderson Jordan, and Prentiss Oakley. Each lawman came prepared for bloodshed, with an automatic rifle, a shotgun, and at least one pistol each. Controversy persists as to whether Ivan Methvin stood beside his pickup truck or was shackled to a nearby tree, preventing a last-minute change of heart.[92]

At 9:15 a.m. their targets appeared, driving north from Sailes in

6. *Trials and Errors* 111

Bonnie and Clyde's vehicle after the ambush, May 23, 1934 (Library of Congress).

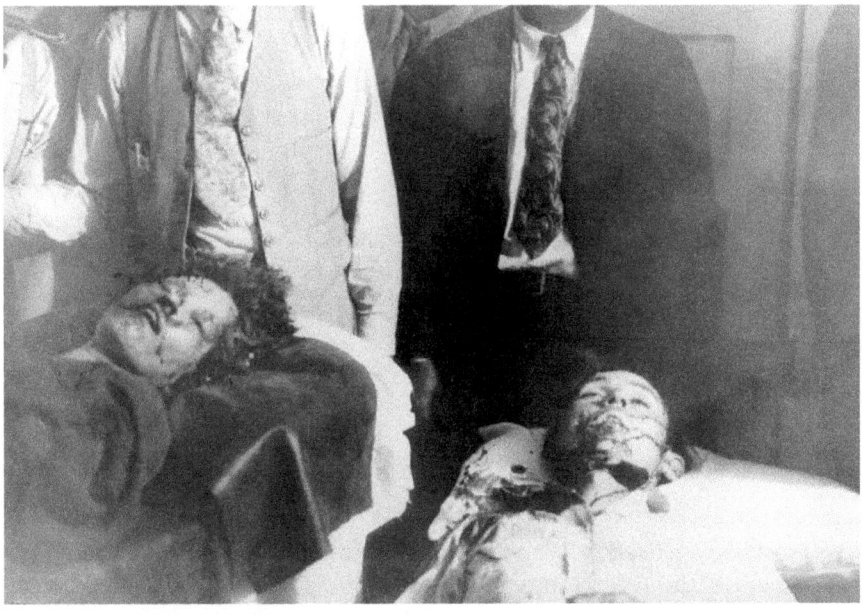

Bonnie Parker and Clyde Barrow in the morgue, May 23, 1934 (National Archives).

Arsenal recovered from the Barrow-Parker car, May 23, 1934 (National Archives).

a stolen Ford V-8 sedan. As Barrow saw Methvin and slowed, the posse opened fire without warning, taking no chances, riddling the car with an estimated 130 shots, pouring lead into the Ford even after it coasted onto the highway's shoulder and stalled. Bienville Parish Coroner Dr. J.L. Wade's autopsy report listed 17 separate entrance wounds on Barrow's body and 26 on Parker's, including multiple head shots for each and one round that severed Clyde's spinal cord. A mob scene ensued at the ambush site, men trying to sever Clyde's ear and his trigger finger, a woman snipping locks of Bonnie's bloodied hair and dress that later sold as souvenirs, others collecting spent shells and glass fragments, carving bullets out of trees along the road. Within hours, Gibsland's population swelled from 2,000 residents to 12,000 gawkers, producing a "circus-like atmosphere." From his Dallas jail cell, W.D. Jones told reporters, "I must admit that I'm relieved."[93]

Clyde and Bonnie wished to be buried together, but Parker's family forbade it. More than 20,000 persons thronged her Dallas funeral on May 26, while cards and funeral wreaths arrived from points nationwide. Dallas city newsboys reportedly purchased the largest wreath, thanking the couple who had helped them sell 500,000 papers within D-Town. A local physician, Dr. Allen Campbell, claimed that wreaths also arrived with cards from John Dillinger and Pretty Boy Floyd, but that remains unverified. Sheriff Schmidt promised the posse members rewards totaling $26,000, split six ways, but most organizations reneged on their pledges, leaving each lawman a paltry $200.23 each.[94]

Barrow's family buried him in a private ceremony beside brother Buck, one day before Bonnie's sendoff. Their stone at Western Heights Cemetery, in Dallas, reads, "Gone but not forgotten."[95]

Lansing fugitive Jim Clark, recovered from his bullet wounds, closed out the month in dramatic style. On May 31, with Frank Delmar, he returned to Kingfisher, Oklahoma, raiding the same bank Clark had previously robbed in August 1933 with Harvey Bailey, Bob Brady, and Wilbur Underhill.[96]

7

Shoot on Sight

The Tri-State Gang made headlines on June 2, 1934, looting guns and ammo from a National Guard armory in Hyattsville, Maryland. Two days later, Baltimore police, unaided by G-men, traced them to a house near the city's fairgrounds, touching off a shootout that left Robert Mais critically wounded by Tommy-gun fire. Walter Legenza and Marie McKeever then surrendered. Mais would survive to face trial for his life with Legenza in Richmond, Virginia.[1]

On June 2, Louis Piquett contacted Dr. Loeser in Chicago, reporting that John Dillinger desired more alterations to his face and fingerprints. Homer Van Meter requested the same treatment. They struck a bargain for fingerprint removal with *aqua regia*—a mixture of hydrochloric and nitric acid—of $100 per finger, totaling $2,000. The work proceeded on June 3, at James Probasco's home, with Dr. Loeser and Dr. Harold Cassidy operating on the fugitives simultaneously. Also present for at least some portion of the work were Piquett, Art O'Leary, Probasco, and his girlfriend, Peggy Doyle. Further work continued on June 5, in the presence of a visitor Loeser later identified as Lester Gillis. Van Meter, suffering and furious, allegedly tried to kill Loeser that night, but was restrained by Dillinger and others while he raged. The fugitives remained at Probasco's home until the last week of June, with occasional visitors. One, a young woman tentatively identified as Chicago prostitute Edythe "Polly" Hamilton, made Van Meter uneasy, Homer warning Dillinger in Loeser's presence against forging new relationships with strange females. Dillinger ignored Homer's advice, which later proved to be prophetic.[2]

On June 4, Chicago police busted Michigan City escapee Joseph Fox, returning him to finish off his prison term in Indiana. That same day, Eddie Bentz and others stole $8,500 from a bank in Danville, Vermont. On Tuesday the 5th, lawmen captured three Dillinger gang "gun molls"—Opal Long, her sister Pat Cherrington, and Jean Burke—at Chicago's Chateau Hotel. Burke kept company with a gang associate, Arthur "Fish" Johnson, previously captured on December 17.[3]

Those events meant little to Dillinger, but Tommy Carroll was a valued member of the gang. On June 6, he checked into the Evening Star Tourist Camp, five miles south of Waterloo, Indiana, with recently paroled girlfriend Jean Delaney, sister of Alvin Karpis's "moll," Dolores Delaney. The next morning, they drove into Waterloo, seeking an optometrist who could fit Jean with glasses. After lunch, Delaney bought a dress, then the couple stopped for gasoline before proceeding to a nearby bar. Unknown to them, the gas station attendant, after noting that their care bore Missouri license plates, saw other plates from sundry states piled up on the backseat. He called police, speaking to ex–Chief P.E. Walker and Detective Emil Steffen, who cruised the district aimlessly without result. Returning to the police department's garage, they were surprised to find the suspect Hudson sedan parked at a beer parlor across the street. A man and woman soon emerged, approaching the Hudson.[4]

Closing in, Walker told Carroll, "You're under arrest." Carroll replied, "The hell I am," drawing a gun, but Walker punched him in the face, causing him to drop his pistol. It slid under the Hudson and Carroll bolted for a nearby alley, Walker and Steffen in pursuit. Taking no chances, the officers shot Carroll four times. Three bullets pierced his chest, one lodging in his lumbar spine. En route to St. Francis Hospital by ambulance, Carroll admitted his identity but would say no more. Dying, he refused to answer questions from police or Black Hawk County prosecutors John Gwynn and Burt Towne. When a reporter butted in with queries of his own, Carroll said, "I'm hit, Buddy. That's all. I'm hit." He died at 6:00 p.m. and was buried at Saint Paul's Oakland Cemetery. On June 9, pregnant Jean Delaney received a 366-day sentence for parole violation, subsequently miscarrying her child.[5]

One of the Bureau's new informers, hired on Hoover's orders, was Arthur Maginnis (or "McGinniss," in some stories) described by Bryan Burrough as a "onetime insurance company snitch," paid by G-man Earl Connelly to hang around Fred Hancock's Indianapolis gas station, waiting to report if John Dillinger stopped by to visit half-brother Hubert. The Bureau didn't get its money's worth from Maginnis, who fed them false tips, once sending Connelly on a wild goose chase to Louisville, Kentucky. Somehow, John Dillinger learned of the spy's treachery and drove from Chicago with Homer Van Meter to murder Maginnis on June 9. The fugitives found their man, then lost him on a crowded street and gave up, returning to the Windy City in frustration.[6]

Three days before that bungled rub-out, on June 6, fugitive Irvin Chapman robbed a bank in Beaumont, Texas. Federal grand jurors delayed nearly three years before indicting him.[7]

In June 1934, Congress passed additional legislation aimed at roving felons. On the 6th, a new statute authorized the Attorney General to offer cash rewards up to $25,000 "to facilitate the apprehension of certain persons charged with crime"—specifically, federal offenses occurring in any state or in Washington, D.C. Twelve days later, another law formally authorized G-men to carry guns, which in fact they had done regularly for the past 26 years. Also on June 18, Congress passed a National Firearms Act, restricting (but not banning) possession of specific "gangster weapons." Included on the list were automatic weapons capable of firing multiple shots "by a single function of the trigger"; shotguns with barrels less than 18 inches long, or measuring less than 26 inches overall; rifles with barrels under 16 inches long or 26 inches in total length; and sound suppressors (commonly called "silencers"), designed to muffle gunfire. Citizens wishing to own such "gangster" weapons were required to register them with the U.S. Treasury Department and pay a $200 "transfer tax" ($3,789 today) each time an item changed hands. FDR signed the new legislation on June 26.[8]

While Washington busied itself with those laws, the "crime war" continued. On June 13 Texas jurors convicted Raymond Hamilton of Major Crowson's murder during the Eastham prison break. One day later, Eastham fugitive Joe Palmer surfaced in Davenport, Iowa, kidnapping Traffic Patrolman Elmer Schleuter and Al Schultze, secretary of the city's baseball club, commandeering their car. En route to Saint Joseph, Missouri, Palmer also snatched Dr. W.H. Fitch, swapped autos, and released his hostages unharmed upon arrival at his destination. Saint Joseph police quickly nabbed him and shipped him back to Texas, where Palmer claimed he would get Hamilton "out of trouble." Instead, he was condemned for Crowson' murder on June 29, joining Raymond at Huntsville Prison's death house.[9]

On June 20, Lansing fugitive Jim Clark robbed a bank in Crescent, Oklahoma, soon rebounding to take $13,000 from the same bank he'd looted with partners Bailey, Brady, and Underhill in July 1933. With Goldie Johnson, Clark was also suspected of hitting a bank in Oxford, Kansas, but neither were charged in that case.[10]

On June 21, Homer Van Meter welcomed paroled girlfriend Marie Conforti home from prison, driving to Calumet City, Illinois, where they rented a room from William and Ella Finerty under pseudonyms. One day later, John Dillinger celebrated his 31st birthday with Polly Hamilton at Chicago's French Casino nightclub. That same day, journalists began calling Dillinger "Public Enemy No. 1," although Hoover's FBI assigned no numerical ranking to its targets. On the 23rd, Dillinger and Hamilton returned to the French Casino, this time celebrating Polly's birthday. June 26 found Dillinger at Wrigley Field, watching the Chicago Cubs defeat

Brooklyn's Dodgers. The 27th sounded sour notes for gang alumni, as Harry Copeland received a 25-year sentence for the Greencastle bank heist from October 1933. The same day, officers arrested Pat Reilly in Saint Paul and he began telling tales of his time with the gang, earning two consecutive sentences totaling 36 months.[11]

In California, meanwhile, jurors convicted Lansing fugitive Ed Davis on sundry charges of burglary, robbery, and kidnapping on June 22. As a habitual criminal, he received a life term at Folsom Prison, but authorities hedged their bets against the possibility of future parole, announcing that they would ship Davis back to Lansing if his release seemed imminent.[12]

Want $50,000? Just Bring Them In

John Dillinger $10,000 — "Baby Face" Nelson $10,000 — Alvin Karper $5,000

Arthur Barker $5,000 — Homer Van Meter $5,000 — "Pretty Boy" Floyd $5,000

Uncle Sam is letting everybody in on the ground floor of an opportunity to make a lot of money, more or less easily. All that is necessary to collect from $1,000 to $50,000 under Uncle Sam's newest plan for relieving unemployment and poverty, is to nab or cause the capture of one of the sextet pictured above. Price tags placed on these outlaws under new law which permits Department of Justice to offer federal rewards are indicated. (Central Press)

The Justice Department enlisted public aid with reward offers for notorious outlaws beginning in June 1933 (author's collection).

On June 23, Attorney General Cummings posted a $5,000 reward for the capture of Lester Gillis, half the price riding on Dillinger's head. Gillis didn't mind, settling briefly with recently-paroled wife Helen near Lake Geneva, Wisconsin. While they idled in the woods, word arrived of Dillinger's next intended bank job, scheduled for June 30.[13]

At noon on that Saturday, four men struck a bank in South Bend, Indiana. Gillis, Van Meter, and an unidentified heavyset man joined Dillinger for the gang's last hurrah, quickly transformed into a chaotic fiasco, leaving one dead and four wounded. Various accounts name the fourth man as John Chase, Fatso Negri, or Gillis childhood friend Jack Perkins (later acquitted), while Negri claimed the add-on was Pretty Boy Floyd.[14]

Whoever tagged along, the heist quickly turned into a wild debacle. Dillinger had planned the raid to be his last, and so it proved to be, although not for the reason intended. Driving a brown Hudson sedan, the bandits struck on time but soon found the action spinning out of control. Initially, Patrolman Howard Wagner, directing traffic nearby, ran toward the bank but died, shot by lookout Van Meter before he could draw his pistol. Emerging from the bank into a hectic street scene—cops on their lunch break rushing from a nearby diner, while motorists, shoppers, and early movie-goers thronged the street—the bandits used bank director Jacob Solomon, head cashier Delos Cohen, fellow cashier Perry Stahley, and customer Bruce Bouchard as human shields. It hardly mattered, though, as nervous cops began firing regardless, wounding all four captives. Jeweler Harry Berg joined the melee with a pistol from his shop, missing twice but striking Gillis with one bullet—useless, since Baby Face wore a steel vest underneath his coat. Seconds later, high school sophomore Joseph Pawlowski leaped onto Gillis's back, trying to choke him, but the outlaw shook him loose and aimed machine-gun fire at the teen as he plunged through a shop's plate glass window, shot through one hand. A police round grazed Bouchard's lip, others wounded Solomon, Cohen, and Stahley, while fire from the bandits struck passing motorist Samuel Toth. Someone's shot grazed Van Meter's head, while others suffered minor injuries from ricochets and shattered chips of pavement. The gang escaped through flying lead, leaving a shattered town behind.[15]

And all for what? Dillinger had hoped to bag $100,000—$1.9 million today—but the final take was only $29,800, just $7,450 each, barely worth the risk and effort.[16]

Back in Chicago, the day after South Bend, a man calling himself "Jimmy Lawrence," allegedly employed at Chicago's Board of Trade, made a date with Polly Hamilton, working from a brothel run by Romanian immigrant Anna Sage (née Cumpănaş). Lawrence had been "dating" Hamilton for two weeks, during which time Sage decided he was Dillinger (while Hamilton allegedly remained oblivious). Facing deportation as an undesirable alien, Sage hatched a plan she hoped would keep her in America.[17]

Prisoner Pat Reilly spent that same Sunday, July 1, spilling everything he knew about Dillinger's gang to Chicago G-men. Aside from details of its interrupted vacation at Little Bohemia, he confided that all addresses and phone numbers gleaned from gang molls were written in a number-substitution code, thereby explaining why the Bureau could not bag its prey.[18]

"Jimmy Lawrence" squired Hamilton to Chicago's Biograph theater on July 2, the same day a Chicago doctor treated Homer Van Meter's

7. Shoot on Sight

head wound in Art O'Leary's presence. Two days later, Lawrence moved into Anna Sage's house, rooming with Polly. On Friday the 6th, Wisconsin jurors convicted Pat Cherrington and Opal Long of harboring Dillinger, resulting in two-year prison terms imposed a day later. Still pining for Billie Frechette despite his new girlfriend, Dillinger met Art O'Leary on the 7th to discuss her appeal. Polly Hamilton waited nearby, but O'Leary declined the offer of an introduction.[19]

July sweltered in Chicago. On the 10th, Dillinger and Van Meter attended the World's Fair with Polly Hamilton and Marie Conforti. The next day, Dillinger met O'Leary at a local park, again discussing Billie's appeal. A carload of policemen passed, staring at the two men, but did not stop. On the 12th, after another baseball game, Dillinger, Polly, and Van Meter huddled once again with Art O'Leary, discussing legal matters.[20]

In the midst of those machinations, on Tuesday the 10th, drive-by machine-gunners blasted Kansas City Mafia boss John Lazia. Physicians could not save him, but they noted his last words: "Why to me, the friend of everybody?" G-men didn't know it yet, but Lazia's assassination would provide a solution of sorts to the Union Station massacre case seven weeks later.[21]

On July 15 members of the Dillinger gang gathered on Wolf Road, near Chicago Municipal Airport (now O'Hare International). All needed cash and hoped to plan another heist, but they were interrupted by Illinois State Police officers Gilbert Cross and Fred McAllister. Lester Gillis opened fire with one of Hyman Lebman's "baby machine guns," wounding both lawmen, and the fugitives scattered. Both policemen survived, Gillis named as their assailant in a later confession from John Paul Chase. The hoped-for "last big score" never occurred.[22]

As July wound down, Anna Sage broached her plan for bagging Dillinger and clearing her problems with Immigration to longtime acquaintance Martin Zarkovich, an East Chicago police sergeant and bagman for underworld payoffs. Seeing green—the $15,000 bounty outstanding by then on Dillinger's head—Zarkovich arranged a meeting between Sage and Melvin Purvis on July 19. Sage agreed to betray Dillinger, aka "Jimmy Lawrence," in exchange for FBI intervention to halt her deportation proceedings. Purvis traded an empty promise for Anna's vow to put Dillinger "on the spot." Almost as if he felt the noose around his neck, Dillinger phoned Louis Piquett on the 21st, for an inconclusive conversation on his possible surrender.[23]

On July 22, Sage spoke to Purvis again, reporting that Dillinger planned to escort her and Polly Hamilton to a movie theater that night. She couldn't say whether they would attend the North Side's Biograph or the West Side's Marbro but promised a follow-up call to let G-men arrive in advance. As a signal, Sage planned to wear an orange skirt, rather than the infamous "red dress" of popular legend. Purvis decided to stake out both theaters, without informing Chicago police. He did, however, ask a team of East Chicago officers, led by Martin Zarkovich, to join the hunt outside their legal jurisdiction. That decision, and the sequence of events to come, ensured no end of controversy spanning future decades.[24]

While Purvis watched the Biograph, Agent Samuel Cowley led a team outside the Marbro. Other G-men, identified as joining in the ambush, included Ralph Brown, Jelly Bryce, Charles Campbell, Herman Hollis, Clarence Hurt, William Ryan, Daniel Sullivan, Raymond Suran, Charles Winstead, and Grier Woltz.[25]

In the end, Dillinger, aka "Jimmy Lawrence," settled on the Biograph, screening *Manhattan Melodrama*, a gangster film starring Clark Gable, William Powell, and Myrna Loy. Contradictory accounts of what transpired that night leave ample room for still-unanswered questions. Dillinger and his two dates reportedly approached the Biograph sometime between 8:15 and 8:30 p.m., whereupon Purvis summoned Cowley's squad to leave the Marbro and join the impending action. Most versions state that Purvis planned to signal his men by lighting a cigar as Dillinger, Hamilton and Sage left the theater between 10:30 and 10:40 p.m. At least one account says Purvis approached the trio from behind, shouting, "Okay, Johnnie, drop your gun!" At that, Dillinger reportedly ran toward a nearby alley, reaching into his trouser pocket for a Colt .380-caliber pistol, and gunshots rang out.[26]

The rest is chaos, with no less than eight "official" accounts of who shot Dillinger and how many times he was hit. All agree that Agents Hollis, Hurt, and Winstead did the shooting, firing four, five, or six shots, of which two, three, or four struck their target. The FBI's website asserts that "Clarence Hurt shot twice, Charles Winstead three times, and Herman Hollis once…. Dillinger was struck four times, with two bullets grazing him and one causing a superficial wound to the right side. The fatal bullet entered through the back of his neck, severed the spinal cord, passed into his brain and exited just under the right eye, severing two sets of veins and arteries." Civilian witnesses contested the Bureau's story of a shouted warning and Dillinger's resistance, telling members of Dillinger's family that agents said nothing, opening fire from a distance of roughly arm's length. One account claims Dillinger died in Agent Hurt's arms, unable to speak.[27]

Matt Leach of Indiana's State Police advanced a *ninth* scenario of Dillinger's death, asserting that the outlaw was shot while unarmed, not by G-men, but by an East Chicago policeman, presumably Martin Zarkovich. Leach also claimed that someone stole $7,000 in cash from Dillinger's corpse. FBI headquarters denies those "myths" to this day, but they live on, growing into full-blown conspiracy theories four decades later (see Chapter 13).[28]

Most versions credit Winstead with the fatal head shot but reports of J. Edgar Hoover's response are confused. One claims the Director praised all three gunmen for their "fearlessness and courageous action," while a letter from Hoover to Winstead, dated July 23, reads: "I have been informed by Mr. Purvis and Mr. Cowley that it was you who shot and killed Dillinger.... We are all indeed proud of you. It is particularly gratifying that Dillinger was shot and killed by one of our own men."[29]

Hoover ignored the fact that his "courageous" agents also wounded two female bystanders, Etta Natalsky and Theresa Paulas. Before an ambulance arrived, transporting Dillinger to Alexian Brothers Hospital and a formal pronouncement of death, a mob scene on par with the deaths of Bonnie and Clyde prevailed outside the Biograph. According to the *New York Times*, "Souvenir hunters madly dipped newspapers in the blood that stained the pavement. Handkerchiefs were whipped out and used to mop up the blood." Later, an estimated 15,000 gawkers filed past Dillinger's slab at the Cook County Morgue, where attendants made at least four plaster death masks of the fugitive's face. Immediately after the slaying, Purvis convened a press conference, while Agent Cowley kept Hoover informed by phone from an adjoining room. Hoover repeatedly told Cowley to halt the press briefing, but Cowley refused.[30]

The spectacle surrounding Dillinger's demise continued after his removal from Chicago to Mooresville's E.F. Harvey Funeral Parlor on July 24. Another public viewing was permitted there, before a hearse transferred the corpse to the Maywood home of Dillinger's sister, Audrey Hancock. She, in turn, allowed more gawkers to observe the fugitive's remains before final interment on the 25th, at Crown Hill Cemetery in Indianapolis. Dillinger's father had the casket covered with three feet of reinforced concrete, to foil potential grave robbers, but vandalism still persisted over time, forcing replacement of Dillinger's chiseled-down headstone several times.[31]

The last days of July wreaked havoc on Dillinger gang survivors. Late on the 22nd, Homer Van Meter left Chicago with Marie Conforti, seeking shelter in Minnesota. Lester and Helen Gillis, with John Chase, fled westward. Stopped for speeding in rural Utah, Baby Face paid a $5 fine and moved on, local police oblivious to his identity and a carload of high-powered weapons. Chicago G-men arrested Dr. Loeser on the 24th, along with James Probasco. Three days later, Probasco "fell or jumped" from a 19th-story window of the Banker's Building, where Purvis maintained his headquarters. Cook County's coroner ruled the death a suicide, but major doubts remain. Probasco's swan dive mimicked Andrea Salcedo's "suicide" at New York City's FBI office in 1920, and more recently, in 1933, another Chicago mobster had complained of being dangled from the same high window by his ankles during "third-degree" interrogation. Agents swore unanimously that they'd left Probasco alone before his leap, surmising that he'd climbed onto a chair and out the unlocked window. The suicide verdict cleared G-men and robbed Probasco's sister of life insurance payments totaling $72,000 ($1.4 million today).[32]

While Dillinger's demise filled headlines, other outlaws vied for attention. In Texas, condemned inmates Raymond Hamilton, Joe Palmer, and Irwin "Blackie" Thompson used smuggled pistols to shoot their way out of the Huntsville death house and escape. While journalists dubbed them "embryonic Dillingers," police grilled Mary O'Dare about the breakout but learned nothing. Two days later, jurors acquitted Floyd Hamilton and Billie Mace—Bonnie Parker's sister—of participating in the Easter slayings of two highway patrolmen at Grapevine.[33]

On July 25, police found alleged Tri-State Gang member Salvatore Serpa murdered in Chicago. His execution may have been internal housekeeping, since New Jersey authorities sought Serpa for a triple murder in their jurisdiction. His victims: fellow gang member Edward "Cowboy" Wallace and two "molls," Ethel Greentree and Florence Miller.[34]

July's last human sacrifice was Chicago's Dr. Joseph Moran, best known for his association with the Barker-Karpis gang and failure to treat dying Red Hamilton in April. Last seen alive while drinking with gang members at a roadhouse near Toledo, Ohio, Moran allegedly told his employers, "I have you guys in the palm of my hand." While no one ever confessed to his slaying, most sources claim that Fred Barker and Alvin Karpis took Moran for a boat ride on nearby Lake Erie and dumped his weighted corpse into its depths.[35]

August started badly for Lansing fugitive Jim Clark. Kansas Governor Alf Landon had posted a $200 reward for his capture, quickly matched by the state banking association. To speed things along, a special police unit organized to pursue Clark, ignoring the niceties of legal jurisdiction. Its officers traced him to Tulsa on August 1, then handed Clark to federal prosecutors who secured his conviction on bank robbery charges, resulting in a 99-year prison sentence.[36]

On August 6, Homer Van Meter and Marie Conforti arrived at Island View Resort in Longville, a tiny hamlet in Minnesota's Cass County, winding their slow way to Saint Paul, 180 farther south.[37]

At 9:40 a.m. on August 11, 60 G-men and deputy U.S. Marshals delivered the first group of 137 prisoners to Alcatraz Island in San Francisco Bay. Brought by train from Leavenworth, then packed onto boats for the 1¼-mile journey offshore, inmates selected for "The Rock" were said to be

7. Shoot on Sight

Alcatraz Island, aka "The Rock," America's toughest federal prison from August 1934 until its closure in 1963 (author's collection).

persistent troublemakers and escape risks from the nation's other federal pens. They were initially outnumbered by 155 staffers, led by Warden James Johnston and Associate Warden Cecil Shuttleworth, both ranked as "iron men" skilled at maintaining security with no thought to "egghead" notions of rehabilitation.[38]

Discovered by Spaniards in 1775 and named "*La Isla de los Alcatraces*"—Island of the Gannets (not pelicans, as often misinterpreted)—Alcatraz comprises 22 stony acres surrounded by swift, cold, shark-infested seas. Mexico ceded it to an American in 1846, on the promise to build a lighthouse, but that goal floundered in 1850, with Alcatraz converted to an army base, then repurposed as a military prison in 1859. The Department of Justice purchased Alcatraz on October 12, 1933, spending $260,000 ($5.2 million today) to modernize its facilities between January and August 1934. By the time it closed for good in March 1963, The Rock housed 1,576 federal prisoners rated America's "worst of the worst," including many of the "crime war" era's "public enemies."[39]

One day after Alcatraz opened for business, police in Paducah, Kentucky, captured ex–Barrow gang member Joe Palmer. In custody, he boasted of a recent bank holdup in Henderson. Later that month, the owner of Bonnie and Clyde's "death car" retrieved her vehicle from police, still covered with blood and flesh fragments—along with an $85 bill for towing and storage.[40]

Eleven days after The Rock's debut as a federal lockup, G-men arrested Oliver "Izzy" Berg at his sister's home in Chicago, charging that he'd helped the Barker-Karpis gang distribute ransom money from the Bremer kidnapping.[41]

One day later, on August 23, Homer Van Meter came to the end of his road in Saint Paul. We know his confrontation with police began at the Saint Paul Auto Company—a dealership alleged to cultivate gangland connections, located at Marion Street and University Avenue—but confused eyewitness statements and police reports obscure the fatal course of events. Some say Homer arrived on foot, others that he came in a car with two other men, one of them alleged to be bank robber Tommy Gannon. It was Van Meter's second visit to the showroom, the first occurring on August 22, when he discussed a trade-in purchase with manager H.H. McGill. McGill said he would need to see Van Meter's current vehicle before a swap could be arranged, and Homer promised to return sometime next day. Unknown to Van Meter, the second trip was a setup, arranged with local officers already under fire for rumors of corrupt involvement with the Barker-Karpis gang and other fugitives.[42]

When he arrived between 4:00 and 5:00 p.m. (accounts differ), Homer found four police officers waiting for him. Chief Frank Cullen, armed with a rifle; Detective Tom Brown, with a Tommy gun; and two unidentified detectives with shotguns had loitered at the dealership since noon. Confronting them—and clearly recognizing Brown, whose losing sheriff's race he had financially supported—Van Meter allegedly drew a pistol (described as a .380 or .45 automatic in conflicting reports) and fled across the street, firing as the officers pursued him. Chief Cullen later claimed he did not return fire, since a female bystander, Mrs. Andrew Stedje, obstructed his view. Van Meter ducked into a dead-end alley and died there seconds later, under circumstances still in doubt.[43]

No civilian witnesses support police claims that Van Meter fired (or even held) a gun when he was slain. Four of them—H. H. McGill, Mrs. Stedje, motorist "D. Peterson," and an unnamed passerby—saw no weapon in Homer's hands at any time, though all claimed he carried a straw "boater" hat. Conflicting police accounts claim he was standing upright or kneeling when a shotgun blast struck him in the face and chest. Ramsey County's coroner listed one machine-gun bullet entry wound and 25 from buckshot on Homer's corpse, all in the back. Additional wounds included one finger severed from his right hand, with another finger and the thumb of that hand "nearly" amputated. Conflicting, unofficial accounts attribute most of Homer's wounds to a Tommy gun or shotgun. Mrs. Stedje described Tom Brown standing over Homer's body, shooting it repeatedly—a claim that made Van Meter's relatives accuse police of using him for "target practice."[44]

All accounts agree Van Meter was set up for execution, suspects variously named as Tommy Gannon, Harry Sawyer, partner Jack Peifer, even Lester Gillis, angry over a recent quarrel with Homer. Motives include silencing Van Meter with regard to Saint Paul P.D.'s corruption and simple greed. Friends claim Homer carried $10,000 ($195,000 today) to the dealership on August 23, while his killers reported confiscating only $1,323 from his corpse. Suspected recipients of the missing cash include the members of his firing squad, Sawyer, and Peifer.[45]

Saint Paul police seized Marie Conforti that same afternoon, charging her with parole violation. Homer was buried in Fort Wayne, Indiana, but separately from his family's plot, as they told reporters, due to shame over his life of crime.[46]

Following Van Meter's death, whatever role he may have played in it, Lester Gillis, his wife, and John Chase embarked on an odyssey that carried them to Chicago, then west to Nevada, and finally eastward again to Manhattan.[47]

Billie Frechette cashed in on her life with Dillinger in August 1934, authorizing a ghostwritten series of articles for the *Chicago Herald Examiner*. The first installment—inevitably titled "Crime Does Not Pay!"—ran on August 27, describing life on the run with Dillinger as the "only one big thing [that] ever happened to me in my life," leading her to prison. That series concluded on August 6, followed in the same newspaper 10 weeks later, when Polly Hamilton climbed aboard the money train, with a one-off piece titled "Dillinger's Last Hours with Me, By His Sweetheart." Her assessment: "John Dillinger, the outlaw? I didn't know him. The man I knew, and loved, was Jimmy Lawrence, a Board of Trade clerk. Jimmy Lawrence wasn't grim, wasn't a killer, any more than he was a Board of Trade clerk. I wouldn't let him call for me, because they thought he was a sissy, with his gold rim glasses and trick mustache that the authorities say now he used for a disguise."[48]

Dr. Loeser, Dr. Cassidy, and Louis Piquett found no takers for their exclusive stories when they faced indictment for harboring Dillinger on August 31.[49]

That same day, G-men Harold Anderson and William Trainor learned from a newspaper story that three gunmen—Jerome Cretes, Robert McCoy, and John Pace—had been arrested while stalking Mafioso Michael "Jimmy Needles" LaCapra. The agents' report reads, "It was obvious from the appearances of the three ... that they had undergone physical punishment, probably at the hands of the Kansas Highway Patrol, as this was stated by the three parties when they were interviewed."[50]

The trio was less talkative than their intended victim, however. LaCapra, held in an adjoining interview room, showed no sign of "third-degree" torture, though Anderson and Trainer reported, "The statements of LaCapra were, of course, very jumbled and rambling and he appeared to be under a very great nervous strain, although he did not appear to be out of his mind in any manner." As author Robert Unger summarizes that recital, by 4:30 a.m. on September 1, Needles "held nothing back. He named names, gave dates, trashed friends, settled old scores, and tried to buy back his life with the only currency left to him."[51]

The result: a "final solution" to the Union Station massacre—at least, to Hoover's satisfaction. Vern Miller's only partners in the crime thus became and would forever be Charles Floyd and Adam Richetti.

8

Wanted Dead

On September 1, 1934, befitting his status as "Dean of American Bank Robbers," authorities moved Harvey Bailey from Leavenworth, 1,800 miles westward to a one-man cage on The Rock.[1]

Fringe members of the Barker-Karpis gang seemed destined to join him that month. On the 4th, fearing the gang more than prison, James Wilson, a cousin of vanished Dr. Joseph Moran, surrendered to G-men in Denver. One day later, Cleveland police nabbed "molls" Wynonna Burdette, Paula "Fat-Witted" Harmon, and Gladys Sawyer for drunk and disorderly behavior at a hotel. Officers advised the feds, but agents failed to capture their fugitive lovers. On the 26th, G-men arrested gambler Cassius McDonald for passing Bremer ransom money in Detroit.[2]

On September 6 J. Edgar Hoover dictated a two-page letter from Washington to Sam Cowley, writing *finis* to the Director's long-running bromance with "Dear Melvin" Purvis. It read:

> I desire that you continue in Chicago in your present capacity of supervision of all remaining angles of the Dillinger case. The Special Agents assigned to this case will work directly under your supervision since I consider this area a special assignment. I expect you to remain personally in control of and directing the activities of the Special Agents assigned to the Dillinger case and desire that thorough and vigorous attention be given to all leads looking to the apprehension of John Hamilton and Baby Face Nelson.
>
> In addition to the supervision of the Dillinger case, I desire that you personally assume direction and control over all investigation of the Bremer kidnaping case and the Special Agents working upon that case. In connection with this case, every possible lead should be promptly followed out in order that subjects Karpis, Barker and other members of the Bremer kidnaping gang may be apprehended at the earliest possible date.
>
> Effective immediately, I also desire that you assume personal supervision of all angles of the Kansas City massacre case, giving this case close supervision and attention.
>
> In the direction and supervision of the above entitled cases, you are now placed in charge of the investigations not only of the Chicago district but in

the districts covered by all other field offices. You are authorized to proceed to St. Paul, Kansas City, Oklahoma City or any other point that you deem desirable in connection with the supervision of these cases. I believe in this regard that it would be advisable for you, as soon as the prosecution of Louis Piquett, Dr. Loeser, Dr. Cassidy, Arthur O'Leary and the other defendants presently in custody upon charges of harboring is completed, to personally visit the St. Paul, Kansas City and Oklahoma City Offices for the purpose of ascertaining just what investigation is being conducted in those districts and organizing the investigative activity in such a manner that a systematic method of handling all leads will be developed....

In the event any question is raised as to your authority to direct the investigative activities in the above enumerated cases, you are authorized to state that these cases are being handled as special assignments and that you, as my personal representative and working directly from my office, are in charge of these cases....[3]

Unstated but clearly intended in Hoover's order, Purvis remained as Chicago's Special Agent in Charge, but every major "crime war" case in progress at the time found him effectively demoted to Cowley's second-in-command, if that.

Remnants of the Barrow gang did not interest Hoover. Sheriff Henderson Jordan had promised to keep hands off Henry Methvin, as long as Henry stayed in Bienville Parish and kept his nose clean. Methvin complied, finding honest work at a sawmill and proposing to a local woman, unaware that Ottawa County, Oklahoma, had indicted him on September 12 for the April 1934 murder of Constable Cal Campbell. Craving extra money for his honeymoon, Methvin was pleased to receive a letter from Shreveport, where a crime "buff" wished to buy one of the guns Henry had carried on the road with Bonnie and Clyde. The message was bait for a trap, Shreveport police arresting him upon arrival and shipping him off to Oklahoma, facing trial for his life.[4]

Another case excluded from Sam Cowley's brief was the still-unsolved Lindbergh kidnapping. Seven months had elapsed since a few ransom bills surfaced at a Federal Reserve Bank, source unknown, then 16 more appeared between August 20 and September 15, passed at various places in Yorkville and Harlem, New York. G-men joined members of New Jersey's and New York's State Police, charting locations on a map and interviewing vendors who'd received the bills. Modern FBI historians claim that descriptions of a single man passing the gold certificates "fit exactly that of 'John' as described by Dr. Condon" in 1932—an exaggeration to say the least, since Condon's descriptions varied over time and contradicted one another.[5]

The last gold certificate, spent on September 15 for gasoline at 125th Street and Park Avenue, intrigued the filling station attendant enough that he wrote the customer's license plate number on the bill's margin. NYPD traced the vehicle to owner Bruno Richard Hauptmann, a German immigrant born in 1899, residing in New York since 1923. Lawmen staked out his home at 1279 East 222nd Street in the Bronx on September 18, watching their suspect emerge at 9:00 a.m. the next day. Apparently spotting a "tail," Hauptmann allegedly began driving erratically, as if to shake off pursuers, but a truck blocked his path on Park Avenue north of Tremont, where detectives placed him under arrest.[6]

Initially, the evidence against Hauptmann seemed damning. He carried a $20 gold certificate in his pocket and admitted spending some of the others around New York. Cabbie Joseph Perrone, mindful of outstanding reward offers, "positively identified" Hauptmann as the man who'd handed him a note for Dr. Condon some 33 months earlier. Dr. Condon chimed in with a corresponding "positive" I.D., but failed to pick Hauptmann from a lineup, and police noted that Hauptmann's common Dodge sedan "resembled" one seen cruising around Hopewell, New Jersey, prior to the Lindbergh abduction.[7]

More telling was the discovery, in Hauptmann's garage, of more ransom money totaling $14,600. Richard claimed the cash was left with him for safekeeping by fellow countryman and sometime business associate Isidor Srul Fisch, born at Leipzig in 1905, who'd immigrated in 1925 and found work as a fur-cutter in New York's Garment District. A notorious con man who frequently tried to involve others in fraudulent business ventures and money laundering schemes, Fisch did so poorly at crime that he relied on stipends from his parents back in Europe to survive. After meeting Hauptmann in 1932, Fisch proposed a merger of their incomes from fur-cutting and Hauptmann's carpentry business to gamble on stocks, producing the first significant profits of his life and entrusting them to Hauptmann. Authorities traced Fisch's movements, learning that he'd applied for a passport on May 12, 1932—the same day Little Lindy was allegedly found dead—and sailed for Germany on December 9, 1933. Tuberculosis claimed his life in Leipzig on March 29, 1934, 25 weeks before Hauptmann's arrest. Unable to question Fisch, U.S. authorities contacted his relatives, who naturally denied his involvement with America's "Crime of the Century."[8]

Meanwhile, lawmen ordered Hauptmann to copy various Lindbergh ransom notes, printing in block letters and replicating various misspellings from those messages, sending them off to the newly-established FBI Laboratory in Washington, where graphologists claimed to find "remarkable similarities in inconspicuous, personal characteristics and writing habits … which resulted in a positive identification." A self-styled "wood expert" removed floorboards from Hauptmann's attic, declaring that Richard—a skilled carpenter—had used the mismatched, ill-fitting pieces to construct a ladder that collapsed under his weight during the Lindbergh kidnapping.

Further "evidence," Dr. Condon's phone number, found penciled inside Hauptmann's closet, was later exposed as a reporter's hoax, written to help sell newspapers, but prosecutors would still use it in court. On September 24, the Bronx Supreme Court indicted Hauptmann for extortion.[9]

A fortnight after Samuel Cowley took control of the Kansas City massacre investigation, on September 22, G-men traced suspected conspirator Dick Galatas and his wife Elizabeth to New Orleans, taking them both into custody for interrogation.[10]

On the day of those Crescent City arrests, Dillinger gangsters Charles Makley and Harry Pierpont made their last bid for freedom from the Ohio State Penitentiary in Columbus. Taking their cue from Dillinger's Crown Point escape, they carved fake guns from bars of soap and blackened them with shoe polish, using the stage props to overpower and assault death row guards. With nothing to lose, they moved on to Russell Clark's cell and released him, along with six other convicts, but met a dead end at a barred door manned by guards with real guns. Clark and the other tagalongs retreated to their cells when gunfire sputtered, bullets striking both Makley and Pierpont. Fat Charley died from his wounds at the scene, bleeding internally, while Pierpont survived multiple slugs to face his scheduled execution date in October. Relatives buried Makley at Leipsic's Sugar Ridge Cemetery.[11]

Tri-State Gang leaders Walter Legenza and Robert Mais had better luck with their breakout plan one week later, on the 29th. Condemned inmates were allowed to receive food mailed from outside, and their last delivery to Richmond's City Jail included two pistols stashed in a can of cooked chicken. Already murderers, the pair shot their way clear, killing Patrolman William Toot and wounding two others as they escaped. Tortured by guilt over his failure to detect and seize the guns, City Night Sergeant Richard Duke later committed suicide.[12]

On October 8, 1934, grand jurors in Hunterdon County, New Jersey, indicted Bruno Hauptmann for murder and kidnapping. Those charges trumped New York's extortion count, and Governor Herbert Lehman signed extradition papers two days later. On the 19th officers transferred Hauptmann to Hunterdon County's jail in Flemington, awaiting trial.[13]

On the same day Hauptmann was indicted, Sam Cowley phoned Director Hoover from Chicago, concerning the Union Station massacre. Hoover's memo of that call says, "He mentioned the fact that if the Kansas City Police Department should break the case it would spoil it for us, and Mr. [U.S. Attorney Maurice] Milligan is of the opinion that this might be done at any time." After ruminating over that, Hoover issued a six-page press release two days later, announcing the FBI's "complete solution" to the murders. It read, in part: "Verne Miller was identified as the leader of the gunmen, and through exhaustive investigation it has been established that the other assassins were Charles Arthur 'Pretty Boy' Floyd and the latter's lieutenant, Adam Richetti.... Floyd was wounded in the skirmish, and since then has successfully remained under cover."[14]

Henceforth, the "facts" were set in stone, immutable.

Twenty-seven hundred miles to the west, in Minden, Nevada, Lester Gillis rejoined John Paul Chase on October 10. Stealing a car, they started toward Chicago, reportedly planning to meet Alvin Karpis and others for a bank raid more rewarding than their last foray at South Bend.[15]

In Texas that week, on Friday the 12th, Tarrant County jurors convicted W.D. Jones as an accomplice to the 1931 murder of Tarrant County Deputy Malcolm Davis. Jones blamed Clyde Barrow for the actual shooting, while state law qualified his role as "murder without malice," sparing him from execution. His prosecutor sought a 99-year sentence but the jury proved more merciful, fixing Jones's penalty at 15 years.[16]

Five days after Jones received his verdict, Harry Pierpont kept his date with the electric chair at midnight on October 17. Pete's mother buried him at Holy Cross and St. Joseph Cemetery in Indianapolis.[17]

Sheriff's deputies in Harrison County, Mississippi, captured fugitive bandit Irvin Chapman on October 19, charging him with bank robbery and burglary. Once again jurors found him guilty, producing a 15-year sentence to Parchman State Farm in the Delta. Before he started serving that time, though, authorities released Chapman to the Ouachita County sheriff's department in Arkansas, pending trial on additional charges.[18]

On the same Friday as Chapman's arrest, normally reliable authors William Helmer and Rick Mattix claim Ohio police named Charles Floyd and Adam Richetti as prime suspects in the afternoon's $500 bank heist at nonexistent "Titusville." They apparently meant *Tiltonsville*, in Jefferson County, where two men robbed a bank on October 19. Meanwhile, Hoover's October 10 announcement naming the pair as Vern Miller's known accomplices in Kansas City forced Floyd, Richetti, and the Baird sisters out of their Buffalo, New York, hideout.[19]

The timeline of what followed was, and is today, hopelessly confused. FBI historians peg their departure date as October 20, nearing Wellsville, Ohio—a journey of 226 miles from Buffalo, 36 miles south of Tiltonsville—"a few hours later." Why the fugitives, allegedly hoping to reach Oklahoma, might double back northward from an Ohio bank holdup remains unexplained, but that presents the first crack in the FBI's timeline. Other versions have Floyd, Richetti, and their women approaching Wellsville on the foggy night of October 18–19. Floyd, driving, struck a roadside telephone pole and damaged their car. He sent the Baird sisters into

Wellsville on foot, to fetch a tow truck and have the vehicle repaired, while he and Richetti waited with their weapons near the crash site.[20]

Sometime between dawn and 10:00 a.m. in differing accounts, motorist Joe Fryman and his son-in-law David O'Hanlon passed the accident scene but saw no car, a wrecker having arrived and towed it into Wellsville with the Baird sisters. Fryman and O'Hanlon *did* see two suspicious men in suits lounging at roadside and either reported it to a neighbor, Lon Israel, or directly to Wellsville Police Chief John Fultz. In one account, Israel alerted Fultz around 10:30 a.m. on October 20. The chief, suspecting he had found the Tiltonsville bandits, proceeded toward the sighting's location with unarmed volunteer policemen William Irwin and Grover Potts, perhaps guided by Lon Israel. As the three (or four) men approached the two strangers, Floyd and Richetti opened fire with pistols, slightly wounding Fultz in the ankle, whereupon his two (or three) companions turned and fled. Believing Chief Fultz to be captured or dead, they armed themselves and returned to the shooting scene, where Floyd alone briefly traded more shots with the posse, wounding Potts in one shoulder, then vanished into the woods, dropping a Tommy gun somewhere along the way. Chief Fultz, meanwhile, reinforced, apprehended Richetti when Adam ran out of bullets. The Baird sisters, hearing of Richetti's capture at the Wellsville garage, left at once for Kansas City. Floyd remained at large with barely 30 hours left to live.[21]

Roughly an hour after his second skirmish with police, around 12:40 p.m., Floyd reached Peterson's garage, a half-mile from the shooting site. He offered several young men $10 for a lift to Youngstown, spinning a tale of his car breaking down nearby. George MacMillen accepted, following backroads, while Floyd inquired, "I suppose you know who I am?" When MacMillen denied it, Floyd displayed a pistol, saying, "The radios are flashing it all over the country, and the papers are full of it." He claimed to be wounded but George saw no blood. As they neared florist James Baum's greenhouse in Wellsville, at 1:00 p.m., McMillen pulled his auto's choke and told Floyd they were out of gas. Floyd asked Baum for some fuel, but Baum had none to spare. Instead, Floyd drew a gun, forcing Baum and McMillen into the florist's car, proceeding toward West Point, nine miles farther north.[22]

As Floyd left Wellsville with his hostages, Sheriff Fultz informed Deputy George Hayes of the woodland shootouts, saying he suspected Pretty Boy of passing through Wellsville. Hayes staked out a nearby crossroads with colleague Charley Patterson and soon spotted a car approaching, two men seated in front, with a third hunched down in the backseat. The deputies gave chase, Floyd shooting out the rear window of Baum's car to stop them, one slug piercing the squad car's windshield between Hayes and

Patterson. Baum slammed on his brakes, while the deputies sprang from their car, shouting for Floyd to surrender. Instead, Floyd exited the stolen car, hiding behind his hostages, while Deputy Patterson shot Baum in one leg. Floyd ducked into surrounding woods and disappeared, while Deputy Hayes handcuffed MacMillen, then summoned reinforcements. The posse scoured backroads until nightfall but found nothing, although one woman glimpsed a man clad in a pinstriped suit crossing her property. The search continued on Sunday, October 21, with no further Pretty Boy sightings.[23]

By then, Sheriff Holtz had alerted the FBI, drawing Melvin Purvis and a team of G-men that included Agents David Hall, Herman Hollis, Winfred "Bud" Hopton, Clifford Risler, plus at least five others. Available Bureau records name two only as "D. DiLillo" and "R. G. McCallum." Sparse media reports refer to three more simply as Agents O'Hare, Reynolds, and Rose. Occupying rooms at the Travelers Hotel in East Liverpool, five miles east of Wellsville, the feds soon irked local lawmen by asserting control of the manhunt—an arrogance that remains a sore point between G-men and "lesser" law enforcement agencies to the present day. Samuel Cowley arrived to help with the search on October 22.[24]

Patrols resumed on country roads at daybreak that Monday, with G-men and local officers riding in separate cars, some county deputies trekking through the woods on foot. Purvis, increasingly pressured by phone calls from Hoover in Washington, left the Travelers Hotel to personally join the search at noon, accompanied by Agents Hall, Hopton, and McKee. By chance, they encountered four members of East Liverpool's police force, including Chief Hugh McDermott with Officers Glenn Montgomery, Herman Roth, Jr., and Chester Smith. While those teams joined forces, feds farther afield raided a home occupied by relatives of Adam Richetti in Dillonville, 46 miles south of East Liverpool, searching the place and then keeping it under surveillance.[25]

Meanwhile, around 10:00 a.m., farmer Arthur Conkle glimpsed a man running through his cornfield. Two hours later, he saw the same man on the property of neighbor Robert Robinson. Around 12:30 Floyd approached Robinson, pleading hunger and seeking a lift to Youngstown. Robinson refused him transportation but had his daughter make their visitor a tomato sandwich. Floyd ate it, thanked his hosts, and went off walking north along the rural highway. With four hours left to live, he was going nowhere fast.[26]

Ninety minutes later, Floyd reached Ellen Conkle's farm on Spruceville Road, two miles south of Clarkson, seven miles northeast of East Liverpool. Ellen was Arthur Conkle's widowed sister-in-law, working in her smokehouse while brother Stewart Dyke ("Stuart Dikes" in some accounts) and his wife Mary labored in Ellen's cornfield. Floyd arrived at 3:00 p.m., pleading hunger and offering money for "meat and bread." He claimed that he'd been out with his brother on Sunday night, hunting "squirrels or rabbits or anything," when they were separated and became lost. Ellen questioned that, reminding Floyd that no one hunted squirrels after sundown, whereupon he said, "To tell the truth lady, I got drunk last night and I don't know where I am exactly." Still skeptical, she led Floyd inside and prepared him a meal of short ribs, potatoes, rice, coffee, and pumpkin pie. Floyd insisted on paying a dollar over Conkle's objections, then asked about getting a ride to Youngstown. Ellen said her brother might drive him part-way there but had to finish working in the cornfield first. Stewart and Mary came in at 4:00 and met Floyd. Stewart refused the lift to Youngstown, but agreed to drive Floyd as far as Clarkson, hoping to remove him from Ellen's property.[27]

As Floyd and Dyke got into Stewart's car, they saw two other vehicles approaching rapidly, Purvis and his agents in one, Chief McDermott and his officers in the other. Floyd drew a pistol, announced, "They are looking for me," and ordered Dyke to drive around behind a corncrib for concealment. It was too late, though, as someone from the posse spotted him and Floyd's pursuers piled out of their cars, shouting for him to halt, throw down his weapon, and approach the road unarmed. Instead, still brandishing his pistol, Floyd bolted for the nearest tree line, some 200 yards distant. Most accounts claim he ran without firing his gun, but Ellen Conkle told reporters Floyd "shot a couple of times at them but I don't think he hit anybody." As he fled, some member of the posse shouted, "Let him have it!" followed by a fusillade of "more than 50 rounds" from Tommy guns, rifles, shotguns, and pistols.[28]

Most of those shots missed their target, a tribute to nerves and poor marksmanship, but Ellen Conkle saw Floyd's right arm jerk from a bullet's impact. He recovered, running for 200 feet or so before he finally collapsed. Melvin Purvis reportedly reached him first, kicking a .45 pistol away from Floyd's hand, while Officer Roth removed another from Floyd's belt and the interrogation began.[29]

Reports of that verbal exchange are predictably confused. Some say that Floyd identified himself as "Murphy" when Purvis asked his name, then grudgingly admitted his identity. He either asked, "Where's Ad?" or "Where's Eddie?" referring to Adam Richetti but got no answers. While Stewart Dyke and Agent Hall went to call an ambulance, Purvis rushed to phone Washington, alerting Hoover that he had Floyd in custody. Officers Montgomery, Roth, and Smith carried Floyd to an apple tree's shade. When asked about the Kansas City massacre, Floyd allegedly replied, "To hell with Union Station." Chief McDermott asked, "How bad are you hurt?" Floyd

8. Wanted Dead

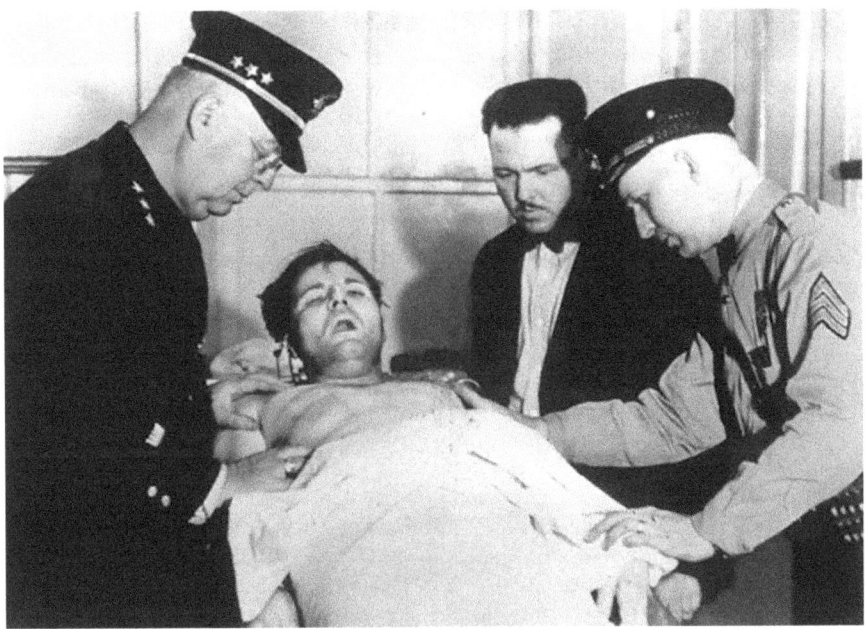

"Pretty Boy" Floyd prior to embalming in East Liverpool, Ohio, October 22, 1934 (author's collection).

supposedly replied, "I'm done. You got me twice. Fuck you!" His last words were "I'm going," whereupon he died at 4:25.[30]

Aside from two pistols, official reports say lawmen recovered $122 in cash from Floyd's pockets, along with a key to his former Buffalo apartment, a loaded .45 magazine, matches, a pocket watch, two apples, and a fifty-cent piece on a chain, allegedly marked with ten hand-carved notches (the latter never photographed or publicly displayed). He also wore a cameo ring, identical to one worn by Richetti. Without waiting for the ambulance, G-men placed Floyd's corpse into the backseat of Agent Hopton's car, wedged between two lawmen, and proceeded to the Sturgis Funeral Home in East Liverpool. There, according to official documents, Columbiana County's coroner logged two .45 caliber bullet wounds—one entering below Floyd's left shoulder, shattering his eighth rib and damaging a lung, the other penetrating from his right and stopping near the other slug, both having nicked his heart. There was no trace of any wounds from Kansas City or his skirmish with Wellsville police.[31]

Richetti, caged while hundreds of gawkers trooped past his cell to stare at him, refused to believe Floyd was dead until officers showed him the headlines. Bewildered then, he said, "I don't see why he struck around so long." From loyalty, perhaps, or maybe Floyd was simply lost. Chief Fultz initially refused to surrender Richetti, put off by the Bureau's high-handed tactics and Purvis allegedly introducing himself with a false name at their first meeting, but finally acceded and saw G-men pack Adam off to Kansas City for trial.[32]

Given Hoover's orders to "exterminate" the Union Station killers, backed by Inspector Quinn Tamm's memo saying Floyd and Richetti should be "knocked off" to solve the massacre case, rumors of Floyd's summary execution lingered in some law enforcement quarters. Still, the stories didn't go public until September 24, 1979, when aged Chester Smith's account appeared in *Time* magazine under the title "Blasting a G-man Myth." It read, in part,

> Last week ... retired East Liverpool Police Captain Chester C. Smith, now 84, came forward with a far different account of Floyd's death. One of six officers who accompanied Purvis that day, Smith was the first to spot Floyd trying to escape. Said Smith: "I knew Purvis couldn't hit him, so I dropped him with two shots from my .32 Winchester rifle." Stunned but not seriously wounded, Floyd sat up and was immediately disarmed by Smith.
>
> Then, said Smith, Purvis ran up and ordered: "Back away from that man. I want to talk to him." Pretty Boy glared and cursed. At which point, said Smith, Purvis turned to G-Man Herman Hollis and said: "Fire into him." Hollis obeyed, said Smith, killing Floyd with a burst from a tommy gun.
>
> Was there a coverup? "Sure was," said Smith, "because they didn't want it to get out that he'd been killed that way." Smith, who was promoted to captain following Floyd's killing, said he decided it was proper to set the record straight now because, of the seven men involved, only he remains alive—and the truth can no longer hurt anyone.[33]

Eight weeks elapsed before the FBI responded indirectly, through a letter to *Time* from retired G-man Winfred Hopton, residing in Tennessee. He wrote:

> I must take issue with the article titled "Blasting a G-Man Myth" about the capture of Charles ("Pretty Boy") Floyd. You reported that Chester Smith, a former member of the East Liverpool, Ohio, police department, said that he decided it was proper to set the record straight now because of the several men involved, only he remains alive.
>
> I was one of the four special agents of the FBI (known at the time as the Division of Investigation) who apprehended Floyd on a farm several miles from East Liverpool on Oct. 22, 1934, and I am very much alive.
>
> To begin with, Mr. Smith did not capture Floyd. The truth is he was shot by two of the four FBI agents present when Floyd aimed his gun at them. After he was shot, two or three members of the East Liverpool police department who were in the immediate area at the time came up to us and offered assistance in directing us to the morgue in East Liverpool. Floyd was then transported to the morgue in my Government-owned car.

According to your article, Smith said that "Purvis ran up and ordered: 'Back away from that man, I want to talk to him.' Pretty Boy glared and cursed, at which point, said Smith, Purvis turned to G-Man Herman Hollis and said: 'Fire into him.' Hollis obeyed, said Smith, killing Floyd with a burst from a tommy gun."

For your information. Agent Hollis, whom I knew personally, was not even present when Floyd was apprehended. The allegation that Purvis ordered an agent to "fire into Floyd" as described above is absolutely false. The truth is that when the several members of the East Liverpool police department came up to where Floyd was lying on the ground, he had already been mortally wounded.[34]

Within hours of Floyd's death, his mother sent a telegram from Oklahoma, asking that his body not be photographed or publicly displayed. Predictably, G-men and Ohio authorities ignored her plea, allowing an estimated 10,000 persons to gape at his corpse through the night of October 22–23. Aside from countless photos, a local pottery worker cast a death mask of Floyd's face, later distributing plaster copies to lawmen involved in his slaying.[35]

The *Liverpool Review* reported "a dozen" gunshot wounds on Floyd's body, contradicting official results of an autopsy performed by Drs. Roy Costello and Edward Miskall at the Sturgis Funeral Home, which logged only the mortal two wounds detailed above, plus a flesh wound to Floyd's right arm. Those injuries aside, several of his fingertips were "frayed," as if by sandpaper, a common means of blurring fingerprints by fugitives without access to acid-wielding surgeons.[36]

Before releasing Richetti to G-men on October 23, Chief Fultz had Adam arraigned on one count of carrying a concealed weapon. Richetti pled guilty, paid the $75 fine out of $98 found in his pockets at capture, then pled not guilty to shooting Fultz with intent to kill, held in lieu of $50,000 bond pending a trial that never occurred. At 11:30 that morning, handlers packed Floyd's corpse into a cloth-lined "rough box of wood" and sent him home to Salisaw, arriving by train on the 26th. That same Wednesday—Melvin Purvis's 31st birthday—a six-car caravan conveyed Richetti to the Columbiana County jail in Lisbon. Hundreds of curious onlookers lined the route of travel, and Fultz stopped the parade at a schoolhouse, calling all students from class for a pit stop lesson that crime doesn't pay. Fultz might have forged ahead with a trial for Richetti, but threats of a federal fine changed his mind, clearing the way for Adam's return to Kansas City. Against all odds, Richetti's cameo ring, identical to Floyd's, found its way to his sister Minnie.[37]

More than 25,000 gawkers—some reports say 40,000—thronged Floyd's funeral on October 28, nearly destroying Akins Cemetery in the process. The *Daily Oklahoman* described the scene as "everything that a funeral ought not be," under headlines reading "Huge throng of curious is disorderly at rites for slain gunman; Morbid thousands create barbaric atmosphere at cemetery." As described by reporter Harold Brown, "They trampled graves, crushed flowers and kicked over foot stones in a mad scramble" to view Floyd's grave. "There was something barbaric about the whole funeral." Afterward, one local wag surmised that based on his posthumous popularity, Floyd "could have been elected governor" the week he died.[38]

Floyd's death and the resultant publicity drove a deeper wedge between J. Edgar Hoover and the agent he'd once addressed as "Dear Melvin." Fearing another Dillinger-style press conference beyond his control, Hoover called Purvis at the Sturgis Funeral Home, recording their conversation in an October 22 memo: "I told Mr. Purvis.... I thought he should go on into Chicago and lay low for a couple of days. Purvis advised that he had been receiving inquiries from newspapers, whereupon I instructed him to tell the newspapers all statements would have to come from Washington." After a second call, to Sam Cowley, Hoover wrote, "Mr. Cowley is to remain [in Ohio] with a few men to clean up the odds and ends. Mr. Purvis is also to leave tonight and the curtain is to be pulled down on publicity there." Purvis obeyed his boss, and received a commendation of sorts on October 23, Hoover declaring, "The courage and the efficiency of the representatives of the Division will I know prove to be of great value to the work which we are all attempting to do in connection with the current warfare against the criminal element."[39]

Purvis's troubles were not over yet, however. On October 26 syndicated gossip columnist Louella Parsons announced that Paramount Pictures planned a film of Melvin's life, titled *Federal Dick*, with Cary Grant portraying Purvis. Worse yet, Parsons claimed that the project had a green light from the Department of Justice. Hoover immediately phoned SAC John Dunn in Los Angeles, demanding an interview with Emanuel Cohen, Paramount's vice president in charge of production. Cohen denied any "concrete plans" for *Federal Dick*, admitting only that a writer had been hired "to bat around ideas." Partially mollified, Hoover then called Purvis in Chicago, summarizing their conversation in a memo that read, "We agreed that it was the most outrageous thing we had ever heard of. Both Purvis and myself view the whole idea with absolute horror and disgust."[40]

If Purvis thought the storm had passed him by, he was mistaken. Even imaginary slights to Hoover's ego were collected, remembered, and nursed as personal grudges.

On October 24, while Floyd's corpse rode the rails between Ohio and Oklahoma, a federal grand jury in Kansas City indicted defendants Herbert Farmer, Richard Galatas and his wife, Vivian Mathias, Frank Mulloy,

Frances Nash, and Louis Stacci on three counts of conspiracy to free Frank Nash from federal custody, thereby causing the Union Station massacre. Deafy Farmer allegedly used $2,500 in Hamm ransom money to hire an attorney, while hinting to G-men that Dock Barker may have been one of the KC gunmen.⁴¹

The Tri-State Gang returned to action on October 26, kidnapping Philadelphia racketeer and nightclub owner William Weiss, demanding $100,000 ransom. After extended haggling, they settled for $8,000 (some accounts claim $12,000), while the victim's associates filed no report of his disappearance.⁴²

Four days later, after finishing his testimony for the state against fellow gang members, Gordon Alcorn returned to Leavenworth for completion of his pending sentence.⁴³

Fresh news from the Urschel kidnapping surfaced on November 2, 1934, when motorist Alvin Scott suffered serious injury in a car crash at Roseburg, Oregon. Police found $1,350 of the Urschel ransom money on his person, with another $6,140 concealed at his home. One week later, G-men searched the Dunsmuir, California, home of Scott cohorts Edward and Clara Feldman, revealing another $1,100, while rigorous interrogation of the pair led searchers to $1,520, hidden near Woodland, Washington. Under continued grilling, Scott coughed up the location of $5,000 more.⁴⁴

The Union Station massacre generated more confusion for Kansas City police in November. City leaders had dismissed Director of Police Eugene Reppert on January 16, 1934, replacing him with former *Kansas City Star* crime reporter Otto Higgins as Acting Chief, confirmed as permanent Director on April 15 and remaining in office for the next five years. On November 4 federal grand jurors indicted Reppert and Chief of Detectives Tom Higgins for perjury, specifically for denying their department's longstanding collusion with organized crime, including charges that they ordered police to "lay off" the massacre investigation. Also indicted was George Rayen, deposed head of the department's Motor Vehicle Theft Bureau, for denying public statements that he "owed more" to corrupt political boss Tom Pendergast than to KCPD. None of those accused faced trial, but their indictments cast doubt upon local efforts to solve the massacre case.⁴⁵

Tri-State gangsters finally collected their meager ransom for William Weiss on November 5, then killed him out of spite the following day, dumping his corpse in Neshaminy Creek near Doylestown, Pennsylvania. Another 13 days passed before a confidential gangland source finally tipped the feds to Weiss's abduction.⁴⁶

Meanwhile, mobster-friendly Saint Paul endured a cleanup launched by investigative journalist Howard Kahn, editor of the *St. Paul Daily News*, exposing the longstanding "O'Connor system" of graft. Mayor William Mahoney fired back, saying, "If there are any gangsters here, it is because they have been invited by the newspapers." That evasion failed to save Mahoney on November 6, when a record 74 percent of local voters turned out to defeat the incumbent, replacing him with lawyer and former state legislator Mark Gehan. The mayor-elect considered hiring businessmen Alexander Jamie—one of Chicago's "Secret Six" who formerly investigated Al Capone—but city councilmen rejected the outsider, whereupon Gehan tried another approach, hiring Jamie's son Wallace—trained in police administration and criminal detection at the University of Chicago and Northwestern University—to investigate Saint Paul corruption on the sly. Surreptitiously, and probably illegally, Jamie tapped police phone lines and hid dictaphones under the desks of prominent city officials, recording their conversations for posterity. Meanwhile, Gehan named Harry "Ned" Warren as Public Safety Commissioner. Warren, in turn, picked shady Michael Culligan as Acting Chief of Police, to everyone's later embarrassment.[47]

On the Tuesday that Saint Paul voters chose reform, Ohio grand jurors charged Adam Richetti with a preliminary count of obstructing justice, then held that charge in abeyance while Missouri prosecutors levied charges of murder for his alleged role in the Union Station massacre. A memo from Director Hoover to his KC office, dated that same day, sought to plug a leak in the Bureau. It read:

> Associated Press dispatches emanating from Kansas City, Missouri, indicate that Jack Jenkins, head of the Identification Bureau, Kansas City, Kansas, Police Department, has given out information to the effect that identifications were made by that Bureau of latent prints taken from beer bottles recovered in the residence of the late Vernon C. Miller, which implicates [*sic*] Miller, Floyd and Richetti....
>
> Of course, the identification of the prints of Miller and Richetti were effected by the Technical Laboratory of the Division and this information was being treated as confidential until such time as it became necessary to disclose the information at the trial of the case. I, therefore, desire that you make every effort to determine the source of Mr. Jenkins's information that the identification had been effected.[48]

Agent William Trainor replied with the non sequitur that "immediately after the massacre" witness Lottie West "positively identified a photograph of Charles Arthur Floyd ... as a likeness of one of the participants in the massacre, and also that she had seen the same individual sitting in her chair at the front of the lobby in the Union Station ... at about fifteen minutes before the massacre. However, it subsequently was stated by various employees of the Union Station, including H. House, a redcap, that the man

8. Wanted Dead

who sat in the chair of Mrs. West was Harry Blanchard, another employee of the Union Station. The photograph of Floyd was not identified by any other witness in a manner which would establish a positive identification." Trainor failed to identify the FBI's leaker, while ducking the fact that no witness had mentioned sighting Richetti.[49]

Hoover, meanwhile, escalated his campaign against Melvin Purvis, sending Inspector James Egan to conduct a "white-glove inspection" of the Chicago field office on November 17, seeking anything that rated criticism. Egan began by noting that Purvis reported for work at 9:30 a.m. on the inquisition's first day, writing, "It is felt that an Agent in Charge should be at his office between 8:30 and 8:43 every morning," with all hands on deck no later than 9:00. Nearly as bad, office stenographers "had not settled down to work until about 9:15. This is very important ... a full and complete explanation is desired." After 10 days, Egan's report "reflect[ed] unfavorably" on Purvis, noting that Melvin "has not been exercising proper supervision over his office ... he is extremely temperamental, egotistical ... he had been giving more time to his own personal interests and to his social activities than he had been to the office which he represents." Specific gripes included, "The road work box is all out of kilter. The ticklers we found dating back as far as June had not been taken out of the file ... dirty underwear and shirts, and so forth, found in some of the cell rooms, and I think they belong to the Agents ... fruit in the desks and one of the stenographers smoking ... desks, file cases and cabinets have been maintained in a terribly lax manner ... dirty dishes were found behind a radiator in the storeroom." Worse still, Egan listed 232 examples of "undue delay in handling cases."[50]

Hoover replied, "Those things you have mentioned ... are really the responsibility of Purvis. He can't alibi that on the ground that he hasn't got enough men. It is absolutely, positively lack of supervision and thought in the management of the office as I can see it. I think these conditions are pretty serious.... I think they are very bad. Yes, very, very bad. I want you to set him down. I'd go down the line—1, 2, 3. It seems to me that he hasn't measured up to what we've been expecting him to do."[51]

Thus far, the amended Lindbergh Law's death penalty clause had not been invoked, but that was about to change. On November 25, 1934, Oklahoma native Arthur Gooch and fellow jailbreak fugitive Ambrose Nix robbed a gas station in Tyler, Texas, of $100. The next day, passing through Paris, 102 miles north of Tyler, their getaway car blew a tire, drawing attention from local policemen R.N. Baker and H.R. Marks, who wrongly suspected the pair of being Barrow gang members. With four arrests and two prison terms on his rap sheet since 1930, Gooch dreaded a return to jail. When Baker and Marks approached him at the auto repair shop, a scuffle ensued, Nix shoving Baker into a glass showcase and gashing his left hip.

The bandits then disarmed both officers, abducted them in their own patrol car, and dropped them off in Oklahoma's Kiamichi Mountains, between Cloudy and Snow in Pushmataha County. Gooch took time to bandage Baker's wound, but it made no difference. The Lindbergh Law's amendment allowed execution for injuring a kidnap victim, no matter how minor the damage inflicted. Manhunters fanned out in search of Gooch and Nix but would not find them until late December.[52]

In Washington, Hoover's campaign against Melvin Purvis escalated on November 21, with receipt of a letter from Henry Suydam, a DOJ publicist and special assistant to Attorney General Cummings, asking Hoover's office to approve a brief biography of Purvis for the department's news "morgue." Hoover refused to comply, responding, "I cannot help but feel that the Department's relations with the Associated Press are being unnecessarily prejudiced"—that is, by promoting Purvis as a hero for bagging Dillinger and Floyd. When Cummings insisted, Hoover reluctantly scanned the short bio, still complaining to his nominal boss, "I well appreciate the fact that in Mr. Purvis' case there has already been much publicity concerning him, and some of the publicity which surrounded the killing of John Dillinger was at least affected through the cooperation of myself and other officials. I think that a mistake was made, however, and should there arise another similar case, it will be my very strong recommendation that no individual be singled out to receive the publicity for the death or capture of a notorious desperado."[53]

Of course, another such case had *already* occurred, with the death of Charles Floyd, but Hoover pressed on in his two-page letter of November 26, first falsely claiming that "such publicity naturally circumscribes the usefulness of the employee in the service for the future," concluding that "no one employee of this Division can ever be responsible for the successful termination of any case."[54]

No one employee but Hoover, that is. All glory must accrue to him alone.

And even as he penned those lines, another headline "public enemy" was running out of time.

Kansas City residents got a grim reminder of the Union Station massacre on Monday, November 26, when Patrolman Myron Fanning, off duty but still in uniform, drunk and raving, commandeered a taxi driven by Charles Alden, ordering his hostage to drive "by a circuitous route" to Union Station. Arriving there, he barged into the commissary, brandishing a pistol, announcing himself as "an officer of the Confederate army" who had come to recruit draftees. Patrolmen Grant Schroder and J.A. Yeaham responded to the alarm, confronting Fanning in the train sheds. As they retreated, Fanning fired six shots, fatally wounding Schroder. Fanning then hijacked another car and wound up at a drug store, where more officers disarmed and handcuffed him. Held without bond on a first-degree murder charge, Fanning denied any memory of the incident, then wept while saying, "I've made a mess of my life. I'm so sorry about what happened last night. Schroeder was my friend. I knew his wife, too. He was a swell kid. It's all so terrible." Colleagues recalled him brooding since the depot murders, telling Officer E.O. Peeney, "They're trying to blame me for some of that killing at the Union Station." Sheriff Bash brought a psychiatrist to examine Fanning, and Jackson County Prosecuting Attorney W.W. Graves Jr., waived the death penalty at Fanning's trial in March 1935. Fanning's attorney offered an insanity defense, buttressed by witnesses who described his client's depression since June 1933 and his "acting crazy" during the November incident. Upon conviction Fanning received a lenient five-year prison term.[55]

Lester Gillis had rendezvoused with John Chase near Minden, Nevada 12 days before Pretty Boy Floyd's last run in Ohio. On November 26, the day of Hoover's letter to Suydam, the pair reached Chicago and stole a Ford V8, allegedly in preparation for a meeting with Alvin Karpis. Lester's professed goal was to rob "a bank a day for a month," then presumably retire to parts unknown.[56]

Before meeting Karpis, Gillis planned to lie low with wife Helen and Chase at the Lake Como Hotel near Lake Geneva, Wisconsin, 84 miles northwest of Chicago. Proprietor Hobart Hermansen, an ex-bootlegger, welcomed gangsters to his hostelry and asked no questions. Meanwhile, Inspector Sam Cowley received a tip that Baby Face and company were somewhere in the general vicinity. Accounts differ as to whether Gillis and his entourage spent their last peaceful night with Hermansen on November 26 or arrived on Tuesday morning, the 27th, and spotted a lone, unarmed G-man watching the Lake Como Hotel. In either case, they swiftly departed for Chi-Town on U.S. Route 12 (now U.S. 14). The unnamed FBI lookout—whose partner had taken their car to fetch breakfast—could not pursue them but managed to alert Cowley by phone.[57]

Cowley dispatched Agents William Ryan and Thomas McDade toward the last sighting point, soon following with Agent Herman Hollis in a second car. Near Fox River Grove, Illinois, 35 miles south of Lake Geneva, around 3:15 p.m., Gillis and company, southbound, passed Ryan and McDade traveling northward. Each party recognized the other and their cars screeched through U-turns, with the result that Gillis wound up chasing his would-be pursuers. An exchange of gunfire followed, shattering windows in both cars but wounding no one, and the agents swerved into a field, taking cover behind their auto and waiting for the gangsters to attack.

Instead, Gillis turned south again and fled, initially unaware that federal bullets had damaged his Ford's radiator or water pump (reports differ).[58]

As Gillis's V8 lost power, manhunters Cowley and Hollis approached in a Hudson sedan, spotting their prey outside Barrington, six miles southeast of Fox River Grove. Hollis, driving, whipped the Hudson through a U-turn and pursued the fugitives, Helen driving the V8 while Chase opened fire on the G-men's car with a Colt Monitor automatic rifle. The Ford gave out at last near at Barrington's North Side Park, where Helen pulled over and stopped. Hollis rolled past, then stopped the Hudson some 150 feet farther south. Helen Gillis bolted for some nearby woods, while Chase fired on the federal car with his rifle, Lester wielding one of Hyman Lebman's "baby machine guns." Hollis carried a shotgun, while Cowley held a Tommy gun. An estimated dozen witnesses observed the final action from hiding nearby.[59]

Moments into the shootout, Nelson's machine pistol jammed, exchanged for another Lebman creation, a .351 Winchester rifle modified to fire full-automatic. Either brave or foolhardy, Gillis left cover and advanced on the agents' vehicle while Cowley and Hollis returned fire, both striking Gillis on open ground. After emptying his shotgun, Hollis drew a revolver and ran for cover behind a nearby electric power pole, dropped by three Winchester slugs to his forehead, stomach and back. Gillis continued his grim march toward Cowley, still firing, bullets striking Cowley in the chest and stomach. Nelson, also gravely wounded, made it to the Hudson with support from Chase and Helen, after which Chase retrieved their mobile arsenal from the ruined Ford and sped off toward a "safe house" on Walnut Street in Wilmette, 25 miles east of Barrington. Bystanders, including off-duty Patrolman William Gallagher of the Illinois State Police, loaded the wounded G-men into separate cars for transport. One delivered Hollis to Barrington Central Hospital, where doctors pronounced him dead on arrival. Another carried Cowley to Sherman Hospital in Elgin, 14 miles southwest of Barrington, where surgeons labored to stanch his internal bleeding.[60]

To this day, controversy endures regarding the placement and nature of Gillis's wounds. A memo from Hoover vaguely estimated "seven to 10 wounds," while modern FBI historians online report that he was hit 17 times. Others drop that tally to nine: one .45 slug from Cowley's Thompson, plus eight buckshot pellets from Hollis's shotgun, spattered across Lester's legs. Whatever the total, Gillis allegedly told Helen, "I'm done for" as they sped toward Wilmette, and his judgment proved correct.[61]

His last hideout belonged to Raymond Henderson—a suspected FBI informer whose home doubled as an underworld mail drop for messages. Henderson invited several other acquaintances of Lester and Helen

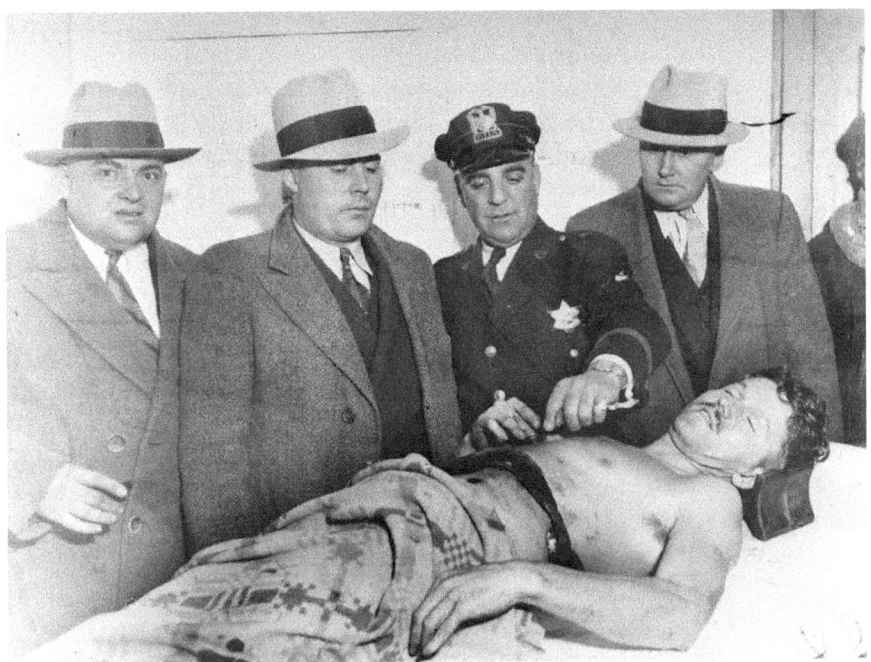

Unidentified lawmen examine the corpse of "Baby Face" Nelson, November 28, 1934.

to attend the outlaw's deathbed. Most remain anonymous today, but one was apparently Father Phillip Coughlin, a Gillis family friend who allegedly administered Catholic last rites to the dying bandit. Sometime between 7:35 and 8:00 p.m., based on divergent reports, Gillis closed his eyes for the last time. Helen helped others strip Lester's corpse, then wrapped it in a blanket because he "didn't like the cold" and left the body in a ditch outside Niles Center (now Skokie), Illinois. Ray Henderson's working alliance with G-men was confirmed when Justice declined to indict him for harboring Gillis or any other fugitives on Walnut Street.[62]

At Sherman Hospital, surgeons failed to repair Sam Cowley's mortal wounds but he survived long enough for Melvin Purvis to reach Elgin from Chicago, hearing Cowley's account of the bloodbath. Cowley died from his wounds around 2:00 a.m. on November 28.[63]

G-men were still raiding suspected hideouts when a passing motorist spied Lester's blanket-shrouded corpse at roadside, around 12:30 p.m., and tipped off manhunters. Again, confusion garbles fact as some reports credit rookie Agent Walter Walsh with discovering the body, while others mention anonymous FBI agents and modern Bureau historians, usually overeager to claim the achievements of others, claim that Lester's body was found by "police." Transported to the same Cook County Morgue that received John Dillinger four months earlier, Lester's body was examined, photographed, and fingerprinted, finally identified beyond all doubt.[64]

Helen Gillis, meanwhile, had parted company with John Chase, transported to Chicago by a gangland friend of Lester's, James Murray, who dropped her off on the North Side. There, Helen hailed a taxi for an aimless drive around Chi-Town, then continued roaming on foot, sat for a while in Humboldt Park, and spent the night of November 28 sleeping in an abandoned building's doorway. At some point she reached out to Lester's sister and brother-in-law, Juliette and Bob Fitzsimmons, who'd been caring for her children, enlisting Bob to negotiate her surrender to G-men. Helen's sole demand: that she be left in peace with family until after Lester's funeral. Hoover reportedly blocked that deal, his men informing Helen that her life was in "extreme danger," translated in headlines to a formal shoot-to-kill order on Lester's spouse. G-men tapped the Fitzsimmons's phone and staked out their house, shadowing the couple as they drove Helen around Chicago for an hour on Thanksgiving Day, November 29. After that final jaunt, Helen surrendered and cooperated partially with her interrogators, describing the Barrington battle and its aftermath, while omitting names of various "people that Les had contact with," lying outright when she called John Chase "a man named George." Charged with violating her parole from the Little Bohemia bust, Helen subsequently drew a 366-day sentence at the Women's Federal Reformatory at Milan, Michigan.[65]

On November 30 John Chase answered a newspaper ad seeking someone to drive a car cross-country from Chicago to Seattle. Acceptance of that offer meant that he required a chauffeur's license, which in turn demanded that he be photographed at a local police station. Lucky for Chase, his only arrest so far was a California drunk driving bust from 1931. Chicago police had no knowledge of that indiscretion, and G-men had failed to provide city lawmen with WANTED posters on Chase, thus clearing him to flee.[66]

Helen Gillis missed her husband's funeral on December 1. Some 200 people crowded the Sadowski Funeral Home's chapel in Chicago beforehand, pallbearers identified as Lester's childhood friends or "professional associates." Three large floral wreaths from relatives stood in for the usual priest, hymns, eulogy, and candles. Afterward, a hearse carried Gillis 15 miles northwest to River Grove's Saint Joseph Cemetery.[67]

J. Edgar Hoover never shied away from contradictions when they served his purpose. His recent letter to Henry Suydam had argued fervently against any lone G-men claiming credit for a bandit's downfall, but Hoover briefly abandoned that stance when he traveled from D.C. to Salt Lake City, addressing Sam Cowley's mourners at Wasatch Lawn Memorial Park cemetery. His eulogy praised Cowley as "brave enough to be scrupulously honest in little things as well as big things. He didn't accept the easy way out, a half-truth, a white lie, or a turned head." A follow-up citation, signed by Hoover and sent to Cowley's widow, stated that Cowley "deserves the credit for perfecting the arrangements that resulted in the location and killing of John Dillinger."[68]

Thus officially forgotten, Melvin Purvis was propelled still further into outer darkness by his former friend "Jayee."

Only one major gang of desperados still remained at large, the Barker-Karpis crew, but G-men missed their shot at one or the outfit's small fry on November 29, when Big Homer Wilson died at home in Chicago, from apparent natural causes. He had passed his bank-robbing career without once being nabbed.[69]

Before feds could locate the Barker crew, Chicago authorities captured Michigan City escapee Joseph Burns. Conflicting reports—one of them misnaming Burns "John"—claim he was arrested on December 4, 12th, and 18th, but the best available information comes from page one of the *Indianapolis News* on December 17, detailing an "all night" interrogation of Burns, presumably pegging the date as December 16. Chief Postal Inspector Walter Johnson suspected Burns of participating in a Brooklyn holdup on August 21, where bandits stole $427,950 ($8.3 million today) from an armored payroll truck, but Burns remained stubbornly silent as he was shipped back to Michigan City. "We haven't given up investigation of the Brooklyn angle," Johnson told reporters, "but whatever is to be done along that line will be handled from Indiana." With Burns's capture, only Joseph Fox remained at large of the September 1933 escapees.[70]

On December 4, Clara Feldman tipped G-men to the location of another $38,460 in Urschel ransom money. Ten days later, federal grand jurors indicted Clara and husband Edward, Ben Laska, James Mathers, and Alvin Scott on charges of conspiracy to violate the Lindbergh Law. Clara pled guilty in Oklahoma City on December 17, with sentencing held in abeyance pending further trials.[71]

From Washington, J. Edgar Hoover continued his campaign to marginalize Melvin Purvis. On December 4 he ordered Earl Connelly—former SAC of Kansas City, named as Sam Cowley's Chicago replacement—to locate quarters for a second "secret" Bureau office away from the Bankers Building on West Adams Street. Connelly chose the New York Life Insurance Building, renting space for $100 monthly, and had the second office operational by December 6. While effectively stripping Purvis of command, Hoover directed Connelly to inform reporters that while Purvis was still Special Agent in Charge, Connelly would be controlling the pursuit of cases formerly entrusted to Sam Cowley. At the same time, Hoover ordered,

"Mr. Purvis is not to accompany raiding parties ... and is to remain in the background generally.... [H]e should remain at home until such time as we can work out something for him to do."[72]

On Thursday December 6, police in Amarillo, Texas, cornered Eastham escapee Blackie Thompson and killed him in an exchange of gunfire.[73]

Five days after Thompson's death, members of the Tri-State Gang raided a National Guard armory in Morristown, Pennsylvania, stealing 13 pistols, three BARs, and 1,000 rounds of ammunition. On the 13th Philadelphia police raided a local hideout, arresting gang members Joseph Darrow, Robert Eckert, Roy Wiley, Beatrice Wilkerson, and Charles Zeid. Robert Mais suffered a gunshot wound, while Walter Legenza leaped from an elevated Wayne Street railroad station, fracturing both feet, but both eluded officers and reached New York City with Marie McKeever. On Monday, the 17th, federal grand jurors in Baltimore indicted Legenza, Mais and McKeever for stealing government property.[74]

On December 8 bandit Irvin Chapman pled guilty to bank robbery in El Dorado, Arkansas, receiving a 15-year prison term that matched his October sentence in Mississippi. As a Razorback prison fugitive, he returned to serve his latest sentence at the notorious prison farm in Tucker, while Magnolia State jailers waited their turn to confine him.[75]

One week after Chapman's guilty plea, on December 15, Indiana Governor Harry Leslie pardoned Anna Sage for her previous prostitution convictions, thus theoretically aiding her legal fight to remain in the Unites States. One week after that, on the 22nd, Marie Conforti received a 366-day sentence for harboring Homer Van Meter.[76]

Also on Saturday, December 22, six bandits robbed two banks in Okemah, Oklahoma, tying up employees and escaping with at least $17,000 (some reports claim $19,000), all without firing a shot. Lawmen, already scouring the Sooner State for fugitives Arthur Gooch and Ambrose Nix, flocked to Okemah, there receiving a tip that bandits responsible for the double heist might be found at a farm four miles west of town, owned by one Lee Mulky. Okemah Chief of Police Frank Gahagen drove to the Mulky spread with Murray Barton, Assistant Superintendent of the Oklahoma State Bureau of Investigation, and mounted covert surveillance on December 23, surprised to see a car approach bearing two men and a young woman. When the woman leapt from the vehicle, screaming, and fled on foot toward the farmhouse, Gahagen and Barton closed in, pistols drawn. Gunfire erupted, with one of the male suspects falling dead, while the other surrendered. Belatedly, the lawmen recognized their prisoners as Gooch and Nix (now deceased), arresting the young woman—Irene Sutton, Nix's girlfriend—for good measure. While Nix went to Okemah's Barry Funeral

Home, officers prepared to transport Gooch from Okemah's jail to Oklahoma City. Before they departed, a passerby tried to kill Gooch, seated in a patrol car, but the gunman's weapon misfired and police disarmed him, identifying him as John Hopkins, owner of a gas station Gooch and Nix had previously robbed. By December 26, confined in Muskogee, Gooch had been indicted for violations of the Dyer Act and Lindbergh Law.[77]

John Chase completed his auto delivery in Seattle, but his time was also running short. FBI agents missed him at the auto drop-off point but circulated among his ex-employers and other associates, demanding prompt notice if Chase surfaced. On December 27 he tried to borrow money from employees at a fish hatchery in Mount Shasta, California, where he'd worked in 1928, and his former friends telephoned authorities. Mount Shasta Chief of Police A.L. Roberts arrested Chase the same day before G-men from the Bureau's San Francisco office could arrive and claim that honor for themselves. Returned to Chicago by New Year's Eve, Chase faced indictment as the first suspect charged with murdering federal agents.[78]

Of the late Lester Gillis gang, only Fatso Negri remained at large, and the date of his apprehension remains shrouded in confusion nine decades after the fact. One vague source claims Negri was captured "soon after" the Barrington shootout, another that lawmen nabbed him sometime "before Christmas" 1934. Both contradict a more specific report, describing the December 29 arrest of San Francisco saloon bouncer "Bull" Kelly, whom G-men roughed up and jailed in their ongoing search for Negri, blacking both of Kelly's eyes. Fatso was seemingly still at large on December 30, when a Kentucky newspaper article announced that "the search for Negri will be continued relentlessly." During said search, G-men misidentified at least one suspect—Ralph de Paoli, aka "Phil Kelly"—as Negri.[79]

New Year's Day of 1935 saw prestigious Little, Brown and Company of Boston publish *Ten Thousand Public Enemies*, allegedly penned by J. Edgar Hoover and Courtney Cooper, largely ghostwritten by flacks from the FBI's Crime Records Division.[80] In the words of *Kirkus Reviews*, it was

> a thriller, of the first water, or rather the substance of which thrillers are model [sic]—the inside story of crime in the United States, and the criminal careers of such famous and notorious characters as Frank Nash, Verne Miller, Harvey Bailey, Machine Gun Kelly, Herb Farmer, Baby Face Nelson, John Paul Chase, Dillinger, William Donald Mayer, and innumerable other headliners of modern times. A tribute to the constructive work being done in the Department of Justice, Division of Investigation, by its director, Edgar J. Hoover [sic]. Factual material, at first hand. For those who like mystery stories, and crime reading; for the vast tabloid public; for the average reader who cannot resist newspaper scareheads. First class journalism, good drama, human interest stuff.[81]

On January 2 Alvin Scott pled guilty to conspiracy in the Urschel kidnapping. His sentence, like Clara Feldman's, was deferred pending decisions on the remaining defendants.[82]

That same Wednesday, G-men released Michael LaCapra from custody, based on his plea bargain that included testimony against other Kansas City massacre participants. On January 4, thanks in large part to LaCapra, Kansas City jurors convicted Union Station plotters Deafy Farmer, Dick Galatas, Frank Mulloy, and Doc Stacci for their roles in the conspiracy to liberate Frank Nash. One day later, the quartet received the maximum penalty under federal law, two years' imprisonment for each, plus $10,000 fines. Female codefendants Elizabeth Galatas, Vivian Mathias, and Frances Nash were also found guilty but granted conditional mercy: two years' probation and fines of $2,000 apiece.[83]

In New Jersey, opening day of Richard Hauptmann's kidnap-murder trial before Judge Thomas Trenchard eclipsed Kansas City's headlines on January 2. The circus atmosphere, described by journalist H.L. Mencken as "the greatest story since the Resurrection," unfolded in an atmosphere that made a fair trial physically impossible. Despite the gravity of the proceedings, prosecutor David Wilentz made do with eleven witnesses, including the Lindberghs; maid Betty Gow; three investigators; Dr. Condon and two more alleged eyewitnesses; one pathologist; and two "experts" for hire: graphologist John Tyrell and private "wood technologist" Arthur Koehler. Against that array, defense attorney Edward Reilly—described in one critical profile as "an over-the-hill alcoholic"—offered only four witnesses: Hauptmann himself, rival graphologist John Trendley, and two persons supporting Hauptmann's alibi.[84]

From beginning to end, the case against Hauptmann was circumstantial throughout and flimsy (or fabricated) at critical points. No witness saw Hauptmann enter the Lindbergh home or emerge with the toddler. Police produced no crime scene fingerprints or murder weapon. D.A. Wilentz also withheld crucial exculpatory evidence from Reilly, including FBI reports suggesting the crime required at least two abductors, the suicide of early suspect Violet Sharpe, and a litany of police blunders including failure to measure two sets of footprints found outside the Lindbergh home.[85] That said, Wilentz appeared to build a fairly solid case against Hauptmann, which included the following elements:

First, the gold certificates paid out as ransom for "Little Lindy," some of which Hauptmann admitted spending, with more found stashed at his home.[86]

Next, the several ransom notes, described by state witness Tyrell as including "many points of similarity" with copies of said notes made by Hauptmann under police direction. Those points included the letter "n"

8. Wanted Dead

drawn backward, plus distinctive misspellings—"boad" for "boat," "latter" for "later," "ouer" for "our," and "were" for "where." No one advised jurors that Hauptmann had been ordered to copy the errors from the original notes verbatim while providing his handwriting samples.[87]

Third, the kidnapper's crude homemade ladder, provoking a sneer from Hauptmann on the witness stand with a reminder that he was a professional carpenter. Arthur Koehler claimed that boards used to build the ladder matched those taken from Hauptmann's attic floor, although Hauptmann had ready access to better commercial lumber. One bit in particular, labeled "rail 16" of the ladder, included holes from four square nails described as "rare" (although billions had been used worldwide since Roman times and their production continues today). Hauptmann's criminal record from Germany also included using a ladder for a second-story burglary soon after World War I, which jurors found significant. Indeed, several jurors claimed they found the wood evidence more persuasive than the ransom notes, eyewitness claims, or Hauptmann's possession of ransom money.[88]

Fourth, alleged eyewitness testimony vaguely linked Hauptmann to the Lindbergh case. Charles Senior never saw his son's abductor but heard "Cemetery John's" voice on one occasion, later claiming that it "sounded like" Hauptmann's. Dr. Condon glimpsed "John" briefly, in a darkened graveyard, and fingered him at trial as Hauptmann, though he'd been unable to identify the suspect in a lineup following Richard's arrest. Two other witnesses, perhaps motivated by outstanding rewards, named Hauptmann as a man seen twice, "prowling around" Lindbergh's home before the abduction, and as the man who passed a note for Dr. Condon to a random New York taxi driver.[89]

Another bit of evidence presented by the state was Dr. Condon's telephone number, found penciled inside a closet at Hauptmann's home. D.A. Wilentz did not inform the court that a crafty reporter—privately identified but never named publicly—had confessed to writing that number himself, in a bid to increase newspaper circulation. That fabrication passed into the court record and into history as further "proof" of guilt. The *New York Times* ran a headline claiming that prior to trial, Hauptmann had "admitted noting" Condon's number and address (not found inside the closet).[90]

Hauptmann did himself no favors by testifying in his own defense, impressing jurors as arrogant and rude in his responses to D.A. Wilentz, stumbling over answers to some basic questions, and granting Wilentz a public platform for mocking Hauptmann's "Fisch story" alibi. At this remove, it is impossible to estimate the impact of juror bias against immigrants—and Germans more specifically, with the world war in mind—but the press seized every opportunity to hype vague or fabricated prosecution evidence, resulting in a preordained conviction and death sentence, both imposed on Saint Valentine's Day.[91]

While America fixated on New Jersey's "Trial of the Century," G-men left out of that drama drew closer to the ruthless Barker-Karpis gang. On January 5 Dock Barker met with William Harrison, a member of the crew deemed unreliable, at a farm near Hanover Park, Illinois, straddling the Cook-DuPage County line. After shooting Harrison, Dock dragged his corpse into a barn and set the barn on fire.[92]

Arthur "Dock" Barker with unidentified federal agent, January 8, 1935 (Library of Congress).

If Harrison's murder was meant to increase gang security, it failed. Three days later, despite his orders to refrain from staging raids, Melvin Purvis led G-men to an apartment on Chicago's Surf Street, arresting Dock and girlfriend Mildred Kuhlman. Simultaneously, other feds besieged a flat on North Pine Grove, fronting Lake Michigan, firing tear gas into lodgings occupied by Russell "Slim Gray" Gibson, William Bryan "Byron" Bolton, and their molls, Clara Fisher and Ruth Heidt. Bolton and the women readily surrendered, while Gibson donned a steel vest and tried to shoot his way out, slain by a Bureau marksman. Some accounts credit Agent Walter Walsh with killing Gibson, while others refute that assertion, naming Agent James "Doc" White as Gibson's slayer, adding that Walsh was present at Dock Barker's capture but not on the subsequent raid. Later in life, Walsh personally claimed both "honors," thus creating a hopeless conundrum of time and space.[93]

In custody, Bryan Bolton couldn't stop talking. Born circa 1898, a farm boy and world war navy seaman turned gangster, Bolton not only robbed banks and dispersed ransom money, but had previously hobnobbed with the Al Capone mob in Chicago. He knew where the bodies were buried and who had planted them, telling all—or most—of what he remembered in a rambling style that left G-men stunned. Among his tales, he spelled out details of 1929's Saint Valentine's Day massacre (still officially unsolved) and the murders that followed that carnage, including that of his mentor and sometime roommate Fred Goetz. Later working with the Barker-Karpis team, Bolton had profited from helping with the Hamm and Bremer kidnappings. He was also suspected of (but never charged with) killing Officer Miles Cunningham in September 1933, after the Barkers looted Chicago's Federal Reserve Bank. Bolton naturally denied that murder, his possible role only coming to light in 1969, with publication of Alvin Karpis's memoirs, which hardly qualified as evidence.[94]

Dock Barker proved more tight-lipped, refusing to say anything, even when G-men allegedly beat him with telephone books. As it happened, though, agents did not require cooperation from their prisoner. A map recovered from Dock's apartment pointed manhunters toward Ocklawaha, Florida, where Fred and "Ma" were hiding out under the surname "Blackburn." The map did not provide an address, but a letter from Fred—also found in Dock's flat—referred to Fred hunting a legendary alligator dubbed "Old Joe," said to inhabit nearby Lake Weir. That lead sent G-men south, questioning residents about newcomers to the region, finally focusing on a rented two-story house at 13250 East Highway C-25.[95]

On the morning of January 16 Earl Connelly invaded Ocklawaha with other members of the Bureau's "Flying Squad," including Ralph Brown, Charles "Jerry" Campbell, Robert Jones, John Madala, Thomas McDade, Sam McKee, John McLaughlin, T.H. Melvin, Alexander Muzzey, Daniel Sullivan, Charles Winstead, James White, and Grier Woltz. All were heavily armed, but only McDade had thought to bring along a camera. The feds hoped to find Alvin Karpis in the bungalow, but he'd departed three days earlier. The only occupants that Wednesday morning were Ma and Freddie. Black handyman Willie Woodbury, hired by the "Blackburns" for $20 weekly, lived with his wife in a small adjacent guest house.[96]

Accounts of the ensuing battle remain hopelessly confused today, nine decades after the fact. Most agree that G-men called out demanding surrender of anyone inside the house, threatening use of tear gas, whereupon someone (male or female) answered, saying, "All right, go ahead!" Some reports claim Fred Barker stepped onto the porch, firing a Tommy gun, and then ducked back inside, while others say he fired first from an upstairs window. Fifteen minutes of "intense firing" followed, until G-men began retreating to a safer distance. The Woodburys cowered under their bed, then escaped. Neighbors to the east, Mrs. A.F. Westberry and her daughter, narrowly escaped death as FBI bullets ripped through their bedroom, escaping on foot to another nearby house while Agent Brown fired machine-gun bursts over their heads. As the morning wore on, agents pumped at least 2,000 rounds into the rented house—one account says "nearly 3,500"—and the Barkers returned fire, moving from window to window, inflicting no casualties. Published estimates of the firefight's duration range from four to six hours, with G-men letting 30 minutes to an hour pass after the Barkers finally ceased firing. As the gun smoke and tear gas cleared, no agents were eager to enter the house. Finally, Earl Connelly summoned Willie Woodbury, handing him a steel vest and demanding that he go inside to see if anyone was still alive. After kicking through a locked door, Woodbury crept from room to room, finally calling through the shattered window of a front bedroom, "They all dead!"[97]

More needless confusion surrounds what G-men found inside the ruined house. Conflicting accounts claim Ma and Fred lay side-by-side, with Ma's arm around Fred (or cradling a Tommy gun). Another says the corpses sat upright, facing one another. Fred had absorbed multiple .45-caliber bullets—at least 11 or "more than a dozen"—while Ma bore only

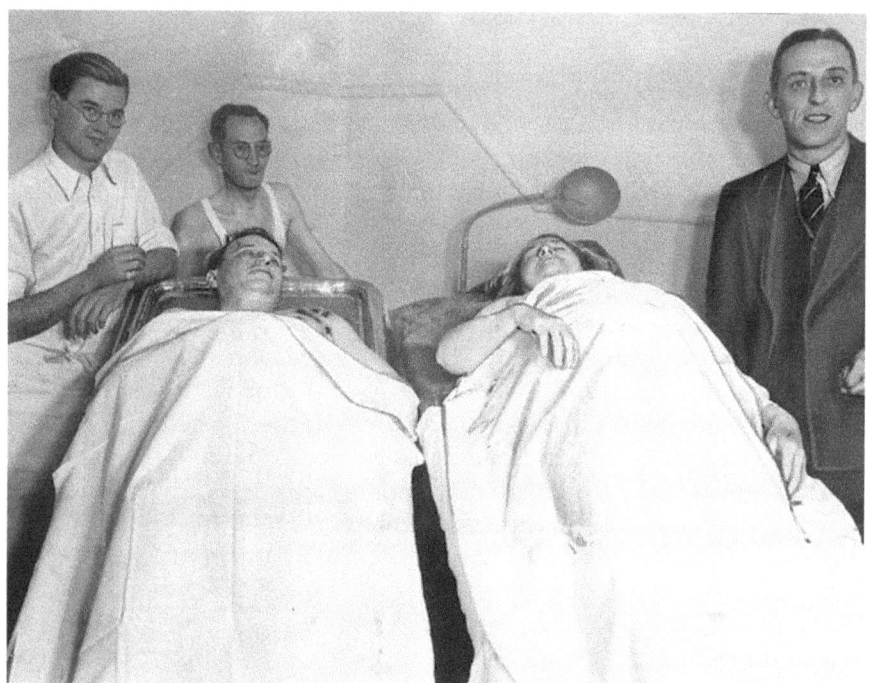

Unidentified morgue attendants pose with Fred and "Ma" Barker after their fatal shootout with FBI agents on January 16, 1935 (National Archives).

8. Wanted Dead

The Barker arsenal retrieved from their rented Florida home on January 16, 1935 (Library of Congress).

a single wound, placed by contradictory reports in her chest or forehead. Stories later circulated that she may have shot herself, as son Herman did in 1927, to avoid arrest. Agent McDade's photographs, published for the first time in 1991, finally resolved some of those riddles, showing Fred face down on the floor, Ma lying on her left side several feet away, with a Tommy gun beside her legs.[98]

A search of the bullet-riddled house revealed a small arsenal including two Tommy guns, two 12-gauge shotguns, one rifle, three pistols, plus various gun magazines and loose ammunition. Reports of other weapons found, including a world war vintage .30–06-caliber Lewis gun, are proved erroneous by McDade's collective photo of the Barker hardware laid out on the porch of their last home. Agents also recovered—or, at least, reported—$14,000 in $1,000 bills, with another $293 in currency of smaller denominations. G-men claimed the $14,000 represented Bremer ransom money, laundered by gang member Cassius McDonald on a sojourn to Havana, Cuba.[99]

A hearse delivered the Barkers to the Pyles Funeral Home in Ocala, where they remained on public display for eight months, unclaimed by family, while gawkers wore out the carpets. Paula Harmon, Fred's girlfriend and widow of bank robber Charles Harmon, suffered a breakdown upon learning of Fred's death, committed on January 20 to a state psychiatric hospital in Rusk, Texas.[100]

Confronted—and surprised—by public condemnation for his agents killing a 63-year-old woman, Hoover mounted an immediate campaign to demonize "Ma" Barker as the iron-fisted queen of a criminal empire. Within 24 hours of the Florida shootout, he told reporters, "She was a jealous old battle axe. She dictated who her four sons' lady friends were to be. We even heard that when they wanted to go out on a party they would go to a different town from the one where she was. There is a legend that she taught her sons never to be taken alive." According to Hoover, Ma also bedded a string of lovers (all anonymous), while serving as "the most vicious, dangerous, and resourceful criminal brain of the last decade."[101]

"Legends" aside, anyone conversant with FBI files released under the Freedom of Information Act will be familiar with the rampant collection of hearsay, rumors, vague claims from unidentified informers (or illegal wiretaps), and unsupported allegations of what agents "heard" or claimed "was said" by persons unknown. Another seeming fabrication is the Bureau's claim that Alvin Karpis, enraged by G-men killing Ma and Fred, sent a letter to Hoover threatening the Director's life. Karpis always denied it, and the alleged threat has never been published or released by Bureau headquarters. When challenged to prove its existence in 1994, the FBI could not. A twist on that story, provided by Alvin's nephew Albert Grooms, claims that Karpis *did* write to Hoover, but *before* the Ocklawaha battle. According to Grooms, "The letter said that Hoover was as queer as a three-dollar bill. Alvin and Ma laughed and laughed about that letter. Alvin said, 'Just imagine how that queer blew his stack.'"[102]

While G-men searched for Karpis nationwide, the hunt for gang stragglers pressed on. Ma and Fred were still under fire on January 16th, when lawmen nabbed Elmer Farmer in Bensonville, Illinois, logging his confession to participation in the Bremer snatch. One day later, in Marion, Indiana, G-men bagged Harold Alderton, owner of the house in Bensonville where Bremer was confined. Bremer himself toured and identified Alderton's home on the 19th. Agents came close to nabbing Karpis and cohort Harry Campbell at Atlantic City's Hotel Danmore ("Dan-Mor" in some accounts) on January 20, but the fugitives shot their way out, Karpis accidentally wounding Dolores Delaney in the process, with a "warning shot." Agents captured Delaney and Campbell's moll, while Karpis and Campbell kidnapped Dr. Horace Hunsicker near Allentown, Pennsylvania, leaving him bound and gagged in Ohio, dumping his car in Monroe, Michigan.[103]

Compensating for that failure, federal grand jurors returned new indictments in the Bremer case on January 22, superseding charges filed in May. Those charged with kidnapping included Harold Alderton, Dock Barker, Bryan Bolton, Harry Campbell, Volney Davis, Elmer Farmer, William Harrison, Karpis, Harry Sawyer, and William Weaver, plus unknown suspects "John Doe" and "Richard Roe." A second indictment, charging conspiracy in the Bremer abduction with deceased participants Fred Barker, Ma Barker, Russell Gibson, and Fred Goetz included Oliver Berg, Philip Delaney, Jess Doyle, John McLaughlin, Dr. Joseph Moran, Edna Murray, William Vidler, James Williams, and someone known only as "Whitey." Doyle and Murray fled to Kansas and dropped out of sight. Doc Moran remained missing, unaccounted for.[104]

In Texas, Miriam Ferguson pardoned an average 100 felons per month during her second term as governor, prompting accusations that she and her husband received bribes in the form of cash and land deeds for those favors. Preparing to leave office for the second and last time in January 1935, she granted mercy to Ralph Fults, wiping his record clean on the 10th. Nine days later, Raymond Hamilton and an unidentified companion stole $500 from a bank in Handley, Texas.[105]

Four days later, Indiana jailers transferred Jim Clark to Leavenworth, where he would spend two years before another move—that time to Alcatraz, as inmate No. 242.[106]

On January 17 G-men arrested Tri-State Gang leader Walter Legenza at Gotham's Presbyterian Hospital, rolling on from there to seize cohorts Edwin Cale and Martin Farrell elsewhere in Manhattan that same afternoon. One day later, agents joined NYPD officers to bag Robert Mais and Marie McKeever at their Manhattan Avenue apartment. Another four days passed before searchers hauled William Weiss's weighted corpse from Neshaminy Creek, in Pennsylvania's Bucks County, raising the charge on Farrell and cohort Frank Wiley from kidnapping to murder. Already facing execution for a Virginia homicide conviction, Legenza and Mais stood before original trial judge John Ingram again on January 24. In lieu of wasting time and money on another trial, Ingram set their execution date for February 2.[107]

Louis Piquett faced trial in January for harboring John Dillinger, conspiring with Drs. Cassidy and Loeser to hide the fugitive while he received plastic surgery. Loeser agreed to testify for the state, despite complaints of FBI "third-degree" tactics that left his nose smashed, causing "a significant change in Loeser's appearance" while confined. Prosecutors called Piquett "the brains of the Dillinger mob," but Piquett caught a break when Loeser missed court, returned to prison for parole violation on his 1913 narcotics conviction. Without his testimony, jurors deliberated for less than four hours, acquitting Piquett—but the feds weren't finished with him yet.[108]

On the last day of January, a new gang made its first known score, taking $3,396 from a bank in Portland, Oregon. Co-founder Joseph Paul "Dutch" Cretzer, born in Montana during April 1911, teamed with Arnold Thomas Kyle—18 months his senior, birthplace uncertain—to lead the outfit, with backup bandits Milton Hartmann and John Oscar Hetzer to start. Most of their heists occurred on the West Coast, and G-men would require some time to launch a manhunt for the crew.[109]

On February 2, 1935, Walter Legenza and Robert Mais kept their date with the electric chair. Mais went first, reportedly "much consoled" by ministrations from the prison's chaplain, while Legenza scorned all rituals, displaying no remorse. Some reports claim Legenza's reputation made his family refuse to claim his corpse, leaving him to be planted beneath a small headstone beside a busy road, in the former front yard of the local mortician's home, his marker shrouded to this day in poison ivy. Public records refute that tale, saying that defense attorney Haley Stanton promised Legenza a decent burial, persuading disgruntled kinfolk to inter him in a corner of the family's private cemetery at Orchid, in Virginia's Louisa County.[110]

Remnants of the Barrow gang kept making news in February. On the 4th, Floyd and Ray Hamilton took $1,000 from a bank in Carthage, Texas. A posse found their Dallas apartment that night, but the brothers escaped. Thirteen days later, Raymond and Ralph Fults hit a National Guard armory in Beaumont, stealing eight BARs, or perhaps Tommy guns (reports differ). On February 22, 23 relatives and friends of Clyde, Bonnie, and Ray Hamilton faced trial in Dallas for harboring federal fugitives. Jurors acquitted Hamilton's sister, Lillian McBride, while convicting defendants Audrey Barrow (Clyde's sister-in-law), Blanche Barrow, Cumie Barrow (Clyde's mother), L.C. Barrow (his brother, Audrey's spouse), Hilton Bybee, James Chambless, Alice Davis (Hamilton's mother), Steve Davis, Joe Bill Francis, Marie Francis (Clyde's sister), Floyd Hamilton, Mildred Hamilton (Floyd's wife), W.D. Jones, Billie Mace (Bonnie's sister), Henry Methvin, James Mullens, Emma Parker (Bonnie's mother), Mary O'Dare Pitts (Ray Hamilton's moll), and S.J. "Baldy" Whatley. Floyd Hamilton drew the maximum sentence, two years and a $10,000 fine. Jones also got two years, to run consecutively with his Texas prison time. L.C. Barrow got 13 months at Leavenworth, wife Audrey 15 days in jail. Billie Mace went off for a year at West Virginia's Alderson Prison. Cumie Barrow, Emma Parker, and Alice Davis drew 30 days apiece. Marie Francis and Mildred Hamilton were ordered to spend one hour behind bars. S.J. Whatley, the odd man out, avoided conviction when he was exposed as a police informer "squealing" on the Barrow gang, a fact that led to later fireworks in Dallas. Two days

8. Wanted Dead 159

Male defendants at Barrow-Parker harboring trial, February 1935. Left to right: Raymond Hamilton, S. J. Whatley, L. C. Barrow, Henry Methvin, William Jones, Joe Francis, James Mullen, Joe Chambless, Steve Davis (National Archives).

after the Dallas verdicts were rendered, Ray Hamilton and Ralph Fults stole a car in Tulsa, then eluded a police ambush in McKinney, Texas.[111]

Still rounding up remnants of the Barker-Karpis gang, G-men captured Volney Davis in Saint Louis on February 6. That same day, Dolores Delaney delivered son Raymond Alvin Karpaviecz in Philadelphia, handing the infant off to her parents in Chicago. On the 7th G-men arrested Jess Doyle and Edna Murray in Pittsburg, Kansas, but Volney Davie balanced the scale by escaping from federal custody at Yorkville, Illinois. Murray's brother, Harry Stanley, was charged with aiding and abetting his sister, subsequently sentenced to six months and fined $1,000. Murray, for her part, was acquitted of conspiracy in the Bremer case but returned to finish off her sentence in Missouri.[112]

On February 13 New Jersey jurors convicted Richard Hauptmann of first-degree murder for slaying Charles Lindbergh, Jr. Judge Trenchard wasted no time in sentencing Hauptmann to die in the electric chair at Trenton's state prison, sometime during the week of March 18 through the 24th. Considering the appeals process, no one expected him to meet his fate on time.[113]

Six days after Hauptmann's sentencing, on the 19th, John Paul Chase

Female defendants at Barrow-Parker harboring trial, February 1935. Left to right: Audrey Barrow, Cumie Barrow, Blanche Barrow, Mary O'Dare (National Archives).

appeared before Judge Philip Sullivan in Chicago, pleading not guilty to the November murders of Agents Cowley and Hollis.[114]

On February 28 G-men received their first notice of a "new" bank-robbing gang at work, this one below the Mason-Dixon Line. Its founders—all born in Sumter County, Florida—included John Riley Gant, his younger brother Hugh Archer Gant, and their brother-in-law Alva Dewey Hunt, married to their sister Katherine since 1914. Three years later, the Gant brothers and Hunt joined the U.S. Army and saw combat in France, returning to the Sunshine State changed men. Their first joint criminal enterprise was an auto theft ring, launched in October 1924. Nine years later they tried burglarizing a store, but lost John Gant in the process, gunned down while fleeing. After a decent mourning period and reconsideration of their "business" model, the surviving gang members raided a bank at Haines City, Florida, on February 28, 1935, escaping with $4,000.[115]

One day after the Florida holdup, on March 1, grand jurors in Kansas City indicted Adam Richetti on four counts of first-degree murder, for allegedly killing Raymond Caffrey, William Grooms, Frank Henderson, and Otto Reed. The panel stalled its charges, hoping that Richetti would be executed for a double murder in Boone County—Sheriff Roger Wilson and Sergeant Ben Booth of Missouri's Highway Patrol—shot while trying to arrest a pair of bank bandits outside Mexico, Missouri, on June 14, 1933. That case collapsed when the actual gunmen—George McNeely and George McKeever (unrelated to the Tri-State Gang's Marie McKeever)— were arrested and confessed in January 1935. McNeely received a life sentence, while McKeever was hanged at New Madrid on December 18, 1936, following rejection of an appeal wherein he tried to place his guilt back on Richetti's head.[116]

One day after Richetti's indictment, on March 2, members of the Irish O'Malley gang raided a bank in Neosho, Missouri. Several gunmen, numbered between four and eight in conflicting accounts, accosted bank janitor Leslie Cooper on his way to work, forcing him to open the safe while other employees arrived and were tied up before the bandits fled with an estimated $8,000 in cash and negotiable bonds. Some reports increase the outlaws' take to $18,000, possibly inflated for FDIC insurance claims.[117]

While reporters were garbling accounts of the Neosho holdup on March 2, a Doylestown, Pennsylvania, jury convicted Tri-State Gang members Martin Farrell and brother-in-law Frank Wiley of murdering "nightlife figure" William Weiss. Defense attorneys pled for mercy, but the panel sentenced both killers to die.[118]

Whatever the date of his capture, Fatso Negri pled guilty to harboring Baby Face Nelson at a San Francisco court hearing on March 4, 1935. Guards kept Negri separated from 12 codefendants facing identical charges, shielding Fatso for his offer to serve as a prosecution witness. Branded a "squealer" by his ex-friends, Negri told reporters, "I'm on the spot and I know it," expecting assassination at any moment.[119]

Eight days after Negri's plea bargain, on March 12, Missouri jurors convicted Harry Stanley and wife May of harboring Harry's sister, Edna Murray. Their judge fined Harry $1,000 and sentenced him to six months in Wichita's Sedgwick County jail, while handing May a five-year suspended sentence.[120]

J. Edgar Hoover loathed John Paul Chase almost as much as he despised Ma Barker, referring to Chase in press releases as "a rat with a patriotic-sounding name." On March 18 Chase went to trial for murdering Agent Sam Cowley, a parallel charge of killing Herman Hollis held in abeyance on the off chance that jurors voted for acquittal. Hoover need not have worried. The panel convicted Chase on March 24 and he entered Alcatraz one week later, as inmate No. 238.[121]

On March 19 Raymond Hamilton and Ralph Fults abducted Houston journalist Harry McCormick, treating him to an exclusive rendition of Hamilton's suffering at the hands of sadistic Texas prison guards. After releasing their captive to write his story, the bandits robbed a grocery store in San Antonio. On the 22nd, en route to Mississippi, Fults and Hamilton stopped at the site where Bonnie and Clyde were ambushed in 1934. Next, they stole a car from Hattiesburg on March 27, then took $933 from a Prentiss, Mississippi, bank the following day. When a 15-man posse pursued them, the duo captured their adversaries, later releasing them unharmed. From there, the fugitives split up, Hamilton returning to Texas, while Fults boarded a train bound for Louisville, Kentucky.[122]

On March 25, in Miami, "gun molls" Wynona Burdette and Dolores Delaney pled guilty to harboring Harry Campbell and Alvin Karpis, respectively, receiving identical two-year sentences at Milan, Michigan's federal lockup. As for Karpis and Campbell, while G-men scoured prospective hideouts nationwide, they were nowhere to be found.[123]

9

Melvin Who?

By April 2, 1935, Kansas City prosecutors Russell Boyle and Michael O'Hern had composed a list of 42 witnesses for Adam Richetti's impending murder trial. The published roster included Melvin Purvis and five other G-men; Kansas City Sheriff Thomas Bash and two of his deputies; Chief Fultz from Wellsville, Ohio; three Union Station employees; Rose Baird (minus sister Beulah); six residents of Hot Springs, Arkansas; and sundry others drawn from far-flung points between Los Angeles, Chicago, and Buffalo. That would not be the *final* list, however, since many would never be called, and others—including G-man Joe Lackey—would be substituted in eleventh-hour efforts to confuse court-appointed defenders James Daleo and Ralph Latshaw.[1]

Also on April 2, Dock Barker pled not guilty to the Bremer abduction in Saint Paul. Trial of 12 defendants commenced on April 15, with two cut from the roster when one pled guilty and Judge Matthew Joyce ruled that another had not been properly arraigned. While proceedings against the remaining 10 suspects dragged on, fugitives Alvin Karpis, Harry Campbell, and Joe Rich robbed a U.S. Mail truck at Warren, Ohio, on April 24, escaping with $72,000 ($1.4 million today). Two days later, police arrested Anthony Labrizetta and George Sargent, Akron residents with long police records, for that holdup, dismissing as false their pleas of innocence.[2]

Two days after Dock Barker's not-guilty plea in Saint Paul, J. Edgar Hoover sent a memo to second-in-command (and rumored paramour) Clyde Tolson, detailing a shake-up of field offices nationwide. Fifteen SAC's were slated for transfers to new assignments, most being promoted to larger offices. The single prominent exception was Melvin Purvis, maintaining his technical rank while Hoover shipped him from Chicago's teeming office to an outpost in Charlotte, North Carolina. Opened in 1908, then closed for lack of activity in January 1925, Charlotte's field office had reopened in February 1928 under ill-fated SAC Reed Vetterli. FBI historians ignore Purvis's transfer, skipping from 1928 to the outbreak of World War II in their history of the Charlotte office. In short, it was a Bureau backwater, making no further headlines until the mid–1950s.[3]

Purvis could vanish there, nearly without a trace.

Cleanup on the Gillis gang continued in San Francisco, where cronies Frank Cochran, Harry "Tex" Hall, Anthony "Soap" Marino, and Thomas "Tobe" Williams received prison terms on April 5 for harboring Baby Face Nelson. The real surprise came with acquittal of Louis "Doc Bones" Tambini and two codefendants.[4]

On the same day, those verdicts were delivered, 1,700 miles southwest of Frisco, Dallas County deputy sheriffs captured Raymond Hamilton at Grapevine, Texas. Ralph Fults, arriving in Springfield, Illinois, that afternoon, immediately boarded the next bus bound for Texas. On the 6th, authorities announced that Hamilton would be executed without any delays for new trials of his offenses committed while a fugitive. Fults reached Fort Worth on April 8, visited his mother in McKinney on the 9th, and stole a car at Renner on the 12th. Two days later, with an unidentified companion, he stole $900 from an oil refinery in Graham. Ralph's latest crime spree ended on April 17, with his capture by Denton County lawmen and a prompt return to Huntsville, pending extradition for trial on bank robbery charges in Mississippi.[5]

While Hoover had scuttled Hollywood's production of *Federal Dick*, he didn't object to films that praised his Bureau generally or himself in particular. On April 18 Warner Brothers released *G-Men*, starring James Cagney as FBI agent James "Brick" Davis, driven by a friend's murder to confront big-city mobsters seldom troubled by the Bureau in real life. Previously known for playing Chicago gangster Tom Powers in 1931's *The Public Enemy*, Cagney pleased viewers on either side of the law. *G-men*, budgeted at $307,000, earned back $1,963,000 at the box office ($37 million now), spawning more films, comic books, radio programs, and even G-men toys.[6]

On April 29, Tri-State Gang members Martin Farrell and Frank Wiley received matching death sentences in Doylestown, Pennsylvania, for William Weiss's murder.[7]

On May 3 FBI agents arrested Barker-Karpis associates Harry and Gladys Sawyer in Pass Christian, Mississippi. Three days later, when the prosecution rested its case, Judge Joyce dismissed all charges against Jess Doyle and Edna Murray as unproven, returning Murray to serve her Missouri sentence while Doyle faced trial for a 1933 bank holdup in Fairbury, Nebraska. (He later pled guilty, receiving a 10-year sentence). Elmer Farmer changed his plea to guilty on May 13, and Saint Paul jurors began deliberating their verdicts on the 16th. One day later they convicted Harold

9. Melvin Who?

Alderton, Dock Barker, Oliver Berg, John McLaughlin, Sr., and James Wilson, while acquitting Philip Delaney and William Vidler. Judge Joyce immediately sentenced Barker and Berg to life imprisonment.[8]

On May 10 Huntsville jailers executed Joe Palmer and Ray Hamilton for murdering Major Crowson during their 1934 escape from Eastham. Palmer went first, followed by a calm Hamilton, whose last recorded words were "Well, goodbye, all."[9]

Twenty days later, on May 30, federal grand jurors indicted Arthur Gooch for "kidnapping and injury by force." The following day, ex–Oklahoma governor turned U.S. district judge Robert Williams received Gooch's not-guilty plea from defense attorney E.M. Frye.[10]

Friday, May 30, found FBI headquarters claiming a triumphant cleanup of "all the major bank robberies in the Middle West"—more specifically, arrests crippling the "Irish O'Malley" gang after a two-year investigation costing $3 million ($58 million today). Conflicting reports claim leader Walter Holland was arrested on the 23rd or 27th. On the 24th agents nabbed Dewey Gilmore in Dallas. G-men found Russell Cooper at Fort Smith, Arkansas, on May 30. The following day, Kansas City SAC Edward Conroy teamed with Jackson County Sheriff Thomas Bash to surprise gang "chief lieutenant" Dapper Dan Heady.[11]

Meanwhile, across country, another kidnapping aroused public ire. Nine-year-old George Weyerhaeuser, Jr., left his Tacoma, Washington, school for lunch on May 24, to meet his sister and his wealthy family's chauffeur at nearby Annie Wright Seminary. but vanished en route. His parents notified police, who called the FBI. That evening, a special delivery letter reached the Weyerhaeuser home. Marked with George's signature on the back, it demanded $200,000 ransom in unmarked $5, $10, and $20 bills, with a classified newspaper ad signed "Percy Minnie" confirming agreement. The Weyerhaeusers complied, receiving a second letter on May 29. Aside from a note penned by George, indicating he was well, the letter ordered George Senior to register at Seattle's Ambassador Hotel and await further instructions.[12]

At 10:00 p.m. on the 29th, a taxi driver brought George Senior another message, directing him to a location where he found four sticks planted in the ground, with a white cloth attached and a note sending him on to another site. Arriving there, he found no further signs but waited for two hours, then returned to the Ambassador. Next morning an anonymous caller chastised him for failure to obey orders, then relented after George Senior explained. At 9:45 p.m. a man with a "European" accent phoned, directing Weyerhaeuser to an address where he found a note inside a tin can. Successive stops followed, ending on a dirt road where he dropped the ransom and retrieved a note promising to release George Junior within 30 hours. Walking back to his car, George Senior heard scuffling sounds and saw a man emerge from shrubbery 100 yards behind him, snatch the payoff, jump into a car, and drive away. At Weyerhaeuser's home, a final anxious wait began.[13]

On Saturday, June 1, FBI outcast Melvin Purvis traced fugitive Volney Davis to a Chicago address and collared him for the Bremer kidnapping. Two days later, Davis pled guilty in Saint Paul and received a life sentence. On June 7, Judge Joyce sentenced Harold Alderton and Elmer Farmer to 25 years, while handing Boss McLaughlin and James Wilson five years each. All were shipped to Leavenworth, before Alderton and Farmer joined Dock Barker and Davis at Alcatraz. Oliver Berg went to complete a prison term in Illinois, with a federal detainer hanging over his head. Wilson started serving his time at the U.S. Industrial Reformatory in Chillicothe, Ohio, then moved on to Northeastern Penitentiary at Lewisburg, Pennsylvania.[14]

On the day of Volney Davis's arrest, June 1, George Weyerhaeuser's kidnappers released him at a shack near Issaquah, Washington. To lawmen, he described his abduction, while taking a shortcut home, when a 40-ish man with brown hair asked him for directions, then dragged him into a car driven by an accomplice. The kidnappers, addressing each other as "Bill" and "Harry," covered George with a blanket and drove around for roughly an hour, then stopped and ordered him to sign the back of an envelope later mailed to his parents. Removing him from the car, his kidnappers blindfolded George Junior and carried him across a rushing stream, then led him by hand through a wooded area and shoved him into a hole four feet square, excavated beneath a large log, his right wrist and ankle chained. Around 10:00 p.m. on June 1 the abductors removed him from that lair, drove him around for another hour or so, then stashed him in another hole at the base of a tree, covered with tarpaper.[15]

Agents later determined that the two men, joined by a woman, placed George into a Ford's trunk on May 26, driving him from Washington to Idaho, finally handcuffing him to a tree near Blanchard, removed later that day to a house where the placed him in a closet. On Friday the 31st, George's captors told him they were leaving, whereupon he glimpsed a watch upon a table, giving the time as 5:55 p.m. Telling George that he would soon be going home, Bill and Harry drove him to the shack near Issaquah and left him there around 3:30 a.m. on June 1.[16]

The case began unraveling on June 2, when someone used one of the $20 ransom bills to buy a train ticket from Huntington, Oregon, to Salt Lake City, Utah. G-men identified the traveler as Harmon Metz Waley, tracking him as more bills surfaced at Salt Lake City discount stores. Founded in 1914 and closed in August 1920, then reopened eight months later, the

FBI's Salt Lake field office was understaffed, requiring aid from local police to stake out various discount outlets. On June 8 detectives caught Margaret Waley, wife of Harmon, passing a ransom bill and retrieved another from her purse. Despite conflicting lies, G-men obtained her home address and captured Harmon there. More lies ensued, before Harmon admitted kidnapping George Junior with William Dainard, a former cellmate from the Idaho State Penitentiary. Harmon claimed that Dainard had cheated him out of $5,000, while another $3,700 was burned in the Waleys's stove. Under further grilling, Harmon admitted buying a Ford roadster in Salt Lake City, registered to "Herman Von Metz," then directed G-men to a buried stash of $90,790, unearthed on June 11.[17]

Agents missed Dainard at the home of Margaret's parents, but fingerprints and other evidence gleaned from various hideouts linked Margaret to the abduction, despite Harmon's denials. Local police spotted Dainard in Butte, Montana, on June 9, but he eluded them, leaving $15,155 ransom money in his abandoned car. The FBI broadcast his description nationwide, with fliers reaching Mexico and Australia. Tacoma grand jurors indicted the trio on June 19. Harmon pled guilty two days later, receiving 45 years for kidnapping plus a concurrent two-year term for conspiracy. Margaret pled not guilty on June 22, her trial scheduled for July.[18]

Trouble continued for survivors of the Barrow gang in June. On the 7th Anna Steve received a three-month jail term for harboring her brother, Raymond Hamilton. On the 27th authorities moved Ralph Fults to Jackson, Mississippi, for trial on bank robbery charges.[19]

Mopping up leftovers from the Urschel kidnapping, Ben Laska and James Mathers faced trial in Oklahoma City on June 10. Their judge directed a verdict of acquittal for Mathers four days later, while jurors convicted Laska. On June 15 Laska received a 10-year sentence, then was freed on $10,000 bond pending appeal. That same day, Clara Feldman received a five-year sentence, matched by identical terms for husband Edward and codefendant Alvin Scott, with all three sentences suspended in favor of probation. Also on the 15th, Denver-based defense attorney Mollie Bert faced a perjury charge for statements made during the Oklahoma City trial. She pled not guilty and was freed on $5,000 bail.[20]

Arthur Gooch tried to change his not-guilty plea on June 8, but Judge Williams—renowned for his "hard-bitten reputation" and "mortal hatred of dishonesty"—rejected the change and scheduled trial for the 10th. That morning, Gooch again tried pleading guilty, but Williams refused once more, telegraphing his intent by saying that "a life sentence was the maximum he could give without a jury verdict." The Lindbergh Law's amendment, more to the judge's liking, specified that defendants "shall, upon conviction, be punished by death if the verdict of the jury shall so recommend." First up for the state was victim R.N. Baker, now chief of police in Paris, Texas, who described his assault and injury by decedent Ambrose Nix. It made no difference to jurors that only Nix had injured Baker, while Gooch bandaged his wound. They convicted Gooch and fixed his penalty at death, presumably pleasing Judge Williams, who set Gooch's execution date for June 19.[21]

Adam Richetti's trial for the Union Station massacre began on the same day as Arthur Gooch's, June 10, but 354 miles to the northwest in Kansas City. If Richetti was convicted, as all seemed to expect, it would write *finis* to the massacre investigation and by implication sanctify all that the FBI had done since then. In preparation for that final act, prosecutors Boyle and O'Hern had stacked the deck with perjured testimony, while defenders Daleo and Latshaw had no access to conflicting statements from shootout survivors, unaware of how the massacre began. It was as if the law of civil procedure, with its pre-trial discovery process, had ceased to exist.[22]

Jury selection proved laborious before Judge Ray Cowan. Few spectators were admitted, as 85 veniremen filled most of the gallery seats. With prosecutors touting their intent to see Richetti executed, each potential juror faced close questioning for suitability to please the state. Of those assembled, 22 were cut for voicing qualms about capital punishment, another 34 for sundry other causes. On June 11 Judge Cowan ordered Sheriff Thomas Bash to call more prospects and the show resumed, continuing into June 12. More veniremen were excused for viewing the films *Public Enemy* and *G-Men,* both of which featured WANTED posters of Floyd and Richetti. Eleven more were cut for admitting bias, one for a plea of poor health. Judge Cowan ordered the remaining 51 prospects held through a lunch break, then whittled that list to 15, with 12 final jurors—all men— seated and sworn in by 2:00 p.m. on June 13.[23]

The trial proper began with G-men packed behind D.A.s Boyle and O'Hern, shoulder to shoulder, grim-faced sentries of federal power. The prosecutor's table virtually overflowed with captured guns, including a Tommy gun lost by Charles Floyd in Ohio woodlands during his final hours. It was the state's task to connect them somehow with the massacre, no easy task if logic were applied. Both sides did their best to titillate jurors with underworld anecdotes, invoking Floyd's ghost for disparate reasons. Boyle fondled Floyd's machine gun frequently, until defense objections finally compelled Judge Cowan to restrain him. Daleo and Latshaw sought to blame Floyd for a share of the massacre, while disassociating their client from his notorious partner.[24]

Richetti's defenders began with a motion to quash Adam's indictment, citing the U.S. Constitution's Fifth, Sixth and Fourteenth Amendments, further claiming that Richetti was denied protection under Missouri's constitution during the grand jury's hearings. For added spice, they also complained that citizens of black, Italian, Greek and Asian extraction were barred from Missouri trial juries, citing the recent Supreme Court case of *Norris v. Alabama*, decided only six weeks earlier, requiring Alabama to admit black jurors. Judge Cowan denied all those motions, whereupon D.A. O'Hern began his recitation of events preceding the Union Station massacre. Too late, Richetti's defenders objected to introduction of Sheriff Killingsworth's abduction and the weapons involved, but by the time Judge Cowan ordered jurors to disregard that part of O'Hern's opening statement, they had already absorbed the information and would not forget it.[25]

The state's first witness, Arthur Muchow, was deputy warden of South Dakota's State Penitentiary at Sioux Falls. He briefed the court on Vern Miller's background, introducing photos and fingerprints taken in 1923, but under cross-examination admitted he was not an expert. Next up, Kansas City Chief of Detectives Tom Higgins recalled arresting Floyd twice in 1929, then admitted showing mug shots of Pretty Boy to Union Station witnesses without result after the massacre, further admitting that in two years' work on the case, Richetti's name had never surfaced. Judge Cowan excused the jury while Michael O'Hern and Ralph Latshaw squabbled over defense questioning of Higgins, finally settled by Cowan sustaining the state's objection. Recalled to the stand, Higgins described guns and scattered cartridges found at the massacre site, then described a search of Vern Miller's home, where G-men joined agents of the private Burns Detective Agency, hired by Higgins, retrieving no identifiable fingerprints.[26]

The day's third witness, Carl Zarder, was a records clerk at Leavenworth, employed since February 1931, called to sketch Frank Nash's record prior to escaping in October 1930. Leavenworth Deputy Warden Fred Morrison followed Zarder to the stand, confirming old mugshots of Nash, admitting minimal knowledge of former massacre suspects Harvey Bailey and Jim Clark. After Morrison's departure, prosecutors sought to introduce a deposition from Sheriff Killingsworth, describing his June 1933 abduction, but defense objections forced the state to call Killingsworth in person.[27]

Most Missourians already knew the tale of Killingsworth's kidnapping nine hours before the Union Station shootout, but prosecutors heightened the drama of its retelling, prompting the sheriff to hold Floyd's captured Tommy gun on his lap while testifying. After relating details of his abduction in Bolivar and safe release in Kansas City, Killingsworth focused on Floyd's submachine gun, noting that the weapon he'd seen in July 1933 had a 20-round magazine, while Exhibit 7 at trial was fitted with a 50-round drum. All Model 1921 Thompsons look alike, but Killingsworth claimed he could identify the gun in court because its model number—not the specific serial number—was "half ground off," an act irrelevant to identification. Judge Cowan overruled defense objections that the scratching proved nothing and permitted each juror to handle the weapon in turn. Next, over more objections, prosecutors handed Killingsworth one of the pistols seized when Floyd was killed, whereupon the sheriff "identified" it from a "contraption" attached to its hammer. Oddly, prosecutors claimed that only one .45 cartridge found at Union Station ballistically matched the confiscated automatic. On cross-examination, Killingsworth admitted that Richetti was drunk when they reached Kansas City, but claimed "he was getting over it."[28]

Mutual Life Insurance agent Walter Griffith a followed Killingsworth to the witness stand, describing his own abduction by Floyd and Richetti hours before the massacre. Naturally alarmed, he initially mistook Jack Killingsworth for an outlaw until passing conversation convinced him otherwise. Like Killingsworth, Griffith "identified" Floyd's pistol by its aberrant hammer, lacking any knowledge of its serial number or alleged ballistic links to Union Station.[29]

Police Chief Fultz was next up for the state, describing his shootout with Floyd and Richetti in October 1934, followed by Adam's surrender, with various firearms retrieved over the next 30–60 minutes. Richetti's defenders challenged the relevance of Fultz's testimony, overruled after O'Hern advised the court that "it don't rain guns" in Ohio. Again, jurors were left with the false impression that any firearms confiscated at Floyd's death must somehow be linked to Union Station.[30]

Melvin Purvis was the state's next witness, testifying that he was "on duty in Cincinnati and Indiana" when summoned to hunt Floyd in Ohio. Again, Richetti's lawyers objected on grounds of irrelevance, noting that Floyd died 15 months after the KC murders, and some 820 miles away. Judge Cowan sided with the prosecution, whereupon Purvis described Floyd's death and identified Exhibit 8 as one of Floyd's pistols—in fact, a "baby machine gun" altered by Hyman Lebman, although the gunsmith's name wasn't mentioned in court. One problem: Purvis never saw the gun until Agent Sam McKee presented it to him at the Travelers Hotel, 90 minutes after Floyd's death. Another glitch: Lebman's customized guns featured a muzzle brake, wooden foregrip, and extended magazine, minus the hammer "contraption" noted by Jack Killingsworth. They also fired full-automatic, raising questions as to why only a single cartridge linked to Floyd's weapon was found at Union Station. Purvis also fumbled other testimony, as in this exchange on cross-examination:

9. Melvin Who? 171

Q: Now, I will ask you to state if you weren't sent full reports from the Kansas City office concerning everything that they gathered in this Union Station killing case in 1933?
A: You mean me personally?
Q: Well, your office then.
A: My office was sent reports. I cannot say that they were sent every report.
Q: You examined them, didn't you?
A: No.
Q: And don't you know it to be a fact, Mr. Purvis, that up until the time of the capture of this defendant, there was never a government report that mentioned him as being implicated in the Union Station killing?
A: Oh, yes, he was mentioned many times before that as being implicated in the killing.
Q: All right. Now, take six weeks afterwards when they made what they called a semi-final report, was either Floyd or Ricchetti mentioned in that?
A: As to the exact length of time after the massacre when they were mentioned, I could not be certain, sir.
Q: A pretty long while, wasn't it, Mr. Purvis?
A: That is a matter of what one might consider a long time, and I can't say just when it was.[31]

As Purvis departed, the state formally introduced Floyd's pistols as Exhibits 8 and 10, Judge Cowan once again overruling defense objections as to relevance. Following Purvis to the stand, Agent Sam McKee echoed his SAC's description of the confrontation the killed Floyd. Again, defense objections were overruled. Thursday's final witness was Harry Wild, an FBI clerk who received Floyd's pistols and three magazines from Purvis at Melvin's home on October 24, 1934. Preparing them for shipment to Washington, Wild logged one's serial number but could find none on the second.[32]

Trial resumed on Friday morning, June 14, with FBI agent Frank Baughman—Assistant to the Director on all firearms-related matters—called to testify. He allegedly received two packages sent by Harry Wild "shortly after" Floyd's slaying, ostensibly two pistols marked as trial Exhibits 8 and 10. Baughman sent both guns to FBI ballistician Seth Wiard for test-firing, after which Director Hoover ordered Baughman to "destroy the firing capabilities of Exhibit 10" before it was lodged in a display case, in Hoover's personal office. Exhibit 8's serial number was missing, but Wiard allegedly restored it "in some fashion, apparently by grinding," although acid was and still remains the standard method in such cases, listing the number as 81479. Exhibit 10's unaltered serial number was 18001.[33]

Seth Wiard followed Baughman at trial. No longer an FBI employee, working instead for Cleveland's Lake Erie Chemical Company, an arms manufacturer, Wiard recalled test-firing both pistols. He marked both bullets and casings with a letter "C," dispatching them to the Bureau's Kansas City office. Again Adam's defenders objected, calling the tests irrelevant, and once again Judge Cowan overruled them. On cross-examination, Wiard admitted spending barely five months with the Bureau, from June 26 to November 27, 1934.[34]

The state's next task was to identify the Union Station gunmen as Miller, Floyd, and Richetti. The link in that chain was Agent Frank Smith, sole unscathed survivor the Union Station bloodbath. When the shooting started, Smith had ducked down in the backseat of Ray Caffrey's Chevrolet, feigning death until the "firing ceased" and the assailants fled. His first report to headquarters, in 1933, declared Smith was "unable to obtain any kind of a description of [the gunman nearest to him] and was unable to see anyone else who did the shooting." Truth was unwelcome at Richetti's trial, however, so Smith's story changed dramatically, identifying Vern Miller as the man who tried in vain to shoot him. He still couldn't name the other gunmen or supply their number, but that wouldn't matter if the state could link Miller persuasively to Floyd and Richetti in the jury's collective mind.[35]

Friday's next witness was Herman McFarland, a Kansas City resident who'd rented a house on Edgevale Road to one "B. C. Moore" in late March 1933, paid in advance through June. McFarland couldn't say when "Moore" moved out, but guessed that it was early June, some 10 days before newspapers reported the massacre. Shown a photo of Miller in court, McFarland identified him as missing tenant "Moore." Mrs. Earl Smith, another Edgevale Road resident, also identified Miller as neighbor "Moore," claiming that he, his wife, and their daughter occupied McFarland's house "continuously up until the day before the massacre." Some 10 days after the killings, a van arrived with two men aboard and removed the "Moore" family's furniture. As Mrs. Smith left the stand, defender Latshaw sought exclusion of all evidence relating to events before the Union Station killings, and specifically objected to the impending testimony of Frances Nash, concerning events at Hot Springs and Joplin after her husband's arrest. Judge Cowan overruled both objections.[36]

Thus cleared to discuss whatever the state might desire, Jelly's widow took the stand next. She described her first meetings with Nash and Vern Miller, both during summer 1931, and admitted sharing digs with Frank, Vern, and Vi Mathias several times, at Lake Geneva, Wisconsin, in New York City, and at Oak Park, Illinois. After Jelly's last arrest, she'd stayed with Deafy Farmer and his wife near Joplin, traveling with Dick Galatas, and had phoned Miller from Farmer's safe house. Around midnight on June 16, 1933, Miller had called back with orders for Frances to visit Louis Stacci's roadhouse, then hide with a cousin in Winona, Illinois. Lawyer Daleo cross-examined Frances, rehashing her movements and relationships from

1931 through Union Station's murders. Frances claimed she'd only learned Jelly's real name from Galatas on June 16, 1933, suggesting that Frances only testified to spare herself from prosecution on Mann Act charges and for harboring her husband. After she was excused, Daleo renewed his objection to testimony on phone calls prior to June 17, 1933, overruled once again by Judge Cowan.[37]

Encouraged, D.A. Boyle called Val Mintun, district manager for Southwestern Bell Telephone Company in Kansas City. He verified "B. C. Moore's" contract for phone service to the rented house on Edgevale Road, continuing from April 4 to July 6, 1933, then validated Exhibit No. 18, a record of a pay phone call from Union Station to Esther Farmer's Joplin home at 12:05 p.m. on massacre day. Richetti's defenders objected, noting that Mintun possessed no record of that conversation, and Judge Cowan disappointed them again. Southwestern Bell operator Verna Felton came next, verifying that call, while admitting that she could not name the parties speaking. SWB manager George Smith and Joplin operator Wilma Swofford added confirmations that the call was made, but neither could identify the caller or receipient.[38]

Proceeding to the actual murders, D.A. Boyle recalled Chief of Detectives Higgins, recording his discovery of "four or five" shell casings, marking each with a "T" before delivering them to freelance ballistician Merle Gill. Before the court recessed for lunch, Higgins also described a mugshot of Frank Nash cohort and early massacre suspect Bernard Phillips, which Higgins had shown to Union Station witness Lottie West before passing it on to Merle Gill.[39]

Louise Brown, ex-maid for the Smiths on Edgevale Road, appeared for the state after lunch. She recalled seeing "a lot of cars coming and going" at the "Moore" home prior to June 17, 1933, and described Miller loading his car with suitcases on June 23, "using only one arm," suggesting an injury.[40]

Merle Gill, denounced in FBI memos from March 1934, followed Brown to the stand—his 191st courtroom appearance—describing his work with KCPD, examining 11,000 guns and 20,000 cartridge casings since 1927. After sketching the basics of ballistic science, Gill identified Exhibits 21 and 22 as .45-calber casings recovered from Union Station, both allegedly bearing marks from the same weapon's firing pin. From there, he "connected" the Tommy gun and a pistol confiscated after Floyd's death to the Union Station murders but did not explain why Floyd might have fired both within a few hectic seconds. As for Adam's pistol, seized from him in October 1934, it matched no evidence from Kansas City. Gill also described two 16-gauge shotgun shells delivered to him by Tom Higgins, one loaded with steel ball bearings identical to one found "in or near" Ray Caffrey's corpse. Gill had requested Otto Reed's shotgun for test-firing, but never received it.[41]

Massacre survivor Reed Vetterli followed Gill to the stand, describing his years of Bureau service and the lead-in to his wounding. Like Frank Smith, Vetterli changed his story for the court, omitting his initial I.D. of Lansing fugitive Bob Brady as one of the Union Station gunmen, belatedly naming Charles Floyd as the only shooter he saw. On cross-examination, Vetterli admitted that neither Floyd nor Richetti were named as massacre suspects in any FBI memos before the Bureau transferred him from his Kansas City post to Indianapolis, serving as SAC of the field office closed in 1929, then reopened in May 1934.[42]

The state's next witness, Lottie West, was also its weakest. We recall her original claim that she'd arrived for work that morning to find Charles Floyd seated at her desk. No other employees saw Floyd, and several contradicted West, coworker Harry Blanchard as the non-suspect in question. After first sighting "Floyd," West repeated her fable of six Benedictine nuns seeking a taxi, seen by no one else either arriving or leaving the depot on June 17. Moments after that imaginary incident, West had told police she heard shots and observed two machine-gunners and a man armed with two pistols—one "blue," the other "nickel-plated"—firing at two parked cars. While all around her fled for cover, West alone—in her account—stood calmly exposed to observe the action. Alas, her original statement, like so many others, was illegally withheld from the defense by Adam's prosecutors. At trial, D.A. O'Hern asked West if she saw in court the man who'd carried two "revolvers"—both actually automatics—at the Union Station ambush. She unhesitatingly picked out Richetti, and with that, Judge Cowan adjourned for the day.[43]

Agent Joe Lackey, reassigned to San Antonio when he regained mobility in September 1933, was the state's first witness on Saturday, June 15. His recitation of the Union Station massacre deviated significantly from his original statements—and from the facts, carefully avoiding a confession that his handling of an unfamiliar weapon had sparked the bloodshed two years earlier. This day in court, Lackey declared he had been carrying a .38 revolver and a 12-gauge shotgun, despite the Bureau's mythical ban on guns before June 1934. He also claimed that Otto Reed carried a 12-gauge but did not refer to borrowing the chief's weapon. After noting that Reed's shotgun was "in the same position as mine," Lackey "secured" the piece, then heard warning shouts of "Up, up, up!" He glimpsed a "heavyset, broad-shouldered" gunman standing near the Chevrolet, while a second man ran north behind the first, whom he now identified in court as Richetti. Gunshots followed "a very short time later," four rounds rather than the three acknowledged earlier striking Lackey *from behind*, two slugs remaining in his body as he testified. He "could not confirm or deny" if Reed's shotgun were ever fired but insisted that he thought it was a

9. Melvin Who?

12-gauge, rather than a smaller 16-gauge. Lackey acknowledged that early Bureau circulars named suspect Harvey Bailey, never mentioning Floyd or Richetti. He couldn't remember his time in the hospital, or an interview he'd granted to the *Kansas City Star* on June 20, 1933, yet declared that he "did not give all of the information to the newspaper reporters as he was not allowed to and he did not tell the truth to the reporters concerning this matter."[44]

That much, at least, was undoubtedly true.

D.A. Boyle's next witness, Jackson County Deputy Sheriff Harry Turner, was assigned to photograph and fingerprint all prisoners booked at the county jail. He readily identified Richetti's booking prints from 1934—which were, in any case irrelevant to the identify of Union Station's murderers.[45]

G-man John Brennen followed Turner, describing a search of Vern Miller's house on Edgevale Road, made with Agent Dwight Brantley and KCPD Chief of Detectives Jack Jenkins 12 days after the killings. Richetti's attorneys objected, citing evidence that Higgins and Reed Vetterli searched the house on June 26 and found nothing, and while Judge Cowan overruled that objection, prosecutors voluntarily withdrew Brennen as a witness, summoning Sheriff Tom Brash in his place.[46]

Brash was meant to circumvent the muddle over searches and discoveries. The best that he could do was recollection of a chat with the defendant when Richetti was transported from Ohio in October 1934. According to the sheriff, Adam first denied that he had ever previously been in Kansas City, then admitted to arriving on the night before the Union Station murders, departing "sometime in the middle of the night, or early morning." Brash could do no more, and after sharing that tale was excused. D.A. Boyle then recalled Agent Brennen, while Richetti's team objected (overruled). A second-generation fingerprint analyst, Brennen described lifting Richetti's prints from two beer bottles—not just one—found on Edgevale Road, state's Exhibits 25 and 26. FBI fingerprint expert Jerry Murphy followed Brennen, citing a "definite match" of Adam's two beer bottle prints, which admittedly proved nothing about *when* the prints were made on bottles found coated with dust.[47]

O'Hern's next witness was Dr. C.G. Leitch, Chief Deputy Coroner for Jackson County. who had autopsied victim Frank Hermanson, finding a single gunshot entry wound on the left side of Hermanson's head, exiting from the rear. Even with no projectile found, Leitch opined that death was caused by a "bullet," not a ball bearing fired from a shotgun. Adam's defenders then recalled Lottie West, questioning her description of victim William Grooms, whom she'd referred to as a "rather slender man" about the height of D.A. Boyle. That clashed with other descriptions of Grooms, a broad-shouldered man much larger than Boyle. Unable to explain yet another flubbed account, West was excused once more and court recessed until Monday morning.[48]

The trial's last day of testimony began at 9:30 a.m. on the Union Station shootout's second anniversary. D.A. Graves recalled Agent Vetterli, seeking to determine when he'd searched the Miller home on Edgevale Road with Tom Higgins, but the best that Vetterli could manage was "sometime in the latter part of June" 1933. "Approximately three days after that," whenever *that* was, Higgins and his boss, then–Director of Police Eugene Reppert—both indicted for perjury about the Union Station case in November 1934—asked Vetterli's permission for another search. Still vague on dates, Vetterli "distinctly remembered" accompanying them "sometime after" his office received beer bottles bearing Richetti's fingerprints. After cross-examination, Ralph Latshaw moved to exclude the bottles and other items of evidence, overruled by Judge Cowan. He then sought a directed verdict of acquittal, based on a faulty indictment (likewise overruled).[49]

Richetti's defenders called their first witness, Union Station employee Theodore Scott, after the state rested its case. He'd been helping a paraplegic traveler into a taxi when shooting began, prompting Scott to seek cover while Patrolman Myron Fanning emerged and fired "a couple of times" at the fleeing gunmen. Scott saw none of the shooters from hiding and refused to identify Richetti but described "two small dark cars" racing away, one with three men in its backseat. Likewise, Scott did not see Lottie West outside the station till she followed Patrolman Fanning, shouting, "Shoot them Mike! Shoot them!" Cross-examined by D.A. O'Hern, Scott insisted that West was not outside when the shooting began.[50]

Next up for the defense, cabbie Robert Fritts was helping "a crippled fellow" into his taxi when gunfire erupted. He saw two triggerman "across the street," and a third crouching behind a car "headed in the wrong direction," under fire from Officer Fanning. Fritts had not seen Lottie West or her imaginary nuns at any time, nor could he pick Richetti from a lineup in October 1934.[51]

The next defense witness was cabbie Harry Orr, who corroborated colleague Fritts in all respects, claiming Richetti bore no resemblance to the fleeing gunman Orr observed. Orr's story held up under cross-examination by D.A. O'Hern.[52]

A third taxi driver, Alava Parman, followed Orr to the stand. He'd seen lawmen escort Frank Nash from the station, approaching two cars when pistol and machine-gun fire rang out. Parman had glimpsed one officer falling, "shot in the face." He could not see the shooters due to parked cars obstructing his view but *did* see one man "walk into the street" seconds later, wearing "a soft hat, a brown suit, and two-toned buttoned shoes." Despite those details, he failed to identify Richetti from an October lineup.[53]

Next, the defense called William Gordon, superintendent of KCPD's Identification Bureau. Following the massacre, he'd issued "pickup orders" for suspected gunmen Harvey Bailey, Bob Brady, Jim Clark, and Bernard Phillips, but none for Floyd or Richetti. Eloise Jones, a clerk at the KCPD Bureau of Records, confirmed those pickup orders and radio logs containing mention of the rumored gunmen named by Gordon.[54]

The defense then called Detective William Eldridge, who'd interrogated Agent Lackey at a local hospital, reporting Lackey's statement that he only glimpsed two gunmen. According to Eldridge, Lackey said, "It was just a flash, and he couldn't state, couldn't tell me just who they were, what they looked like, or anything, it was done too—just a flash. The only description that he could give was that these men appeared to be Americans."[55]

After the lunch break, Ralph Latshaw recalled Eloise Jones, who went over the KCPD radio logs. They were vague at best, describing "two white males, neatly shaven, wearing blue shirts, driving a dark Chevrolet coup/sedan with a Missouri license plate of 428–329 or 428–239 heading south through Penn Valley Park, probably headed for Kansas." Next up, Leroy Smith, continuity editor for local KMBC Radio, confirmed that nebulous description of the slayers.[56]

Latshaw then introduced the first federal indictment against Union Station conspirators, dating from September 1933, which omitted his client's name from a list including Harvey Bailey, Robert Brady, Louis Conner, Esther and Herbert Farmer, Richard Galatas, Vern Miller, Frank Mulloy, Frances Nash, Louis Stacci, and Wilbur Underhill. Richetti's belated indictment, dated November 5, 1934, added his name and Charles Floyd's to the previous list, while including Adam's account of his first visit to Kansas City. In Richetti's words, he admitted entering KC on the night of June 16, 1933, but mistook it for Lee's Summit, 20 miles farther southeast. He admitted the Killingsworth-Griffin abductions, but said he was already drunk on arrival and smoked marijuana that same night with Floyd and a man Richetti didn't know. From there, before dawn on the 17th, Richetti claimed that Floyd had driven him to Texarkana, Texas, staying at an address he could not recall. Dismissing Adam's tale as false, grand jurors had charged him with four counts of murder, presumably omitting victim Jelly Nash.[57]

Judge Cowan overruled Latishaw's latest attempt to quash Adam's indictment, then issued his charge to the jury. It covered 10 points of law, with No. 2 the most critical, stating, "All persons are equally guilty who act together with a common intent in the commission of a crime, and a crime so committed by two or more persons acting jointly is the act of all and each one so acting." Before day's end, the panel returned its verdict: "We, the jury find the defendant, Adam Richetti, guilty of murder in the first degree, and assess his punishment at death." Judge Cowan duly sentenced him to hang, while Adam's defenders prepared an appeal.[58]

Elsewhere in June, more cases ran their course. On June 4, Chicago police captured Joseph Fox, the last remaining fugitive from Michigan City's September 1933 breakout. Louis Piquett faced trial for harboring Homer Van Meter on June 18, convicted one week later, and received a two-year prison term, topped with a $10,000 fine, on the following day.[59]

June 10 was a hectic day for starting trials, Ben Laska and James Mathers facing judgment in Oklahoma City for conspiring in the Urschel kidnapping. Mathers won a directed acquittal on the 14th, based in insufficient evidence, but jurors convicted Laska the next day, resulting in a 10-year prison term.[60]

On June 20, Bruno Hauptmann's attorneys appealed his conviction to New Jersey's Supreme Court.[61]

The cleanup of Saint Paul's Augean stables moved forward on June 24, Police Commissioner Harry Warren declaring that city officers had maintained a "startling" alliance with felons since 1900. He instantly suspended Chief Culligan and four other officers, while demanding resignations from four more.[62]

Two days later, in Edwardsville, Illinois, kidnapper "Irish O'Malley" interrupted his trial to plead guilty in the Luer abduction. Circuit Judge Dick Mudge wasted no time in pronouncing a life sentence.[63]

On July 5, in Tacoma, Margaret Waley pled not-guilty to charges of kidnapping George Weyerhaeuser, Jr. Jurors disagreed, convicting her on the 9th, whereupon she received two concurrent 20-year sentences at Milan, Michigan's federal lockup.[64]

One day later, Melvin Purvis gave ex-friend "Jayee" Hoover what he'd been seeking for months, resigning from the FBI. That did not fully separate him from the Bureau, though. In 1936 he hosted a children's radio program called "Junior G-Men," then became the public face of breakfast cereal Post Toasties promotional detective club, inviting children to become "secret operators" in his "Law and Order Patrols." Some Boy Scout troops attached themselves to Junior G-man clubs, while Parker Brothers released "Melvin Purvis' 'G'-Men Detective Game" in 1937. Three years later, Universal Studios screened a *Junior G-Men* serial, followed in 1942 by *Junior G-Men of the Air*. One may only imaging Director Hoover's simmering fury as his castoff former friend and confidante continued in the public eye beyond the "crime war's" end.[65]

In early July, fear of mob violence prompted officers to transfer Arthur Gooch from Muskogee's jail to McAlester's state prison for safekeeping.

9. Melvin Who?

Bankrolled by an uncle—also named Arthur Gooch—"Little Arthur" retained attorneys W.F. Rampendahl and Chal Wheeler, who submitted an Assignment of Errors to the Tenth Circuit Court of Appeals, listing 14 alleged mistakes committed by Gooch's trial court. Included on that list were claims that police had no cause to accost Gooch and Nix, that they possessed no valid arrest warrant, that Gooch and Nix rightly resisted an illegal arrest, that Officer Baker was trespassing when injured, and that his injury occurred prior to the kidnapping. With time running short, Gooch settled in to wait.[66]

By mid–July, Jamie Wallace's transcribed recordings of Saint Paul police conversations filled 3,000 typewritten pages. Harry Warren passed them to Mayor Gehan. The *Daily News* published its first in a series of exposés on the 24th, prompting once-suspended Police Chief Culligan's resignation. His replacement, 23-year SPPD veteran Gustave Harfuss, served as Acting Chief until June 2, 1936, by which time the "O'Connor lay-over system" was a fading memory.[67]

On August 1, the Hunt-Gantt gang returned to action, looting an undisclosed amount of cash from a bank in Mulberry, Florida.[68]

Alvin Karpis kept moving after his escape from G-men in Atlantic City, hiding in a Toledo brothel run by Edith Barry until June 1935, then idling in Hot Springs, Arkansas. With new accomplice Fred Hunter, Karpis visited Saratoga Springs, New York, in August, sighted on the 13th, but he eluded capture once again. Running back to Hot Springs, he found shelter with another brothel madam, Grace Goldstein, while Hunter roomed with Connie Morris, one of Goldstein's working girls. *Liberty* magazine offered a $5,000 reward for Karpis dead, emphasizing that proviso with no mention of live capture, but G-men were no closer to their prey.[69]

On August 16 Agent Nelson Klein, with several other feds, went hunting for interstate stolen-car dealer George Barrett at West College Corner, Indiana. They missed him at his brother's home, then cornered Barrett at a local garage soon afterward. Agent Klein suffered mortal wounds but returned fire, striking Barrett in both legs, resulting in his capture and hospitalization.[70]

Five days later, at New Pike, New York, police found Union Station massacre plotter-turned-stoolpigeon Jimmy Needles LaCapra murdered by persons unknown, likely in retaliation for his plea bargain.[71]

Arthur Gooch caught a break in late August, when federal judges Sam Bratton, George McDermott, and Orie Phillips certified two points of his appeal for consideration by the U.S. Supreme Court.[72]

On August 27 Hoover's publicity department trumpeted the final break-up of the "Irish O'Malley" gang, with a total of 19 arrests. All were run to ground by G-men save for Otto Jackson, collared while drunk on

August 1 by two Kansas City patrolmen. Even then, the Bureau was confused, however, counting the "O'Malley" crew as one gang, while identifying several cohorts as members of a "closely associated" outfit dubbed "Six Daring Bandits, Inc."[73]

One day later, acting on information supplied by Volney Davis and Edna Murray, G-men unearthed Red Hamilton from his grave near Oswego, Illinois. The decomposed remains, identified from prison dental records, failed to end rumors of Hamilton's survival and escape to Canada.[74]

Pursuit of Barker gang stragglers continued with the September 1 arrests of fugitives William "Lapland Willie" Weaver and Myrtle Eaton by G-men in Allandale, Florida, residing as "Mr. and Mrs. J.W. Osborne." Two days later, Oklahoma authorities paroled bank robber Sam Coker, allegedly after receiving payoffs from friends of Alvin Karpis. On the 26th, a man's badly decomposed corpse washed ashore from Lake Erie at Crystal Beach, Ontario. While never formally identified, the body was presumed by some authorities to be the last remains of Dr. Joseph Moran. (Alvin Karpis contradicted that assumption in his 1971 autobiography, claiming that Dock and Fred Barker planted Moran in a Michigan lime pit.) One day later, on the 27th, Ohio jurors wrongfully convicted Anthony Labrizetta and George Sargent of the April mail truck robbery Karpis and cronies committed. Before pronouncement of their 25-year sentences, U.S. Attorney Emerich Freed told reporters, "Because of their past records, these men should be put away where there will be no chance of their getting out for a long time."[75]

On September 3, Mississippi jurors convicted Ralph Fults of bank robbery, resulting in a 50-year sentence at Parchman prison farm.[76]

Two days later, three bandits tried to rob a bank in Blythedale, Missouri, foiled when cashier Truman White escaped and raised the alarm. G-men and Missouri Highway Patrol officers trailed the fugitives to their hideout, backed by armed civilians, and a shootout ensued. Robert Jones, age 25, used a borrowed rifle to wound gunman Raymond Fletcher in the hip, disabling him, then shot accomplice Clarence Sparger, who escaped through a cornfield and was rescued by a fourth accomplice passing in a car, believed to be bandit John Langan ("Langdon" in some reports). Captured with Fletcher was Charles "Bad Eye" Arbogast, nicknamed for a cataract, who'd been imprisoned from 1923 to '31, before Governor Henry Caulfield commuted the remainder of his 36-year robbery sentence. Langan and Sparger escaped from the trap, while Arbogast and Fletcher went to jail.[77]

Mid–September witnessed a series of drugstore robberies in Kansas City, Missouri, carried out by a man and woman. Witnesses identified the female bandit from mugshots as Vivian Chase—dubbed "Girl Bandit No. 1"—but police had no luck tracing her.[78]

9. Melvin Who?

On September 19 rumors spread that Fatso Negri had been murdered for testifying against Lester Gillis's accomplices at trial. An anonymous note sent to DOJ agents "through underworld channels" in Reno declared, "Negri's mouth has been slit—because he squealed." Charles Upton, Negri's probation officer, told reporters he hadn't heard from Fatso since Wednesday the 11th, adding, "He is supposed to report to me, in person or by mail, at least once a week. Never before has he allowed more than seven days to pass between reports." While speculation ran rampant, authorities freed Helen Gillis from prison on the 26th.[79]

On September 21, Art O'Leary pled guilty to harboring John Dillinger, sentenced to one year's probation. That same day, Dr. Harold Cassidy received an identical sentence for aiding in Dillinger's plastic surgery, while Dr. Wilhelm Loeser was released from custody.[80]

The bodies of Kate and Fred Barker lay unclaimed in Ocala for eight months, until relatives grudgingly retrieved them on October 1, 1935, interring them next to Herman at Williams Timberhill Cemetery in Welch, Oklahoma. Ten days later, Chicago jurors convicted Bremer kidnapping accomplice Brian Austin, resulting in a life prison term.[81]

On October 2 Basil Banghart and two fellow inmates, armed with scissors from the Menard Prison tailor shop, commandeered a laundry truck, crashing through the gate to freedom. Police recaptured them on the 12th, wounding Banghart in the process. Upon recovery, he was transferred to maximum security at Joliet.[82]

On October 9 New Jersey's Supreme Court rejected Bruno Hauptmann's appeal, affirming his conviction and sentence. Six days later his defense team took their case to the U.S. Supreme Court.[83]

While Hauptmann's team fought on against all odds, a new gang—small but ruthless and determined—organized in Indiana. It started with three friends, conceived by Alfred James "Al" Brady, born near Kentland in 1910. His father died in 1912, whereupon Brady's mother moved to Indianapolis and remarried. She died in 1926, and Brady's stepfather killed himself two years later. High school classmates later said Al "didn't seem to be particularly interested in gangsters but talked a lot about big-shot bootleggers." Alone in the world, Brady worked at a clothing store, then as a photographer's errand boy, sold hot tamales, and sorted mail for the *Indianapolis Star* during 1931 and '32. Drifting thereafter, he was jailed for vagrancy on July 10, 1934, under the alias "James Reid." Friends persuaded police to drop that charge, but Al was back behind bars 11 days later, charged with possessing stolen property. That rap sent him to the state farm at Greencastle for 180 days. A conflicting report claims Brady stole a car in 1930, spending time at the Indiana Reformatory in Pendleton. In either case, upon release, he visited an acquaintance's farm near

Alfred Brady expressed a desire to "make John Dillinger look like a piker" with multiple robberies and murders (National Archives).

Hanover, where he befriended next-door neighbor Rhuel James Dalhover. FBI historians claim he next surfaced in August 1935, back in Indianapolis, working briefly at a mattress factory and as a welder for an auto factory, then told relatives he was hitting the road as an insurance inspector.[84]

Rhuel Dalhover, born in 1906 at Madison, Indiana, lived and attended classes there until 1917, when he and brother George were sent to reform school at Plainfield for robbing a rural grocery store at Madison County's Plow Handle Point. Released in December 1918, Rhuel joined his mother in Cincinnati, holding various jobs through spring 1926, and married in December 1925, fathering two children. His wife's grandfather was a moonshiner, Dalhover making liquor deliveries until a Kentucky arrest saw him sentenced to 100 days and a $100 fine. Three weeks into his sentence, Rhuel escaped with accomplice-brother George, obtained a car in Madison, Indiana, then stole another when the first broke down in New Mexico. Captured there, the brothers received two-year terms for assault with intent to kill. Released before Thanksgiving 1929, Rhuel returned to moonshining in Ohio. January 1931 found him in California, holding legitimate jobs through June 1932, then he ran home to Madison and more bootlegging through 1934. He met Al Brady in early 1935, before revenue agents raided Dalhover's farm in March and saw him sentenced to another 60 days, released in September. By October, he'd agreed to join Brady in a campaign

9. Melvin Who?

Indiana WANTED poster for Brady gang founders Al Brady, James Dalhover, and Clarence Shaffer, Jr. (author's collection).

of armed robberies. Claims that Dalhover "turned Brady to crime" ignore Al's first arrests a year before they met.[85]

The gang's third and youngest member, born in 1916, was Indianapolis native Clarence Lee Shaffer, Jr. His parents divorced two years later, leaving grandparents to raise him, and Clarence logged his first arrest for auto theft at age 12, continuing that trade into his teens. Later, he ran a hamburger stand, mowed lawns, and hauled coal with the gang's fourth recruit, Charles Geiseking, born in 1900, whose early life remains obscure. During summer 1935 Shaffer impregnated a younger girlfriend but ignored his mother's plea to wed and settle down.[86]

Once those four men allied, they forged a unit meant to make John Dillinger "look like a piker." Brady, in particular, enjoyed deriding Dillinger, calling him "a creampuff" and "a guy who parts his hair in the middle," adding, "They should have given Dillinger a lollipop." That said, the foursome started small, with weekend holdups of grocery stores, gas stations, and pharmacies. Later, in custody, Dalhover claimed the gang had pulled at least 150 robberies across Indiana and Ohio without drawing FBI attention. On October 12, 1935, they took $18 from a movie theater in Crothersville, Indiana, splitting $16 after "expenses," then rebounded on the 14th by stealing $190 from a Sellersburg grocery. Along the way, obsessed with guns, the gang collected an impressive arsenal. An Indiana State Police captain ultimately warned reporters, "They will make the Dillinger gang look like neophytes."[87]

On October 13, U.S. marshals transported Floyd Hamilton from Leavenworth to Fort Tyler, Texas, for trial on more bank robbery charges. Jurors acquitted him in that case, returning Hamilton to his cell in Kansas.[88]

Around the same time, G-men betrayed their promise to rescue Anna Sage from deportation. Although she'd collected $5,000 for putting Dillinger "on the spot," G-men claimed they couldn't intervene due "lack of influence over the Department of Labor," which controlled immigration matters. She appealed the deportation ruling on October 16 but lost. Meanwhile, Doris Hinkley—ex-secretary to Melvin Purvis—married Agent Allen Lockerman, quit the Bureau, and launched a journalistic career with the *Chicago Tribune*. Her premiere series, titled "A Girl Among Manhunters," started strong, with snippets of "inside" information, but climaxed by regurgitating Hoover's lies about Ma Barker: "She planned their crimes. Hers was the iron hand that ruled that evil brood."[89]

October 1935 closed with two federal indictments against members of the "Irish O'Malley" gang in Oklahoma. The first count charged defendants Russell Cooper, Dewey Gilmore, Jack Miller, "Leo O'Malley, alias Irish," and Leonard Short with bank robbery at Okemah in December 1934. The second charge accused Dan Heady, Virgil "Red" Melton, Jack Miller, and Fred Reese with putting bank officers in jeopardy during the same incident.⁹⁰

Fugitive Vivian Chase reached the end of her run on November 3, 1935, when Kansas City police found her dead in a stolen sedan parked near Saint Luke's Hospital, shot once in the neck with a .45-caliber pistol, the slug exiting from her chest. Beneath her body, officers found a handbag containing a .38-caliber "Spanish-type" pistol, 25 rounds for that gun, and 20 more .45-caliber rounds like the one that killed her. Detectives announced an "intensified" search for cohort and fugitive bank robber John Langan, suspected of wounding a policeman in a September shootout where Langan's wife was slain. Without citing evidence, the manhunters also labeled Chase "an associate of Alvin Karpis." Chase initially seemed destined for a pauper's grave, until the funeral home holding her corpse received an anonymous phone call asking about interment expenses. The next morning, morticians received a parcel containing sufficient cash, plus a blue dress and undergarments identified as belonging to Chase. Nine mourners joined journalists and police for the funeral, none seeing fit to sign the guestbook.⁹¹

On November 7 Alvin Karpis teamed with John Brock, Harry Campbell, Sam Coker, Fred Hunter, and Ben Grayson to rob an Erie Railroad mail train of $34,000 at Garrettsville, Ohio. From that flashback to Jesse James, the crew broke new ground one day later, becoming the first outlaws to use a private airplane for their getaway, flying from Port Clinton, Ohio, to Hot Springs, Arkansas. Upon arrival, Karpis gave the plane to his hired pilot and drove toward Paris, Texas, while the others scattered, Campbell bound for San Antonio. On the 27th, a federal grand jury in Saint Paul indicted Cassius McDonald—captured in Detroit two months earlier—on charges of exchanging Bremer kidnap ransom money in Cuba.⁹²

"Irish O'Malley" gang members faced multiple trials in Oklahoma. One jury convicted Russell Cooper and Dewey Gilmore on dual counts for robbing the Okemah bank, producing concurrent sentences of 20 and 25 years for each defendant. A separate panel convicted Leonard Short of one count in the same case, while acquitting him on the second. A third jury convicted Dapper Dan Heady on both charges.⁹³

On November 29 Doug Cretzer, Arnold Kyle, and Milton Hartman robbed a Las Angeles bank, escaping with $2,765.⁹⁴

One day later, the Brady gang looted a bank in Anderson, Indiana. Although never charged, the bandits were also suspected of killing local Patrolman Frank Levy on November 25, when he stopped to investigate a "suspicious" car on his beat. That homicide remains officially unsolved today.⁹⁵

On December 2, Tri-State Gang members Martin Farrell and Francis

Wiley died in the electric chair at Pennsylvania's Rockview State Prison, for the kidnap-murder of William Weiss.[96]

Formal sentencing of the convicted Tri-State Gang defendants was scheduled for December 9, but some decided not to wait around. Six days earlier, Dan Heady's wife, "Pretty Betty," slipped him a pistol during a jailhouse visit. Dapper Dan used the gun for a breakout with codefendants Cooper, Gilmore, and Short, mortally wounding Muskogee Chief of Detectives Ben Bolton, who died two days later. A dragnet of G-men, police, and airborne spotters tracked the fugitives into Pushmataha County's Kiamichi Mountains, capturing Cooper 12 miles north of Clayton on the 5th. One day later, manhunters cornered Gilmore and Heady at a farmhouse near Weathers. Both resisted, whereupon authorities killed Heady and Gilmore surrendered. He, in turn, led officers to Short, within two miles of the farm where Heady died. In a peculiar twist of fate, Short had suffered critical burns from an accidental fire on the night of December 5, then drowned when a boat procured to evacuate him accidentally capsized. The gang's survivors received their sentences as scheduled, on December 9.[97]

On the same day, the U.S. Supreme Court rejected Bruno Hauptmann's appeal.[98]

Five days later, in San Francisco, Helen Gillis pled guilty to harboring her husband and received a sentence of one year's probation.[99]

The Brady gang continued its Midwestern depredations through December 1935, operating chiefly from Rhuel Dalhover's farm. Leary of using stolen cars, Brady ordered Dalhover to legally purchase an auto. Around the same time, alarmed by Shaffer's drinking and loose talk, Brady reportedly dropped him from the roster, replaced full-time by Geiseking.[100]

Facing trial for the 1934 murder of Constable Campbell, Henry Methvin and a cellmate planned to escape from Oklahoma's Ottawa County jail, using a smuggled pocketknife. Jailer Tom Armstrong surprised them, overpowering both men with the aid of another inmate. Methvin received a death sentence for Campbell's murder on December 20.[101]

Ten days later, 1935 ended on a sour note for Barker gang survivors, as "Boss" Laughlin died at Leavenworth while serving time for the Bremer abduction.[102]

10

Old Creepy

A second trial of Bremer kidnapping conspirators began in Saint Paul on January 6, 1936, including defendants Cassius McDonald, Harry Sawyer, and William Weaver. All feigned innocence, but unconvincingly. McDonald admitted laundering cash in Havana but denied knowing it was ransom loot. Sawyer and Weaver both admitted associations with the Barker-Karpis gang, while disclaiming any knowledge of the kidnapping. Jurors convicted the trio on January 24, Sawyer and Weaver receiving life terms the same day with a one-way trip to Leavenworth. McDonald got off "easy" with 15 years but was shipped off to serve it at Alcatraz.[1]

New Jersey's Court of Pardons heard and denied Bruno Hauptmann's plea for clemency on January 11. With his death scheduled for the 17th, Hauptmann appealed to Governor Harold Hoffman for a stay on the 16th and received a 30-day postponement.[2]

On January 13 and 14th the U.S. Supreme Court considered two objections to Arthur Gooch's death sentence, specifically whether holding and transporting a policeman in interstate commerce to avoid arrest, without any ransom demands, constituted a capital crime under the amended Lindbergh Law. The panel voted against commutation of his sentence to a life prison term.[3]

On the Tuesday when Gooch's appeal went up in smoke, the Hunt-Gant gang stole $4,000 from a bank in Cross City, Florida.[4]

Nine days later, Dutch Cretzer, Arnold Kyle, and Milton Hartmann took $6,000 from an Oakland, California, bank. One day later, they struck again, looting $1,475 from a bank in Los Angeles.[5]

In Muskogee, Oklahoma, a new January indictment charged Russell Cooper and Dewey Gilmore with murdering Ben Bolton during their abortive jailbreak.[6]

January dealt another blow to Anna Sage, as an appellate court upheld her deportation order. On the 30th, Evelyn Frechette completed her two-year prison term and joined remnants of John Dillinger's family on a traveling "Crime Does Not Pay" tour spanning the next five years.[7]

Through January and February 1936 G-men hunted Alvin Karpis, using their typical combination of illegal wiretaps and tips from informers seeking leniency in court. The taps covered outlaw casinos around Cleveland, where Karpis worked part-time as "security" for the Moe Dalitz mob, while informers included Bryan Bolton, Volney Davis, and Oklahoma gangland middleman George "Burrhead" Keady. From those sources and others, Bureau headquarters prepared a profile of Karpis ranking him as "a good conversationalist, never calls person by correct name; refers to person by some place or incident (note: this trait evidently was to avoid implicating others in crimes). Smokes one pack of Chesterfield cigarettes per day; drinks canned beer and expensive whiskey; gets drunk; never talks when drunk; does not use narcotics; reads all newspapers; reads *Detective Story* and *True Story* magazines; desires female company regularly and likes to maul them; gambles—dice and poker; usually stays at tourist camp when traveling." Along the way, George Keady betrayed train-robbing cohort John Brock who, in turn, gave up Ohio brothel madam Edith Barry and spilled details of the U.S. Mail train heist. Still, Karpis and Harry Campbell remained one jump ahead of G-men following their trail.[8]

January saw the Brady gang continue its Indiana raids, with a foray to Danville, Illinois, robbing two grocery stores in one night. Fleeing the latter of those heists, Al Brady fired on pursuing lawmen with an automatic rifle, but he also dealt with crooked cops when seeking to augment his arsenal. A jaunt to Newport, Kentucky, secured a Tommy gun from a bartender who identified his source as a policeman in what FBI reports call "a large city in Ohio." The gang later bought more guns from the officer directly, until his sideline was discovered, resulting in dismissal.[9]

On February 15, a red-haired man tried to exchange $300 in Weyerhaeuser ransom money at a bank in Seattle. He fled, leaving the cash, when a teller went to check serial numbers against a list provided by the Bureau. G-men identified the runner as Edward Fliss, an associate of William Dainard, also known as "Frank 'Red' Lane," an ex-con who'd kidnapped newly-elected Idaho Lieutenant Governor William Kinne in June 1929. Kinne had escaped and furnished information sufficient for Fliss's conviction, then died three months later from peritonitis caused by a ruptured appendix. With a new target on their radar, G-men redoubled their efforts.[10]

Two days after Fliss's near miss in Seattle, Bruno Hauptmann's trial judge resentenced him to die, with execution scheduled for March 30.[11]

In February, Al Brady's gang reprised their last double-play holdup, stealing $600 in one night from two Springfield, Illinois, grocery stores. Driving to New Orleans for Mardi Gras, they partied with strangers, while Brady made a love connection with local housewife Margaret

Larson, explaining his cache of weapons by claiming that he, Dalhover, and Geiseking were federal agents. Smitten at first sight, Margaret abandoned her husband and four-year-old son, returning north with Brady when the gang left town.[12]

On February 26, a federal grand jury in Tampa, Florida, indicted Myrtle Eaton for harboring Barker gang member William Weaver.[13]

March began with a spate of widely-separated robberies. On the 2nd, the Cretzer-Kyle gang scored their biggest-ever take, $6,100, from a bank in Los Angeles. One day later, the Hunt-Gant gang did better, taking $30,459 ($567,000 today) from a bank in Ybor City, Florida. On the 4th, Al Brady's trio stole gems valued at $8,000 from a jewelry store in Greenville, Ohio.[14]

Also on the 4th, Louis Piquett began serving his two-year term at Leavenworth for harboring Homer Van Meter.[15]

Verna Bentz left husband Eddie in March, tired of life on the run, and went home to South Milwaukee, traced by G-men and interrogated there. She provided the address of Eddie's Brooklyn hideout and raiders found him there on March 13, hiding in a dumbwaiter. Bentz confessed two bank holdups but refused to name accomplices, accepting a 20-year term on conviction. At sentencing, he asked for a cell at Alcatraz, telling the judge, "All my friends are there."[16]

Pleased with their haul from Greenville, the Brady gang reprised that effort on March 19, looting jewelry worth an estimated $6,800 from a shop in Lima, Ohio. During that heist, an employee jumped onto Brady's back, scuffling with him until Brady shook him off, dropping behind a display case. As he began to rise, an unidentified accomplice fired at Brady, narrowly missing his head, and earning instant dismissal from the gang as soon as they'd escaped.[17]

Following recuperation from his gunshot wounds from August 1935, George Barrett, slayer of G-man Norman Klein, was transported to Indianapolis, where he became the first person condemned for killing a federal agent on duty. Authorities hanged him there on March 24, then planted him in an unmarked grave at Holy Cross and St. Joseph Cemetery.[18]

Following conviction for his role in the Bremer kidnapping, Ben Laska posted $10,000 bond pending appeal. On March 27 the 10th Circuit Court of Appeals in Denver upheld his conviction and sentence.[19]

When that verdict came down, Alvin Karpis and Fred Hunter occupied a rented house seven miles southeast of Hot Springs, Arkansas. "Flying Squad" G-men led by Earl Connelly, with postal inspectors and a Kansas state policeman, traced them there on March 30 but arrived too late, finding the place vacant. On the 31st they interrogated brothel madam Grace Goldstein, who furnished some details on Hunter and moll Connie Morris, while falsely denying any knowledge of Karpis.[20]

In a sideshow to the main event, on March 30, Edna Murray's son, Preston Paden received a life sentence for killing a night watchman during a Kansas robbery.[21]

That same day, New Jersey's Court of Pardons rejected Bruno Hauptmann's second clemency petition.[22] On March 31 Hauptmann penned a final letter to Governor Hoffman, reading:

> Your Excellency:
>
> My writing is not for fear of losing my life, this is in the hands of God, it is His will. I will go gladly, it means the end of my tremendous suffering. Only in thinking of my wife and my little boy, that is breaking my heart. I know until this terrible crime is solvet [sic], they will have to suffer unter [sic] the weight of my unfair conviction.
> I beg you, Attorney General [sic], believe at least a dying man. Please investigate, because the case is not solvet, it only adds another death to the Lindbergh case.
> I thank your Excellency, from the bottom of my heart, and may God bless you,
>
> Respectfully,
> Bruno Richard Hauptmann[23]

Hauptmann kept his date with the electric chair on April 3. His final statement read: "I am glad that my life in a world which has not understood me has ended. Soon I will be at home with my Lord, so I am dying an innocent man. Should, however, my death serve for the purpose of abolishing capital punishment—such a punishment being arrived at only by circumstantial evidence—I feel that my death has not been in vain. I am at peace with God. I repeat, I protest my innocence of the crime for my soul and I am happy in Him."[24]

On the same day Hauptmann died, J. Edgar Hoover railed against congressional efforts to trim the FBI's budget. Specifically, he forecast a new "wave of kidnapping" if the Bureau's funding were not augmented, claiming further that an immediate increase in crime "would cripple law enforcement and place a premium on lawlessness." He backed that grim prediction with a skewed claim that G-men alone had solved 62 kidnappings since June 1932, resulting in 136 convictions.[25]

The Brady gang's rampage continued in April. Operating from an Indianapolis rooming house, its members carried their weapons in banjo and violin cases, persuading other boarders that they were musicians. On the 9th, Brady, Dalhover, Geiseking, and Shaffer drove a stolen car to Dayton, looting a jewelry store. Dalhover later claimed the gems bore price tags totaling $68,000 ($1.3 million today), though fences offered only $22,000. Arriving for that meeting in Chicago, the thieves themselves were robbed by gunmen who dismissed them as harmless "punks." Underworld gossip soon revised that opinion, but while the hijackers negotiated to return the loot, it never happened.[26]

On April 22 Al Brady and Rhuel Dalhover robbed two small grocery stores in Ohio. The first take disappointed them, so they drove to nearby Piqua, in Miami County, Brady entering through the front door, Dalhover through the back. Some 35 customers were present when clerk Edward Lindsay ("Linsey" in some reports) emerged from the basement and asked what was happening. Brady shot him and pushed him back downstairs, fatally wounded, later telling Dalhover the victim had "jumped" him.[27]

Five days later, the gang made their second raid on the Lima, Ohio, jewelry store they'd previously robbed in March. That time, they bagged gems worth $8,000 and fled, firing an automatic rifle at police who pursued them. Geiseking suffered a gunshot wound to one leg, while the patrol car crashed under fire, injuring Patrolman Edward Swaney. From Piqua the gang drove 130 miles to Indianapolis and the home of Dr. E.E. Rose, persuading him to treat Geiseking's wound with the lie that it was inflicted by "a jealous boyfriend." After taking Geiseking home, Brady, Dalhover, and Shaffer returned to Rose's house, seeking to ensure his silence, but in the meantime Dr. Rose had called police as required by law. The bandits found officers waiting and a shootout ensued, killing Sergeant Richard Rivers before the trio fled again. Burning two getaway cars outside Indianapolis, the gang drove in another toward Chicago, where they fenced their latest haul for $12,000. Meanwhile, jewelry boxes from the Lima holdup surfaced near Geneva, Indiana, permitting G-men to enter the case on grounds of stolen property crossing state lines.[28]

Brady and girlfriend Margaret lingered at a Chicago hotel, where police arrested both on April 29. One day later, officers found some of the Lima loot in a Chicago safe deposit box, and more at the home of the box's renter, jewelry salesman Jack Becker, charging Becker and wife Laura as accessories. While reporters dubbed Margaret and Laura "new Dillinger molls," Margaret, released from a vagrancy charge, apparently forgot her vow to "follow Al into Hell," finding work in a Chicago tavern, never seeing him again.[29]

Arrests continued through April in the Hamm kidnapping. On the 9th, G-men collared accomplice Charles Fitzgerald in Los Angeles. Eight days later, Bensenville, Illinois Postmaster Edmund Bartholmey confessed his role in the abduction, after Hamm identified Bartholmey's home as the place where he'd been held captive. Saint Paul gangster Jack Peifer joined the rest in jail on the 18th. Four days later, a federal grand jury indicted Bartholmey, Dock Barker, Bryan Bolton, Elmer Farmer, Alvin Karpis, and Peifer for kidnapping Hamm. That same day, the DOJ offered $5,000 rewards for the capture of Karpis and Harry Campbell. On the 27th, U.S. Postmaster General James Farley raised the ante by $2,000 for Karpis's arrest.[30]

"Old Creepy," meanwhile, remained elusive. On April 10 he met Grace Goldstein in Hot Springs, dispatching her to recover Tommy guns stashed at her brother's home in Paris, Texas, and convey them to Karpis in New Orleans. Upon arriving in the Crescent City, she reported failure, telling Karpis that the FBI was staking out her brother's farm and that the weapons had been buried on his property, remaining inaccessible.[31]

While Karpis waited in vain for the guns, J. Edgar Hoover took his yearly plea for cash to the Senate Appropriations Committee, where he met stiff resistance from Tennessee Senator Kenneth McKellar, chairman of the panel's Justice Subcommittee. Aside from condemning Hoover's exaggerated tabulation of the "crime war's" death toll on both sides, McKellar criticized Hoover's employment of DOJ publicists to hype his reputation, and scored Hoover for rising to control the FBI without ever attending "crime school" or personally arresting a single suspect during his 19 years and counting with Justice. Hoover left the hearing humiliated and fuming, with $225,000 ($4.3 million today) pared from his original request for funds, snapping orders at Clyde Tolson. First, he demanded that when Alvin Karpis was located, no attempt to nab him should be made until Hoover himself arrived, to make his first-ever "personal" arrest.[32]

His second order called for G-men to unearth whatever "dirt" they could compile against McKellar, for use in political blackmail that Hoover had already honed to an artform. One juicy item was McKellar's attendance, as an honored guest, at the 1924 wedding of Ku Klux Klan lobbyist W.F. Zumbrunn to a Tennessee woman at Dyersburg. Whatever else agents uncovered still remains unclear, but history records that Senator McKellar dropped his opposition to the Bureau and its director, appearing as guest speaker at the FBI Academy's 1943 graduation ceremony, where he praised "this great instrument of law and order that has been built up by the grand man who is your director." McKellar retained his office until January 1953, rising to chairman of the Appropriations Committee (1945–1947, and 1949–1953), as well as the Civil Service Committee (1943–44). His record stands today as the only Tennessee senator to have completed more than three full terms, and he never again trimmed a cent from Hoover's budgetary requests.[33]

While Karpis remained at large, on April 21 G-men waged a "fierce machine-gun battle" in the Kansas City suburb of Hickman Mills, Missouri, with "Irish O'Malley" gang members John Langan and Charles Sparger. Both were captured, Sparger after suffering three bullet wounds. G-man George Franklin also took a slug from Sparger in his left thigh during that firefight, though Washington initially withheld his name.[34]

On April 27 Anna Sage passed through Fostoria, Ohio, on a guarded train bound for Ellis Island, bearing 80 other aliens earmarked for deportation from lockups spanning the eastern United States. They reached their destination that same day, scheduled for departure to their respective homelands on May 2.³⁵

After briefly visiting Florida, Alvin Karpis drove Grace Goldstein back to Hot Springs on April 25, then embarked on a fishing trip to Mississippi, returning to New Orleans on May 1, where he and Fred Hunter (with Connie Morris) occupied separate apartments under pseudonyms. G-men gleaned that information on April 30—perhaps from Goldstein—and began reinforcing the New Orleans office that same day, while Director Hoover chartered a flight south from Washington.³⁶

Agents mounted surveillance on both apartments, ready and waiting when Karpis emerged and approached his car soon after 5:00 p.m. on May 1. In Hoover's version of events, he rushed the car alone, pistol in hand, and arrested Alvin as Karpis tried to reach a rifle lying on the backseat of his vehicle. Karpis disputed that claim, asserting that a crowd of agents surrounded him, then summoned Hoover from concealment in a nearby alleyway. He also claimed there was no rifle in his car, and that the Plymouth coupe had no backseat (a fact confirmed by photographs online, although there *was* narrow floor space behind the car's front seats). The muddle continued as Hoover ordered Karpis handcuffed, but no G-man present had "bracelets" on hand, compelling one to shed his necktie and bind Alvin's wrists hostage-style. Next, G-men lost their way en route to the New Orleans post office, whereupon Karpis chimed in, "If it's the *new* post office you want, I know how to get there. I was planning to hold it up." Hoover wanted the *old* post office instead and sought directions from a pedestrian in reaching his destination.³⁷

While Director Hoover was thus engaged, other agents captured Fred Hunter and Connie Morris (née Ruth Robinson) and held them for transportation. Six days later, Hoover led his second raid in Toledo, Ohio, "personally" arresting fugitives Harry Campbell and Sam Coker. That same afternoon, May 7, Karpis faced arraignment for the Hamm and Bremer kidnappings in Saint Paul, held in lieu of $500,000 bond. Authorities returned Coker to Oklahoma's McAlester Prison on the 9th, to complete his 30-year term for bank robbery. On May 27 Fred Hunter pled guilty to harboring Karpis, receiving a two-year sentence.³⁸

Ralph Fults led an inmate strike at Parchman Prison on May 5, earning a punitive sentence to solitary confinement.³⁹

One day later, employees at two San Francisco banks reported a customer exchanging altered bills linked to the Weyerhaeuser ransom. Tellers noted the man's license number, issued to local resident "Bert E. Cole." G-men scoured the neighborhood, spotting the car and staking it out on

May 7. They pounced on "Cole" when he appeared, relieving him of a .45 automatic and identifying him as fugitive William Dainard, recovering $37,374.47 in cash that Dainard admitted swapping for ransom money. He also directed them to another $14,000 in $100 bills, buried in Utah. Transferred to Tacoma on May 9, Dainard pled guilty on two counts, receiving concurrent 60-year terms at McNeil Island's federal prison, later transferred to Leavenworth, where he was judged insane and confined to an asylum.[40]

Alvin Karpis (right) with federal agents on May 3, 1936, following J. Edgar Hoover's staged and fraudulent "personal" arrest in New Orleans two days earlier (Library of Congress).

On May 7 Arthur Gooch appeared before Judge Williams for sentencing in Muskogee. After condemning Gooch to hang, Williams asked if he wished to make a statement. Gooch replied, "I didn't commit a crime for which I should be executed. I admit my life hasn't been what it should have been, but I don't think I should die." Unmoved, Williams advised Gooch to "make peace with your God."[41]

On May 8, in Kansas City, Judge Albert Reeves set a tentative date for Clarence Sparger's bank robbery trial. U.S. Attorney Maurice Milligan described the case against Sparger as "concrete."[42]

On Monday, May 11, police arrested Clarence Shaffer at his home near Indianapolis. Four days later, Chicago officers captured Rhuel Dalhover. Both fugitives joined leader Brady in Indiana's Marion County Jail, awaiting trial for murder.[43]

On June 3 Florida jurors convicted Myrtle Eaton of harboring Barker gang member William Weaver, resulting in a six-month sentence and $1,000 fine. Three days later, Lawrence DeVol and 15 other inmates staged a breakout from St. Peter Hospital for the Criminally Insane (now Minnesota Security Hospital) in Nicollet County, 10 miles north of Mankato.[44]

On June 15 federal prosecutors charged Denver attorney Mollie Bert with furnishing false testimony at Ben Laska's Oklahoma City trial. She pled not guilty and was freed on $5,000 bail.[45]

Arthur Gooch appealed for presidential clemency from his death sentence, rejected by FDR on the recommendation of Attorney General Cummings. Gooch kept his date with the gallows on June 19, slowly strangling for 26 minutes before a clutch of four doctors confirmed he was dead. Hangman Rich Owens, who claimed the death rope as a trophy, explained, "You pull a chicken's head off and he flops around like everything. That's the way it was with Gooch. He just had to have time to die." To date, Gooch remains the only federal inmate executed under the Lindbergh Law.[46]

On July 1 Dutch Cretzer, Arnold Kyle, and Milton Hartmann stole $1,996 from a bank in Los Angeles. On the 27th they strayed 1,135 miles from their home base to score their best take yet, escaping from a Seattle bank with $14,581. Witnesses identified all three bandits on both jobs.[47]

July 8 found Lawrence DeVol and fellow asylum escapee Don Reeder robbing a bank in Turon, Kansas, then pausing to celebrate at a tavern in Enid, Oklahoma. The suspicious proprietor, an ex-policeman, called former colleagues, whereupon DeVol opened fire with a .38, killing Patrolman Cal Palmer and wounding partner Ralph Knarr. Fleeing on foot, DeVol commandeered a passing car while more police gave chase. In a second firefight, DeVol slightly wounded Officer Lelon Coyle before other policemen shot him nine times, killing him.[48]

At his kidnapping trial in Saint Paul, Alvin Karpis initially pled not guilty, then, on July 14, told lawyer Thomas Newman he'd plead guilty to conspiracy if the government dropped kidnapping charges from the Hamm case. The court approved that deal on July 27, imposing a life prison term. Four days later, Charles Fitzgerald received a matching sentence for the Hamm abduction. Jack Peifer got 30 years, then killed himself in jail with poisoned chewing gum. Edward Bartholmey received a six-year term. Bryan Bolton, who had turned state's witness, drew concurrent three- to five-year terms for the Bremer and Hamm abductions.[49]

While those cases proceeded, Detective Tom Brown faced charges of collusion with Saint Paul's kidnappers. Bryan Bolton testified against him, joined by Edna Murray, leading to Brown's suspension on July 17. He fought that judgment before a Civil Service board, resulting in permanent dismissal on October 9. Even then, Brown faced no criminal charges for any of his numerous offenses.[50]

On July 25 U.S. Attorney Maurice Milligan filed charges against Juanita Sparger and accomplice Fay Fulbright for harboring Sparger's husband and cohort John Langan. Fulbright owned the tourist camp where G-men captured Langan and Clarence Sparger in March. By that time, both bandits were serving 25 and 10 years respectively for separate Missouri holdups.[51]

Ticking another box on the Urschel kidnapping case, Ben Laska surrendered to Oklahoma City's U.S. marshal on August 1 and was transferred to Leavenworth the same day. Alvin Karpis formally pled guilty to conspiracy two days later, reaching Alcatraz on August 7. Media claims that the Midwest "gangster era was winding to a close" with his imprisonment would prove spectacularly premature.[52]

Proving that point, trustee Irvin Chapman escaped from Cummins Prison Farm in Arkansas on August 25, using a pistol stolen from the warden's office. One week later, in Atlanta, Texas, Chapman teamed with Hugh Lindsey and Louis Sadler to rob a local bank. A clamoring alarm drew armed citizens to the scene, engaging in a battle that left Chapman and four innocent bystanders wounded. Police arrested Chapman and Lindsey on the spot, while Sadler briefly escaped.[53]

On September 12, police in Henderson, Kentucky, captured Charles Geiseking, packing him off to Indianapolis, where Al Brady, Rhuel Dalhover, and Clarence Shaffer awaited trial for murdering Sergeant Rivers. Twelve days later, fate intervened as Brady, Dalhover and Shaffer were moved to the Hancock County jail in Breensfield, Indiana. Geiseking, absolved of the Rivers slaying, wound up in Ohio, facing armed robbery charges. Upon conviction there, he drew a sentence of 10 to 25 years, served his time, then was paroled and permanently vanished from the public eye.[54]

On September 18 Texas Governor James Allred commuted Henry Methvin's death sentence to life imprisonment.[55]

Oklahoma City wrote the final chapter of the Urschel case on October 1, 1936, when Mollie Bert switched her not-guilty plea to *nolo contendere* ("no contest"), receiving a 366-day prison term, suspended on condition of one year's good behavior. The final tally for the Urschel prosecutions included 21 persons convicted, receiving six life sentences and lesser terms totaling 58 years, two months, and three days.[56]

Eight days later, federal grand jurors at Tyler, Texas, indicted Irvin Chapman, Hugh Lindsey, and Louis Sadler for bank robbery. Subsequently convicted at trial in Linden, Chapman, Lindsey, and Sadler received prison terms of 65, 75, and 25 years, respectively—but Chapman was not finished yet.[57]

On October 11 Al Brady, Rhuel Dalhover, and Clarence Shaffer assaulted Hancock County's sheriff during breakfast service in jail, grabbing his pistol and escaping to begin another year-long crime spree. On the

13th G-men joined the manhunt, tracking the fugitives for Dyer Act and National Stolen Property Act violations. By then, the three were back in Ohio, where they burglarized a home in Gallipolis, then drove to Wheeling, West Virginia. There, Dalhover later said, they "cased" a jewelry store but reconsidered, driving on to Baltimore, settling in to live quietly for a time. In mid–October Shaffer began dating teenage waitress Minnie Raimondo, identifying himself as "George Riley," vacationing co-owner of a furniture store in Bangor, Maine, with traveling companions "Edward Maxwell" (Brady) and "Herbert Schwartz" (Dalhover). Soon, Dalhover became involved with Minnie's sister, Mary, and both couples were engaged within two weeks.[58]

With aid from defendant William Dainard, G-men traced Weyerhaeuser kidnapping accomplice Edward Fliss to a San Francisco hotel on October 23. Transferred to Tacoma, Fliss was charged as an accessory after the fact for passing ransom money after the abduction. He pled guilty on November 14, claiming he had been "hard up" when he exchanged thousands of dollars and pocketed 15 percent of the take. Already an ex-convict, Fliss received the maximum 10-year sentence and $5,000 fine, whereupon Washington closed the case.[59]

In Missouri, on November 13, Juanita Sparger interrupted jury selection for her harboring trial with a guilty plea. Codefendant Fay Fulbright proceeded to trial, while Juanita—now a state witness against her ex-friend—saw her sentencing deferred until Fulbright's case was completed.[60]

Despite trying to keep a low profile, the Brady gang supported its "vacation" by robbing several Maryland grocery stores, choosing marks distant from Baltimore. Next, they decided to raid a bank in North Madison, Indiana, first stealing a 1937 Buick sedan from its owner and his female companion. On November 23, with Shaffer driving getaway, the trio took $1,630 from their Hoosier target, then returned to Baltimore. Five days later, Dalhover and Shaffer decided to wed the Raimondo sisters, Rhuel neglecting to mention that he already had a wife and two children. The double ceremony occurred at Elkton on November 30, with Al Brady and a third Raimondo sister, Josephine, serving as witnesses. Back in Baltimore, the newlyweds moved in with the gangsters' mother-in-law, while Brady found separate lodgings. Within a week, the Raimondo home felt too crowded, whereupon the two couples rented a house. Shaffer constructed a basement "workroom" for their ever-growing arsenal, kept perpetually locked.[61]

On November 26 Texas authorities moved Irvin Chapman from Huntsville to Clarksville, facing a kidnapping charge. Conviction on that count earned him another 25-year sentence and return to Huntsville, followed shortly by another transfer to the Eastham Prison Farm near Weldon.[62]

On November 27 witnesses identified Arnold Kyle and Milton Hartmann as the thieves who tapped another bank for $8,000. Dutch Cretzer apparently missed that outing.[63]

After J. Edgar Hoover redeemed himself by "personally" nabbing Alvin Karpis, it was alter-ego Clyde Tolson's turn in the spotlight. The targets: Harry Walter Brunette and Merle Vandenbush, branded "public enemies" for robbing a series of New York City banks and kidnapping New Jersey State Trooper William Turnbull. On December 14 NYPD traced the duo to an apartment on West 102nd Street, notifying the Bureau as a point of professional courtesy. By mutual agreement, Hoover and NYPD Commissioner Lewis Valentine agreed to raid the flat in unison at 2:00 p.m. on the 15th, then Hoover jumped the gun by 14 hours, arriving with his troops at midnight, hurling tear gas grenades that set the apartment ablaze. Firefighters arrived on a chaotic scene, during which one G-man jabbed his Tommy gun into a uniformed fireman's stomach, prompting the response, "Dammit, can't you read? If you don't take that gun out of my stomach I'll bash your head in!" Brunette briefly returned fire, then surrendered while Tolson posed with his catch for press cameras. When journalists queried the premature strike, Hoover "merely shrugged his shoulders." Commissioner Valentine issued a statement condemning federal endanger-

Clyde Tolson (left) with constant companion and rumored paramour J. Edgar Hoover. Following the capture of Alvin Karpis, Hoover staged a "personal arrest" for Tolson, targeting bandit Harry Brunette in December 1936, but the raid went awry and Brunette escaped (Library of Congress).

ment of innocent lives, dismissed by Hoover as "unjustified and petty criticism." Vandenbush came home with the raid in progress and escaped in the confusion, later claiming that he briefly stood close enough in the crowd to "tap J. Edgar Hoover on the shoulder."[64]

The Brady gang's last target for 1936 was a bank in Carthage, Indiana. After stealing fresh plates for their getaway car, they left Baltimore on December 15 and stopped overnight at a tourist camp in Marietta, Ohio, then drove 270 miles to Carthage on the 16th. Their reported take from that job: $2,154 and some silverware stolen as an afterthought. From there, it was back to Baltimore and lying low on their faux vacation from Maine.[65]

11

Mopping Up

January 1937 was a slow month for the FBI's "crime war" until the 28th, when Dutch Cretzer, apparently acting alone, stole $2,870 from a Los Angeles bank.[1]

Ten days later, Little, Brown and Company announced the publication of J. Edgar Hoover's second book, *Persons in Hiding*, once again penned for him by agents of his Crime Records Division. The *New York Times* was not enthusiastic, warning, "It is time that Mr. Hoover gave his ghost some fresh material. This book is washed over and dimmed by banalities. Those who take it up after reading Courtney Riley Cooper's earlier books will hardly escape the conviction that they have read it before."[2]

Kirkus Reviews was more encouraging, telling its readers, "The director of the Federal Bureau of Investigation presents a series of well-known crime cases to illustrate various points he wishes to make. He takes up such angles on crime as the relation of environment to the criminal, professional men and criminals (Dillinger's doctor and his attorney, for instance), the women behind the crime, the criminal at your elbow, hero worship as an impetus to crime, the evils of the parole system, extortion and blackmail, etc. He has certain constructive suggestions, such as increased police force, education of the public, treatment of crime as a social problem, taking the matter out of politics. This is not an inside picture of the workings of the Federal Bureau or the G-men in operation but should appeal to that market and to those interested in criminology."[3]

On February 25 Merle Vandenbush, Hoover's latest "Public Rat No. 1," teamed with Anthony Rera (misidentified as "Joseph Stuzza" in one report) to loot $17,600 from a bank in Katonah, New York. Brother George Rera drove the getaway car but they didn't get far. Twelve miles to the south, in Armonk, local officers stopped them 22 minutes later, arresting the trio without resistance when they found Vandenbush and Anthony Rera huddled in the vehicle's trunk. One day later, grand jurors in White Plains indicted the three for first-degree robbery, prosecutors announcing their hope to impose 70-year sentences.[4]

11. Mopping Up

Two weeks later, on March 13, "three cool bandits" robbed the same Katonah bank but managed to escape where Vandenbush and company had failed, bagging more than $18,000. Investigation identified two of the three as Glenn John Applegate (aka "Alfred Powers") and Robert Suhay. Meanwhile, justice moved swiftly for Merle Vandenbush and the Rera brothers, all three pleading guilty as charged on the 17th. Vandenbush and Anthony Rera drew matching 45-year prison terms, while George's sentence was deferred until a later date.[5]

On March 19, a grand jury in Beaumont, Texas, indicted Irvin Chapman for another bank robbery, that one occurring in mid–June 1934.[6]

Ten days later, outlaw John Oscar Hetzer made his debut with Arnold Kyle and Milton Hartmann, netting $18,195 from a bank in Portland, Oregon. It was the gang's best take to date, again with Dutch Cretzer seemingly on hiatus. The end was nearing, however. G-men captured Hetzer on April 6, at a Los Angeles garage. They cornered Hartmann at L.A.'s Stuart Hotel one day later, whereupon he shot and killed himself.[7]

On the day of Hetzer's capture, April 6, the Sixth Circuit Court of Appeals affirmed the wrongful convictions of Anthony Labrizetta and George Sargent for the Karpis gang's Ohio mail robbery. If Karpis heard the news on Alcatraz it didn't lift his spirits. Seventeen days later he incurred a penalty for brawling with a fellow inmate.[8]

On April 16 New York bandits Glenn Applegate and Robert Suhay entered the U.S. Post Office in Topeka, Kansas, presumably intending to rob it. G-man Wimberly Baker and another agent, unidentified in press reports, were at the scene coincidentally and sought to arrest the gunmen. Powers and Suhay fired at Baker, while Baker's partner joined in the battle. Both bandits escaped but were captured that night in Plattsmouth, Nebraska. Agent Baker died from his wounds on the 17th.[9]

In early April, the Brady gang passed through Chicago, pausing to consider legal purchase of a submachine gun from a sporting goods store, but the price and registration rules dissuaded them. Returning to Baltimore, they stopped to steal a fresh getaway car. On April 26, in Farmland, Indiana, they used that ride to loot another bank of $1,427, then backtracked to Maryland.[10]

On May 11, driving the Chevrolet they'd stolen during their Greenfield, Indiana, jailbreak, the gang traveled to Bellefontaine, Ohio, in search of another vehicle. The following day, they stole a Ford from two girls, then drove to Hamilton and torched the Chevy. From there, they went to Moscow, Ohio, stole a deactivated .30-caliber machine gun from an American Legion post, and restored it to working order. A week later, they repeated that theft at another Legion post in Felicity, Ohio, then fled briefly back to Baltimore.[11]

May 23 found them back on the road, en route to rob a bank in Sheldon, Illinois, but it had closed its doors for good before they got the chance. Two days later, in Goodland, Indiana, they lifted $2,528 from another bank. Fifteen miles into their getaway, the bandits met an Indiana State Police car, firing several shots at the officers in passing. Trooper Paul Minneman pursued them, with ride-along passenger Deputy Sheriff Elmer Craig of Cass County. The bandits stopped at a crossroads, piling out of their car, Brady with a Tommy gun, Shaffer and Dalhover armed with automatic rifles. Trooper Minneman stopped to confront them, facing a storm of rapid fire, hit 20 times (some reports claim more). Deputy Craig, also wounded, collapsed and lay helpless as Dalhover approached, asking his friends, "Should I finish this guy, too?" Craig heard one of them reply, "No, come on. Let's get the hell out of here." Taking Minneman's revolver and Craig's shotgun, plus a first-aid kit from the patrol car, the gunmen escaped. Craig would recover from his wounds, but Trooper Minneman died on May 27.[12]

On June 1, 1937, Agent Truett Rowe received a tip that fugitive Guy Osborne was hiding out on his brother's ranch at Gallup, New Mexico. The Bureau wanted Osborne for a Dyer Act violation in Fort Smith, Arkansas, and for breaking out of Eufaula, Oklahoma's jail on April 22. Accompanied by Gallup's police chief, Agent Rowe located and confronted Osborne, who produced a hidden gun and shot Rowe. Gallup's chief tried to return fire but his pistol misfired and Osborne fled on foot. Rowe died while the chief rushed him toward a local hospital, but Osborne was running out of time. Some two hours after the shooting, a posse that included Navajo trackers found him in the desert outside Gallup, arresting him without further resistance.[13]

Back in Baltimore—alias "Charm City" or "Mobtown"—the Brady gang bought a small motorboat and a motorcycle, spending the next two months at sea, cruising the roads, or visiting local roller skating rinks. Al Brady loved skating so much that he purchased custom-made skates and carried them habitually in his car. He also bought a tavern under an assumed name, personally running it until the charm wore thin and he sold it. Meanwhile, on June 15, Attorney General Cummings offered $1,500 for information leading to the trio's capture—or $500 per head—and the FBI sent thousands of WANTED fliers nationwide, to police departments and skating rinks alike. Feeling the heat, the fugitives left Baltimore for Buffalo, New York, then traveled on to Nashville, Tennessee, and Milwaukee, Wisconsin. Dalhover and Shaffer told their wives the road trips were related to their far-flung furniture business.[14]

On June 7, bandits Floyd Hamilton and Ted Walters robbed a bank in Bradley, Arkansas.[15]

On June 23, 19 "hard-boiled" convicts fled a work detail from Eastham's prison farm in Texas, eluding a small army of men and bloodhounds dispatched to retrieve them. Hilton Bybee and James Rice led the breakout, overpowering the detail's lone guard as he rolled a cigarette, stealing his weapons, uniform, and horse. Three other guards were running 20 minutes late for work as the pair, followed by 17 tagalong prisoners—four of them lifers like Bybee—broke for freedom mounted on mules. Within a week, all but Bybee, Rice and one Harry Roberts were safely back in custody.[16]

Two days after the Eastham breakout, federal jurors in Topeka, Kansas, convicted Glenn Applegate and Robert Suhay of murdering G-man Wimberly Baker, fixing their penalty at death. Both were sent to Leavenworth, pending resolution of their appeal.[17]

In Cleveland, on June 30, defendants Arthur Hebebrand and John "Sharky" Gordon pled guilty to federal charges of harboring Alvin Karpis and Harry Campbell. Gordon received a three-year term, with two years for Hebebrand, both also paying $1,000 fines.[18]

Eastham prison farm suffered its second breakout in 16 days on July 8, 1937. This time, Irvin Chapman and seven other inmates on another work detail retrieved two rifles planted by free world accomplices, wounding one guard while return fire killed convicted chicken thief J.D. Reed. Leaders of the break, with Chapman, were lifer Fred Tindol and notorious Oklahoma badman Roy "Pete" Traxler, serving time for armed robbery. The trio reached a nearby farmhouse, wounding the property's owner and taking him hostage, fleeing in his car to Trinity, Texas, where they robbed the City Marshal, then stole a Texas Highway Patrol car. On July 15 they surfaced in Ada, Oklahoma, abducting motorist Baird Markham, Jr., dropping him in Sapulpa and going on in his car. Chapman ditched Tindol and Traxler before July 23, when they robbed and kidnapped two Kingston residents, but the rigors of flight made the fugitives careless, permitting one captive to seize a gun, killing Tindol and wounding Traxler. By early August, only Chapman remained alive and at large of the nine escapees.[19]

Fay Fulbright appealed her conviction for harboring fugitives John Langan and Clarence Sparger. On July 13 the Eighth Circuit Court of Appeals reversed that verdict and remanded her case for retrial. Research for this volume failed to uncover the new trial's result.[20]

Six days later, President Roosevelt pardoned inmates Anthony Labrizetta and George Sargent from their wrongful convictions for U.S. Mail robbery. That belated mercy followed a two-month review of their case by Attorney General Cummings and federal pardon attorney Daniel Lyons.[21]

On the same day Labrizetta and Sargent received their pardons, three bandits robbed a bank at Weiner, Arkansas, in Poinsett County. Soon afterward, they were seen buying gas and groceries in Selma, 159 miles south of Weiner. Drew County Sheriff W.C. Cruce organized a ten-man posse, including Sergeants Buck Mooney and Neil Shannon from Arkansas State Police Intelligence Division headquarters, speeding ahead of the rest in pursuit of the suspects' getaway car. The bandits ambushed their advance pursers, Hilton Bybee shooting Shannon in the chest with a rifle before Mooney cut him down with a Tommy gun, also shooting a weapon from James Rice's hand. Harry Roberts escaped on foot during the firefight, vanishing into woodlands. The other officers arrived to find Bybee's head "riddled with bullets," James Rice bleeding and in handcuffs. Available sources list Bybee's final resting place as "unknown."[22]

The Brady gang returned to action on August 7 but hit an immediate snag. Driving their "hot" Ford to Baltimore's outskirts, they were transferring guns and clothes from that car to a 1931 Buick, purchased legally, when a pair of city patrolmen surprised them and gave chase. Gunfire disabled the patrol car, then the gang ditched their Buick, leaving a rifle inside it. From the car's registration and other clues, G-men identified the fugitives, moving on to grill Dalhover's and Shaffer's wives, along with other acquaintances, launching what modern FBI historians call "one of the biggest manhunts in history." Still, agents were no closer to their prey on August 23, when the gang stole $7,000 and a security guard's revolver from a bank in Thorp, Wisconsin. From there, they drove to Buffalo, hiding out until September 3, when they moved on to rent an apartment in Bridgeport, Connecticut.[23]

Floyd Hamilton and Ted Walters struck again on August 12, robbing a Coca-Cola office in Lewisville, Arkansas, fleeing in a Ford stolen from a Crittenden County deputy sheriff in Marion. Three days later they encountered a police roadblock at Ashdown, Arkansas, losing their Ford in the firefight but fleeing in another stolen ride. On the 16th another checkpoint blocked their progress near De Queen, forcing the bandits to ditch their latest car and escape on foot, pursued by officers with dogs. Five days later, still in Sevier County, the fugitives hopped a train bound for Texarkana, riding the rails from there to Dallas. Their run ended on the 22nd when Dallas officers arrested them.[24]

J. Edgar Hoover's brooding wrath caught up with Matt Leach on September 4, when Indiana State Police Superintendent Donald Silver demanded his resignation, citing 13 separate charges of failure to cooperate with G-men. Hoover added an accusation that Leach told Hoosier citizens to stonewall agents during the Dillinger manhunt, pursuit of the Brady gang, and the gruesome 1936 "heads and hands" murder that sent four men to Michigan City's electric chair. Leach refused to leave voluntarily, so Silver fired him on the 16th.[25]

Three days later, on September 19, Ed "Old Deafy" Davis and four

11. Mopping Up

other convicts—Fred Barnes, Robert Cannon, Albert Kessell, and Eudy Wesley—seized Folsom Prison's Warden Clarence Larkin and Officer Harry Martin at knifepoint, demanding liberation. Other guards called their bluff, opening fire and killing the hostages, with two of the would-be escapees—before Davis and his surviving cohorts surrendered. Under California's "felony murder" rule, while guards did the actual killing, Davis and his cronies were convicted and sentenced to die.[26]

On September 21, the Brady gang arrived in Bangor, Maine, home of their mythical furniture business. Brady and Dalhover entered Dakin's Sporting Goods Store on Central Street, Brady flashing a fat wad of bills at clerk Lewis Clark, claiming they were hunters who needed equipment. They bought a rifle, two .45 automatics, and some ammunition, while ordering a third .45 and 500 rounds of .30-caliber ammo. Clark made the sale, told his customers to come back later for the rest, then watched them leave and rushed to speak with owner Everett Hurd. Hurd telephoned Bangor Police Chief Thomas Crowley, who said his hands were tied since the strangers had broken no laws.[27]

On the 22nd, Brady and Dalhover visited another shop, Rice and Miller on Broad Street, where they purchased three .32 automatics from clerk C.E. Silsbury. Silsbury in turn called Chief Crowley, who belatedly passed the information on to G-men. Four days later, the bandits returned to Dakin's, bought another rifle, and asked Everett Hurd if he stocked Tommy guns. Certain now that they were criminals, Hurd put them off, requesting that they return "within a few days," and passed word again to Chief Crowley.[28]

While the Bureau's Boston field office plotted a reception for the Brady gang, Bonnie Parker's ex-husband made headlines in Texas. Roy Thornton had received a five-year burglary sentence to Eastham in March 1933, tiring of confinement with only five months left on his term. Doubtless encouraged by summer's bust-outs from the prison farm, he tried an escape of his own on October 3 but guards killed him on the spot, warding off any further bad press for the moment.[29]

Two days later, Albuquerque jurors convicted Guy Osborne of murdering G-man Truett Rowe. Prosecutors seemed surprised when the panel recommended life imprisonment. Osborne arrived at Leavenworth on October 6.[30]

On October 9, Bangor witnessed a covert influx of 15 FBI agents, accompanied by Maine and Indiana State Police. By then, Everett Hurd, Lewis Clark, and other gun store personnel had identified mugshots of Brady and Dalhover, expecting the fugitives to return and collect a nonexistent Tommy gun on the 11th or 12th. On the 11th a phone call told Hurd to expect his customers the following morning, on Columbus Day.[31]

What happened next is local history, still celebrated annually, fictionalized half a century later by best-selling author Stephen King in his horror novel *It*.

The setup was elaborate, with G-men lurking around Dakin's, several of their number inside, impersonating employees. At 8:30 a.m. a Buick bearing Ohio license plates appeared, circled twice around the block, then parked near Dakin's. Al Brady remained in the backseat, while Dalhover entered the store and Shaffer stood guard on the sidewalk. The G-men "clerks" immediately drew their guns, relieved Dalhover of two automatics, handcuffed him, and asked where his "pals" were. Shaffer, outside, noted the commotion and fired through the shop's front door with a .32 pistol, wounding one agent in the shoulder. The G-men returned fire, mortally wounding Shaffer where he stood, while others closed in on the Buick, Maine, and Indiana State Police cars screeching up to seal off the block. From the Buick, Al Brady called, "Don't shoot, don't shoot, I'll get out," but when he emerged he was firing murder victim Paul Minneman's service revolver, two automatics hidden beneath his jacket. One of his .38 slugs pierced an agent's coat and holster, then a storm of federal bullets cut him down, sprawling lifeless in the street.[32]

Overall, the firefight had lasted less than four minutes, but confusion surrounds it to the present day. Many media reports name G-man Walter Walsh as the agent wounded in Dakin's, further crediting him with killing both gangsters that day, plus "at least" nine others before his retirement to join the Marine Corps in 1942, but as previously seen (Chapter 10) another agent claimed credit for slaying Russell Gibson in Chicago and no published record of Walsh's other purported kills exists. Indeed, given the number of feds firing at Shaffer and Brady during their last stand, it seems unlikely that Walsh alone killed either fugitive. Modern Bureau historians still credit no specific agent or agents from bringing down either bandit. Other G-men present at the fight included SAC Earl Connelly, Almon Barber, Christopher Callan, Rufus Coulter, Vernon Criss, Walter Devereaux, Myron Gurnea, Joseph Johnson, Kenneth Logan, and Arthur Reeder.[33]

We *do* know that Al Brady, with no surviving relatives except a distant uncle who refused to claim his corpse, lay unclaimed in Bangor's morgue until his pauper's burial on October 15. Shaffer's family interred him at Madison, Indiana's Fairmount Cemetery.[34]

Ed Davis and his fellow Folsom breakout bunglers reached San Quentin's death row on December 8, awaiting decisions on their appeals.[35]

On January 11, 1938, Louis Piquett left prison minus his law license, finding work as a bartender. That same Monday, G-men captured Hugh Gant and Alva Hunt in Houston, Texas.[36]

11. Mopping Up

Al Brady lies dead in Bangor, Maine, after his gang's shootout with FBI agents on October 12, 1937 (National Archives).

Two weeks later, officers in Pittsburg, California, arrested Edna Cretzer—bandit Dutch's wife—for running a brothel under the alias "Kay Wallace." She posted bond and walked free.[37]

March 28 saw Alvin Karpis back in solitary on The Rock, after guards found a knife in his cell. That punitive sentence lasted four days.[38]

On April 5, the 10th Circuit Court of Appeals rejected a bid by Glen Applegate and Robert Suhay to reverse their death sentences for killing G-man Wimberly Baker. Their first execution date had elapsed by then, so the panel remanded their case to the trial court for scheduling of a new date. They tried again in vain, their bid for a rehearing denied on April 25.[39]

Five days after that defeat, Floyd Hamilton, Ted Walters, and horse-thief Ervin Goodspeed escaped from jail in Montague County, Texas, where Hamilton awaited trial for auto theft. Goodspeed stabbed the sheriff's son in one leg during breakfast service, and victim Kenneth Chandler refused first-aid for his wound, whereupon the trio fled on foot, then stole a Ford V-8, leaving Goodspeed behind. Reaching a roadblock, Walters lay down behind the front seat, while Hamilton pulled a hat low on his face, passing unrecognized by careless manhunters.[40]

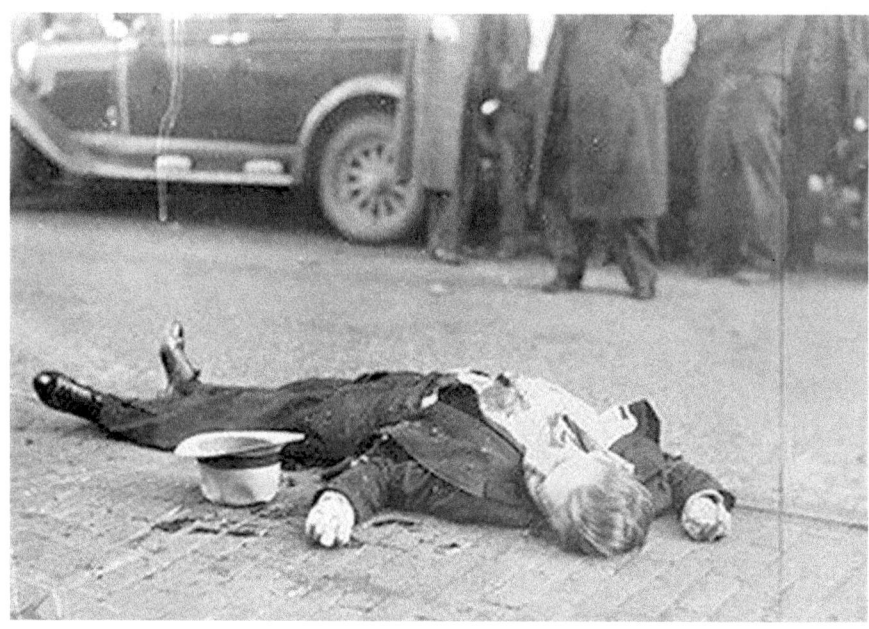

Clarence Shaffer, slain in the same Bangor gunfight, October 12, 1937 (National Archives).

Unidentified FBI agents with weapons captured after the Brady gang's demise in 1937 (National Archives).

11. Mopping Up

In Penfield, Illinois, on May 3, G-man William Ramsey, a partner, and local police tried to arrest Joe Earlywine and John Hulett, suspects in a Lapel, Indiana, bank robbery from December 1937. Hulett surrendered without resistance at Earlywine's home, but Earlywine shot Ramsey multiple times before return fire killed Joe on the spot. Ramsey died at a local hospital the next morning.[41]

Also on May 3, Missouri's Supreme Court affirmed Adam Richetti's murder conviction and death sentence.[42]

June 7 found Floyd Hamilton and Ted Walters back in action, perhaps with fugitive Irvin Chapman, stealing $865 from a bank in Bradley, Arkansas. Authorities initially suspected the same trio of taking $8,000 from a Minden, Louisiana, bank on the 8th, but filed no charges in that case. On June 14 police captured Chapman in New York City.[43]

Nine days later, in Little Rock, Connie Morris pled guilty to harboring Alvin Karpis, receiving a 366-day prison term.[44]

On July 21, after a skirmish with highway patrolmen at Wills Point, Texas, three suspected bandits eluded capture. Witnesses identified one as Floyd Hamilton. Ten days later, officers of the Missouri Highway Patrol pursued three suspects but lost them, naming two as Hamilton and Ted Walters.[45]

Hamilton and Walters, with an unidentified companion, reportedly held up a bank messenger in Wood River, Illinois, on August 5, escaping with $34,000 ($607,000 today). Five days later, the duo, minus their sidekick allegedly engaged in a shootout with police near Fort Worth, Texas.[46]

While lawmen scurried in pursuit of Hamilton and Walters, outlaw Benjamin Dickson married 15-year-old Estelle "Stella Mae Irwin" Redenbraugh—12 years his junior—before a police judge in Pipestone, Minnesota. Ben, the son of a Topeka high school teacher, had already served time for auto theft in Kansas and bank robbery in Missouri, but his clean-cut appearance, coupled with Stella's perpetual smile, produced a classic image of the boy and girl next door, when in fact they had more in common with Bonnie and Clyde. Stella knew Ben first as Chicago insurance salesman "Johnny O'Malley," but he spilled the truth within weeks of their meeting, then fled to California ahead of an assault charge, sending Stella money to join him. They wed while on vacation with her seemingly oblivious parents at Lake Benton, near Pipestone.[47]

Three weeks after their nuptials, one day before Stella turned 16, a Ford with California license plates stopped outside a bank in Elkton, South Dakota, disgorging an angry-looking young woman. She wore a straw hat, dark glasses, and men's overalls, walking with "a pronounced hip movement" as she crossed the street. She carried a package wrapped in newspaper, "about the size of a machine gun," prompting one witness to surmise she was "a gun moll." Ben Dickson, similarly clad, entered the bank soon afterward, producing a white sugar sack and demanding that clerk Robert Petschow fill it with bills from the cashier's registers. Advised that the vault's time lock would not open for another 30 minutes, Dickson said he would wait. Stella entered soon thereafter, while Ben chatted with customers. Once the time lock disengaged, the Dicksons bagged more cash, then shut the bank's employees and customers inside the vault. Within 15 minutes of the thieves' departure, carrying $17,592.99 in cash, plus stocks valued at more than $16,000, FBI agents had been informed of the holdup. From Elkton, Ben and Stella drove to her parents' home in Topeka, Kansas, remaining there until their return to southwestern South Dakota two months later. While G-men began tracking the still-unidentified raiders, Ben spent his time between heists attending night school and taking correspondence courses, as if preparing for a legitimate future.[48]

On August 13 Leavenworth officials hanged Glenn Applegate and Robert Suhay, the first double execution in Kansas since brothers Jake and Joe Tobler, hanged in November 1888.[49]

Adam Richetti received his second death sentence on August 31, but by then, Missouri's mode of execution had changed, supplanting the gallows with a lethal gas chamber. Authorities transferred him from Kansas City's jail to Jefferson City's state prison on September 3.[50]

One day after Adam's transfer, in Dallas, a "Kentucky-style family feud" enveloped the Barrow family. L.C. Barrow, lately released

Stella Dickson poses with firearms, emulating the late Bonnie Parker (National Archives).

from prison, had entered a tavern with brother Jack, where they quarreled with former gang traitor S.J. "Baldy" Whatley. Later that night, September 4, Whatley fired shots into the home of Clyde Barrow's parents, blinding mother Cumie in one eye and nearly killing her, inflicting lesser wounds on her nephew, Lewis Francis. Police jailed Whatley for attempted murder, then released him on $18,500 bond. Later, they hauled him back repeatedly, accused of dynamiting Henry and Cumie's home, then twice firebombing the family's filling station. Whatley finally received a 12-year sentence, then escaped from Huntsville, living with his wife in Dallas for 10 months before officers retrieved him. Back in custody, Baldy confessed to using his free time for a series of jewelry store holdups.[51]

As Adam Richetti's time ran out, Ben Dickson concocted a plan to free him from Jefferson City. Formerly a worker in the prison's repair shop, Dickson schemed to pack a damaged couch with a revolver, 50 rounds of ammo, and a stick of dynamite, smuggling it into the lockup where friends on the inside would use the hardware to free Richetti and stage a mass breakout. Unknown to Dickson, that job went to free world repairman Milo Waltz, brother of Cole County's sheriff, who found the contraband and blew the whistle. On October 7 Jeff City officials gassed Richetti on schedule, making him Missouri's first inmate executed via cyanide, thereby endorsing the FBI's frameup.[52]

On October 29, federal jurors in Little Rock convicted Grace Goldstein, Hot Springs Police Chief Joseph Wakelin, Chief of Detectives Herbert "Dutch" Akers, and Lieutenant Cecil Brock on charges of harboring Alvin Karpis. The four received identical two-year prison terms. That same day, Lloyd Barker was paroled from Leavenworth at age 40, settling with his father George in Joplin, Missouri.[53]

Two days later, on Halloween morning, Ben and Stella Dickson pulled their second South Dakota holdup in Brookings. They caught assistant bank manager John Torsey arriving for work and got the drop on him, finding manager Richard DePuy, teller Curtis Lovre and his wife, bookkeeper Dorothy Lovre, already inside. As at Elkton two months earlier, the bandits waited patiently for the vault's time lock to wind down, watching oblivious customers come and go, escaping with $47,233 in cash and bonds. Employees at a nearby gas station saw Stella waving goodbye while she scattered roofing nails behind their car to stall pursuers. In bygone days, both the Dillinger and Barker-Karpis gangs had taken similar precautions.[54]

While the Dicksons cashed in at Brookings, Irvin Chapman fought a skirmish with police near Williamsville, Mississippi, eluding capture once again.[55]

On November 3, 1938, in Fort Smith, Arkansas, Floyd Hamilton and

Ted Walters pled guilty to bank robbery, receiving 30 years apiece. Hamilton entered Leavenworth on the 4th to start serving his time.[56]

Two weeks later, on Wednesday the 18th, Rhuel Dalhover died in Michigan City's electric chair for murdering Indiana State Police Officer Paul Minneman. He was buried at Fairmount Cemetery in North Madison (now simply Madison), Indiana.[57]

Six days after Dalhover's execution, police spotted Ben and Stella Dickson vacationing with relatives in Topeka for Thanksgiving. The fugitives escaped separately, Stella hiding under a bridge, while Ben drove to Clinton, Iowa, stole another car there, and returned to pick up Stella on the 25th. Over the successive days, they engaged in two running firefights with Michigan authorities, Stella flattening the tires of one patrol car and earning the nickname "Sure Shot." They also hijacked a car in Michigan, then two more in Indiana, finally buying another one there and making for New Orleans. Despite a massive media campaign, G-men lost track of them and settled in to wait for the couple's next move.[58]

During two weeks in December 1938, California executed four perpetrators of the failed Folsom prison break that killed Warden Clarence Larkin and Officer Harry Martin. Robert Cannon and Albert Kessell paid their debt in San Quentin's gas chamber—its first-ever occupants—on the 2nd. Fred Barnes and Eudy Wesley went next, in another double-header on December 9. Ringleader Ed Davis brought up the rear on the 16th, finally closing the book on his long life of crime. A note left in his death row cell read, "No regrets for Old Ed. All considered, my conscience is now resting easy."[59]

January 1939 witnessed another bungled prison break, this one on The Rock. On the 13th, Dock Barker joined inmates William "Ty" Martin, Rufus McCain, Dale Stamphill, and Henri Young in a bid for freedom. Already segregated as troublesome prisoners, the five sawed through four sets of bars, scaled walls under cover of nocturnal fog, and made their way to the beach. There, they split into pairs and tried to swim for the mainland, soon defeated by the tides. Next, they tried to build a raft from scrap wood, bound with pieces of their shirts, but a tower guard finally spied them as the fog cleared. He and other guards aboard a patrol boat opened fire when the convicts ignored demands for surrender, wounding Stamphill, striking Barker in the head and one leg. Martin, McCain, and Young landed in solitary, while Barker and Stamphill went to the prison infirmary. There, doctors tried to give Dock a blood transfusion, but he pulled the tubes out and died soon thereafter.[60]

Authorities buried Barker at Olivet Memorial Park in Colma, California. Henri Young, in retrospect, called Dock "one of America's most dangerous men. I knew, however, that he was determined and ruthless, and that once he started on anything nothing could stop him but death. I couldn't think of anyone else I'd rather have with me on a break from Alcatraz."⁶¹

On February 8 Arnold Kyle stole $9,115 from a bank in Wichita, Kansas.⁶²

Despite his expression of "absolute horror and disgust" at the prospect of a movie praising Melvin Purvis, J. Edgar Hoover had no qualms about approving four separate Hollywood features based on his ghostwritten volume *Persons in Hiding*, all of which put unacknowledged money in his pocket. Paramount Studios—formerly bullied into dropping *Federal Dick*—released the first, also titled *Persons in Hiding*, fictionalizing the Urschel kidnapping, on February 10, 1939, starring J. Carrol Naish as "Freddie 'Gunner' Martin," pressured into trying the snatch racket by avaricious girlfriend "Dorothy Bronson"—Patricia Morison in her debut role as "the WOMAN behind the KILLER behind the GUN!" Posters trumpeted that "J. Edgar Hoover tells her story," although William Lipman and Horace McCoy penned the screenplay.⁶³

Four months later, on June 9, Paramount's first sequel hit U.S. theaters. *Undercover Doctor* starred Naish again, this time as a thinly-disguised Wilhelm Loeser ("Dr. Bartley Morgan"), servicing various felons in league with "Eddie Kator" (Broderick Crawford), aided by nurse "Margaret Hopkins" (Janice Morgan). Once again, posters gave top billing to "author" Hoover, while Lipman and McCoy wrote the script.⁶⁴

Eight months elapsed before release of Paramount's next sequel, *Parole Fixer*, on February 2, 1940. Billed as Hoover's exposé of a corrupt parole system, the film focused on gangster "Francis 'Big Boy' Bradmore," played by Anthony Quinn, who receives undeserved clemency, then quickly murders a fictional FBI agent. As before, screenwriters Lipman and McCoy crafted the drama, while ceding top marquee credit to Hoover.⁶⁵

Finally, on June 28, 1940, Paramount released *Queen of the Mob*, a highly fictionalized pastiche of the Barker-Karpis gang. "Ma Webster" (Blanche Yurka) lives quietly with husband Eddie (James Seay), while she masterminds the criminal rampage of sons Bert, Charlie, Tom, and Billy, portrayed respectively by William Henry, Richard Denning, Paul Kelly, and Tommy Conley. J. Carol Naish returns as "George Frost," standing in for Alvin Karpis as the only gang member not spawned from Ma's loins. In a Christmas Eve finale, G-men surround Ma and Eddie at a rural hideout, killing Eddie and capturing Ma alive to face trial. Hoover's name appeared on posters once again, while Lipman and McCoy did the actual writing.⁶⁶

If Paramount had suffered any loss from scuttling *Federal Dick*, the studio regained Hoover's favor and profited handsomely from its revisions

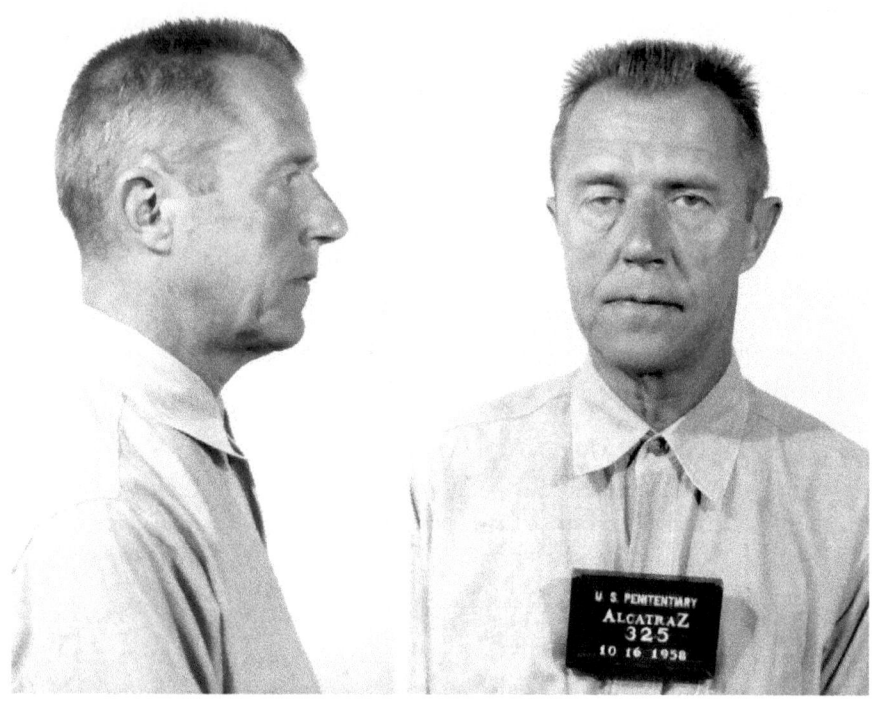

Prison mugshot of Alvin Karpis taken eleven years prior to his 1969 parole and deportation to Canada (National Archives).

of *Persons in Hiding*. No one can say how much of the box office proceeds ultimately found their way to Hoover's hands.

In the midst of that movie marathon, on March 30, 1939, attorneys argued the case of *United States v. Miller* before the U.S. Supreme Court. That case involved "Irish O'Malley" gang member Jackson Miller, tried and convicted for violating the National Firearms Act, specifically by transporting a sawed-off shotgun from Oklahoma into Arkansas. Miller claimed that law violated the Constitution's Second Amendment right to "keep and bear arms" on behalf of a "well-regulated Militia ... necessary to the security of a free State." While that assertion seemed bizarre on its face, posed by a lifelong felon, the panel pondered it for nearly seven weeks, then reversed Miller's conviction and remanded the case for retrial on May 15, but Jack never saw the inside of another courtroom. Before his retrial could be scheduled, hikers found his bullet-riddled corpse on the bank of Spencer Creek, in Oklahoma's Rogers County, apparently executed by underworld rivals.[67]

G-men searched in vain for Ben and Stella Dickson after their second bank holdup, until April 6, when a tip sent four agents to a hamburger shop

11. Mopping Up

near Forest Park in midtown St. Louis. There, they saw Ben sitting with a woman identified only as "Naomi," sister of a former cellmate from Jefferson City, who doubled as a paid police informer. When Ben left the restaurant, Stella waiting for him in a car nearby, one agent shot him twice in the back and side, killing him.[68]

Bureau reports claimed that Ben saw the agents as he left the café and "crouched," reaching for a hidden gun and forcing the unnamed G-man to kill him in self-defense. The sole civilian witness, burger joint waitress Gloria Cambrón, saw things differently. In her initial account, the agents confronted Dickson, whereupon Ben turned and ran toward an apartment north of the café, where a locked door defeated his effort to enter. Only *then* was he shot, still without threatening the agents. Local police arrived on the scene, making a "technical arrest" of two agents, while G-man Gerald Norris, in charge of the case, refused to answer questions until he'd spoken with his superiors in Washington. Gloria Cambrón shared her tale with several reporters over the next 24 hours, whereupon Bureau Assistant Director Edward Tamm ordered Rogers "that this woman should be brought into the office and given a good scare and that she should be told that she has been quoted in the newspapers as telling some stores [sic] that were not true and that if we are going to have to prosecute her for perjury or something, we will do so." At the subsequent coroner's inquest, omitting Cambrón from the witness roster, Agent Norris supported the Bureau's version of events under oath. Washington's account compounded those lies, denying that any hired informer was present the day Dickson died, and the jury ruled his killing justifiable. A memoir penned later by ex–Agent Louis Cochran listed Dickson's crimes in detail, while omitting any mention of "Naomi" or Gloria Cambrón.[69]

After witnessing her husband's summary execution, Stella Dickson sought to reach her mother's home in Topeka, hiring a man to serve as her driver. Meanwhile, the *Kansas City Star* reported that "Estelle [sic] Dickson is wanted just as badly as her husband was," giving her chauffeur an idea for instant profit, calling ahead and parking his car less than a block from the Bureau's KC field office. Stella later said, "I knew the minute he stopped he was going to get a federal man to arrest me. I didn't care. I just sat in the car. I knew if I got out and tried to get to Topeka by myself I wouldn't get there alive, and I wanted to see my mother." Swarmed by waiting agents, Stella surrendered peaceably, carrying a poem of sorts written by ben, which read, "In the eyes of men I am not just, but in your eyes, O Life, I see justification. You have taught me that my path is right if I am true to you."[70]

On April 10, after a doctor's examination and protracted questioning without her mother or a lawyer present, Stella appeared before a federal commissioner in KC with her mother and stepfather, waiving extradition

WANTED poster for Benjamin and Estelle Dickson, final bandits of the FBI's "crime war" era (author's collection).

to South Dakota while held under $25,000 bond returnable at Sioux Falls. On April 13 she revised her first confession, blaming husband "Johnny" for their holdups, committed against her will, adding that he "frequently got mad at me and said if I left him he would kill me and said he would kill anybody who helped me leave him."[71]

On April 16 agents raided the Chicago home of ex–Dillinger associate James Murray and jailed him for robbing a Clintonville, Pennsylvania, bank of $85,000 ($1.5 million today) six months earlier, with companions John Dorsch and George Slade. In addition to harboring Dillinger, Murray, a sometime local politician, had reportedly helped transport Lester Gillis's corpse in November 1934. A two-time loser, previously convicted for a $2 million train robbery at Rondout, Illinois, in 1924 ($30 million today), Murray was convicted and received a 10-year sentence.[72]

Two days after Murray's capture, Minneapolis police caught Arnold Kyle driving drunk under the alias "Raymond Palmer," but identified him from fingerprints and surrendered him to FBI agents. On June 7 Kyle pled guilty to bank robbery, receiving a 25-year sentence at McNeil Island, Washington.[73]

Stella Dickson appeared before federal judge Alfred Wyman on August 21, in Deadwood, South Dakota. Age 17 by then, she pled guilty on two counts of bank robbery and received twin concurrent 10-year terms at the U.S. Women's Reformatory in Alderson, West Virginia. Six days later, she arrived there and started serving her time. FBI headquarters approved the plea bargain, apparently hoping to whitewash Ben Dickson's death and prevent witness Gloria Cambrón from trying to clear her conscience with more public revelations.[74]

On August 24, J. Edgar Hoover scored another "personal" arrest and logged the FBI's only capture of a Syndicate gangster since Al Capone, charged with contempt of a federal court in Miami ten years earlier. This time, the subject was labor racketeer Louis "Lepke" Buchalter, who in fact arranged his own surrender in Gotham through gossip columnist Walter Winchell, a close friend of Hoover's. Despite false claims that Hoover "walked alone" to meet and arrest Lepke, Winchell actually drove him to the meeting site on Fifth Avenue, while a carload of armed G-men shadowed their every move.[75]

Three days after Lepke turned himself in, FBI agents arrested Dutch Cretzer in Chicago. Like partner Kyle before him, he pled guilty to bank robbery before Judge Leon Yankwich and received a matching 25-year-sentence at McNeil Island.[76]

On September 6, 1939, Irvin Chapman shot his way out of a police trap near his hometown of Philadelphia, Mississippi. Later accounts claiming he was tagged as No. 1 on the FBI's "Most Wanted" list are erroneous, since that roster did not exist before March 1950.[77]

Two months later, on November 7, Edna Cretzer pled guilty to harboring her fugitive husband and received an 85-day jail term. That same day, Dutch pled guilty to one of the gang's Los Angeles holdups before Judge Leon Yankwich, who'd previously sentenced Edna's brother, Arnold Kyle, to 25 years at McNeil Island. Dutch received a matching term and joined his partner there, where they soon began plotting a breakout.[78]

12

Scorched Earth

No one escapes from war unscathed. Even survivors leave the battlefield with physical and psychic scars. As for the dead, in April 1936 Director Hoover told the Senate that since June 1934 "there have been eight desperadoes killed by our agents and we have had four agents killed by them."[1]

In fact, both stats were wrong. Agents killed seven fugitives during the 21 months in question. Eight G-men died in combat during the "crime war," but only three—Agents Cowley, Hollis, and Klein—fell between June 1934 Hoover's public claim.[2] As for the gangsters who survived arrest....

Fred "Killer" Burke developed diabetes in prison and died from a heart attack on July 10, 1940.[3]

Two survivors of Dock Barker's abortive 1939 Alcatraz escape bid, Rufus McCain and Henri Young, served time in solitary, somehow becoming enemies. On December 3, 1940, Young fatally stabbed McCain with a sharpened spoon, refusing to disclose his motive. Convicted of that slaying, he remained in solitary until 1948, when he was transferred to the Medical Center for Federal Prisoners at Springfield, Missouri. Washington State claimed him in 1954, to serve time for a 1933 homicide. Released in 1972, he jumped parole and vanished. The 1995 film *Murder in the First* portrays a fictionalized version of Young's time at Alcatraz.[4]

Lansing escapee Lewis Bechtel received a full pardon from Kansas Governor Payne Ratner on January 11, 1941, and vanished thereafter from the public record.[5]

Irvin Chapman remained on the FBI's wanted list, profiled in the Bureau's July 1940 *Law Enforcement Bulletin* as a fugitive from bank-robbing and Dyer Act charges, traveling under 15 known aliases. He returned to Mississippi in January 1942, wounding a Meridian patrolman the 17th, then ran out of luck in his native Neshoba County on February 22. Stopped at a roadblock by calls for surrender, Chapman and comrade Alfred Ward responded differently, Ward raising his hands while Chapman came out shooting. Three G-men and 15 other officers replied in kind, riddling

Chapman with bullets. Dying, he snarled, "Go ahead and shoot, you bastards," then expired. Relatives buried him in nearby Sandtown.[6]

It took six years for the 10th Circuit Court of Appeals to rule on Irish O'Malley gang member Dewey Gilmore's appeal of his January 1936 indictment with co-defendant Russell Cooper, wherein both were charged and later convicted of escaping from Muskogee, Oklahoma's jail in December 1935, killing Chief of Detectives Ben Bolton in the process. The appellate court affirmed the indictment and conviction on June 29, 1942, leaving Gilmore to complete his 25-year prison term.[7]

Leslie Homer served his time for the Racine mail holdup, then passed into obscurity after release in 1943.[8]

Lansing escapee Cliff Dopson received a pardon from Governor Andrew Schoeppel in 1943 and vanished from the public record.[9]

Union Station conspirator Louis Stacci died at 50 in Chicago, on August 15, 1943, buried there as "Louis Stacey," a frequent alias.[10]

Multiple sources report that Walter "Irish O'Malley" Holland was declared insane while serving a life term for the August Luer kidnapping. All agree that he died sometime in 1944, but none provide any further details.[11]

Some observers predicted a short lifespan for Joseph Negri, based on his testimony against members of the Gillis gang, but no one moved against him. Instead, he married happily and in 1940 wrote a three-part article for *True Detective Magazine* on his life as a gangster, titled "In the Hinges of Hell." Penned with aid from Bureau PR flacks, that series bore the subtitle "How G-Men Ended Crime's Reddest Chapter." Negri served with the Merchant Marine during World War II, then disappeared into obscurity, his fate unknown.[12]

Herbert Farmer spent two years at Alcatraz for his role in the Kansas City massacre, then returned to his wife in Missouri. He died in Joplin at 55, on January 12 or 24, 1948 (reports differ).[13]

Texas commuted Henry Methvin's death sentence to life imprisonment in September 1936, then paroled him in March 1942. November 1945 saw him jailed for carrying a shotgun and fighting. In October 1946 Shreveport police arrested him for attempted robbery and drunk driving. Intoxicated again on April 19, 1948, he was struck and killed by a train in Sulphur, Louisiana. Stories differ as to whether he fell asleep on the tracks, tried to cross in a stupor, or was murdered for his role in the slayings of Bonnie and Clyde.[14]

A fellow Alcatraz inmate stabbed Albert Bates to death on July 4, 1948.[15]

Lloyd Barker was paroled from Leavenworth in time to serve as a U.S. Army cook during World War II, at a Michigan prisoner of war camp, receiving a Good Conduct Medal and an honorable discharge. Moving to Denver with his wife, Lloyd worked as market manager until she shot and killed him on March 18, 1949, afterward committed to the Colorado State Insane Asylum.[16]

After many disciplinary infractions at Lansing, Harold "Billie Woods" Harris received a full pardon from Governor Payne Rattner on February 28, 1941. Illinois police detained him on suspicion of burglary in 1942, then dropped the case, after which he moved to St. Louis and opened a hamburger restaurant. After a series of local break-ins, a highway patrolman caught Harris near Bluffton with a small arsenal in his car. Convicted of burglary and larceny, he received an eight-year sentence, released in 1944. Reverting to the "Woods" pseudonym, he moved to Kansas City, tried selling cars during World War II, then remarried and moved to Eminence, Missouri, as a professional hunter. Obsessed with 15-year-old neighbor Lila Fanser, he abducted her from home in 1950, killing her older brother and wounding her mother in the process. Stopped at a police roadblock on August 9, Harris resisted arrest and died from a sniper's gunshot. Officers recovered his victim unharmed.[17]

Thomas Holden left Alcatraz in November 1947 and returned to Chicago. On June 5, 1949, in a drunken row, he fatally shot his wife and her two brothers. Named to the FBI's new "Ten Most Wanted" list on March 14, 1950, he was captured in Oregon on June 23, 1951. Sentenced to life at Joliet, he died there from a heart attack on December 18, 1953.[18]

George Kelly served 17 years at Alcatraz, then was transferred to Leavenworth, where a heart attack killed him on his 59th birthday, July 18, 1954. In his obituary, an unnamed FBI spokesman repeated the lie that agents found Kelly "cowering in a corner with no gun handy. His face twitched and got white. He was whimpering. He lost his bravado. He reached up his hands toward the ceiling, trembled and said, 'Don't shoot, G-Men, don't shoot.'"[19]

President Roosevelt pardoned Robert "Boss" Shannon "owing to ill health" in 1944, but Shannon survived for another 12 years, described by acquaintance Stephen Barnes as "a basket case," predicting oil strikes on his property. Thrice married, he died on Christmas Day 1956, age 79, and was buried in Cottondale between his first two wives, sisters Mary and Maud Jackson.[20]

"Big Tom" Brown was never prosecuted for his crimes. He moved to Morris, Minnesota, and ran a liquor store until dying from a heart attack on January 5, 1959.[21]

Edward Shouse died from heart disease in Chicago, on September 13, 1959, and was buried in an unmarked grave in Terre Haute, Indiana.[22]

Roger Touhy staged a prison break from Joliet Prison on October 6,

1942, with Basil Banghart and five other inmates, using guns tossed over the wall by one escapee's brother. G-men captured one fugitive on December 16, then traced the rest to a Chicago rooming house 12 days later. Two escapees died fighting, while the rest surrendered, Touhy receiving an additional 199 years for the breakout. On August 9, 1954, a federal district court ordered Touhy's release, finding that Jake Factor's kidnapping was a hoax, prosecuted with perjured testimony. Briefly free, Touhy returned to prison 50 hours later, when an appellate court denied the district court's jurisdiction. The Supreme Court upheld that decision on February 14, 1955. On July 19, 1957, Governor William Stratton commuted Touhy's original 99-year sentence to 72 years and reduced his 199-year sentence to three years. Touhy left Joliet on November 24, 1959, but a federal judge sought to reverse the parole two days later, despite clear evidence of perjury and prosecutorial misconduct. Before that case was litigated, on December 16, 1959, shotgunners fatally wounded Touhy and a bodyguard in Chicago. Touhy's last recorded words: "I've been expecting it. The bastards never forget!"[23]

Harry Copeland was intoxicated when a car struck and killed him in Detroit, on December 7, 1963.[24]

Edna Murray passed her Missouri prison time by giving interviews with titles such as "I Was a Karpis-Barker Gang Moll" and befriended fellow inmate Blanche Barrow. Paroled on December 20, 1940, she moved to San Francisco and died there in 1966, at age 68.[25]

Urschel kidnap conspirator Armon "Potatoes" Shannon went "straight" after receiving a suspended sentence in 1933. He died in Paradise, Texas, at 56, on August 11, 1968, and was buried with his father in Cottondale.[26]

Russell Clark served 34 years in prison, paroled for health reasons on August 14, 1968. He died in Detroit on December 24 of that year. Conflicting reports blame cancer and heart disease.[27]

Authorities transferred John Paul Chase from Alcatraz to Leavenworth in September 1954. Director Hoover called for immediate trial on a pending indictment for Herman Hollis's murder, but a federal judge in Chicago dismissed that charge on October 17, 1955, ruling that prosecutors failed in their requirement for a speedy trial. Paroled on October 31, 1966, Chase worked as an infirmary custodian in Palo Alto, California, until cancer claimed his life on October 5, 1973.[28]

Jim Clark operated a gambling and loan-sharking racket at Leavenworth until January 1948, when he received a disciplinary transfer to Alcatraz, then returned to Leavenworth in 1960 and finally wound up incarcerated at Seagoville, Texas, in 1969. Paroled on December 9 of that year, he moved to Oklahoma, married his brother's widow, and worked as

12. Scorched Earth

a ranch hand until age rendered him useless, then managed a local bank's commercial parking lot until his death on June 9, 1974.[29]

Authorities paroled W.D. Jones in time for World War II but the army rejected him due to preexisting bullet wounds and fragments. He returned to Houston, married, and appeared to settle down. Widowed in the 1960s, he sued Warner Brothers for "maligning his character" in *Bonnie and Clyde* (case dismissed), turned to drugs and entered rehab in 1971. On September 13, 1973, federal judge James Noel sentenced Jones to six months in prison and 4½ years' probation for illegal possession of barbiturates. On August 20, 1974, Jones met a young woman at a bar and drove her to the home of her ex-boyfriend, where an argument ensued and she told her ex that she was with a Barrow gangster who was armed. Jealous boyfriend George Jones (no relation) killed William with a shotgun. George received a 15-year sentence, then committed suicide prior to entering prison.[30]

Bryan Bolton served his time and reunited with wife Vera in California, working at a Lakewood furniture store in the 1950s as William B. Bolton. Tuberculosis claimed his life in 1977. Vera outlived him by six years.[31]

Released in 1948, Francis Keating returned to Minneapolis, working in a flower shop, then as a union organizer in Saint Paul. A heart attack killed him at a nursing home in Saint Louis Park, Minnesota, at 79, on July 25, 1978.[32]

From Alcatraz, Harvey Bailey was transferred to Leavenworth in 1946, then to a Texas lockup in 1960. Released on March 30, 1964, he married and resumed the cabinet-maker's trade he'd learned as a youth. His autobiography, published in 1973, absolved Fred Burke of participation in the St. Valentine's Day massacre, claiming Bailey and Burke were planning a robbery when the murders occurred. Bailey died peacefully in Joplin, Missouri, at age 91, on March 1, 1979.[33]

Esther Farmer outlived her husband and married ex-convict Harvey Bailey in 1966. Records indicate that she died in Joplin two days after Bailey, on March 3, 1979, and was interred near first love "Deafy."[34]

Volney Davis was in poor health when he left Alcatraz in the late 1950s. On May 21, 1960, he married Daisy Graham in California's Contra Costa County and they settled in Guerneville. He died in Sonoma County on July 20, 1979.[35]

Authorities transferred Alvin Karpis from Alcatraz to Leavenworth for six months during 1958, then returned him to The Rock until April 1962, recording numerous fights with other inmates during his 26 years—a record—at Alcatraz. In April 1962 he moved again, to McNeil Island Penitentiary in Washington State, where he gave guitar lessons to car thief Charles Manson. Paroled in 1969, his lack of fingerprints delayed deportation to his native Canada. Karpis coauthored a memoir in 1971 and moved to Spain in 1973, dying there from a drug overdose on August 26, 1979. Pathologists performed no autopsy, but a coroner changed the initial verdict of suicide to death by natural causes and Karpis was buried the following day. A second memoir hit bookstores in 1980.[36]

Bandit Frank Sawyer appealed his Fort Scott robbery conviction in vain, despite published claims from Alvin Karpis pronouncing him innocent of that charge. Kansas governor Robert Docking pardoned him on September 18, 1969, based on a sworn affidavit from Karpis, and Sawyer sued the state for false imprisonment, but that case still awaited litigation at his death on August 27, 1979.[37]

Eddie Bentz left Alcatraz in 1948, but not for freedom. Open charges in Massachusetts saw him confined until 1954, followed by an eight-year sentence in Wisconsin, before a federal parole violation jailed him at Sandstone, Minnesota, in 1962. Free at last by 1967, he returned to his native Tacoma, where he died on October 31, 1979, at age 81. His death certificate lists his occupation as "salesman" of "specialty advertising."[38]

Upon leaving prison, Urschel kidnap conspirator Ora Shannon settled in Tecumseh, Oklahoma. She died there, age 91, on May 21, 1980.[39]

Following his 1934 testimony, Gordon Alcorn was transferred from Leavenworth to Alcatraz. Paroled and deported to Canada in 1949, he settled in Vancouver to lead "a quiet and law-abiding life." Published obituaries for his relatives report him living in 1972 but deceased when his brother died July 1983. Sparse records indicate he died in 1982, date uncertain, at age 76 or 77.[40]

Floyd Hamilton served time for harboring the Barrow gang, then returned to Leavenworth and Alcatraz before eventual release in 1958, following a failed attempt to make him serve a 25-year Texas sentence handed down 30 years earlier. He emerged as a Christian convert, running a halfway house for ex-convicts and touring as an itinerant preacher, earning kudos as "a fine man" for religious work. Hamilton died in Tarrant County, Texas, at 76, on July 24, 1984.[41]

Kathryn Kelly won parole in 1958 and settled in Tecumseh, Oklahoma, residing as "Lera Cleo Kelly" until her death at 81, on May 28, 1985. She was interred with her mother at Tecumseh, Oklahoma.[42]

Despite spending time in solitary for leading a prison strike, Ralph Fults received a pardon in 1944 and found "straight" work as a security guard and laundry manager at a Dallas orphanage. There, he converted to Christianity and lectured young inmates on the perils of crime. In 1960 he helped create a local TV show called *Confession*, later nationally syndicated, featuring Texas officials, business leaders and lawyers on issues related to ex-convicts' employment. Fults died in Dallas at 82, on March 16, 1993.[43]

12. Scorched Earth

Stella Dickson remained in prison until age 26, in 1958. She later settled in Raytown, Missouri, working as a grocery store clerk and remarrying several times before emphysema claimed her life in 1995, at age 72. Her exploits with first husband Ben allegedly inspired the Thomas Strubel, founder of a Brookings, South Dakota, micro-brewery, to name his new firm "Heist Brewing Company" in 2010.[44]

John Dillinger remains the "crime war's" superstar. Nephew Michael Thompson sought permission to exhume his uncle's corpse in 2019, claiming he had "evidence" that the remains were not Dillinger's. Indiana's Department of Health approved on July 3, while A&E Networks announced plans to cover the exhumation on its History Channel, but great-nephew Jeff Scalf opposed the "despicable" effort in court, backed by objections from Crown Hill Cemetery's staff. Thompson's permit expired in September, but another was issued in October, permitting exhumation and reburial before December 31. The FBI, meanwhile, weighed in with a statement calling Dillinger's alleged survival "a common myth." A&E abandoned the project and Thompson dropped his efforts in January 2020. The mysteries surrounding Dillinger's death endure (see Chapter 13).[45]

Gang wives and "molls" faced their own travails after the "crime war."

Deported to Romania, Anna Sage died there from liver disease on April 25, 1947.[46]

Housekeepers found Patricia Cherrington dead in her room at Chicago's Burton Hotel on May 3, 1949, survived by a daughter in New York.[47]

Ray Hamilton's sister Margie, while not a Barrow gang member, had legal problems of her own. In 1946 she shot and killed first husband Andy Robinson but grand jurors declined to indict her. In June 1952 she killed second spouse Michael Zeglen with the same pistol, again pleading self-defense, receiving a five-year sentence that November. Released early, she opened a bar in Houston and shot customer Jessie Muirhead in January 1953, after he "insisted on finding out how tough she is." Muirhead survived and no charges resulted. After relocating to Bogalusa, Louisiana, Margie died there at age 50, on March 4, 1966.[48]

After a short-lived career on the lecture circuit, Evelyn Frechette succumbed to cancer in Shawano, Wisconsin, on January 13, 1969. She was 61.[49]

Polly Hamilton went into hiding after Dillinger's death but eventually returned to Chicago under an assumed name and married salesman Michael Black. As "Edyth Black," she died there on February 19, 1969.[50]

Herbert Farmer's wife Esther served no time for helping "Deafy" run a safe house for 1930s "public enemies." Upon his release from Alcatraz they reunited, sold their farm, and moved to Joplin, Missouri. Widowed in 1948, she married Harvey Bailey in October 1966. Esther died on March 3, 1979, age 90 or 91, and was buried with Bailey at Joplin's Forest Park Cemetery. Deafy Farmer lies nearby.[51]

Helen Gillis returned to Chicago after her release from federal prison in December 1936. She died there at 79, on July 3, 1987, one week after suffering a stroke, and was buried beside husband Lester.[52]

After prison, Blanche Barrow returned to Dallas and in 1940 married Eddie Frasure. They adopted a son in 1965, later estranged due to his legal issues. Although displeased by her portrayal in the 1967 film *Bonnie and Clyde*, she remained good friends with star Warren Beatty. Cancer killed Blanche on December 24, 1988, one week before her 78th birthday. Her memoirs appeared posthumously in 2004.[53]

Other gangster relatives and accomplices met the Reaper in their turn, beginning with Chicago gunsmith Oswald von Lengerke on July 19, 1932, at age 71.[54]

Cumie Barrow, Clyde's mother, served 30 days for harboring her son and avoided legal problems thereafter. She died on August 14, 1947, age 67. Husband Henry, never charged, survived her by a nearly a decade, dying at 83 on June 19, 1957. By then all but two of her seven children were dead or imprisoned.[55]

John Wilson Dillinger died at 79, on November 3, 1943, and was buried next to his son.[56]

Emma Parker, Bonnie's widowed mother, joined various family members and relatives of other outlaws on the "Crime Does Not Pay" circuit, then returned to Dallas. She died at 59, on September 21, 1944, and rests beside Bonnie in an unmarked grave.[57]

Douglas Cretzer confessed to a Los Angeles bank heist in January 1940, receiving a 26-year sentence at McNeil's Island with brother-in-law Arnold Kyle. He entered the prison on February 15 with no plans to stay. On April 11, the pair hijacked a prison truck and escaped but were recaptured after three days near the McNeil Island schoolhouse. During their trial for that offense, on August 22, they tried to flee again, assaulting Deputy U.S. Marshal A.J. Chitty, but were caught before fleeing the courthouse. Chitty's death from a heart attack earned them both life sentences at Alcatraz, where they failed at a third escape attempt, on May 22, 1941. On May 2, 1946, Cretzer joined five other inmates in his last escape attempt, touching off a two-day melee dubbed "the Battle of Alcatraz," murdering two guards and injuring 14 more. U.S. Marines joined prison guards to suppress the rebellion, killing Cretzer and accomplice Bernard Coy on May 4. Edna Cretzer claimed her husband's remains, had him cremated, and interred his ashes at Coloma, California's Cypress Lawn Memorial Cemetery. Inmates Sam Shockley and Miran Thompson were convicted of murder, executed at

12. Scorched Earth 227

San Quentin on December 3, 1948. Survivor Clarence Carnes received an extended sentence, was paroled, then returned to prison twice for parole violations. He died from AIDS–related complications at the Medical Center for Federal Prisoners in Springfield, Missouri, on October 3, 1988.[58] Meanwhile, Dr. Harold Cassidy, Dillinger's anesthetist, committed suicide in Chicago on July 30, 1946.[59]

Passersby found Ivan Methvin dead in Shreveport, Louisiana, on December 28, 1946. Accounts differ on whether he was beaten or struck by a still-unidentified hit-and-run driver.[60]

One source describes Elvin "Jack" Barrow, Clyde's eldest brother, as "a law-abiding and peaceful man," while another says he received a 99-year sentence for a West Dallas murder in 1940. He died on April 26, 1947, at 52.[61]

Lawyer Louis Piquett appealed his sentence all the way to the Supreme Court, which upheld it in April 1936. President Harry Truman pardoned him in January 1951 and a heart attack killed Piquett on December 31 of that year.[62]

Gunsmith Louis Scaramuzzo quit Chicago for Tucson's warmer climate and died there at age 73, long divorced from the Tommy-gun trade, on March 5, 1963.[63]

Hubert Parker, two years Bonnie's senior, faced no charges after returning his sister to Dallas for burial. He outlived Bonnie by three decades, dying on March 10, 1964.[64]

Arthur O'Leary, Louis Piquett's lead investigator, received a suspended sentence for his role in the Crown Point jailbreak, in exchange for testimony against his ex-employer. He moved to Dubuque, Iowa, and died there in 1966.[65]

Chock Floyd's ex-wife Ruby remarried after his death and time spent lecturing that "Crime Does Not Pay." She died in Bixby, Oklahoma, at 63, on July 29, 1970.[66]

Arnold Kyle spent 20 years at Alcatraz, then transferred back to McNeil Island, finally considered for parole in 1961. First, however, he pled guilty to a Wichita bank heist from October 1938 and served more time for that offense. Released in August 1963, Kyle died in Lynnwood, Washington, at age 71, on November 30, 1980.[67]

Clyde Barrow's older sisters, Artie and Nell, avoided prosecution for harboring, despite evidence that Nellie, at least, met with Clyde while he was on the lam. They subsequently co-owned a Dallas beauty parlor, and Nell published a family memoir titled *Fugitives* before she died at 63, on November 16, 1968. Artie survived until March 3, 1981, 27 days before her 82nd birthday. The sisters rest beside their husbands in separate cemeteries.[68]

Leon Barrow followed older brothers Buck and Clyde into a life of crime, serving time for various offenses until his mother's death, when he married and went "straight" as a truck driver. Leon died at 66, on September 3, 1979, surrounded by his wife, four children and 15 grandchildren.[69]

Machine Gun Kelly's first son, George Jr., reportedly never forgave his father for physical and emotional abuse, plus the humiliation heaped upon their family. He married and fathered five children, three of whom died from muscular dystrophy. A heart attack killed him on June 6, 1989, while en route to his grandson's high school graduation. Sibling Stephen Barnes reports that Kathryn's daughter Pauline Frye "grew up to be a fine professional woman with high moral standards and a commitment to serve humanity."[70]

Texas firearms innovator Hyman Lebman remained in San Antonio until his death on September 22, 1990, at age 87.[71]

Bonnie Parker's youngest sister, Billie Jean, was married and a mother at 16, in 1928, but her young sons died within days of each other in 1933. Billie spent part of that year nursing Bonnie's critical burns and faced charges for a murder the gang committed while she was with them, but prosecutors dropped those charges after the Gibsland ambush. Convicted at the harboring trial, she served 366 days and emerged a lifelong friend of Blanche Barrow. Her first husband, Frederick Mace, also served time on unrelated charges. Upon release Billie returned to Dallas, divorced Mace, and married Arthur Moon in 1957. She died in Henderson, Texas, at 80, on May 21, 1993.[72]

Lillian Barrow, Clyde's youngest sibling, attended her family's meetings with the fugitives and served various brief jail terms. At the harboring trial she was sentenced to one hour in a Deputy U.S. Marshal's custody, then went on the obligatory speaking tour, trailed by husband Joe Francis. She later divorced him and remarried, dying in Mesquite, Texas, on February 3, 1999, at age 80.[73]

Charles Dempsey Floyd, born to parents Charles and Ruby in December 1924, was often called "Jack" after the boxer who inspired his middle name. He died in Vacaville, California, at age 74, on March 23, 1999, survived by his wife, two children and nine grandchildren.[74]

Anna Hauptmann never stopped trying to vindicate her husband in the Lindbergh kidnapping, petitioning New Jersey to release suppressed evidence from the case in 1981 and filing a wrongful-death lawsuit against various state officials in 1982, claiming more than $100 million in damages (dismissed in 1984). Mrs. Hauptman died in Lancaster, Pennsylvania, at 95, on October 10, 1944. She was cremated and her ashes scattered.[75]

G-men who survived the "crime war" followed diverse courses through the Bureau and beyond.

12. Scorched Earth

J. Edgar Hoover ruled the FBI for 48 years, growing ever more capricious and abusive, helped along by daily "vitamin" injections that contained amphetamines. In 1956 he launched a series of "counterintelligence programs," dubbed COINTELPRO, against groups he deemed "subversive," tactics ranging from burglaries and wiretapping to character assassination, frame-ups and abetting murder. One crackpot effort, "Operation Hoodwink," tried to incite gang warfare between the Mafia and Communist Party. Exposed in 1971 by burglars who stole COINTELPRO files and gave them to the media, those crimes were ostensibly canceled, but similar tactics continue today.[76]

Hoover died at home on May 2, 1972, allegedly from "hypertensive cardiovascular disease," but rumors persist that he was murdered, a claim supported by Watergate conspirators who admit discussing that prospect when Hoover, jealous of power, refused to grant President Nixon unfettered control over the FBI.[77]

Clyde Tolson, Hoover's constant companion and rumored gay lover, suffered a stroke in 1964 but stayed on the job by Hoover's sufferance, receiving the President's Award for Distinguished Federal Civilian Service in 1965. At Hoover's death, Tolson inherited $551,000 and served two days as Acting Director. He died from kidney failure on April 14, 1975, age 74.[78]

Union Station survivor Reed Vetterli never regained Hoover's trust, leaving the FBI in 1935. After a failed congressional campaign in Utah he served as Salt Lake City's police chief from 1940 to 1945, then worked as a radio distributor. He died at 45, on June 16, 1949.[79]

Melvin Purvis served as a U.S. Army intelligence officer in World War II, afterward compiling evidence for the Nuremberg war crimes trials. He died by gunshot in Florence, South Carolina, on February 29, 1960, two months after publication of a memoir titled *The Violent Years*. Debate continues as to whether he committed suicide or suffered a gun-cleaning accident.[80]

Charles Winstead, purported slayer of John Dillinger, struggled with Bureau discipline after the "crime war." Following a cantankerous lecture at the FBI Academy in 1941, a counselor voiced "very serious" doubts about further public speaking assignments, fearing that Winstead "might go too far and say something that would prove embarrassing to the Bureau." Transferred to Albuquerque, in 1942 he called a female reporter a "screwball" and accused her of communist sympathies. Hoover reprimanded him and ordered a disciplinary transfer to Oklahoma City, whereupon Winstead cursed the director and resigned that December. He joined U.S. Army Intelligence, working as a security officer for the Manhattan Project at Los Alamos, serving in postwar years as a sheriff's deputy and private investigator. On August 3, 1973, he died at the Albuquerque Veteran's Hospital from pneumonia or lung cancer (reports differ).[81]

Jacob "Jelly" Bryce advanced to serve as Special Agent in Charge of El Paso, San Antonio, Albuquerque and Oklahoma City before he retired from the FBI in 1958. He lost Oklahoma's gubernatorial race that November and returned to hometown Mountain View as a rancher, dying there at 67 on May 12, 1974.[82]

Clarence Hurt retired from the FBI in 1958 to operate a farm at McAlester, Oklahoma, also serving three terms as Pittsburg County's sheriff. In 1973 he served as a consultant to the movie *Dillinger*, filmed locally. Cancer claimed his life at 78, on November 4, 1975. During the funeral, burglars ransacked his home in what newspapers called "underworld revenge."[83]

FBI "Flying Squad" member Charles Campbell opened the Bureau's Palo Alto, California, office in 1946 and retired from that post in 1965, joining a local firearms company and moonlighting as a shooting advisor to various police departments. Congestive heart failure killed him at 84, on January 1, 1991.[84]

Walter Walsh ranked among the "crime war's" most celebrated survivors. Aside from participation in various high-profile cases, he also won several pistol-shooting championships in 1939–40, then joined the Marine Corps in 1942 and spent two years training recruits before he requested combat duty. Deployed to Okinawa in April 1945, he rescued his platoon from sniper fire by killing their assailant with a single 80-yard pistol shot. Walsh briefly returned to the FBI in 1945, but applied himself increasingly to competitive shooting, winning numerous awards through 1997 and coaching U.S. Olympic teams until 2000. Walsh died in Arlington, Virginia, on April 29, 2014, ranked as both the oldest former G-man and oldest U.S. Olympian. Son Gerald told obituary writers that his father killed "between 11 and 17 fugitives" during his years with the Bureau, but published accounts claim only three, and in fact G-men slew only 10 all told during his active service years, most without Walsh present.[85]

State and local officers are generally overlooked in Bureau histories, but each of them, for good or ill, continued on with life.

Maney Gault rejoined the Texas Rangers in 1937 and took charge of the Lubbock detachment. He held that post, as captain, until his death at 61, in Austin, on December 4, 1947.[86]

Matt Leach spent years planning a book on Dillinger without success. While returning from a visit to a New York publisher, on June 14, 1955, Leach and wife Mary died in a head-on collision near Somerset, Pennsylvania. Two persons in the other vehicle also succumbed. The Leaches were buried in Merrillville, Indiana.[87]

12. Scorched Earth

After ambushing Bonnie and Clyde, Frank Hamer worked for various corporations as a union-buster, leading a force of 20 ex–Rangers and sheriffs. In 1939 he was one of 49 ex–Rangers who offered to help defend Britain from Nazi invaders. He briefly rejoined the Rangers in 1948, to quell election disturbances, then finally retired in 1949. He suffered a stroke in 1953 but survived two more years, dying at 71 on July 10, 1955.[88]

Barrow posse member Henderson Jordan served as sheriff of Bienville Parish, Louisiana, until retiring in 1940. He died in a car crash at Arcadia on June 13, 1958, at age 61.[89]

Posse member Prentiss Oakley succeeded Jordan as Bienville Parish sheriff, serving until his death at 52, on October 15, 1957. He often voiced regret over firing on Bonnie and Clyde without a verbal warning.[90]

Bob Alcorn left law enforcement after the Barrow ambush and ran a used-car dealership. He died in Dallas at age 66, on the 30th anniversary—and almost to the hour—of the Gibsland ambush.[91]

Martin Zarkovich, named in various conspiracy theories as Dillinger's actual slayer (or murderer of a stand-in "patsy") remained with East Chicago's police department until his promotion to chief probation officer of the City Court. The FBI denied his involvement in the case and never prosecuted him on allegations of corruption. Zarkovich died at 73, on October 30, 1969, and is buried in Calumet City.[92]

Ted Hinton remained in law enforcement for several years after the Gibsland ambush, remaining friendly with members of the Barrow family he'd known from childhood. Later, he took flying lessons and trained fighter pilots during World War II, then ran a trucking company, and finally managed a motel in Irving, Texas. He finished a manuscript on the Barrow ambush shortly before dying in Dallas at 73, on October 27, 1977.[93]

Most wealthy kidnap victims from the "crime war" resumed their affluent lives upon release.

The exception, perhaps, was Charles Lindbergh, Jr., apparently murdered on the night of his abduction. His parents subsequently had five more children (not counting eight sired out of wedlock by Charles Senior with at least three other women). Prior to Pearl Harbor, Charles Senior resigned his U.S. Army Air Force commission and served as spokesman for the isolationist, pro-Hitler America First Committee, severely damaging his hero's reputation. After the war, the Lindberghs traveled widely, ending up in Hawaii where Charles Senior died on Maui at 72, on August 26, 1974. Wife Anne survived him by a quarter-century, dying at Passumpsic, Vermont, on February 7, 2001, age 94.[94]

As for Charles Junior, presumably murdered, his partial remains were never properly identified prior to cremation, with the ashes scattered at sea.

That fact spawned numerous conspiracy theories, including claims that "Little Lindy" survived the abduction and grew to adulthood, perhaps recognized by his family but shunned for financial reasons. Between 1981 and 2010 at least five aged men claimed to be Charles Junior, while FBI headquarters declined to release any files containing "Little Lindy's" fingerprints or other conclusive identifying marks. So far, none of the claims are scientifically confirmed.[95]

Edward Bremer of Saint Paul continued in business, moving to Pompano Beach, Florida, when he retired. He died there at 67, on May 4, 1965.[96]

William Hamm, Jr., remained in Minnesota, dying in Saint Paul at 79, on August 20, 1970.[97]

Charles Urschel moved his family to San Antonio, running the Slick-Urschel Oil Company and engaging in philanthropy. He died at 80, on September 26, 1970.[98]

John Factor enjoyed the most colorful career after his fake abduction and frame-up of the Touhy gang. Convicted of mail fraud in 1945, he served 10 years, then emerged to serve as manager for the Stardust Hotel in Las Vegas, fronting for Moe Dalitz and his Cleveland crime partners. After selling his interest there, he moved to California, becoming active in politics and ostensible philanthropy. Like other mobsters, he contributed heavily to John Kennedy's 1960 presidential campaign and reaped his reward two years later, with a December 1962 pardon sparing him from impending deportation. Factor died in Los Angeles at 91, on January 22, 1984. Mayor Tom Bradley and ex–Governor Edmund Brown joined other luminaries at his funeral.[99]

Landmarks of the "crime war" and its aftermath survive.

The most famous—or infamous—is Alcatraz, in San Francisco Bay. "The Rock" remained in service as a federal prison until March 21, 1963, when it closed and its remaining inmates were transferred to other lockups, where maintenance totaled $3 daily, versus $10 on the island. Native American activists briefly occupied Alcatraz in March 1964, then returned in November for a protest lasting 19 months. During that occupation, fire destroyed several buildings. In 1972 The Rock became part of Golden Gate National Recreation Area, designated as a National Historic Landmark in 1986. Weather and safety conditions permitting, daily cruises transport visitors to Alcatraz for guided tours of the prison buildings that remain.[100]

Little Bohemia Lodge also endures, on U.S. Highway 51 South in Manitowish Waters, Wisconsin. Its kitchen serves three meals daily, varying by season, open holidays, with facilities available for banquets, private parties, and weddings. Vintage newspapers decorate the walls and bullet holes remain from the 1934 shootout.[101]

12. Scorched Earth 233

Gibsland, Louisiana, offers tourists the Bonnie and Clyde Ambush Museum on Main Street, run by L.J. Hinton from 2005 until his death in 2016, owned today by Perry Carver. Exhibits include some of Clyde's guns and a faux "death car" standing in for the 1967 movie version that moved to Washington, D.C.'s Crime Museum in 2008, then on to Pigeon Forge, Tennessee, in 2016. The original death car, along with Clyde's bloody shirt (purchased for $75,000) are displayed at Whiskey Pete's Hotel and Casino in Primm, Nevada.[102]

The former Sturgis Funeral Home in East Liverpool, Ohio, operates today as a bed-and-breakfast, tempting guests since 1998 with a small Sturgis House Mortuary Museum including a death mask of Pretty Boy Floyd and other tokens of his fatal visit to the area.[103]

In Ocklawaha, Florida, Gator Joe's Beach Bar and Grill is named for the reptile allegedly hunted by Ma and Fred Barker, featuring live music and a view of Lake Weir. The Lake Weir Chamber of Commerce stages an annual "Ma Barker Shootout" in January, on "Ma Barker Day," in a building near the 1935 battle site. The original "death house" went on sale in 2012 with a reserve of $1 million but failed to sell. In 2015 Florida's state senate considered a bill for $500,000 in repairs but failed to pass the measure. In October 2016 buyers moved the house across Lake Weir by barge, to Carney Island, opened for "limited tours" in January 2019.[104]

The best-known "crime war" tourist attraction is Indiana's Dillinger Museum, opened by Dillinger biographer Joseph Pinkston in tiny Nashville, Indiana, in 1976. Featuring weapons, vintage photographs, Dillinger's alleged wooden gun and wax figures of various outlaws (plus G-man Charles Winstead), the original museum operated until Pinkston's death, apparently a suicide, in 1996. The Lake County Convention and Visitors Bureau purchased Pinkston's artifacts and opened a new museum at Hammond's Indiana Welcome Center in 1997, but a lawsuit filed by Dillinger great-nephew Jeffrey Scalf closed that facility in 2006. It reopened as a collaborative venture in March 2008 but controversy continued. In July 2015 a new John Dillinger Museum opened in Crown Point, competing with a smaller display at the venerable Old Sheriff's House and Jail Museum. Locals were surprised when the new museum closed suddenly and without explanation on August 31, 2017.[105]

13

Redacting History

The FBI's publicity machine, refined across 113 controversial years, has never stopped perpetuating myths. If anything, its methods now are more sophisticated, with substantial aid from the mass media.

Esteemed author Bryan Burrough calls the years 1933–34 "America's greatest crime wave," hyperbole perhaps employed for drama's sake but clearly disregarding southern terrorism during Reconstruction (1865–77), Prohibition's rampant lawlessness (1920–33), racist mayhem of the Civil Rights era (1954–68) and the urban riots of "long hot summers" (1964–69).[1]

Regarding gang-specific crimes during the Great Depression, William Breuer writes that during 1932 banks were robbed at a rate of "12 to 16 each month"—i.e., 144 to 192 for the year. Don Whitehead claims that 1933's bank raids totaled "almost two per day," approaching 730. Neither credits any source for those statistics, but we may compare them to the work of independent authors not beholden to the FBI for aid.[2]

Those detailed timelines of "public enemy" activity from 1930 to 1938 claim a total of 18 and 21 bank heists respectively for 1932, with 23 and 29 for 1933. Their totals for the nine-year period are 65 versus 110. Even allowing for some minor local holdups overlooked, it seems improbable they could be off by hundreds during any given year.[3]

Today the FBI provides no stats for 1930s robberies. It *does* publish breakdowns of yearly daylight bank jobs for the years 2003–2018. During that period, bandits robbed 86,680 American banks—an average of 9,631 yearly or 26 per day. By that standard, the 1930s pale except for the publicity evoked by holdup gangs.[4]

While Hoover and ghostwriter Courtney Cooper both published best-selling tomes on "public enemies" during the Thirties, the FBI's first "official" history, penned by journalist Don Whitehead, appeared in 1956. Titled *The FBI Story: A Report to the People*, it featured a five-page foreword allegedly penned by Hoover, noting that "[t]o do the job properly, [Whitehead] had to have access to the record, within the bounds of security and policy considerations." That said, Whitehead presented a singularly laudatory view of FBI operations, including standard mythology on the Kansas City massacre, George Kelly's arrest, Little Bohemia, the deaths of Charles Floyd and the Barkers (reduced to footnotes)—all without a single mention of Melvin Purvis spanning 357 pages.[5]

In the process, Whitehead also foisted other fabrications on "the people," including a claim that with arrival of Prohibition "it fell to the FBI to take over leadership in the drive against the gangsters." The tally, with regard to Syndicate overlords: a 1929 arrest of Al Capone for flaunting a federal subpoena (dismissed); the capture of small-time car thief and cop-killer Charles Durkin; and the 1939 surrender of "Murder, Inc." shot-caller Lepke Buchalter. In the latter case, Whitehead falsely claims that "Hoover walked alone through New York City's streets" to collar Lepke, when in fact he rode with Walter Winchell to the rendezvous, trailed by armed G-men. In a similar vein, Whitehead "debunked" Attorney General–designate Thomas Walsh's intent to fire Hoover as his first act in office, citing a letter penned to the *Washington Herald* by a D.C. attorney and nephew of Walsh, claiming Walsh had changed his mind "after long consideration," dismissing prior reports of his late uncle's statements as "a gross inaccuracy."[6]

Whitehead pleased the FBI well enough to land more books in a similar vein. One, *The Dow Story* (1968), praised the inventors of napalm at the height of protests against Dow's providing 388,000 tons of "liquid fire" dropped over Vietnam. Two years later, he published *Attack on Terror: The FBI Against the Ku Klux Klan in Mississippi*, again consulting Bureau files while carefully omitting any mention of its illegal "COINTELPRO" campaigns.[7]

When Mervyn LeRoy Productions bought film rights to *The FBI Story*, Hoover served as a co-producer of sorts, supervising casting for the film with stars James Stewart and Myrna Loy, forcing LeRoy—a personal friend—to reshoot various scenes which, in Hoover's judgment, portrayed G-men in a less than "appropriate" light. Two agents remained with LeRoy for the duration of filming and Hoover personally reviewed every frame of the two-and-one-half-hour feature before its release. Stories persist that despite their friendship, Hoover only allowed LeRoy to direct after confirming that "we had enough dirt to control him." While LeRoy ducked that issue, he later admitted, "Everybody on that picture, from the carpenters and electricians right to the top, everybody, had to be okayed by the FBI."[8]

It comes as no surprise, then, that the film not only preaches the straight Bureau line, but goes farther, fabricating certain incidents and warping historical chronology in the guise of "dramatic license." Stewart plays the lead, fictional G-Man "Chip Hardesty," who stands in for missing Melvin Purvis at Dillinger's slaying and other incidents. In one scene from the 1920s, Hardesty—disguised in a KKK robe—arrests a truckload of Klan vandals for trashing a newspaper office, depicting a clear violation of the FBI's authority with an incident that never happened anywhere, at any time. History takes another hit when scriptwriters move passage of the 1934 crime bills two full months ahead of the April raid on Little Bohemia, thus disguising the fact that G-Men engaged in an epic shootout (and killed an innocent man) before they were technically "authorized" to carry guns. Likewise, in the round-up scenes of "public enemies," the script identifies George Kelly as "one of the last to go," when his September 1933 arrest preceded the deaths of Dillinger, Floyd, Nelson and the Barkers by 10 to 16 months (a seemingly pointless deviation from truth).[9]

Few if any Americans noticed. The film cleared $3.5 million at the box office, equivalent to $31 million today.[10]

While Warner Brothers was producing *The FBI Story* to Hoover's nit-picking specifications, a competitor called Visual Drama Inc. beat them to the punch by releasing *Guns Don't Argue* in December 1957. A full hour shorter than LeRoy's epic, the film limited coverage to moralistic treatment of the Bureau's "crime war" without courting Hoover's favor and cast narrator James Davis—later "Jock Ewing" on *Dallas*—as fictional Texas Ranger "Captain Stewart." The feature "recreated" FBI pursuit of Dillinger and Homer Van Meter, the Barrow and Barker-Karpis gangs, Floyd, Richetti and Gillis. Most names of "molls" were fabricated, and the film was rife with other inaccuracies—e.g., Agent Raymond Caffrey named as the first G-man killed on duty, dying on his first day with the Bureau. Although strongly pro–Hoover, *Guns* never mentions his name, replacing him with veteran actor Sam Flint as the anonymous "FBI Chief." Visual Drama had produced only one prior film, 1950's *Sins of Pompeii*, and later recycled clips from *Guns* in its TV series *Gang Busters*. It impressed future award-winning director Martin Scorsese enough for him to say, "It's an amazing film. It's to be studied, because it shows you how to make a film on a low budget."[11]

In the same month *The FBI Story* hit theaters, October 1959, ABC Television aired the first episode of *The Untouchables,* a crime drama starring Robert Stack as Eliot Ness, narrated by Hoover's pal Walter Winchell, produced by Desilu Studios under actor/musician Desi Arnaz and his wife, comedian Lucille Ball. The small-screen offering, which ran 118 episodes before its cancellation in May 1963, immediately lit a fuse at FBI headquarters.[12]

For starters, Hoover loathed Ness in real life, a former Prohibition agent from Chicago sometimes hyperbolically hailed as "the man who got Capone," ignoring the fact that tax auditors sent Scarface Al to prison, working on the sly, while Ness and his allegedly "untouchable" raiders, seized booze trucks and raided breweries. Later, moving on to other law enforcement posts in Cleveland and beyond, Ness craved a G-man's badge but found himself excluded from the club by Hoover, unwilling to share publicity with another potential Mel Purvis. Ness eventually collaborated with author Oscar Fraley on a fictionalized version of his Chicago campaign, *The Untouchables*, but died before its publication and sale of 1.5 million copies in 1957.[13]

From that tome sprang the TV series, veering even farther from fact as Ness confronted mobsters whom he never met—Dutch Schultz, Lucky Luciano, Lepke Buchalter, et al.—in cities where he never served, long after his Chicago team dissolved. Worse yet, the program's second episode, aired on October 22, had Ness tracking down "Ma Barker and Her Boys" to end their holdup spree in Florida. In the first season's ninth episode, "The Tri-State Gang," Ness stepped on Bureau toes again.[14]

Hoover was livid, and his staff fell into line accordingly. Headquarters compelled Desilu to insert a disclaimer following the Tri-State episode, admitting that the FBI had primary jurisdiction over that case, rather than the defunct Prohibition Bureau. Over the next four years, G-men "monitored" each episode of *The Untouchables*, highlighting any errors they perceived, meanwhile collecting press clippings when prominent Italian Americans, ranging from Frank Sinatra to mobster Antonio "Tough Tony" Anastasio, lobbied successfully to minimize use of Italian names for fictional gangsters portrayed on the show. The war also turned personal, when agents illegally obtained results of Lucille Ball's pregnancy test, rushing to alert Arnaz to his impending fatherhood before Lucy could break the news herself.[15]

Despite stern opposition from the FBI's Crime Records Division, some authors did diverge from the official party line. One of the strangest offerings, 1988's *Machine-Gun Man*, professed to tell the story of George Kelly's "incredible survival into the 1970s," when official records claim he died at Leavenworth on his 59th birthday, in 1954. Purported author "John H. Webb" claimed that a body-switch allowed him to escape from custody and start life over with his second wife, Cindy, in Arizona. Sadly, or conveniently, Webb was deceased before the book appeared under the byline of "George Kelly" and collaborator Jim Dobkins. A segment producer for the long-running TV series *Unsolved Mysteries* flew to Phoenix, hoping to launch NBC's new season with the "Kelly" case, huddling with Cindy Webb, Dobkins, and associate Ben Jordan. The unnamed segment producer promised a call-back "next week," then lapsed into silence. When Dobkins finally reached him by phone, the still-anonymous NBC staffer allegedly "admitted that the FBI, which had a close advisory relationship with *Unsolved Mysteries*, had directed the producers" to sever contact with Webb and Dobkins. There the matter rests today, with sparse book

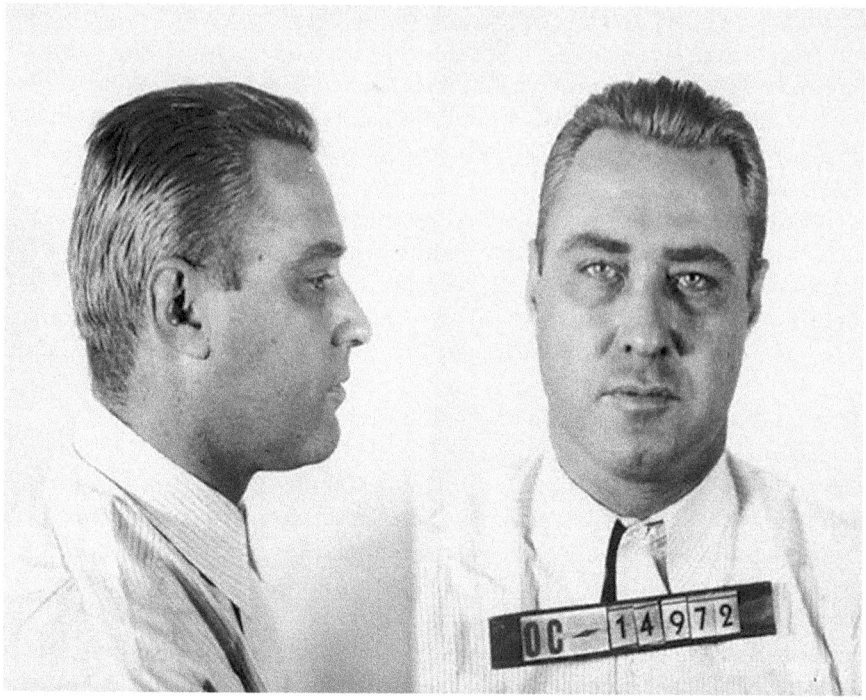

Federal prison records state that "Machine Gun" Kelly died at Leavenworth on July 18, 1954, but a ghostwritten book, published 34 years later, claims that Kelly faked his death, escaped, and lived at large until the 1970s (National Archives).

reviews online ranging from "excellent" to "curious" and "a pile of cow dung."[16]

No modern author has defied official FBI history more outspokenly than Jay Robert Nash, once hailed by the *Chicago Tribune* as the "dean of American crime writers," self-described as "one of the world's foremost historians, encyclopedists and leading crime experts." Sundry reviewers disagree, citing innumerable errors scattered throughout his 60-odd publications released as reference works since 1973. A *New York Times* review of his premiere volume, *Bloodletters and Badmen,* notes that "Mr. Nash makes enjoyable mistakes, not without panache." Another, examining his catalog of natural disasters, *Darkest Hours* (1976), deemed information from his entry on a Lisbon earthquake "simply false." Reviewer Richard Maxwell also noted "numerous errors, omissions, inconsistencies, and anomalies" in Nash's *Encyclopedia of Western Lawmen & Outlaws* (1994).[17]

That volume followed Nash's magnum opus, a six-volume *Encyclopedia of World Crime* (1990), which collated and repeated errors from his earlier works, later subdivided for retail circulation with specific volumes on murder, the Old West, and so on. Sally Waters of Florida's Stetson University Law Library reviewed the collection for *Library Journal*, writing:

> This mammoth undertaking makes available in one source almost every major crime in history.... There are errors, however, ranging from somewhat minor (William Cruse's murder spree was in Palm Bay, Florida, not Bartow) to more egregious (a murderer named Hickman is the subject of two entries—a two-page one with photos, and a shorter one under the misspelled name Hinkman). Such errors, combined with a claim on the copyright page that the set has somehow been "seeded with information to detect any unauthorized use or duplication," make this a fascinating yet flawed set, useful mainly as a background source for information to be verified elsewhere.[18]

"Errors," whether accidental or intentional, are less germane to Nash's treatment of 1930s "public enemies" than his advancement of purported information challenging the FBI's reports. First and foremost (see Chapter 7) is his claim that Dillinger was not killed by G-men in 1934 but lived for decades afterward, married, and built a "normal" life under an alias. He took that claim so seriously—and professed to "own" it legally—that he sued CBS TV for "stealing" it in a March 1984 episode of *Simon and Simon* that considered Dillinger's survival 50 years after his trip to the Biograph. The U.S. Seventh Circuit Court of Appeals dismissed that case in April 1990, ruling that Nash had no claim upon a "speculative" theory, adding, "His own books are largely fresh expositions of facts looked up in other people's books."[19]

Nash cited various "proofs" for Dillinger's survival, beginning with alleged misidentification of the outlaw's corpse on July 22, 1934. After formal pronouncement of death at the Alexian Brothers Hospital, logged at 10:30 p.m., Dillinger's body was transferred to the Cook County Morgue for autopsy. Dillinger's father and sister Audrey were reportedly unable to recognize him there, attributed by FBI historians to his plastic surgery by Drs. Loeser and Cassidy. FBI historians claim agents were able to make "positive identification" of Dillinger's fingerprints despite efforts to obliterate them, although the fugitive's fingerprint card was "misplaced" at the morgue for more than three decades. Nash goes further, claiming that pathologists found "Jimmy Lawrence" taller than Dillinger's recorded height, with different-colored eyes, and a rheumatic heart condition which, Nash says, should have prevented Dillinger from joining the navy or playing baseball in prison. Dr. Patrick Weeks, a physician and psychiatrist at Michigan City during Dillinger's tenure there, rebutted Nash's claim by saying he discovered the heart disease early on and warned against any future strenuous activity that might endanger his life.[20]

Another sticking point for Nash was the .380 automatic Dillinger allegedly carried on the night he died. Nash reported that the pistol on display at FBI headquarters bore a serial number proving it was manufactured and sold for the first time *after* Dillinger's death. That was true, in fact, whereupon sundry FBI spokespersons offered various explanations for the discrepancy. One unsubstantiated claim asserts that Hoover, enamored of fawning celebrities, gave the original Biograph Colt to an unnamed wealthy admirer, later replacing it with a lookalike of later manufacture. Former G-man Larry Wack later related three alternative theories: (a) that Dillinger ground off the original gun's serial number (which can still be seen with applications of acid); (b) that Hoover ordered the Dillinger pistol's slide welded shut, "concealing" the serial number (which in fact appears on the left side of the outer frame, above the trigger); and/or (c) that once Dillinger's gun mysteriously "disappeared," it was replaced by one belonging to Volney Davis. FBI historian John Fox, Jr., added another twist, claiming the Biograph gun would appear at the FBI Experience, a self-guided tour of Bureau memorabilia in Washington, a claim allegedly substantiated by Fox and Wack in November 2007.[21]

Nash was still at it in August 2009, with a scathing review of the new film *Public Enemies,* penned under the aegis of critic Roger Ebert, titled "Film wrong! Dillinger not killed by FBI! Fact: Hoover coverup!" In that broadside, he debunked the myth of George Kelly coining the nickname "G-men," then accused Hoover and Purvis of first falling prey to a trick by corrupt East Chicago police—faux Dillinger's actual slayers—and then mounting a cover-up that outlived both plotters to placate Bureau critics in the U.S. Senate, leaving real-life Dillinger at large to live happily ever after. In closing, he could not resist adding, "Johnny Depp as John Dillinger? What a joke. The producers of that film would have been better served if Moe Howard was still alive and had been cast in that role—he would have been far more entertaining!"[22]

Another famous crime, the Lindbergh kidnapping, is frequently associated with the FBI despite the Bureau's relatively minor role, and it remains a point of controversy to the present day, with FBI sources still defending the prosecution's shaky evidence at Bruno Hauptmann's show trial.[23]

Literary dissection of Hauptmann's case began with Anthony Scaduto's *Scapegoat* in 1976 (not 1974, as claimed by FBI reviewers). Without naming an alternate suspect, Scaduto deemed Hauptmann innocent, accusing police of suppressing vital evidence and manufacturing fake "leads."[24] Ludovic Kennedy published *The Airman and the Carpenter* in 1985, filmed in 1996 as *Crime of the Century,* suggesting that a member of the Lindbergh household accidentally killed Charles Junior, precipitating a deadly frame-up. British author William Norris refined that theory in 2013 with

A Talent to Deceive, pointing the finger of suspicion at Ann Lindbergh's brother Dwight Reeve, Jr., initiating a cover-up to spare the Lindbergh clan from scandal.[25]

Thankfully, from the Bureau's perspective, ex-agent Jim Fisher, later interim Vice President of Academic Affairs at Pennsylvania's Edinboro University, produced two books defending Hauptmann's prosecutors: *The Lindbergh Case* (1987) and *The Ghosts of Hopewell* (1999). J. Edgar Hoover had serious doubts regarding Hauptmann's guilt and the "evidence" arrayed against him (see Chapter 9), but Fisher assures his readers, "Today, the Lindbergh phenomena [sic] is a giant hoax perpetrated by people who are taking advantage of an uninformed and cynical public. Notwithstanding all of the books, TV programs, and legal suits, Hauptmann is as guilty today as he was in 1932 when he kidnapped and killed the son of Mr. and Mrs. Charles Lindbergh."[26]

While the exploits of "public enemies" inspired various films with some still remaining at large, biopics using real names (more or less) did not begin appearing until 1945. Since then, as of 2019, a total of 24 feature-length films have screened in theaters or on TV. John Dillinger leads the pack with eight (including one filmed in Romanian), followed by four each for the Barrows, the Barker-Karpis gang and Chock Floyd, two each for Lester Gillis and George Kelly. Estelle Parsons won an Academy Award for Best Supporting Actress, as Blanche Barrow in 1967's *Bonnie and Clyde*, although real-live consultant Blanche complained that the film "made me look like a screaming horse's ass."[27]

Hollywood seldom honors historicity, and real-life outlaws are not spared from meddling. At least three films—*Young Dillinger* (1965), *Dillinger* (1973) and *Public Enemies* (2009)—have Floyd and Gillis slain before Dillinger's Biograph ambush. *Dillinger* raises the ante by having Floyd join the gang at Little Bohemia, before vigilantes slay Homer Van Meter and police kill Charles Makley, while Melvin Purvis personally executes Wilbur Underhill and Jack Klutas, then captures George Kelly. In *Public Enemies*, Purvis alone kills Floyd before drawing the Dillinger assignment, Dillinger covers the Michigan City escapees with Tommy-gun fire, Gillis shoots his first G-man inside a rooming house, then Purvis kills him at Little Bohemia. Dillinger and Gillis join the Barker gang in *Ma Barker's Killer Brood* (1960), vying to outwit rival George Kelly while Fred Barker has an affair with Kelly's wife "Lou." Kelly killed no one in real life, but in *Machine Gun Kelly* (1958), again with wife "Lou," he slays several Syndicate mobsters. Dock Barker dies with Ma and Fred in 1970's *Bloody Mama*. *Bonnie and Clyde* melds gang members William Jones and Henry Methvin into composite character "C.W. Moss," while the title characters kidnap Frank Hamer to snap embarrassing photos.[28]

A sampling of posters for Hollywood films recounting (and fictionalizing) the lives of 1930s "public enemies" (author's collection).

Television was no better. *Gang Busters,* first out of the gate, ran half-hour episodes from March 1952 to October 1963. In April 1952 viewers saw a lone G-man (not Hoover) capture Alvin Karpis during an attempt to flee via rowboat. Six months later, successive installments charted the downfall of Dillinger and Homer Van Meter. In *The Untouchables*' Ma Barker episode, Arthur, Fred and Lloyd face federal guns with Ma in Florida, Fred shooting Lloyd when he tries to surrender. *The Witness,* on CBS (1960–61), paraded outlaws including Roger Touhy, Ma Barker and Dillinger before a fictional "committee" of lawyers for inconclusive mock trials. During 1966, *Batman* pursued the thinly-disguised "Ma Parker" gang. CBS ran *The Manhunter* during 1974–75, starring Ken Howard as a vengeance-driven P.I. hunting gangsters across the Midwest. Its early episodes featured the "Ma Gantry" gang and a fugitive madman who emulates John Dillinger, even dressing his girlfriend in red. 1974's *The Kansas City Massacre* closes with Melvin Purvis (Rory Calhoun) cornering Chock Floyd (Bo Hopkins), then releasing him to track down Vern Miller (Matt Clark). Disney's *DuckTales* (1987–90) featured multiple episodes with "Ma Beagle" and her felonious sons. In

December 2016 A&E ordered a pilot for *Baby Face*, starring co-author and producer Freddie Highmore, but the program had not aired by press time.²⁹

Few actors have portrayed two "public enemies" on film. Martin Sheen heads the list, with starring roles as Chock Floyd in 1974 and Dillinger in 1995, opposite Eric Roberts as Al Capone. Stephen Graham portrayed Lester Gillis in *Public Enemies* and Al Capone in HBO's *Boardwalk Empire* (2010–14). Versatile Harris Yulin played George Kelly in *Melvin Purvis: G-Man* (1974), then switched sides to become J. Edgar Hoover that same year, in *The FBI Story: The FBI Versus Alvin Karpis, Public Enemy Number One*.³⁰

In spite of all historical revisionism in the media, the FBI and "friendly" journalists remain committed to established myths. Little has changed from Courtney Cooper's writing in the 1930s or Don Whitehead's 20 years later.

The first author to follow Whitehead's lead was Ralph de Toledano, a close friend of Richard Nixon and editor of the ultraconservative *National Review*. One of his 26 books, 1973's *J. Edgar Hoover: The Man in His Time*, closely followed Hoover's death and verged upon false advertising with its paperback tagline promising "The Biggest Exposé of the Year." What readers got for their money, instead, was a strictly doctrinaire recitation of Hoover's flawless career that might have been penned by Cooper or Whitehead decades earlier. He tries to credit Hoover with solving the Lindbergh case, repeats the fable of George Kelly's coining the "G-men" nickname, exaggerates the Bureau's role in tracking the Barrow gang, parrots Hoover's purple prose about Ma Barker (misstating the number of her fatal wounds) and his staged "solo" capture of Alvin Karpis, and whitewashes the Harry Brunette fiasco. Only in discussing Thomas Walsh does de Toledano deviate a fraction from the Bureau line, admitting that Walsh's nomination as FDR's attorney general posed "a crisis which might have changed the course of history" for Hoover and his FBI. Walsh's sudden death kept Hoover at the Bureau's helm and thus averted decades of catastrophe.³¹

In 1995 William Breuer published his laudatory history of *J. Edgar Hoover and His G-men* during the Depression, rehashing all the usual exaggerations of Ma Barker's brilliant "lectures" on crime to her sons, her death in desperate battle, detailing Hoover's tirades against "sentimental moo-cows" who objected to shoot-on-sight orders—in short, recycling every FBI myth created by Hoover and Cooper, later warmed over by Whitehead and de Toledano. An epilogue condemns the "biased and grotesquely twisted broadsides" of journalists recounting Hoover's widespread

COINTELPRO crimes, including multiple frame-ups and murders, concluding that "the true measure of Hoover rests" with 8,000 members of the Society of Former Agents of the FBI. "These men and women," Breuer declares—forgetting that Hoover fired the Bureau's female agents in 1924, with no more hired until after he died—"view J. Edgar Hoover as one of America's towering heroes."[32]

Cartha DeLoach joined the FBI as a clerk in 1942, thus playing no part in the "crime war," but advanced to serve as Assistant Director in 1959 and Director for Investigations in 1965, considered as Hoover's successor by President Lyndon Johnson before LBJ declined to seek reelection in 1968 and victor Richard Nixon kept Hoover on past mandatory retirement age. In 1997 DeLoach published *Hoover's FBI,* ignoring the Depression years until his chapter on allegations of Hoover's closet homosexuality. Biographer Anthony Summers cited Hoover's early intimate letters to Melvin Purvis (see Chapter 6) as "a homosexual courtship," but DeLoach takes umbrage, declaring the racier passages "clearly part of the bantering between two bachelors interested in women."[33]

Meanwhile, at Bureau headquarters, little has changed regarding propagation of "crime war" mythology. One effort to adjust archaic legend led to some confusion on the FBI's website. An entry on the capture of George Kelly offers up a sentence fragment reading "In 1956, when reporter Don Whitehead wrote *The FBI Story*...." Whatever the unknown webmaster meant to say, that partial sentence ends with a hyperlink leading to a "1985 revision of the official case write-up," but clicking on the link takes readers to an error message reading "Page Not Found." Instead, a final sentence, also hyperlinked, declares, "In recent years, we've been correcting the story—see our article here on this website in 2003."[34] That link, in turn, tells visitors:

> On September 26th, "Machine Gun" Kelly was found in a decrepit Memphis residence. Some early press reports said that a tired, perhaps hung-over Kelly stumbled out of his bed mumbling something like "I was expecting you." Another version of the event held that Kelly emerged from his room, hands-up, crying "Don't shoot G-Men, don't Shoot." Either way, Kelly was arrested without violence. The rest is history. The more colorful version sparked the popular imagination and "G-Man" became synonymous with the special agents of J. Edgar Hoover's Federal Bureau of Investigation.[35]

The webmaster's final conclusion: "Good myths, though, die hard, and this one does make a great story!"[36]

Meanwhile, another page on the same website still proclaims, erroneously, "The legal tools given to the FBI by Congress, as well as Bureau initiatives to upgrade its own professionalism and that of law enforcement, resulted in the arrest or demise of all the major gangsters by 1936."[37]

Half a century since Hoover's death, change at Bureau headquarters still moves at glacial speed when it transpires at all. Above all else, the image must endure: Fidelity, Bravery, Integrity.

The truth is incidental and of small concern.

Chapter Notes

Chapter 1

1. DOJ; USSS; LOA.
2. FBIH.
3. Gentry, 111, 114; FBIH.
4. FBIH; LOA; Mansky/Boissoneault.
5. LOA; FBIH.
6. FBIH.
7. *Ibid.*
8. *Ibid.*; Gentry, 79.
9. FBIH.
10. Whitehead, 95; Gentry, 124.
11. FBIH; Gentry, 127.
12. Mansky/Boissoneault; FBIH; LOA.
13. FBIH.
14. *Ibid.*
15. *Ibid.*
16. *Ibid.*
17. Gentry, 118–20, 148.
18. *Ibid.*, 154–55.
19. FBIH.
20. OED.
21. *Ibid.*
22. Gentry, 71–73, 75–80, 104–5.
23. Charles, 62.
24. Wack.
25. *Ibid.*
26. *Ibid.*

Chapter 2

1. MWD; Helmer/Mattix, 291, 298–99.
2. Newton, 143–44, 170–71.
3. FG.
4. *Ibid.*; OJ.
5. OJ.
6. *Ibid.*
7. MACM; FG.
8. Helmer/Mattix, 123, 134.
9. *Ibid.*, 141, 378.
10. *Ibid.*, 179–80; DE.
11. Helmer/Mattix, 104–105, 161, 165.
12. OJ.
13. DE; EOA; Helmer/Mattix, 170–80.
14. AH; Biography.
15. GI; OJ; GESP.
16. FBI Barker-Karpis Gang File; GESP; Mahone, 57; RAAI.
17. FBI Barker-Karpis Gang File; RAAI; Newton, 137–38; J. G. Autographs, Inc.
18. DE; Helmer/Mattix, 148–9, 164, 168, 173, 178.
19. AH.
20. LOA; OJ; SS; WHP.
21. DE; FG.
22. *Ibid.*
23. DE; Helmer/Mattix, 175–82.
24. HL; Helmer/Mattix, 6.
25. MACM.
26. *BP*, 7/5/2019; FG; *ND*, 2/5/2019.
27. FG.
28. GT; *SJ*, 11/9/33.
29. Helmer/Mattix, 17, 136, 164, 175; *SJ*, 11/9/33; *CE*, 9/8/27; BIB.
30. PT; Sifakis, 244–45; Breuer, 106–09.
31. OJ; JDF; FBIH.
32. Matera, 26, 28; Girardin/Helmer, 18.
33. Toland, 17–18; King, *Rise*, 19; IADC.
34. OJ; JDF.
35. OJ.
36. *Ibid.*; IADC.
37. OJ.
38. JDF.
39. IADC.
40. *Ibid.*
41. *Ibid.*
42. *Ibid.*
43. Toland, 27–31; Matera, 37–39.
44. IADC; Matera, 37–39.
45. IADC; Helmer/Mattix, 182.
46. CAF.
47. *Ibid.*

48. *Ibid.*
49. Newton, 93.
50. *Ibid.*, 197–98.
51. *Ibid.*, 34–35,
52. *Ibid.*, 261–62; FBIH.
53. LOA; OJ; FBIH.
54. *Ibid.*
55. *Ibid.*
56. OJ; FBIH.
57. *Ibid.*; *SFE*, 7/3/2016.
58. OJ.
59. Sifakis, 509; Helmer/Mattix, 17; Toland, 29–31.
60. *Ibid.*
61. OJ.
62. FBIH.
63. *Ibid.*
64. *Ibid.*
65. Morgan, *Irish O'Malley*, 1–2.
66. *Ibid.*, 4–6.
67. Answers; MOH; SAIB.
68. AH; FG; MFH; Newton, 272–73; *WT*, 2/2/34.
69. HBM; MNHS; *WT*, 2/2/34.
70. FBIH; AM.
71. *Ibid.*
72. OJ.
73. *Ibid.*
74. *Ibid.*
75. *Ibid.*
76. FBIH.
77. *Ibid.*
78. HBM.
79. *Ibid.*
80. Breuer, 53; *HT*, 6/2/33; *NT*, 6/5/33.
81. Newton, 39–41; Wallis, 299, 321, 323, 326.
82. *LT*, 6/1/33.
83. Newton, 76–77; Wallis, 326.
84. *HN*, 5/31/33; RAAI.
85. *HT*, 6/2/33.
86. Breuer, 34, 50, 54; Newton, 273–74; PDC, 9/17/23.
87. *HN*, 5/31/33.
88. *NT*, 6/5/33; NHYS, 6/5/33; RAAI.
89. FBI Bremer Kidnapping and Kansas City Massacre files.
90. MNOPEDIA.
91. 3AM.
92. Helmer/Mattix, 90–95.
93. MACM.
94. *Ibid.*
95. YWSYEO; FG.
96. FBI Kansas City Massacre File.
97. FBI Barker/Karpis Gang File.
98. 3AM.
99. CAF.

Chapter 3

1. FBI Kansas City Massacre File; AMM; FG; *KCS*, 6/17/33; Clayton, 113–14.
2. Edge, 2; OJ; Clayton, 119.
3. FBI Kansas City Massacre File.
4. FBIH; FG; Clayton, 119
5. Smith, *Lawman*, 116; Edge, 3; Unger 57, 222–23; Kirchner, 33.
6. FBIH; Edge, 4; Kirchner, 79–80, 107; FG; Smith, *Lawman*, 117.
7. FBIH; Kirchner, 32–33; Unger, 223–24.
8. FBIH; Smith, *Lawman*, 117; FG; Edge, 4.
9. Kirchner, 109; Smith, *Lawman*, 118; FG; FBIH; Unger, 228.
10. Kirchner, 111; Smith, *Lawman*, 118; OJ.
11. Kirchner, 112.
12. *Ibid.*, 135–36; OJ.
13. Unger, 55–56.
14. *Ibid.*, 56; ELL.
15. Unger, 52; ELL.
16. ELL.
17. Clayton, 146; Unger 133; Kirchner, 18–19, 28–29.
18. ELL; Kirchner, 18–19, 28–29, 107.
19. Kirchner, 109–11.
20. FBIH; Kirchner, 96.
21. Kirchner, 33–34; Unger, 53–54.
22. Kirchner, 34; Unger, 54–55.
23. Unger, 55.
24. *Ibid.*, 78.
25. Kirchner, 18–19.
26. OJ.
27. Kirchner, 18; *SLT*, 6/18/49; Unger 51; FBI Kansas City Massacre File.
28. Kirchner, 26, 34–35; Clayton, 148, 159.
29. MACM; FG.
30. Clayton, 140, 143; Kirchner, 28, 98–99' Unger, 58.
31. Clayton, 155; OJ; Kirchner, 105.
32. Clayton, 144; Unger, 52, 80.
33. *KCJP*, 6/20/33; Kirchner, 113–14, 135–36.
34. Unger, 67.
35. Fox, 337; Unger, 21.
36. HGM; Unger, 57.
37. Unger, 165.
38. Newton, 158.

39. Unger, 82.
40. *Ibid.*, 85.
41. *Ibid.*, 71–72.
42. Kirchner, 95; U.S. Census Bureau.
43. Helmer/Mattix, 90–95.
44. Kirchner, 130–31.
45. *Ibid.*, 107; FBI Kansas City Massacre File; FG; Unger, 52, 85, 170, 228.
46. Unger, 86, 164.
47. *Ibid.*, 165.
48. *Ibid.*
49. Kirchner, 91–92.
50. Edge, 4.
51. Kirchner, 62, 94, 97, 131.
52. *Ibid.*, 79, 122, 124–26.
53. Butts, 73–80.
54. *Ibid.*
55. Unger, 223, 225–27.
56. Unger, 225–27.
57. *Ibid.*, 169–70.
58. *Ibid.*, 168–70.
59. *Ibid.*, 169–70, 228.
60. *Ibid.*, 229; PG.
61. FG.
62. *FMDD*, 9/10/2019.

Chapter 4

1. JDF; OJ.
2. *ND*, 2/5/2014.
3. Guinn, 199–205.
4. RAAI; *SJ*, 7/1/33, 7/14/33; Helmer/Mattix, 186.
5. Helmer/Mattix, 186.
6. *Ibid.*, 186–87; MACM; Unger, 67–68; FBI Kansas City Massacre file.
7. *BCE*, 7/17/33; *ESG*, 7/20/33; *SJ*, 7/21/33; *SLPD*, 9/13/2012.
8. *EG*, 7/14/33; *LJS*, 7/14/33; *SJ*, 7/14/33; RAAI.
9. JD; OJ.
10. FBI Bonnie and Clyde File; OJ.
11. FBI Machine Gun Kelly File; FBIH.
12. *Ibid.*
13. JD; OJ; AE.
14. Newton, 58–59, 76–77.
15. *NYT*, 8/9/33; Unger, 80.
16. FBI Machine Gun Kelly File.
17. Unger, 86.
18. AM.
19. LOA; OJ; HL.
20. *KT*, 8/25/33.
21. FBI Bonnie and Clyde File; Patch.
22. Unger, 115–16.
23. LOA; 3AM.
24. FBI Barker-Karpis Gang File; Helmer/Mattix, 190–91.
25. OJ; Guinn, 235.
26. FBIH.
27. *NYT*, 9/23/33; *GT*, 9/30/33; *ATU*, 9/30/33; *SLPD*, 9/9/2012.
28. Unger, 86.
29. JD; OJ; FBIH.
30. OJ.
31. *SA*, 9/24/33.
32. FBI Machine Gun Kelly File.
33. *Ibid.*
34. *Ibid.*
35. *Ibid.*; *MF*, 9/25/2007.
36. FBI Machine Gun Kelly File.
37. IADC; OJ; JD.
38. Newton, 76–77.

Chapter 5

1. OJ; FBIH.
2. *Ibid.*
3. *Ibid.*
4. *Ibid.*
5. *Ibid.*
6. DE; JD; OJ.
7. *Ibid.*; AE.
8. OJ; *SJ*, 10/7/33; Burrough, 55, 92, 146.
9. JD; OJ; LOA.
10. OJ; SDPB; Unger, 91–101, 114–15.
11. OJ; Newton, 38.
12. *SJ*, 11/9/33; *SA*, 11/12/33; *HIR*, 11/12–13/33, 11/21/33; *FS*, 11/13/33; *NYS*, 11/13/33; *MT*, 11/27/33.
13. SDPB; GR; OJ; FBIH.
14. FBIH; Newton, 12–13.
15. Touhy, 87.
16. *CDT*, 7/22/33, 11/29/33.
17. JD; JDF.
18. FBIH; OJ; AP, 11/25/33; *DMT*, 11/23/33. 11/26/33, 1/23/34.
19. FBIH.
20. *NYP*, 12/4/33.
21. OJ; ODMP; JDF.
22. JDF; OJ.
23. *Ibid.*
24. FBIH.
25. OJ, HGM; FG; *BCE*, 12/31/33.
26. *Ibid.*; Unger, 109–13.
27. OJ; HGM.

Chapter 6

1. FBI Kansas City Massacre File.
2. *Ibid.*

3. *Ibid.*
4. Unger, 153–54.
5. *NYP*, 12/4/33; *HIR*, 1/7/34; *BCE*, 1/8/34; OJ; IADC; *CDT*, 1/11/34; *SSS*,1/24/34.
6. Newton, 143–44.
7. HGM.
8. *Ibid.*
9. JD.
10. *Ibid.*
11. *Ibid.*
12. *Ibid.*
13. *Ibid.*; AE.
14. *NYT*, 12/13/51; *CST*, 3/4/2020.
15. *CDT*, 1/16/34, 2/3/34.
16. LOA; *OCA*, 9/19/2016; ODMP; FG/LOA.
17. LOA.
18. THN.
19. TRHF.
20. FBIH.
21. *Ibid.*; 3AM.
22. Newton, 58–59; RAAB.
23. *PP*, 2/1/34.
24. *Ibid.*
25. *WT*, 2/2/34; *JS* ,2/3/34; *HT*, 2/9/34; *Time*, 2/19/34.
26. *PP.* 2/1/34; FBIH.
27. FBIH; LOA.
28. Purvis, *Vendetta*, 17–19, 46.
29. *Ibid.*, 51, 53
30. *Ibid.*, 51.
31. *Ibid.*, 52.
32. *Ibid.*.
33. *Ibid.*, 54–55.
34. Newton, 58–59.
35. DE; JDF.
36. Unger, 121.
37. *Ibid.*, 122–23.
38. FBIH.
39. OJ.
40. FBIH.
41. LOA; TRHF; FG; *AMN*, 5/22/34.
42. *TDN*, 3/4/34.
43. DE; JD; OJ.
44. *Ibid.*; FBI John Dillinger File.
45. *Ibid.*
46. *Ibid.*
47. *Ibid.*
48. FG; SNPM; S&S.
49. FBIH; LOA.
50. H.
51. Unger, 161–62.
52. *Ibid.*, 163–64.
53. FG; MACM.
54. SLPH; *MS*, 3/7 and 3/9/34; Burrough, 243–44.
55. *RNR*, 7/9/2009.
56. Wallis, 226; FG.
57. OMDP.
58. OCA; OJ, LOA.
59. *Ibid.*
60. *Ibid.*
61. Purvis, *Vendetta*, 59–60.
62. Burrough, 274–78.
63. *Ibid.*
64. Unger, 134.
65. DE; JDF.
66. *Ibid.*; OJ.
67. MW.
68. JD; OJ.
69. *Ibid.*
70. *Ibid.*; FBIH; MW.
71. *Ibid.*
72. *Ibid.*
73. *Ibid.*
74. *Ibid.*
75. *Ibid.*
76. *Ibid.*
77. *Ibid.*
78. *Ibid.*
79. *Ibid.*
80. *Ibid.*
81. *Ibid.*
82. Purvis, *Vendetta*, 134–36.
83. *Ibid.*, 136.
84. FBIH.
85. Purvis, *Vendetta*, 150–51; HGM.
86. DE; JDF; OJ.
87. *Ibid.*
88. JDF; AE.
89. DE; JDF; OJ.
90. FBIH.
91. *Ibid.*; *AMN*, 5/21/34.
92. LOA, *OCA*, 9/19/2016.
93. *OCA*, 9/19/2016.
94. *Ibid.*
95. FG.
96. Newton, 58–59.

Chapter 7

1. Helmer/Mattix, 216; S&S.
2. DE; JDF.
3. Helmer/Mattix, 199, 216; JDF.
4. *Ibid.*; OJ.
5. *Ibid.*; FG.
6. Burrough, 294; JDF.
7. *FBILEB*, Vol. 9, No. 7 (July 1940).
8. AE; FBIH; HGM.
9. DE; Helmer/Mattix, 217; *UDC*, 6/15/34; DE.

Notes—Chapter 8

10. DE; Newton, 58–59.
11. DE; JDF.
12. DE.
13. FBIH; JDF.
14. DE; JDF; OJ.
15. *Ibid.*; FBIH.
16. *Ibid.*
17. JDF; OJ.
18. JDF.
19. *Ibid.*; DE; Helmer/Mattix, 217.
20. DE; JDF.
21. Unger, 134–36.
22. WP.
23. DE.
24. FBIH; JDF; OJ.
25. FBIH; HGM.
26. *Ibid.*; JDF; OJ.
27. FBIH; HGM; JDF; TTW.
28. AE.
29. HGM; FBI Dillinger File.
30. FBIH; *NYT*, 7/23/34.
31. FBIH; JDF.
32. OJ; Helmer/Mattix, 220; *CDT*, 7/27/34; CCSP.
33. DE; Helmer/Mattix, 217–20.
34. Helmer/Mattix, 220.
35. Breuer, 145; Matera, 291.
36. DE; Helmer/Mattix, 221.
37. DE.
38. AH.
39. *Ibid.*
40. DE; Helmer/Mattix, 221; OJ.
41. Helmer/Mattix, 223.
42. DE; OJ.
43. *Ibid.*
44. *Ibid.*
45. *Ibid.*
46. DE; FG.
47. LOA; OJ.
48. *CHE*, 8/27–30/34.
49. DE.
50. Unger, 137.
51. *Ibid.*, 137–38.

Chapter 8

1. DE.
2. Helmer/Mattix, 224–25.
3. FBIH.
4. OJ.
5. FBIH.
6. *Ibid.*
7. *Ibid.*
8. *Ibid.*
9. *Ibid.*
10. Helmer/Mattix, 225.
11. DE; OJ; FG.
12. Helmer/Mattix, 225; S&S.
13. FBIH.
14. Unger, 163.
15. OJ.
16. DE.
17. *Ibid.*; FG.
18. *ND*, 2/5/2014, 2/12/2014.
19. Helmer/Mattix, 225.
20. FBIH; OJ.
21. *Ibid.*
22. TKCM.
23. *Ibid.*; FBIH; OJ.
24. *Ibid.*
25. *Ibid.*
26. *Ibid.*
27. *Ibid.*; UPI, 10/23/34.
28. *Ibid.*
29. *Ibid.*
30. *Ibid.*
31. *Ibid.*
32. *Ibid.*
33. *Time*, 9/24/79.
34. *Ibid.*, 11/19/79.
35. OJ.
36. *Ibid.*
37. *Ibid.*; TKCM.
38. TKCM; *DO*, 10/28/2014.
39. Purvis, *Vendetta*, 235, 244.
40. *Ibid.*, 245.
41. OJ; Burrough, 109–10.
42. S&S; Helmer/Mattix, 225.
43. MFH.
44. FBIH.
45. KCPD; *NYT*, 11/4/34; *EP*, 11/5/37; *KCS*, 3/8/35.
46. Helmer/Mattix, 225.
47. 3AM; PG.
48. Unger, 132–33.
49. *Ibid.*, 133.
50. Purvis, *Vendetta*, 248–49.
51. *Ibid.*, 249.
52. Jones, 49–55.
53. Purvis, *Vendetta*, 246–47.
54. *Ibid.*, 247.
55. *IR*, 11/27/34, ODMP; *JG*, 3/28/35.
56. FBIH; OJ; *TRC*, 8/22/2016.
57. FBIH; OJ.
58. *Ibid.*; HGM; LOA.
59. FBIH; LOA.
60. FBIH; OJ.
61. FBIH; Nickell/Helmer, 341–60; *NYT*, 12/6/34.
62. FBIH; OJ.
63. OJ.

64. Nickell/Helmer, 357–62; *NYT,* 4/30/2014; LOA; FBIH; OJ.
65. OJ; *CHT,* 11/30/34; LOA.
66. OJ.
67. OJ; FG.
68. FG; Purvis, *Vendetta,* 261.
69. Helmer/Mattix, 226.
70. *Ibid.,* 221, 229; JD; OJ; *IH,* 12/17/34.
71. FBIH.
72. HGM; Purvis, *Vendetta,* 263–64.
73. Helmer/Mattix, 226.
74. *Ibid.;* S&S.
75. *FBILEB,* July 1940; WP.
76. FBI John Dillinger File; JD.
77. *NYT,* 12/23/34; Jones, 55–57l *AWN,* 12/27/34.
78. FBIH; Helmer/Mattix, 226; OJ.
79. OJ; *OT,* 2/2/35; *BH,* 12/30/34; *CJ,* 12/30/34.
80. Gentry, 176.
81. *Kirkus Reviews,* 1/1/35.
82. FBIH.
83. *Ibid.;* Helmer/Mattix, 226; OJ.
84. FAT.
85. *Ibid.*
86. *Ibid.*
87. *Ibid.*
88. *Ibid.;* BM.
89. FAT.
90. *Ibid.; NYT,* 9/26/34.
91. FAT.
92. Helmer/Mattix, 226.
93. *Ibid.,* 226–27; *NYT,* 5/1/2014; HGM.
94. SL.
95. *Ibid.*
96. HGM; *OS,* 1/11/98.
97. Burrough, 506–07; CE; FBIH; HGM; Gentry, 253; *MM,* 1/16/35; OKHS; *OS,* 1/11/98; *OSB,* 1/1/2003.
98. CE; *OSB,* 1/1/2003.
99. CE; HGM.
100. *OSB,* 1/1/2003, 1/23/2019; Mahoney, 165.
101. *NP,* 1/18/35; Maccabee, 105.
102. OH.
103. Helmer/Mattix, 227.
104. *Ibid.;* OJ.
105. THT; DE; Helmer/Mattix, 227.
106. AH.
107. Helmer/Mattix, 227–28; S&S.
108. *NYT,* 6/28/35.
109. Helmer/Mattix, 227; FG.
110. Helmer/Mattix, 228; S&S; FG.
111. Helmer/Mattix, 227; TH; *OCA,* 9/19/2016.
112. Helmer/Mattix, 228; OJ.
113. FBIH; *NYT,* 2/14/35.
114. OJ.
115. Parish, 1–5; Helmer/Mattix, 228.
116. FBIH; TKCM; ODMP; *State v. McKeever,* 101 S.W.2d 22 (Mo. 1936).
117. *JP,* 3/3/35; *NDN,* 5/31/2009; MOH.
118. *NYT,* 3/3/35.
119. HT, 3/4/35.
120. Helmer/Mattix, 228.
121. FBIH; OJ; AH.
122. Helmer/Mattix, 228–29; DE.
123. Helmer/Mattix, 228.

Chapter 9

1. TKCM; ELL, 1/24/2019.
2. DE; *NYT,* 4/16/35, 4/25/35; Helmer/Mattix, 229; OJ; NRE.
3. Purvis, *Vendetta,* 273; FBIH.
4. Helmer/Mattix, 229.
5. *Ibid.; MT,* 4/6/35; DE.
6. IMDB.
7. *HTE,* 4/29/35.
8. *Ibid.;* FBI Bremer Kidnapping File.
9. THT; LOA.
10. Jones, 57–67.
11. *NYT,* 6/1/35; *CC,* 8/27/35; *SLPD,* 9/13, 2012.
12. Breuer, 1–10.
13. *Ibid.*
14. Helmer/Mattix, 229, 231; DE; FBI Bremer Kidnapping File.
15. Breuer, 1–10.
16. *Ibid.*
17. *Ibid.,;* FBIH.
18. Breuer, 1–10.
19. DE.
20. FBIH.
21. Jones, 61–67.
22. Helmer/Mattix, 229; TKCM; ELL, 1/24/2019.
23. TKCM.
24. *Ibid.;* ELL, 1/24/2019.
25. TKCM.
26. *Ibid.*
27. *Ibid.;* ELL, 1/24/2019.
28. *Ibid.*
29. TKCM.
30. *Ibid.*
31. *Ibid.*
32. *Ibid.*
33. *Ibid.*
34. *Ibid.*
35. *Ibid.;* ELL, 1/24/2019.
36. TKMC.

37. *Ibid.*
38. *Ibid.*
39. *Ibid.*
40. *Ibid.*; ELL, 1/24/2019.
41. TKCM.
42. *Ibid.*; ELL, 1/24/2019; FBIH.
43. ELL, 1/24/2019; TKCM.
44. TKCM.
45. *Ibid.*
46. *Ibid.*
47. *Ibid.*
48. *Ibid.*
49. *Ibid.*; NYT, 11/4/34.
50. TKCM.
51. *Ibid.*
52. *Ibid.*
53. *Ibid.*
54. *Ibid.*
55. *Ibid.*
56. *Ibid.*
57. *Ibid.*
58. *Ibid.*
59. RI, 6/5/34; DE; NYT, 6/26–28/35.
60. FBIH.
61. FAT.
62. NYT, 6/25/35.
63. NYT, 6/27/35; NFG, 6/27/35.
64. Breuer: 1–10.
65. Helmer/Mattix, 229; Purvis, *Vendetta*, 273–74; IMDB.
66. Jones, 66–67.
67. 3AM; SPPHS.
68. Helmer/Mattix, 229.
69. OJ; DE.
70. FBIH.
71. Helmer/Mattix, 229.
72. Jones, 67.
73. CC, 8/27/35.
74. DE; Helmer/Mattix, 229.
75. Helmer/Mattix, 229; FBI Barker-Karpis File; NRE.
76. DE.
77. JG, 9/6/35.
78. NYT, 11/4/35.
79. HT, 9/19/35.
80. DE; JD.
81. OSB, 1/1/35, 1/23/35; FG; FBI Bremer Kidnapping File.
82. YS, 10/13/35.
83. FAT.
84. FBIH; CE; IS, 6/28/2018.
85. FBIH; IS, 6/28/2018.
86. *Ibid.*; OJ.
87. FBIH; IS, 6/28/2018; OJ; Helmer/Mattix, 230.
88. DE.
89. CNN, 8/19/2008; WW.
90. *Gilmore v. United States*, 124 F.2d 537 (10th Cir. 1942).
91. NYS, 11/4/35; FG.
92. DE; FBIH.
93. *Gilmore v. United States*, 124 F.2d 537 (10th Cir. 1942).
94. Helmer/Mattix, 231.
95. *Ibid.*; ODMP.
96. S&S; DPUSA.
97. Frye; ODMP.
98. FBIH.
99. DE.
100. Helmer/Mattix, 230; FBIH.
101. DE.
102. Helmer/Mattix, 231.

Chapter 10

1. FBI Barker-Karpis File.
2. FAT; FBIH.
3. Jones, 67–69; *Gooch v. United States*, 297 U.S. 124 (1936).
4. Helmer/Mattix, 232.
5. *Ibid.*
6. *Gilmore v. United States*, 124 F.2d 537 (10th Cir. 1942).
7. DE.
8. OJ.
9. FBIH.
10. *Ibid.*
11. *Ibid.*
12. *Ibid.*
13. FBI Barker-Karpis File.
14. Helmer/Mattix, 232.
15. DE.
16. Helmer/Mattix, 232; HL.
17. Helmer/Mattix, 232; OJ.
18. FBIH; FG.
19. FBIH.
20. EOA; OJ.
21. Helmer/Mattix, 232.
22. FBIH; FAT.
23. FAT.
24. *Ibid.*; FBIH.
25. Jones, 69–70; IS, 6/28/2018; FBIH.
26. Helmer/Mattix, 232; OJ; FBIH.
27. Helmer/Mattix, 233; FBIH; IS, 5/28/2018.
28. FBIH; OJ; OMPD.
29. Helmer/Mattix, 233; FBIH; IS, 5/28/2018; CE.
30. Helmer/Mattix, 232–33.
31. OJ.
32. Gentry, 182–87; FBIH; TKF; OJ.

33. Chalmers, 283; Gentry, 194; PG.
34. *EG*, 4/21/36; *NYT*, 4/22/36; HGM.
35. SCHS; *NYT*, 4/28/36.
36. Helmer/Mattix, 233; DE; OJ; FBIH; di Toledano, 133–34.
37. Helmer/Mattix, 233; DE.
38. *Ibid.*
39. DE.
40. FBIH; Breuer, 1–10.
41. Jones, 70.
42. *JG*, 5/9/36.
43. Helmer/Mattix, 233; FBIH.
44. FBI Barker-Karpis File; Helmer/Mattix, 233.
45. FBIH.
46. Jones, 71–80; DPUSA.
47. Helmer/Mattix, 234.
48. *Ibid.*; *LJW*, 7/9/36.
49. *SPDN*, 7/14/36; EOA; *MDT*, 7/29/36; Helmer/Mattix, 234.
50. FG.
51. *JG*, 7/26/36.
52. FBIH; Helmer/Mattix, 234; MNO.
53. WP; *FBILEB*, July 1940.
54. Helmer/Mattix, 234; OJ; FBIH.
55. DE.
56. FBIH.
57. *FBILEB*, July 1940.
58. Helmer/Mattix, 234; OJ; FBIH.
59. FBIH.
60. *SLPD*, 11/13/36.
61. FBIH; OJ.
62. *FBILEB*, July 1940.
63. Helmer/Mattix, 234.
64. *Ibid.*; Cook, 196–200; Messick, 65–66.
65. FBIH.

Chapter 11

1. DE.
2. Gentry, 176.
3. *KR*, 2/7/37.
4. *NYT*, 2/26–27/37; *CH*, 2/26/37; *MNR* 2/26/37; *CC*, 3/4/37.
5. *NYT*, 3/13/37; *CDS*, 3/17/37; *Suhay v. United States*, 95 F.2d 890 (10th Cir. 1938).
6. *FBILEB*, July 1940.
7. Helmer/Mattix, 234–35.
8. NRE; DE.
9. FBIH.
10. *Ibid.*; Helmer/Mattix, 235; OJ.
11. FBIH; OJ.
12. *Ibid.*; *IS*, 6/28/2018.
13. FBIH; *NYT*, 6/2/37.
14. FBIH; OJ.
15. DE.
16. DE; *BPP*, 7/25/2019.
17. *NYT*, 6/26/37.
18. Helmer/Mattix, 235.
19. *FBILEB*, July 1940; *BB*, 7/5/2019.
20. *Fulbright v. United States*, 91 F.2d 210 (8th Cir. 1937).
21. NRE.
22. *LNJ*, 7/21/37; FG.
23. Helmer/Mattix, 235; FBIH; OJ.
24. DE.
25. AE; WW; *NYDN*, 11/26/2017.
26. DE; DPUSA.
27. FBIH; OJ; BF; NEHS.
28. *Ibid.*
29. DE; Helmer/Mattix, 235.
30. FBIH; OJ; Helmer/Mattix, 235.
31. FBIH; BF.
32. *Ibid.*; *NYT*, 10/13/37.
33. FBIH; OJ; *NYT*, 4/30/2014; HGM.
34. *NYT*, 10/16/37; FG.
35. DE.
36. *Ibid.*; Helmer/Mattix, 235.
37. Helmer/Mattix, 235.
38. DE.
39. *Suhay v. United States*, 95 F.2d 890 (10th Cir. 1938).
40. DE; EFCA.
41. FBIH.
42. *Ibid.*
43. Helmer/Mattix, 235; *GR*, 6/14/38.
44. Helmer/Mattix, 235.
45. *Ibid.*
46. *Ibid.*, 235–36.
47. *Ibid.*; Cecil, "In the Eyes of Men."
48. *Ibid.*
49. *NYT*, 8/13/38.
50. FBIH.
51. RAAI; *OCA*, 9/19/2016.
52. TKCM; FBIH.
53. Helmer/Mattix, 236; ELL.
54. Cecil, "In the Eyes of Men."
55. *FBILEB*. July 1940.
56. *RMS*, 11/4/38; DE.
57. FBIH; *NYT*, 11/18/38.
58. Helmer/Mattix, 236; Cecil, "In the Eyes of Men."
59. DPUSA; RAAB.
60. Helmer/Mattix, 236; Ward Davis, 487.
61. FG; Ward Davis, 487.
62. Helmer/Mattix, 236.
63. IMDB.
64. *Ibid.*
65. *Ibid.*

Notes—Chapter 12

66. *Ibid.*
67. *United States v. Miller* 59 S.Ct. 816 (1939); "An Oklahoma Gangster's Impact on U.S. Gun Laws," TV Channel 6 (Tulsa), 1/29/2008.
68. Cecil, "In the Eyes of Men."
69. *Ibid.*
70. *Ibid.*
71. *Ibid.*
72. Helmer/Mattix, 236–37.
73. *Ibid.*, 237.
74. Cecil, "In the Eyes of Men."
75. Helmer/Mattix, 237.
76. *Ibid.*,; HL.
77. MNHS.
78. Helmer/Mattix, 237; HL.

Chapter 12

1. Gentry, 185.
2. FBIH.
3. MACM.
4. AH.
5. Edge, 224.
6. MHS; *DMR*, 2/24/42; FBIH; *BBP*, 7/5/2019; FG; WP.
7. *Gilmore v. United States*, 129 F.2d 199 (10th Cir. 1942).
8. JD.
9. Edge, 228.
10. FG.
11. MOH; *NDN*, 1/5/2013.
12. *SFW*, 7/3/2016.
13. JD; FG.
14. JD.
15. AH.
16. FG.
17. Edge, 228–33.
18. *Ibid.*; OJ.
19. CM; JDF; FG.
20. OJ; FG.
21. FG.
22. JDF.
23. FBIH; LOA.
24. JDF.
25. *Ibid.*; LOA.
26. FG.
27. FG; JDF.
28. JD; OJ.
29. Newton, 58–59.
30. JD; *HC*, 9/14/73.
31. SL.
32. FG.
33. JD.
34. FG.
35. OJ.
36. *SDS*, 8/27/79.
37. IJ; FG.
38. HL.
39. FG.
40. *HIR*, 9/21/41; *SSP*, 10/20/56; RAAI; FG.
41. JD; *DMN*, 12/15/56, 7/28/84; *MH*, 7/28/84; FG.
42. FG.
43. HL.
44. Jones, 173.
45. AP, 7/30, 8/1 and 8/6/2019; *USAT*, 12/4/2019; *RS*, 1/6/2020.
46. JDF.
47. FG.
48. *Ibid.*; UG.
49. JDF.
50. FG.
51. *Ibid.*
52. *Ibid.*; OJ.
53. JD.
54. QH.
55. FG.
56. *Ibid.*
57. *Ibid.*
58. AH; HL; FG.
59. JD.
60. *Ibid.*; FG.
61. FG; *OCA*, 9/16/2016.
62. *NYT*, 12/13/51.
63. FG.
64. JD.
65. *Ibid.*
66. OJ; FG.
67. FG.
68. JD; FG.
69. *Ibid.*
70. JD.
71. FG.
72. *Ibid.*; JD.
73. *Ibid.*
74. OJ; FG.
75. FAT; FBIH; FG.
76. Gentry, 442–45, 562–66, 595, 618–23, 692–93.
77. *Ibid.*, 36; *LAT*, 11/2/97.
78. JG; FG.
79. *Ibid.*
80. HGM; JDF.
81. HGM; OC.
82. HGM; FG.
83. HGM.
84. *Ibid.*
85. *NYT*, 4/30/2014; FG.
86. JG; FG.

87. FG; AE.
88. TRHF.
89. FG.
90. JD.
91. FG.
92. *Ibid.*
93. *Ibid.*; JD.
94. FG.
95. *NYT,* 2/15/81; *WP,* 7/30/2000; *LAT,* 10/3/2004; *SCS,* 2/11/2010.
96. FG.
97. *Ibid.*
98. *Ibid.*
99. *Ibid.*
100. AH.
101. LBL.
102. RA; HSW.
103. AO.
104. GJ; *OSB,* 10/27/2016, 1/16/2019.
105. RA; *NIT,* 3/29/2008; *IS,* 3/16–17/2015, 7/28/2015, 8/31/2017.

Chapter 13

1. Burrough, title page.
2. Breuer, 25; Whitehead, 96.
3. DE; Helmer/Mattix, 161–230.
4. FBIBCS,
5. Whitehead, xi–xv, 97–101, 333–34.
6. *Ibid.*, pp. 82–84, 86, 110, 111, 336.
7. WHO.
8. IMDB; Gentry, 384, 446–47.
9. IMDB.
10. *Ibid.*
11. *Ibid.*
12. *Ibid.*
13. Collins/Schwartz, 521–24.
14. IMDB.
15. FBI Desi Arnaz file; Gentry, xi–xiii, 384–85.
16. Amazon.com; BN.
17. JRNAC; *NYT,* 7/29/73; Wikipedia; *Journal of American History,* 81, No. 4 (March 1995): 1885–1887.
18. *Library Journal,* August 1990.
19. *Nash v. CBS, Inc.*, No. 89–1823 (1990).
20. JD.
21. CF; JD; MGB.
22. RE.
23. JRNAC.
24. *Ibid.*
25. FBIH.
26. *Ibid.*; Gentry, 160–63l; JFOW.
27. IMDB.
28. *Ibid.*
29. *Ibid.*
30. *Ibid.*
31. De Toledano, 95–100, 112, 127–39, 143.
32. Breuer, 29, 147–9, 225–26.
33. DeLoach, 66–69.
34. FBIH.
35. *Ibid.*
36. *Ibid.*
37. *Ibid.*

Bibliography

Books

Algren, Gregory, and Stephen Monier. *Crime of the Century: The Lindbergh Kidnapping Hoax.* Wellesley, MA: Branden Books, 1993.
Alix, Ernest. *Ransom Kidnapping in America, 1874–1974: The Creation of a Capital Crime.* Carbondale, IL: Southern Illinois University Press, 1978.
Barnes, Bruce. *Machine Gun Kelly: To Right a Wrong.* Perris, CA: Tipper Publications, 1992.
Barrow, Blanche, and John Phillips. *My Life with Bonnie and Clyde.* Norman, OK: University of Oklahoma Press, 2012.
Behn, Noel. *Lindbergh, The Crime.* New York: Atlantic Monthly Press,1993.
Blumenthal, Karen. *Bonnie and Clyde: The Making of a Legend.* New York: Viking Books, 2018.
Boessenecker, John. *Texas Ranger: The Epic Life of Frank Hamer, the Man Who Killed Bonnie and Clyde.* New York: Thomas Dunne Books, 2016.
Breuer, William. *J. Edgar Hoover and His G-Men.* Westport, CT: Diane Publishing, 1995.
Brooks, Bill. *Pretty Boy: The Epic Life of Pretty Boy Floyd.* New York: Forge Books, 2017.
Burgess, Marjorie. *Charles "Pretty Boy" Floyd: In His Own Words from the Other Side.* Pittsburgh, PA: PublishAmerica, 2005,
Burrough, Bryan. *Public Enemies: America's Greatest Crime Wave and the Birth of the FBI, 1933–34.* New York: Penguin, 2004.
Butts, Edward. *Running With Dillinger: The Story of Red Hamilton and Other Forgotten Canadian Outlaws.* Toronto, ON: Dundurn Press, 2008.
Cahill, Richard Jr. *Hauptmann's Ladder: A Step-by-Step Analysis of the Lindbergh Kidnapping.* Kent, OH: Kent State University Press, 2014.
Cecil, Matthew. *The Ballad of Ben and Stella Mae: Great Plains Outlaws Who Became FBI Public Enemies Nos. 1 and 2.* Lawrence, KS: University Press of Kansas, 2016.
_____. *Hoover's FBI and the Fourth Estate: The Campaign to Control the Press and the Bureau's Image.* Lawrence, KS: University Press of Kansas, 2014.
Chalmers, David. *Hooded Americanism: The History of the Ku Klux Klan.* Durham, NC: Duke University Press, 1987.
Charles, Douglas. *The FBI's Obscene File: J. Edgar Hoover and the Bureau's Crusade against Smut.* Lawrence, KS: University Press of Kansas, 2012.
Clayton, Merle. *Union Station Massacre: The Shootout That Started The FBI's War On Crime.* Indianapolis: Bobbs-Merrill, 1975.
Collins, Max, and A. Brad Schwartz. *Scarface and the Untouchable: Al Capone, Eliot Ness, and the Battle for Chicago.* New York: William Morrow, 2018.
Condon, John. *Jafsie Tells All!* New York: Jonathan Lee Publishing, 1936.
Cook, Fred. *The FBI Nobody Knows.* New York: Macmillan, 1964.
Cooper, Courtney, and J. Edgar Hoover. *Ten Thousand Public Enemies.* Boston: Little, Brown, 1935.
Cromie, Robert, and Joseph Pinkston. *Dillinger: A Short and Violent Life.* New York: McGraw-Hill, 1962.

Bibliography

Culleton, Claire. *Joyce and the G-Men: J. Edgar Hoover's Manipulation of Modernism.* New York: Palgrave Macmillan, 2004.
Davis, Jonathan. *Bonnie and Clyde and Marie: A Sister's Perspective on the Notorious Barrow Gang.* Nacogdoches, TX: Stephen F. Austin State University Press, 2014.
Davis, Ward. *Alcatraz: The Gangster Years.* Berkeley: University of California Press, 2009.
DeFord, Miriam. *The Real Ma Barker.* New York: Ace Books, 1970.
DeLoach, Cartha. *Hoover's FBI.* Washington, D.C.: Regnery Publishing, 1995.
De Toledano, Ralph. *J. Edgar Hoover: The Man in His Time.* Westport, CT: Arlington House, 1973.
Edge, L. L. *Run the Cat Roads: A True Story of Bank Robbers in the Thirties.* New York: W. W. Norton, 1981.
Edwards, Wallace. *The Trail's End: The Story of Bonnie and Clyde.* Scotts Valley, CA: CreateSpace, 2013.
Enss, Chris, and Howard Kazanjian. *Ma Barker: America's Most Wanted Mother.* Lanham, MD: TwoDot Books, 2016.
Ernst, Robert. *Robbin' Banks and Killin' Cops: The Life and Crimes of Lawrence DeVol and His Association with Alvin Karpis and the Barker-Karpis Gang.* Pittsburgh, PA: PublishAmerica, 2009.
Fisher, Jim. *The Ghosts of Hopewell: Setting the Record Straight in the Lindbergh Case.* Carbondale, IL: Southern Illinois University Press, 1999.
_____. *The Lindbergh Case.* Morristown, NJ: Rutgers University Press, 1987.
Fox, Stephen. *Blood and Power: Organized Crime in Twentieth-Century America.* New York: Penguin Books, 1989.
Gardner, Lloyd. *The Case That Never Dies: The Lindbergh Kidnapping.* New Brunswick, NJ: Rutgers University Press, 2004.
Gentry, Curt. *J. Edgar Hoover: The Man and the Secrets.* New York: W. W. Norton, 1991.
Gilmore, John, and Marshall Terrill. *On the Run with Bonnie and Clyde.* Los Angeles: Amok Books, 2013.
Girardin, G. Russell, and William Helmer. *Dillinger: The Untold Story.* Bloomington, IN: Indiana University Press, 1994.
Gorn, Elliott. *Dillinger's Wild Ride: The Year That Made America's Public Enemy Number One.* New York: Oxford University Press, 2009.
Guinn, Jess. *Go Down Together: The True, Untold Story of Bonnie and Clyde.* New York: Simon & Schuster, 2009.
Hamilton, Stanley. *Machine Gun Kelly's Last Stand.* Lawrence, KS: University Press of Kansas, 2003.
Harrington, Roger. *The Real Bonnie and Clyde: America's Most Infamous Criminal Double-Act.* Pittsburgh, PA: Shoal Creek Publishers.
Helmer, William, and Rick Mattix. *Public Enemies: America's Criminal Past, 1919–1940.* New York: Checkmark Books, 2006.
Hendley, Nate. *Bonnie and Clyde: A Biography.* Westport, CT: Greenwood Press, 2007.
Herion, Don. *Touhy vs. Capone: The Chicago Outfit's Biggest Frame Job.* Cheltenham, UK: The History Press, 20117.
Herzberg, Bob. *The FBI and the Movies: A History of the Bureau on Screen and Behind the Scenes in Hollywood.* Jefferson, NC: McFarland, 2006.
Hoover, J. Edgar. *Persons in Hiding.* Boston: Little, Brown, 1938.
Hunt, Brian. *G-Men, Gangsters, and Gators: The FBI Flying Squad and the Deaths of Ma and Fred Barker in Florida.* Scotts Valley CA: CreateSpace, 2012.
Jett, Robin. *Traveling History with Bonnie and Clyde: A Road Tripper's Guide to Gangster Sites in Middle America.* Lewisville, TX: Red River Historian Press, 2008.
Karpis, Alvin, and Bill Trent. *The Alvin Karpis Story.* Toronto, ON: McClellan and Stewart, 1971.
Karpis, Alvin, and Robert Livesey. *On the Rock: Twenty-Five Years in Alcatraz.* New York: Beaufort Books, 1980.
Kelly, George, and Jim Dobkins. *Machine-Gun Man: The True Story of My Incredible Survival Into the 1970's.* Prescott, AZ: UCS Press, 1988.

Bibliography 259

Kennedy, Ludovic. *The Airman and the Carpenter: The Lindbergh Kidnapping and the Framing of Richard Hauptmann*. New York: Viking, 1985.
King, Jefferey. *The Life and Death of Pretty Boy Floyd*. Kent, OH: Kent State University Press, 1997.
_____. *The Rise and Fall of the Dillinger Gang*. Nashville, TN: Cumberland House, 2005.
Kirchner, L. R. *Triple Cross Fire: J. Edgar Hoover and the Kansas City Union Station Massacre*. New York: Janlar Books, 2000.
Knight, James, and Jonathan Davis. *Bonnie and Clyde: A Twenty-First-Century Update*. Fort Worth: Eakin Press, 2014.
Koblas, John, and Rick Mattix. *"Ma": The Life and Times of Ma Barker and Her Boys*. St. Cloud, MN: North Star Press, 2008.
Koch, Michael. *The Kimes Gang*. Bloomington, IN: AuthorHouse, 2005.
_____. *A Murder in Tulsa: The Sherrill Murder Case and The Rise of the Barker-Karpis Gang*. Pittsburgh, PA: PublishAmerica, 2008.
Louderback, Lew. *The Bad Ones: Gangsters of the '30s and Their Molls*. New York: Fawcett, 1968.
Maccabee, Paul. *John Dillinger Slept Here: A Crooks' Tour of Crime and Corruption in St. Paul, 1920–1936*. Saint Paul: Minnesota Historical Society Press, 1995.
Mahoney, Tim. *Secret Partners: Big Tom Brown and the Barker Gang*. St. Paul, MN: Minnesota Historical Society Press. 2013.
Matera, Dary. *John Dillinger: The Life and Death of America's First Celebrity Criminal*. Boston: Da Capo Press, 2005.
Messick, Hank. *John Edgar Hoover: An Inquiry into the Life and Times of John Edgar Hoover, and His Relationship to the Continuing Partnership of Crime, Business, and Politics*. New York: David McKay, 1972.
Milligan, Maurice. *Missouri Waltz: The Inside Story of the Pendergast Machine by the Man Who Smashed It*. New York: Charles Scribner's, 1948.
Milner, E. R. *The Lives and Times of Bonnie and Clyde*. Carbondale, IL: Southern Illinois University Press, 1996.
Morgan, R. D. *The Bad Boys of the Cookson Hills*. Stillwater, OK: New Forums Press, 2003.
_____. *The Bandit Kings of the Cookson Hills*. Stillwater, OK: New Forums Press, 2002.
_____. *Irish O'Malley and the Ozark Mountain Boys*. Stillwater, OK: New Forums Press, 2011.
Morgan, R. D., and Rick Mattix. *The Tri-State Terror: The Life and Crimes of Wilbur Underhill*. Stillwater, OK: New Forums Press,, 2005.
Nash, Jay. *The Dillinger Dossier*. Highland Park, IL: December Press, 1983.
_____. *Look for the Woman: A Narrative Encyclopedia of Female Poisoners, Kidnappers, Thieves, Extortionists, Terrorists, Swindlers and Spies from Elizabethan Times to the Present*. Lanham, MD: M. Evans & Company, 1981.
Nash, Jay, and Ron Offen. *Dillinger: Dead or Alive?* New York: Henry Regnery, 1970.
Newton, Michael. *The Encyclopedia of Robberies, Heists, and Capers*. New York: Facts on File, 2002.
Nickel, Steven, and William Helmer. *Baby Face Nelson: Portrait of a Public Enemy*. Nashville, TN: Cumberland House, 2016.
Norris, William. *A Talent to Deceive: Who Really Killed the Lindberg Baby?* Columbia, TN: SynergEbooks, 2013.
Oliver, Willard. *The Birth of the FBI: Teddy Roosevelt, the Secret Service, and the Fight Over America's Premier Law Enforcement Agency*. Lanham, MD: Rowman & Littlefield, 2019.
Parish, Samuel. *Central Florida's Most Notorious Gangsters: Alva Hunt and Hugh Gant*. Cheltenham, UK: The History Press, 2008.
Parker, Emma, and Nell Cowan. *The True Story of Bonnie and Clyde*. New York: Signet, 1968.
Phillips, John. *Running With Bonnie and Clyde: The Ten Fast Years of Ralph Fults*. Norman, OK: University of Oklahoma Press, 2014.
Poulsen, Ellen, and Lori Hyde. *Chasing Dillinger: Police Captain Matt Leach, J. Edgar Hoover and the Rivalry to Capture Public Enemy No. 1*. Jefferson, NC: Exposit, 2018.
Powers, Richard. *G-Men: Hoover's FBI in American Popular Culture*. Carbondale, IL: Southern Illinois University Press, 1983.

Purvis, Alston. *The Vendetta: Special Agent Melvin Purvis, John Dillinger, and Hoover's FBI in the Age of Gangsters*. Philadelphia: Perseus Books, 2009.
Purvis, Melvin. *The Violent Years*. New York: Hillman Books, 1960.
Quimby, Myron. *The Devil's Emissaries*. New York: A. S. Barnes, 1969.
Ramsey, Winston. *On the Trail of Bonnie and Clyde Then and Now*. Essex, UK: After the Battle, 2003.
Richardson, Selden. *The Tri-State Gang in Richmond: Murder and Robbery in the Great Depression*. Cheltenham, UK: The History Press, 2012.
Scaduto, Anthony. *Scapegoat: The Lonesome Death of Bruno Richard Hauptmann*. New York: Putnam, 1976.
Scee, Trudy. *Public Enemy # 1: The True Story of the Brady Gang*. Camden, ME: Down East Books, 2015.
Schneider, Paul. *Bonnie and Clyde: The Lives Behind the Legend*. New York: St. Martin's Griffin, 2009.
Schrager, Adam. *The Sixteenth Rail: The Evidence, the Scientist, and the Lindbergh Kidnapping*. Golden, CO: Fulcrum Publishing, 2013.
Sifakis, Carl. *The Mafia Encyclopedia*. New York: Checkmark Books, 2005.
Smith, Brad. *Lawman to Outlaw: Verne Miller and the Kansas City Massacre*. Pittsburgh, PA: Jona Books, 2002.
Smith, W. D., and Tony Stewart. *The Barker-Karpis Gang: An American Crime Family*. Seattle: Amazon.com, 2016.
Steele, Phillip, and Marie Scoma. *The Family Story of Bonnie and Clyde*. Gretna, LA: Pelican Publishing Company, 2000.
Stewart, Tony. *Ma Barker in Ocklawaha*. Raleigh, NC: Lulu.com, 2018.
Theoharis, Athan, and John Cox. *The Boss: J. Edgar Hoover and the Great American Inquisition*. Philadelphia: Temple University Press, 1988.
Thompson, Julie. *The Hunt for the Last Public Enemy in Northeastern Ohio: Alvin "Creepy" Karpis and His Road to Alcatraz*. Cheltenham, UK: The History Press, 2019.
Thurman, Steve. *"Baby Face" Nelson*. New York: Monarch Books, 1961.
Tippet, Pam. *Run Rabbit Run: The Edna Murray Story*. Scotts Valley, CA: CreateSpace, 2013.
Toland, John. *Dillinger Days*. New York: Random House, 1963.
Touhy, Roger, and John Touhy. *The Stolen Years*. McLean, VA: Litchfield Library Books, 2020.
Unger, Robert. *The Union Station Massacre: The Original Sin of J. Edgar Hoover's FBI*. Kansas City, MO: Andrews McMeel Publishing, 1997.
Urschel, Joe. *The Year of Fear: Machine Gun Kelly and the Manhunt That Changed the Nation*. New York: Minotaur, 2015.
Wallis, Michael. *Pretty Boy: The Life and Times of Charles Arthur Floyd*. New York: St. Martin's Press, 1992.
Wellman, Paul Jr. *A Dynasty of Western Outlaws*. Lincoln, NE: University of Nebraska Press, 1986.
Whipple, Sidney. *The Trial of Bruno Richard Hauptmann*. Lewisville, NC: Gryphon Notable Trials Library, 1991.
Winter, Robert. *Mean Men: The Sons of Ma Barker*. Ocala, FL: Netsource Distribution, 2000.
Young, Jason. *Wanted: The Hunt for Dillinger and His Stash*. Minneapolis: Two Harbors Press, 2008.
Zorn, Robert. *Cemetery John: The Undiscovered Mastermind of the Lindbergh Kidnapping*. New York: Harry N. Abrams, 2012.

Articles

Cecil, Matthew. "'In the Eyes of Men': Ben and Stella Mae Dickson, Bank Robbers." *South Dakota History* Vol 29, No. 2 (1999): 155–173.
Frye, Bruan. "The Peculiar Story of *United States v. Miller*." *NYU Journal of Law & Liberty*, 3:48 (2008): 45–82.
Jones, Leslie. "Arthur Gooch: The Political, Economic, and Social Influences That Led Him

to the Gallows." (Unpublished Master's Thesis): Edmond, OK: University of Central Oklahoma, 2010.
Mansky, Jackie, and Lorraine Boissoneault. "Has the FBI Ever Been Divorced from Politics?" *Smithsonian Magazine.* May 11, 2017.

FBI Files

Alvin Francis "Creepy" Karpis: No. 62–43010
Barker/Karpis Gang: No. 7–77
Bonnie and Clyde: No. 26–4114
Bremer Kidnapping: No. 7–576
Charles Arthur (Pretty Boy) Floyd: No. 32–16393
Desi Arnaz: No. 94–52549
Eliot Ness: No. 77–314
Evelyn Frechette: No. 62–47968

George (Machine Gun) Kelly: No. 7–115
Herman Barker: No. 26–9961
John Dillinger: No. 62–29777
John (Jake the Barber) Factor: No. 62–25802
Kansas City Massacre: No. 62–28195
Lester Joseph Gillis (Baby Face Nelson): No. 91–57
Lloyd William Barker: No. 62–89785
Melvin Purvis: No. 67–7489

Periodicals

(Abbreviations correlate to reference notes)

Abilene Morning News (AMN)
Ada Weekly News (AWN)
Albany Times-Union (ATU)
Arizona Republic (AR)
Associated Press (AP)
Bangor Daily News (BDN)
The Banner-Press (BP)
Brenham Banner-Press (BBP)
Brownsville Herald (BH)
Buffalo Courier-Express (BCE)
Calexico Chronicle (CC)
Chicago Daily Tribune (CDT)
Chicago Herald Examiner (CHE)
Chicago Sun Times (CST)
Cincinnati Enquirer (CE)
Circleville Herald (CH)
Cornell Daily Sun (CDS)
Courier-Journal (CJ)
Daily Oklahoman (DO)
Dallas Morning News (DMN)
Dallas Morning Tribune (DMT)
Des Moines Register (DMR)
Edwardsville Intelligencer (EI)
Elmira Star-Gazette (ESG)
Emporia Gazette (EG)
Evening Independent (EP)
FBI Law Enforcement Bulletin (FBILEB)
Fitchburg Sentinel (FS)
Fort Madison Daily Democrat (FMDD)
Gettysburg Times (GT)
Greensburg Record (GR)
Harrisburg Telegraph (HTE)
Healdsburg Tribune (HT)
Helena Independent Record (HIR)

Houston Chronicle (HC)
Hutchinson News (HN)
The Independent (TI)
Indianapolis Herald (IH)
Indianapolis Star (IS)
Iola Register (IO)
Joplin Globe (JP)
Journal News (JS)
Kansas City Journal-Post (KCJP)
Kansas City Star (KCS)
Kokomo Tribune (KT)
Lawrence Journal World (LJT)
Leavenworth Times (LT)
Lincoln Journal Star (LJS)
Longview News-Journal (LNJ)
Los Angeles Times (LAT)
Madera Tribune (MT)
Manhattan Mercury (MM)
Marion Leader-Tribune (MLT)
Memphis Flyer (MF)
Miami Herald (MH)
Miami News-Record (MNR)
Minneapolis Daily Tribune (MDT)
Minneapolis Star (MS)
Nashua Telegraph (NT)
Neosho Daily News (NDN)
Neshoba Democrat (ND)
New York Daily News (NYDN)
New York Post (NYP)
New York Sun (NYS)
New York Times (NYT)
News-Press (NP)
Niagara Falls Gazette (NFG)
Oak Cliff Advocate (OCA)

Bibliography

Ocala Star Banner (OSB)
Orlando Sentinel (OS)
Pawhuska Daily Capitol (PDC)
Pittsburgh Press (PP)
The Record-Courier (TRC)
Reno News & Review (RNR)
Richmond Item (RI)
Rockford Morning Star (RMS)
Rolling Stone (RS)
St. Louis Post-Dispatch (SLPD)
Saint Paul Daily News (SPDN)
Salt Lake Tribune (SLT)
San Francisco Examiner (SFE)
Santa Cruz Sentinel (SCS)
Saratoga Springs Saratogian (SSS)
Saskatoon Star Phoenix (SSP)
Spokane Daily Sentinel (SDS)
Syracuse American (SA)
Syracuse Journal (SJ)
Tulsa Daily News (TDN)
United Press International (UPI)
Urbana Daily Courier (UDC)
USA Today (USAT)
Washington Post (WP)
Winnipeg Tribune (WT)
Yuma Sun (YS)

Internet Sources

(Abbreviations correlate to reference notes)

Alabama.com, https://www.al.com
Alcatraz History (AH), https://www.alcatrazhistory.com
Amazon.com, https://www.amazon.com
American Experience (AE), https://www.pbs.org/wgbh/americanexperience
American Mafia (AM), https://web.archive.org/web/20101014234000/http://americanmafia.com
Answers, https://www.answers.com
Atlas Obscura (AO), https://www.atlasobscura.com
Bangor in Focus (BF), http://www.bangorinfo.com/Focus/focus_brady_gang.html
Barnes & Noble (BN), https://www.barnesandnoble.com
Biography, https://www.biography.com
Blue Island Bang-Up (BIB), https://blueislandbangup.blogspot.com
Building Moxie (BM), https://www.buildingmoxie.com/old-square-nails
Captured and Exposed (CE), https://capturedandexposed.com/tag/al-brady
Charles Arthur Floyd (CAF), https://sites.google.com/site/imcharlesarthurfloyd
The Chicago Crime Scenes Project (CCSP), https://chicagocrimescenes.blogspot.com
Chris Enss (CE), https://chrisenss.com/ma-barkers-last-day
CNN, https://www.cnn.com/2008/LIVING/wayoflife/08/19/mf.snitches.in.history/index.html
Colt Forum (CF), https://www.coltforum.com
Crime Museum (CM), https://www.crimemuseum.org
Death Penalty USA (DPUSA), http://deathpenaltyusa.org
The Dillinger Era (DE), http://wwww.geocities.com/~jdillinger/outlaws1.html
Early Ford V-8 Club of America (EFCA), http://clubs.hemmings.com
Edmond Life & Leisure (ELL), http://edmondlifeandleisure.com/index1.htm
The Encyclopedia of Arkansas (EOA), https://encyclopediaofarkansas.net
Famous American Trials (FAT), http://law2.umkc.edu/faculty/projects/ftrials/hauptmann/Hauptmann.htm
FBI Bank Crime Statistics (FBIBCS), https://www.fbi.gov/investigate/violent-crime/bank-robbery/bank-crime-reports
FBI History (FBIH), https://www.fbi.gov/history
Find a Grave (FG), https://www.findagrave.com
Gangster Report (GR), https://gangsterreport.com
Gator Joe's Beach Bar and Grill (GJ), https://www.gatorjoesocala.com
Genealogy Trails (GT). http://genealogytrails.com
GENi (Geni), https://www.geni.com/discussions/93353
The Handbook of Texas (THT), https://tshaonline.org/handbook/online/articles/ffe06
Historical G-Men (HGM), http://historicalgmen.squarespace.com

Bibliography 263

History (H), https://www.history.com
History Link (HL), https://www.historylink.org
Home Brewed Mojo (HBM), https://homebrewedmojo.blogspot.com
How Stuff Works (HSW), https://www.howstuffworks.com
Indiana Archives Dillinger Collection (IADC), https://www.in.gov/iara/2839.htm
Jay Robert Nash Annals of Crime (JRNAC), http://annalsofcrime.com
Jim Fisher Official Website (JFOW), http://jimfisher.edinboro.edu
John Dillinger, Public Enemy No. 1 (JD), http://johndillinger.com
The John Dillinger File (JDF), https://www.oocities.org/athens/olympus/4172
Kansas City Police Dept. (KCPD), https://www.kcpolicememorial.com/history/chiefs
The Knoxville Focus (TKF), https://knoxfocus.com/archives
Legends of America (LOA), https://www.legendsofamerica.com
Little Bohemia Lodge (LBL), http://www.littlebohemialodge.com
Machine Gun Boards (MGB), http://www.machinegunboards.com
Merriam-Webster Dictionary (MWD), https://www.merriam-webster.com/
A Mess of a Massacre (AMM), https://kchistory.org/week-kansas-city-history/mess-massacre
Midwest Weekends (MW), https://midwestweekends.com/index.html
Minnesota Good Age (MGA), https://www.minnesotagoodage.com
Minnesota Historical Society (MNHS), https://www.mnhs.org
Missouri and Ozark History (MOH), http://ozarks-history.blogspot.com
MNOPEDIA (MNO), https://www.mnopedia.org
Moffat Family History (MFH), https://www.moffatfamilyhistory.com
My Al Capone Museum (MACM), http://www.myalcaponemuseum.com
National Registry of Exonerations (NRE), https://www.law.umich.edu/special/exoneration/Pages/about.aspx
New England Historical Society (NEHS), https://www.newenglandhistoricalsociety.com
News Center Maine (NCM), https://www.newscentermaine.com
Officer Down Memorial Page (ODMP), https://www.odmp.org
Oklahoma Historical Society (OHS), https://www.okhistory.org
1930s Gangster Era In St. Paul (GESP), https://haileym7.weebly.com
Online Etymology Dictionary (OED), https://www.etymonline.com
Our Campaigns (OC), https://www.ourcampaigns.com
Out History (OH), http://outhistory.org/exhibits/show/fbi-history/1930–1939#
The Outlaw Journals (OJ), https://www.babyfacenelsonjournal.com
Patch, https://patch.com
Political Graveyard (PG), http://politicalgraveyard.com
Prohibition Tours (PT), https://www.prohibitiontours.com
Quinn History (QH), https://www.quinnhistory.com
Read All About It (RAAI), https://www.major-smolinski.com
Roadside America (RA), https://www.roadsideamerica.com/story/10864
RogerEbert.com (RE), https://www.rogerebert.com/roger-ebert/film-wrong-dillinger-not-killed-by-fbi-fact-hoover-coverup
Sagamon Link (SL), https://sangamoncountyhistory.org/wp/?p=10565
Saint Louis Park Historical Society (SLPH), http://slphistory.org
Saint Paul Police Historical Society (SPPHS), http://www.spphs.org/history
Sam I Am Blog (SIAB), https://samwarren55.wordpress.com
Sangamon Link (SL), http://sangamoncountyhistory.org/wp/?p=10565
Seneca County Historical Society (SCHS), https://www.facebook.com/senecacountymuseum
Smithsonian National Postal Museum (SNPM), https://postalmuseum.si.edu
Soft Schools (SS), https://www.softschools.com
South Dakota Public Broadcasting (SDPB), https://www.sdpb.org
Sword and Scale (S&S), https://www.swordandscale.com
Texas Hideout (TH), texashideout.tripod.com
Texas History Notebook (THN), https://texoso66.com
Texas Ranger Hall of Fame and Museum (TRHF), https://www.texasranger.org
3:AM Magazine (3AM), https://www.3ammagazine.com

Bibliography

Tickle the Wire (TTW), https://www.ticklethewire.com
The Trial of the Kansas City Massacre (TKCM), http://fredsustik.com/AdamTrialKC.html
United States Department of Justice (DOJ), https://www.justice.gov
United States Marshals Service (USMS), https://www.usmarshals.gov
United States Secret Service (USSS), https://www.secretservice.gov
Unknown Gender History (UG), http://unknownmisandry.blogspot.com
Wack, Larry. "FBI Firearms & The Myth Of The 1934 Crime Bill," https://static1.squarespace.com/static/54dc6b0be4b0d364a5ee20e0/t/575aa8c12fe13175d880c0bd/1465559233746/weapons.pdf
War History Online (WHO), https://www.warhistoryonline.com
Wikipedia, https://www.wikipedia.org
World History Project (WHP), https://worldhistoryproject.org
Worth Point (WP), https://www.worthpoint.com
The Writers of Wrongs (WW), http://www.writersofwrongs.com
You Will Shoot Your Eye Out (YWSYEO), youwillshootyoureyeout.com

Index

A&E Networks 225
ABC Television 236
Adams, Ike (Skeet) 38
Adams, John 84
Akers, Herbert (Dutch) 45, 211
Alcatraz Island (The Rock) 122, 123, 157, 161, 166, 187, 189, 196, 201, 207, 212, 213, 219, 220, 221, 222, 223, 224, 225, 226, 227, 232
Alcorn, Gordon 93, 139, 224
Alcorn, Robert 82
Alden, Charles 142
Alderton, Harold 156–157, 165, 166
Allen, William 8
Allred, James 196
Anastasia, Albert 81
Anastasio, Antonio (Tough Tony) 237
Anderson, Harold 125
Anzone, Adolphe 87
Appel, Charles 58, 99
Applegate, Glenn (Alfred Powers) 201, 203, 207, 210
Arbogast, Charles (Bad Eye) 180
Arnaz, Desi 236
Arnold, Geraldine 73, 77
Arnold, Hilda 73, 77
Arnold, Luther 73
Ash, Rose (née Baird) 31, 32, 72, 131, 132, 163
Ash, Wallace 30
Ash, William 30
Atlanta Federal Prison 37
Audett, James (Blackie) 62, 64
Austin, Brian 181
Aye, George (Mad Dog) 3, 36

Baby Face (TV series) 243
Badgely, Frank 28
Bailey, Harvey 3, 16, 17, 18, 19, 20, 23, 35, 38, 40, 42, 49, 52, 53, 54, 58, 61, 67, 69, 70, 71, 72, 75, 76, 78, 84, 113, 116, 127, 149, 169, 175, 177, 223, 225, 226
Baird, Beulah 29–30, 72, 131, 131, 163
Baker, R.N. 141, 168
Baker, Wimberly 201, 203, 207
Ball, Lucille 236, 237

Banghart, Basil (The Owl) 37, 38, 65, 70, 81, 93, 98, 99, 181, 222
Barber, Almon 206
Barker, Arizona (Ma) 2, 16, 17, 153, 154, 155, 156, 157, 161, 184, 233, 237, 241, 242, 243
Barker, Arthur (Dock) 2, 16, 17, 18, 71, 92, 106, 107, 139, 152, 153, 157, 163, 165, 166, 180, 191, 212, 219, 241
Barker, Fred 2, 16, 17, 86, 122, 153, 154, 155, 156, 157, 180, 181, 233, 241, 242
Barker, George 16, 211
Barker, Herman 16, 155
Barker, Lloyd 16, 17, 211, 220–221
Barker-Karpis gang 2, 16, 18, 19, 20, 34, 42, 44, 54, 70, 71, 72, 73, 81, 92, 99, 102, 122, 123, 124, 127, 147, 152, 153, 159, 164, 187, 211, 213, 236, 241
Barnes, Fred 205, 212
Barnes, George, Jr. 228
Barnes, Stephen 221, 228
Barrett, George 179, 189
Barrow, Artie 227
Barrow, Audrey 158, 160
Barrow, Blanche 2, 21, 68, 158, 160, 222, 226, 228, 241
Barrow, Clyde 2, 21, 22, 68, 71, 82, 84, 90, 91, 96, 101, 108, 109, 110, 111, 113, 121, 128, 131, 158, 162, 209, 211, 220, 223, 226, 227, 228, 231, 233, 241
Barrow, Cumie 158, 159, 160, 211, 226
Barrow, Elvin (Jack) 227
Barrow, Henry 211, 226
Barrow, L.C. 158, 159, 210
Barrow, Leon 228
Barrow, Lillian 228
Barrow, Marvin (Buck) 2, 21, 66
Barrow, Nell 227
Barrow gang 2, 21, 43, 60, 66, 67, 71, 82, 90, 92, 99, 101, 123, 128, 141, 158, 167, 224, 225, 243
Barry, Edith 179, 188
Bartholmey, Edmund 2, 191, 195
Barton, Murray 148
Bash, Thomas 51, 143, 161, 165, 168,
Bates, Albert 2, 20, 2325, 68, 69, 76, 220

265

266　Index

Baughman, Frank 171
Baum, James 132–133
Baum, Willis 106
Beatty, Warren (actor) 226
Bechtel, Lewis 40, 219
Becker, Jack 191
Becker, Laura 191
Becker, William 64
Behrens, William 26
Benge, Jim 80
Bentz, Edward 2, 20, 23, 33, 35, 70, 114, 189, 224
Bentz, Verna 189
Berg, Harry 118
Berg, Oliver (Izzy) 123, 157, 165, 166
Bergl, Joseph 73
Berman, Edward (Barney) 70, 76
Berry, Walt 52
Bert, Mollie 167, 195, 196
Berta, Charles 35
Bielaski, Alexander 8
Birch, Tyler 84
Birdwell, George 3, 31, 80
Blair, Albert (The Alabama Kid) 25
Blanchard, Harry 51, 141, 166, 174
Blease, Coleman 94
Bloody Mama (film) 241
Blumenfeld, Isadore (Kid Cann) 70, 76
Boardwalk Empire (TV series) 243
Boettcher, Charles II 37, 93
Bohn, Haskell 37
Boisenau, Eugene 105
Bolton, Ben 2, 186, 187, 220
Bolton, Vera 223
Bolton, William Bryan (Byron) 2, 152, 153, 157, 188, 191, 195, 223
Bonaparte, Charles 7, 8
Bonaparte, Napoleon 7
Bonnie and Clyde (film) 223, 226, 241
Bonnie and Clyde Ambush Museum 233
Booth, Ben 161
Borenstein, Herman 81
Bouchard, Bruce 118
Boyd, Percy 101
Boyle, Russell 163, 168, 173, 175–176
Bradley, Tom 232
Brady, Alfred 3, 181, 182, 183, 184, 185, 186, 188, 189, 190, 191, 194, 196, 197, 199, 202, 205, 206, 207
Brady, Robert (Big Bob) 40, 50, 54, 58, 67, 69, 70, 72, 78, 92, 113, 116, 174, 177
Brantley, Dwight 175
Bratton, Sam 179
Bray, Hal 56
Bremer, Edward 92, 99, 102, 123, 127, 153, 155, 156, 157, 159, 163, 166, 181, 185, 186, 187, 189, 193, 195, 232
Brennen, John 58, 72
Breuer, Anthony (author) 25
Bridgewater, Everett 26
Brock, Cecil 211

Brock, John 185, 188
Bronx Home News 10
Brooks, James 76
Brothers, Leo 90
Brown, Edmund 232
Brown, Louise 173
Brown, Ralph 120, 153
Brown, Stanley 35
Brown, Thomas (Big Tom) 42, 71, 124, 195, 221
Brunette, Harry 198, 243
Bryant, Frank 84
Bryce, Jacob (Jelly) 84, 85, 108, 120, 230
Buchalter, Louis (Lepke) 81, 217, 235, 237
Budlong, C.V. 89
Burdette, Wynonna 127
Burke, Curtis 30
Burke, Fred (Killer) 23, 24, 219, 223
Burke, Jean 114
Burns, Joseph (né John Heaps) 1, 27, 74, 147
Burns, William 9
Burns Detective Agency 169
Burrough, Bryan (author) 100, 115, 234
Butts, Edward (author) 62
Bybee, William Hilton (W.H.) 90, 96, 109, 158, 203, 204
Byers, Joseph 27

Caffrey, Raymond 45, 46, 47, 48, 50, 51, 52, 57, 59, 60, 61, 63, 160, 236
Cagney, James 164
Calhoun, J.R. 52, 242
Callan, Christopher 206
Cambrón, Gloria 215, 217
Campbell, Allen 113
Campbell, Charles (Jerry) 88, 108, 120, 153, 230
Campbell, Harry 2, 156, 157, 162, 163, 185, 188, 191, 193, 203
Campbell, William 101
Cannon, Robert 205, 212
Capone, Al 16, 25, 37, 43, 65, 67, 81, 90, 94, 103, 140, 153, 217, 235, 236, 243
Cargin, Frank 103
Carnes, Clarence 227
Carroll, Thomas 1, 33, 70, 79, 80, 83, 88, 97, 103, 106, 108, 109, 115
Carver, Perry 233
Casey, Will 78
Cassidy, Harold 107, 109, 114, 125, 128, 157, 181, 227, 239
Catlett, John 68, 77
Cavanaugh, Charles 97
CBS TV 239, 242
Central Park Gang 18
Century of Progress World's Fair 67, 72, 119
Cernocky, Louis 103, 104
Chait, Abraham 81
Chambless, James 158, 159
Chapman, Irvin (Charlie) 24, 65, 115, 131, 148, 196, 197, 201, 203, 209, 211, 217, 219, 220

Index

Chase, George 24
Chase, John Paul 1, 33, 79, 83, 88, 97, 100, 117, 119, 121, 125, 131, 143, 144, 146, 149, 159, 161, 222
Chase, Vivian 3, 24, 67, 181, 185
Cherrington, Patricia 99, 104, 105, 114, 119, 225
Chessen, Charles 4, 72
Chessen, Lillian 4, 72
Chicago Crime Commission 16
Chicago Herald Examiner 125
Chicago Tribune 90, 184, 238
Chitty, A.J. 226
Christensen, Carl 106
Christman, Earl 2, 19
Clanton, Newton (Newt) 80
Clark, James (Oklahoma Jack) 1, 27, 28, 34, 41, 54, 58, 67, 69, 74, 75, 78, 92, 95, 113, 116, 122, 157, 169, 177, 222
Clark, Lewis 205
Clark, Russell (Boobie) 1, 26, 27, 28, 29, 74, 82, 84, 88, 89, 130, 222
Clarrity, Phil 104
Clegg, Hugh 86, 104, 105, 106, 107
Cochran, Frank 164
Cochran, Louis 215
Cohen, Delos 118
Cohen, Emanuel 138
Coker, Sam 2, 180, 185, 193
Coleman, Cassey 73, 74, 78
Coleman, Frank (Weinie) 35
College Kidnappers 3, 25, 27, 80, 83, 87
Colorado State Insane Asylum 221
Colver, Merle 38
Colvin, Ralph 14, 53, 73, 80, 84, 85
Condon, John 10, 39, 128, 129, 150, 151
Confession (TV series) 225
Conkle, Arthur 133
Conkle, Ellen 134
Conn, Kenneth (Lewis Thagard) 40, 67
Connell, Doris 34
Connell, Emory 34
Connelly, Earl 115, 147, 153, 154, 189, 206
Conner, Lou 70, 72
Conner, Louise 177
Connors, Charles (Ice Wagon) 65, 81, 99
Conroy, Edward 95, 165
Cooper, Courtney 149, 234, 243
Cooper, Leslie 161
Cooper, Russell 3, 165, 184, 185, 186, 187, 220
Copeland, Harry 1, 67, 69, 72, 78, 82, 117, 222
Costner, Ike 98–99
Coughlin, Phillip 145
Coulter, Rufus 98, 206
Cowan, Ray 168, 169, 170, 171, 172, 173, 174, 175 176, 177, 178
Cowley, Samuel 87, 120, 121, 127, 130, 133, 138, 143, 144, 145, 146, 147, 160, 161, 219
Coy, Bernard 226
Coyle, Lelon 195
Craig, Elmer 202

Crawford, Broderick (actor) 213
Cretes, Jerome 125
Cretzer, Douglas 185, 226
Cretzer, Edna (Kyle) 207, 218
Cretzer, Joseph (Dutch) 4, 158, 187, 195, 198, 200, 201, 217
Crick, Francis 58
Criss, Vernon 206
Cross, Gilbert 119
Crouch, Hilton 1, 67, 69, 72, 83
Crowley, Thomas 205
Crowson, Joe 90, 116, 165
Cruce, W.C. 204
Cullen, Frank 124
Culligan, Michael 140, 178
Culp, Frank 108
Culver Bandits (gang) 27
Cummings, Henry 98
Cummings, Homer 11, 55, 70, 107, 117, 142, 195, 202, 203
Cunningham, Miles 153
Curtis, George 35

Dahill, Thomas 93
Daily Oklahoman (newspaper) 137
Dainard, William 167, 188, 194, 197
Daleo, James 163, 168, 172, 173
Dalhover, George 182
Dalhover, Rhuel (James) 3, 182, 183, 184, 186, 189, 190, 191, 194, 196, 197, 202, 205, 206, 212
Dalitz, Moe 188, 232
Darrow, Joseph 148
Daugherty, Harry 9
Davis, Alice 158
Davis, Edward (The Fox, Old Deafy) 3, 40, 41, 54, 58, 69, 75, 100, 117, 204, 205, 206, 212
Davis, James (actor) 236
Davis, Jeff 41
Davis, Malcolm 83, 131
Davis, Mort 15
Davis, Steve 158, 159
Davis, Volney (Curley) 2, 18, 34, 107, 157, 159, 166, 180, 188, 223, 240
Deadrick, Kelly 84, 85
Delaney, Dolores 115, 156, 162
Delaney, Jean 103, 115
Delaney, Philip 157, 159, 165
Delmar, Frank 92, 95, 113
DeLoach, Cartha 244
Denning, Homer 61, 62
Denning, Maurice (Morris) 61, 62, 64
Denning, Richard (actor) 213
de Paoli, Ralph (Phil Kelly) 149
DePuy, Richard 211
Desilu Studios 236, 237
Detective Story magazine 188
de Toledano, Ralph (author) 243
de Truffin, Mina 11
Devereaux, Walter 206
De Vol, Lawrence 18, 35

Index

Dickson, Ben (Johnny O'Malley) 209, 210, 211, 212, 214, 215, 216
Dickson, Stella (Sure Shot) 210, 211, 212, 214, 215, 216, 225
Dietrich, Walter 3, 25, 27, 34, 74, 87, 88
DiLillo, D. 133
Dillinger (film) 230, 241
Dillinger, Hubert 102, 103, 108, 115
Dillinger, John Herbert 1, 25, 26, 27, 28, 29, 33, 34, 43, 65, 67, 68, 69, 72, 74, 75, 78, 82, 83, 84, 88, 89, 90, 91, 95, 96, 97, 98, 102, 103, 104, 106, 107, 108, 109, 113, 114, 115, 116, 117, 118, 119, 120, 121, 125, 127, 142, 146, 149, 157, 181, 182, 184, 204, 211, 217, 225, 229, 236, 239, 240, 241, 242, 243
Dillinger, John Wilson 83, 226
Dillinger Museum 233
Dobkins, Jim 237
Docking, Robert 224
Doll, Edward 3, 20, 25
Dopson, Clifford 41, 42, 220
Dorsch, John 217
Douglass, Frank 67
Doyle, Eddie 71
Doyle, Jess 2, 157, 159, 164
Dresser, Louis 92
Duke, Richard 130
Dunbar, Edgar 32
Dunlop, Arthur 16, 19
Dunn, John 138
Durkee, Otto 40
Durkin, Charles 235
Durrill, Grover 35
Dyke, Stewart 133, 134

Eads, Bill 84
Earlywine, Joe 209
Eaton, Myrtle 180, 189, 194
Ebert, Roger 240
Eckert, Robert 4, 148
Edgar, J.M. 84
Edge, L.L. (author) 60, 61
Egan, James 141
Egan's Rats gang 22, 36
Eggebrecht, Henry 87
Eldridge, William 177
Elliott, Aussie 31, 32, 80
Ellis, Arthur 65
Espionage Act (1917) 8
Estill, Robert 90, 91, 95
Eye, Charles 82

Factor, Jerome 65
Factor, John (Jake the Barber) 65, 67, 70, 82, 93, 99, 232
Fanning, Myron (Mike) 48, 60–61, 64, 142, 143, 176
Fanser, Lila 221
Farland, A.C. (Gyp) 86
Farley, James 191
Farmer, Elmer 2, 156, 157, 164, 166, 191

Farmer, Esther 46, 56, 67, 70, 72, 173, 177, 223, 225
Farmer, Herbert (Deafy) 42, 46, 56, 67, 70, 72, 139, 149, 150, 172, 177, 220, 225–226
Farrell, Martin 3, 157, 161, 164, 185
The FBI Story 5, 234, 235, 236, 243, 244
FBI Story: The FBI Versus Alvin Karpis, Public Enemy Number One, The (film) 243
Federal Deposit Insurance Corporation (FDIC) 44
Federal Dick (film) 138, 164, 213
Federal Kidnapping Act (Lindbergh Law) 11
Feeney, Albert 69
Feinberg, Michael 91
Feldman, Clara 139, 147, 167
Feldman, Edward 139
Felton, Verna 173
Ferguson, Miriam (Ma) 91, 101, 157
Finch, Stanley 7, 8
Finerty, Ella 116
Finerty, William 116
Fisch, Isidor 129
Fisher, Charles 79
Fisher, Clara 152
Fisher, Jim 241
Fitch, W.H. 116
Fitzgerald, Percy (Dice Box Kid) 67
Fitzsimmons, Bob 146
Fitzsimmons, Juliette 146
Fletcher, Raymond 180
Flint, Sam (actor) 236
Fliss, Edward 188, 197
Flowers, Margaret 52
Floyd, Charles (Pretty Boy) 3, 29, 30, 31, 32, 44, 46, 50, 51, 53, 54, 57, 60, 61, 62, 71, 72, 80, 90, 99, 102, 113, 117, 122, 126, 131, 132, 133, 134, 135, 136, 137, 138, 140, 141, 142, 158, 168, 169, 170, 171, 172, 173, 174, 175, 177, 233, 235, 236, 241, 242
Floyd, Charles Dempsey 228
Floyd, Ruby 29, 227, 228
Flynn, William 8, 9
Forrestal, Clem 3, 46
Fox, John, Jr. 240
Fox, Joseph 28, 114, 147, 178
Fox, Peter (Charles Penders) 27
Fox Lake massacre 81
Fraley, Oscar 237
Francis, Joe 2, 158, 159, 228
Francis, Marie 158
Franklin, George 84, 192
Frasure, Eddie 226
Frazer, George 26
Frechette, Mary (Billie) 78, 82, 83, 88, 89, 95, 97, 98, 102, 103, 108, 119, 125, 189, 225
Frisch, Roy 100
Fritts, Robert 176
Frye, E.M. 165
Frye, Pauline 228
Fryman, Joe 132
Fulbright, Fay 196, 197, 203

Index 269

Fults, Ralph 2, 21, 157, 158, 159, 161, 162, 164, 167, 180, 193, 224
Fultz, John 132, 135, 137, 163, 170

G-Men (film) 164
Galatas, Elizabeth 130, 138, 150
Galatas, Richard 44, 45, 46, 72, 86, 87, 130, 138, 150, 172, 173, 177
Gandy, Helen 94, 95, 102
Gang Busters (TV series) 236, 242
Gann, Red 38
Gannon, Harry 104
Gannon, Tommy 124
Gant, Hugh 160, 187, 189, 206
Gant, John 160, 187, 189
Gator Joe's Beach Bar and Grill 233
Gault, Benjamin (Maney) 96, 109, 110, 230
Gehan, Mark 140, 179
Geiseking, Charles 184, 186, 189, 190, 191, 196
Gibson, Russell (Slim Gray) 3, 18, 152, 157, 206
Giggal, Mabel 101
Gill, Merle 59, 60, 63, 64, 99, 173, 174
Gallagher, William 144
Gillis, Helen (née Wawrzyniak) 103, 108, 121, 144, 146, 181, 186, 226
Gillis, Lester (Baby Face Nelson) 1, 23, 30, 32, 43, 70, 79, 83, 88, 97, 100, 103, 104, 106, 108, 114, 117, 118, 119, 121, 124, 125, 127, 131, 143, 144, 145, 149, 161, 164, 181, 217, 226, 241, 243
Gilmore, Dewey 3, 165, 184, 185, 186, 187, 220
Glass, George 31
Gleckman, Leon 42, 92
Goetz, Fred (Shotgun George Ziegler) 2, 18, 19, 54, 99, 153, 157
Goldstein, Grace 179, 189, 192, 193, 211
Goldstein, Sam 1, 29
Gooch, Arthur 141, 142, 148, 149, 165, 168, 178, 179, 194, 195
Goodfellow, Bob 42
Goodfellow, Lois 42
Goodling, Mrs. J.E. 48
Goodman, Leona 102
Goodspeed, Ervin 207
Gordon, John (Sharky) 203
Gordon, William 177
Gow, Betty 10, 150
Graham, Stephen (actor) 243
Graham, William 100
Grant, Cary 138
Graves, W.W., Jr. 143
Grayson, Ben 185
Green, Bessie 102
Green, Harold (Eddie) 1, 18, 70, 88, 97, 102, 108
Green, William 35
Greentree, Ethel 122
Gregory, Thomas 8
Griffin, William (Reddy) 42, 177
Griffith, Walter 170
Grooms, Albert 156

Grooms, William (Red) 45, 46, 47, 48, 55, 59, 64, 160, 175
Gross, Bill (Red) 102
Guns Don't Argue (film) 236
Gurnea, Myron 206
Gwynn, John 115

Hackett, James 25, 83, 87
Hall, David 133, 134
Hall, Harry (Tex) 164
Hamer, Francis (Frank) 91, 92, 96, 109, 110, 231, 241
Hamilton, Edythe (Polly) 114, 116, 118, 119, 125, 225
Hamilton, Floyd 90, 122, 184, 202, 204, 207, 209, 211, 212, 224
Hamilton, John (Red) 1, 26, 27, 28, 74, 78, 82, 83, 88, 103, 106, 122, 127, 180
Hamilton, Margie 225
Hamilton, Mildred 158
Hamilton, Raymond 2, 21, 90, 96, 97, 100, 101, 116, 120, 122, 157, 158, 159, 161, 162, 164, 165, 167
Hamm, William, Jr. 44, 67, 70, 71, 72, 81, 82, 92, 139, 153, 191, 194, 232
Hancock, Audrey 121
Hancock, Fred 108
Hanson, Paul 84, 85
Harding, Warren 9
Harfuss, Gustave 179
Harmon, Charles 35, 156
Harmon, Paula (Fat-Witted) 127, 156
Harper, Francis 64
Harper, William 66
Harris, Harold (Billie Woods) 41, 221
Harrison, William 2, 152, 157
Harrison Narcotics Tax Act 107
Hart, Brooke 81
Hartman, Al 83
Hartmann, Milton 4, 185, 187, 195, 198, 201
Hauptmann, Anna 228
Hauptmann, Bruno Richard 129, 130, 150, 159, 187, 190, 240, 241
Hayes, George 132, 133
Heady, Betty 186
Heady, Daniel (Dapper Dan) 3, 165, 184, 185, 186
Hebebrand, Arthur 203
Heidt, Ruth 152
Heist Brewing Co. 225
Helmer, William (author) 23, 131
Henderson, Frank 160
Henderson, Raymond 144
Henry, William (actor) 213
Hermansen, Hobart 143
Hermanson, Frank 45, 46, 47, 48, 55, 59, 60, 63, 64, 175
Hetzer, John 158, 201
Higgins, Tom 54, 139, 169, 171, 174, 175, 176
Hinton, L.J. 233
Hinton, Ted 83, 110, 231

Hoffman, Harold 187, 190
Hoffman, John 105
Hogan, Daniel (Dapper Dan) 42
Holbrook, P.B. 36
Holden, Thomas 2, 20, 35, 221
Holland, Walter (Irish O'Malley) 36, 165, 220
Holley, Lillian 90, 97, 98
Hollis, Herman 88, 120, 133, 136, 137, 143, 144, 160, 161
Homer, Leslie 82, 220
Hoover, John Edgar 9, 11, 13, 14, 16, 23, 43, 50, 54, 55, 56, 60, 63, 64, 67, 69, 70, 80, 86, 87, 93, 94, 95, 99, 101, 102, 104, 107, 109, 121, 127, 128, 130, 133, 134, 138, 140, 141, 142, 144, 146, 147, 149, 156, 161, 163, 164, 171, 178, 190, 192, 193, 198, 199, 200, 204, 213, 217, 219, 222, 229, 234, 235, 236, 237, 240, 241, 242, 243, 244
Hopton, Winfred (Bud) 133
Houser, Neal 68
Hovious, Charles 29
Howard, Rex 81
Hughes, Russell 3, 25, 80
Hulett, John 209
Humphrey, Henry 65
Hunsicker, Horace 156
Hunt, Alva 206
Hunter, Fred 2, 179, 185, 189, 193
Hunter, W.H. 34
Hurd, Everett 205
Hurt, Clarence 84, 85, 108, 120, 230
Hyde, Herbert 76

Indiana Department of Health 225
Indiana Reformatory 26
Indiana State Clemency Commission 70
Indiana State Police 69, 83, 184, 202, 204, 205, 206, 212
Indiana State Prison (Michigan City) 27, 28, 29, 67, 74, 75, 78, 82, 83, 100, 114, 147, 239, 241
Indianapolis Star 181
Industrial Workers of the World 13
Inman, Elmer 16, 84, 87
Irish O'Malley Gang 3, 36, 67, 161, 165, 178, 179, 184, 185, 192, 214, 220
Irwin, William 132
Israel, Lon 132

Jackson, Mary 221
Jackson, Maud 221
Jackson, Otto 179
James, R.H. 97
Jameson, J.D. (Red) 52
Jamie, Alexander 140
Jarrett, Walter 68, 80
Jenkins, Jack 140, 175
Jenkins, James 1, 67, 74, 75
Johnson, Arthur (Fish) 114
Johnson, Goldie 92, 116
Johnson, Joseph 206

Johnson, Lyndon 244
Johnson, Walter 147
Johnston, James 123
Jones, Eloise 177
Jones, George 223
Jones, Gus 54, 56, 60, 63,
Jones, Julius (Babe) 3, 25, 80, 83
Jones, Robert (FBI agent) 153
Jones, Robert (posse member) 180
Jones, William Daniel (W.D.) 2, 65, 66, 68, 71, 82, 91, 113, 131, 158, 159, 223
Jordan, Ben 237
Jordan, Henderson 96, 110, 128, 231
Joyce, Matthew 163, 164, 165, 166
Judiciary Act (1789) 7
Junior G-Men (film serial) 178
Junior G-Men of the Air (film serial) 178

Kahn, Howard 140
Kansas City Journal-Post 51
Kansas City massacre 45–64, 69, 70, 72, 80, 81, 84, 86, 127, 130, 134, 150, 220, 235
The Kansas City Massacre (film) 242
Kansas City Star 43, 50, 51
Kansas Highway Patrol 125
Kansas State Prison (Lansing) 17, 38, 39, 40, 41, 53, 54, 58, 61, 67, 69, 74, 92, 95, 113, 117, 122, 174, 219, 220, 221
Karpaviecz, Raymond 159
Karpis, Alvin (Old Creepy) 2, 16, 17, 18, 19, 20, 33, 44, 71, 86, 122, 127, 131, 143, 153, 156, 157, 162, 163, 179, 180, 185, 187, 188, 189, 191, 192, 193, 194, 195, 196, 198, 201, 203, 207, 209, 211, 213, 214, 223, 224, 242, 243
Kator, Albert 93, 213
Keady, George (Burrhead) 188
Keating, Francis 2, 20, 35, 223
Keeling, Earl 64
Kefauver Committee 56
Keith, Hale 97
Keith, John 95
Keller, Ella 24
Kelley, Ervin 30
Kelly, "Bull" 149
Kelly, Edward 80
Kelly, George (Machine Gun Kelly) 2, 19, 20, 21, 23, 25, 35, 68, 69, 71, 72, 73, 74, 76, 77, 79, 149, 221, 236, 237, 238, 240, 241, 243, 244
Kelly, Kathryn (née Lera Brooks) 2, 19, 20, 68, 69, 70, 72, 73, 74, 76, 77, 79, 96, 224
Kelly, Paul (actor) 213
Kennedy, Duff 38
Kennedy, John 232
Kennedy, Ludovic (author) 240
Kerr, George 84
Kessell, Albert 205, 212
Kidder, Theodore 100
kidnapping *see* individual victims by name
Killingsworth, William 44, 169, 170, 177
Kimes, Matthew 16
Kinder, Margaret 84

Index

Kinder, Mary 29, 84, 88, 89, 95
Kinkead, M.F. 93
Kirchner, L.R. (author) 51, 55, 56, 61
Kirkus Reviews (magazine) 149, 200
Klein, Nelson 179, 189, 219
Klutas, Theodore (Handsome Jack) 3, 25, 80, 81, 83, 87, 241
Knarr, Ralph 195
Koehler, Arthur 40, 150, 151
Koerner, Alvin 106
Korecek, Alex 43
Kozberg, Sam 70, 76
Kraft, James 35
Kronick, Sam 70, 76
Ku Klux Klan 5, 192, 235
Kuhlman, Mildred 152
Kunkel, Louis 74
Kyle, Arnold 4, 158, 185, 187, 195, 198, 201, 213, 217, 218, 226, 227

Labrizetta, Anthony 163, 180, 201, 203
LaCapra, Michael (Jimmy Needles) 55, 125, 150, 179
Lackey, Francis Joseph (Joe) 44, 45, 46, 47, 48, 50, 57, 59, 63, 64, 163, 174, 175, 177
Lamm, Herman (Baron) 27, 28, 33, 34
Landon, Alfred (Alf) 122
Landy, G.W. (Dad) 34
Lang, G.W. 106
Langan, John 3, 180, 185, 192, 196, 203
LaPorte, George 104
LaPorte, Lloyd 104
Larkin, Clarence 205, 212
Larson, Margaret 189
Laska, Ben 147, 167, 178, 189, 196
Latshaw, Ralph 163, 168, 169, 172, 176, 177
Lauer, Frank 81
"Lawrence, Jimmy" (John Dillinger alias) 118, 119, 120, 125, 239
Lazia, John 55, 56, 61, 119
Leach, Matthew 69, 78, 89, 120, 204, 230
Leavenworth prison 20, 33, 35, 55, 76, 86, 107, 122, 127, 139, 157, 158, 166, 169, 184, 186, 187, 189, 194, 196, 203, 204, 211, 212, 220, 221, 222, 223, 225, 237, 238
Lebman, Hyman 43, 80, 144, 170, 228
Legenza, Walter 3, 98, 114, 130, 148, 157, 158
Lehman, Herbert 130
Leitch, C.G. 175
LeRoy, Mervyn 235
Leslie, Harry 220
Levy, Frank 185
Lewis, Cecil 96
Lewis, Clarence 109
Liberty (magazine) 179
Limerick, Thomas 64
Lindbergh, Anne 10, 11, 241
Lindbergh, Charles, Jr. 10, 39, 93, 128, 129, 150, 151, 159, 231, 232, 240
Lindbergh, Charles, Sr. 10, 151, 241
Lindsay, Edward 191

Lindsey, Hugh 196
Lingle, Jake 90
Lininger, Harvey 92
Link, Samuel 52, 53, 71
Lipman, William (writer) 213
Little Bohemia Lodge 103, 104, 105, 106, 108, 118, 146, 232, 235, 236, 241
Little, Brown and Co. 149, 200
Liverpool Review (newspaper) 137
Lloyd, Jack (Tom) 84
Lockerman, Allen 184
Lockerman, Doris (Hinkley) 184
Loeser, Wilhelm 107, 109, 114, 121, 125, 128, 157, 181, 213, 239
Loftis, Harry 20
Logan, Kenneth 206
Long, Alice 64
Long, Opal 84, 88, 97, 114, 119
Longnaker, Mary 67, 72
Lovre, Curtis 211
Lovre, Dorothy 211
Lowall, Gene 62
Loy, Myrna 120, 235
Luce, Frances 35
Luer, August 67, 72, 178, 220
Lyons, Daniel 203

Ma Barker's Killer Brood (film) 241
Mace, Billie 122, 158
Mace, Frederick 228
Machine Gun Kelly (film) 241
Machine-Gun Man (book) 239
MacMillen, George 132, 133
Madala, John 153
Mafia 55, 56, 119, 229
Maginnis, Arthur 113
Magness, Louise 96, 107
Mahoney, William 42, 140
Mais, Robert 3, 98, 114, 130, 148, 157, 158
Makley, Charles (Fat Charlie) 1, 26, 27, 28, 74, 78, 82, 84, 88, 89, 95, 97, 130, 241
Marino, Anthony (Soap) 164
Marks, H.R. 141
Martin, Harry 205, 212
Martin, William (Ty) 212
Mathers, James 147, 167, 178
Mathias, Vivian 46, 58, 80, 81, 99, 138, 150, 172
Mattern, Helen 92
Mattix, Rick (author) 131
Maxwell, Bud 41
Maxwell, Richard 238
May, Clayton 98, 103, 108, 186
McAllister, Fred 119
McBride, Lillian 158
McCain, Rufus 212, 219
McCallum, R.G. 133
McCarty, A.H. 67
McCarty, Isaac 67
McClean, Evalyn 11
McCormick, Harry 161

272 Index

McCoy, Horace (writer) 213
McCoy, Robert 125
McDade, Thomas 88, 143, 153
McDermott, George 179
McDermott, Hugh 133, 134
McDonald, Cassius 127, 155, 185, 187
McElroy, Henry (Judge) 54
McElroy, Mary 62
McFadden, Eddie (Chicken) 66, 82, 83
McFarland, Herman 172
McGill, H.H. 124
McHenry, Roy 15
McKay, Jim 100
McKee, Sam 133, 153, 170, 171
McKeever, George 161
McKeever, Marie 114, 148, 157, 161
McKellar, Kenneth 192
McLaughlin, John 153, 157, 165, 166
McMahon, Earl 3, 87
McNeely, George 161
McNeil Island Penitentiary 217, 218, 223, 226, 227
McNutt, Paul 69, 79
Means, Gaston 11, 12
Melton, Virgil (Red) 3, 184
Melvin, T.H. 153
Melvin Purvis: G-Man (film) 243
Mencken, H.L. 150
Methvin, Henry 2, 90, 91, 96, 100, 101, 109, 110, 112, 128, 158, 159, 186, 241
Methvin, Ivan (Ivy) 109, 110, 227
Miller, Florence 122
Miller, Jack 3, 184
Miller, Parnie (Millikan) 46, 49, 59, 63
Miller, Vernon 17, 49
Miller, William (Billy the Killer) 31
Milligan, George 81
Milligan, Maurice 60, 131, 194, 196
Minneman, Paul 202, 212
Minnima, Howard 81
Mintun, Val 173
Missouri Waltz (book) 60
Mitchell, E.J. 106
Mohler, Clifford 1, 29
Montgomery, Glenn 133, 134
Moon, Arthur 134
Mooney, Buck 204
Moore, Bobbie 81
Moore, Eugene 90
Moore, John 41
Moran, Joseph 19, 107, 122, 127, 157, 180
Morgan, Janice (actor) 213
Morison, Patricia (actor) 213
Morris, Connie (Ruth Robinson) 179, 189, 193, 209
Morris, John 105
Morrison, Fred 169
Morrison, Ralph 64
Morse, Robert 26
Mortensen, Nels 97
Muchow, Arthur 169

Mudge, Dick 168
Muirhead, Jessie 225
Mulky, Lee 148
Mullins, Jimmy 90
Mulloy, Frank (Fritz) 46, 67, 70, 72, 95, 138, 150, 177
Mulvihill, Francis 108
"Murder, Inc." 81, 235
murders *see* individual victims by name
Murphy, Holloway 100, 101, 134
Murray, Edna (Rabbit) 34, 107, 157, 159, 161, 164, 180, 195, 222
Murray, Jack 34
Murray, James 1, 146, 217
Musiala, Anna 3, 67
Musiala, Michael 3,
Muzzey, Alexander 153

Naish, J. Carrol (actor) 213
Nalls, Rosser (Rusty) 98
Nash, Frances 46, 67, 72, 139, 150, 172, 177
Nash, Frank (Jelly) 2, 3, 34, 45, 46, 47, 49, 52, 54, 60, 62, 63, 177
Nash, Jay Robert (author) 238
Natalsky, Etta 121
Nathan, Harold (Pop) 67, 70, 94
National Firearms Act 116, 214
National Motor Vehicle Theft Act (Dyer Act) 8, 24, 33, 37, 71, 97, 149, 197, 219
NBC Television 237
Neel, Charles 74, 75
Negri, Joseph (Fatso) 1, 33, 117, 149, 161, 181, 220
Nelson, George (Baby Face) *see* Gillis, Lester
Ness, Eliot 236, 237
New Jersey State Police 10, 198
New York Times 200, 238
Newman, Jay 106
Newman, Thomas 195
Nichols, Lena 87
Nitto, Frank (The Enforcer) 37, 38, 107
Nix, Ambrose 142, 146, 148, 149, 168, 179
Nixon, Richard 229, 243, 244
Noel, James 223
Nordbye, Gunnar 108
Norris, Gerald 215
Norris, William (author) 240
Norris v. Alabama (court case) 169
Northern, Earl 26, 29
Norvell, Randol 67, 72
Notesteen, Edward 102

Oakley, Prentiss 110, 231
O'Brien, Martin 108
O'Connor, John 42
O'Dare, Mary 90, 96, 101, 122, 158, 160
O'Hanlon, David 132
O'Hern, Michael 163
"Ohio Gang" 9, 11
Oitcho, Christ 3, 72

Index

Oklahoma State Prison (McAlester) 40, 41, 44, 193, 230
O'Leary, Arthur 89, 97, 107, 109, 114, 119, 128, 181, 227
O'Leary, Martin 29
O'Malley, George (Mickey) 3, 36, 67, 161, 165, 178, 179, 180, 184, 187, 192, 220
O'Malley, William 88, 89, 95
Orr, Harry 53, 176
Osborne, Guy 202, 205
Owens, Rich 195
Ozark Mountain Boys gang 3, 36

Pabst, William 66
Pace, John 125
Paden, Preston 34, 190
Palmer, Alexander 8, 9
Palmer, Cal 195
Palmer, Joe 2, 90, 101, 116, 122, 123, 165
Paramount Pictures 138, 213, 231
Parente, Joe 33
Parker, Billie Jean 228
Parker, Bonnie 2, 21, 22, 68, 82, 84, 90, 91, 92, 96, 101, 108, 109, 110, 111, 113, 121, 122, 123, 128, 158, 162, 205, 209, 210, 220, 223, 226, 227, 228, 231, 233, 241
Parker, Emma 158, 226
Parker, Hubert 227
Parker, Paul 29
Parker Brothers Co. 178
Parman, Alava 51, 176
Parole Fixer (film) 213
Parsons, Louella 138
Patterson, C.C. 31
Patterson, Charley 132–133
Paulas, Theresa 121
Pawlowski, Joseph 118
Payton, Alvie (Sonny) 41, 67
Peeney, E.O. 143
Peifer, Jack 2, 124, 125, 191, 195
Perkins, Jack 2, 117
Perkins, James 73
Perrin, Howard 83
Perrone, Joseph 10, 129
Persons in Hiding (book and film) 200, 213, 214
Petschow, Robert 210
Phares, Louis 101
Phillips, Bernard (Big Phil; Phil Courtney) 2, 19, 20, 173, 177
Phillips, Orie 179
Pierpont, Harry (Pete) 1, 26, 27, 28, 29, 71, 74, 78, 82, 84, 88, 89, 95, 97, 130, 131
Pinkston, Joseph 233
Piquett, Louis 89, 90, 95, 97, 107, 114, 119, 125, 128, 157, 178, 189, 207, 227
Portley, Ed 67
Post Toasties "Law and Order Patrols" 178
Potts, Grover 132
Prather, Kirk 40
prison breaks *see* individual prison by name

Probasco, James (Cabaret) 107, 114, 121, 122
Prohibition 9, 16, 19
"public enemies" 16, 39, 87, 123, 149, 198, 225, 234, 236, 239, 240, 241, 242, 243
Public Enemies (film) 243
The Public Enemy (film) 164
Purple Gang 23
Purvis, Melvin, Jr. (Little Mel) 54, 67, 71, 87, 93, 94, 101, 102, 103, 104, 105, 106, 107, 119, 120, 121, 127, 128, 133, 134, 136, 137, 138, 141, 142, 145, 147, 148, 152, 163, 164, 166, 170, 171, 178, 184, 213, 229, 235, 237, 240, 241, 242, 243, 244

Queen of the Mob (film) 213
Quinn, Anthony (actor) 213

Raimondo, Josephine 197
Raimondo, Mary 197
Raimondo, Minnie 197
Rampendahl, W.F. 179
Ramsey, Langford 73, 74, 78, 124
Ramsey, William 209
Raney, William 73
Rap Sheet (book) 62
Rattner, Payne 221
Reed, Otto 44, 46, 63, 161, 174
Reeder, Arthur 206
Reeder, Don 195
Reese, Fred 3, 185
Reeves, Albert 194
Reilly, Albert (Pat) 1, 103, 104, 105, 117, 119
Reilly, Edward 150
Reppert, Eugene 54, 139, 176
Rera, Anthony 200, 201
Rera, George 200, 201
Ricca, Paul (The Waiter) 37
Rice, James 203, 204, 205
Rich, Joe 2, 163
Richetti, Adam (Eddie) 3, 31, 44, 60, 61, 72, 80, 96, 99, 102, 126, 131, 132, 133, 136, 137, 140, 141, 160, 161, 168, 169, 170, 172, 174, 175, 176, 177, 178, 210, 211, 236
Riley, Robert 3, 36
Riley, Walter (Irish O'Malley) 3, 36
Risler, Clifford 133
Rivers, Richard 191, 196
Roberts, A.L. 149
Roberts, Eric (actor) 243
Roberts, Harry 203, 204
Robinson, Andy 225
Robinson, Robert 133
Roe, Ralph (Raymond) 84
Rogers, Will 106
Rolph, James, Jr. 81
Roosevelt, Franklin 11, 44, 70, 107, 108, 203, 221
Roosevelt, Theodore 7
Rorer, William, Sr. 73, 102
Rose, E.E. 191
Roth, Herman, Jr. 133, 134

274 Index

Rowe, Truett 202, 205
Rusick, Mike 35
Russell, Ivy 36
Ryan, Mickey 84
Ryan, William 120, 143

Sadler, Louis 196
Sage, Anna (Cumpănaș) 118, 119, 120, 148, 184, 187, 192, 225
Saint Paul Daily News 140, 179
Saint Valentine's Day massacre 18, 24, 43, 100, 152, 153, 223
Salsedo, Andrea 13
Salt, Augusta 98, 103, 108
Salt Lake Tribune 53, 59
Salyers, Ansel 65
Sammons, James (Fur) 67
Sankey, Rio Verne 4, 36, 37, 92, 93
Sarber, Jesse 78
Sargent, George 163, 180, 201, 203
Sawyer, Gladys 127, 164
Sawyer, Harry (Dutch) 2, 92, 104, 124, 125, 157, 187
Sawyer, James (Frank) 3, 41, 42, 224
Scaduto, Anthony (author) 240
Scaramuzzo, Louis 43, 227
Schaefer, Gustav (Gloomy Gus) 66, 82, 83, 93
Schieffer, William 101
Schleuter, Elmer 116
Schlotman, Ed 92
Schmidt, Robert (Smoot) 82, 83, 113
Schoeppel, Andrew 220
Schroder, Grant 142
Schultze, Al 116
Schwarzkopf, Herman 10
Scorsese, Martin 236
Scott, Alvin 139, 147, 150, 167
Scott, Theodore 176
Seay, James (actor) 213
Sedition Act (1918) 8
Selective Service Act (1917) 8
Serpa, Salvatore 3, 122
Shaffer, Clarence, Jr. 3, 183, 184, 190, 191, 194, 196, 197, 202, 206
Shanley, William 83
Shannon, Armon (Potatoes) 2, 69, 76, 222
Shannon, Neil 204
Shannon, Ora 76, 224
Shannon, Robert (Boss) 2, 68, 76, 221
Sharkey, William (Wee Willie) 66, 82, 83
Sharpe, Violet 10, 150
Shaw, Earl 65
Shaw, William 1, 29
Sheen, Martin (actor) 243
Sheldon brothers (gang) 80
Sheppard, Bill 41
Shockley, Sam 226
Shoemaker, William 43
Short, Dewey 36
Short, George (Shock) 3, 36
Shouse, Edward 1, 28, 74, 78, 83, 221

Shuttleworth, Cecil 123
Silbert, Art (Abe Silver) 27
Silsbury, C.E. 205
Silverman, Alan (Al Silvers) 80, 81
Simmons, Lee 90
Simon and Simon (TV series) 239
Sinatra, Frank 237
"Six Daring Bandits, Inc." (gang) 180
Skeer, Thaddeus 26
Skelly, Clifford 70, 76
Slade, George 217
Smalley, L.C. (Blackie) 31
Smalley, W.A. 31
Smith, Chester 133, 136, 137
Smith, Earl 19, 58
Smith, Mrs. Earl 58
Smith, Frank 44, 45, 46, 47, 48, 50, 57, 84, 134, 172, 174
Smith, George 173
Smith, Leroy 177
Smith, Marion (Red) 26
Solomon, Jacob 118
Souder, Frank 3, 25, 80, 87
Southward, H.H. 34
Sparger, Clarence 3, 180, 192, 196, 203
Spear, Monte 45, 86
Spencer, Ethan Allen 35, 41, 214
Stacci, Louis (Doc) 46, 69, 70, 72, 139, 150, 177, 220
Stack, Robert (actor) 236
Stahley, Perry 118
Stamphill, Dale 212
Stanley, Harry 159, 161
Stanley, May 161
Stanton, Haley 158
Stark, Lloyd 64
Stedje, Mrs. Andrew 124
Steffen, Emil 115
Stein, Samuel (Jew Sammy) 35
Steve, Anna 167
Stewart, Charles 27
Stewart, James 235
Stone, Don 84
Stone, Harlan 9
Stratton, William 222
Stroud, Paul 87
Strubel, Thomas 225
Sturgis House Mortuary Museum 233
Suhay, Robert 201, 203, 207, 210
Sullivan, Daniel (Sully) 88, 91, 92, 120, 153
Sullivan, Joseph (Diamond Joe) 34
Sullivan, Philip 160
Suran, Raymond 54, 56, 57, 120
Sutton, Irene 148
Suydam, Henry 142, 143, 146
Swaney, Edward 191
Swofford, Wilma 173
Swolley, Gale 25, 80, 87

Tambini, Louis (Doc Bones) 164
Tamm, Edward 215

Index

Tamm, Quinn 99
Teapot Dome scandal 11
Ten Thousand Public Enemies (book) 149
Terrill, Ray 16
Thayer, Earl 35
Thayer, Steve (author) 42
Thompson, Irwin (Blackie) 122, 148
Thompson, Michael 225
Thompson, Miran 226
Thompson, William (Big Bill) 90
Thornton, Roy 205
Tichenor, J.C. 78
Time magazine 93, 136
Tindol, Fred 203
Tolson, Clyde 163, 192, 198, 229
Toot, William 130
Torsey, John 211
Touhy, James, Jr. 37
Touhy, Roger (The Terrible) 37, 43, 65, 66, 70, 71, 72, 81, 82, 83, 86, 90, 93–94, 103, 221, 222, 232, 242
Towne, Burt 115
Trainor, William 51, 125, 140, 141
Trant, Leo 81
Traxler, Roy (Pete) 203
Traynor, James 3, 36
Trenchard, Thomas 150, 159
Trendley, John 150
Tri-State Gang 38, 98, 114, 122, 130, 139, 148, 157, 161, 164, 185, 186, 237
Tribble, James 72
True Detective Magazine 220
True Story magazine 188
Truman, Harry 227
Turnbull, William 198
Turner, Harry 175
Turner, Michelle 52
Twelve Point Crime Package (1934) 107
Tyrell, John 150

Undercover Doctor (film) 213
Underhill, Frank 38
Underhill, George 38
Underhill, Hazel 84
Underhill, Wilbur, Jr. (The Tri-State Terror) 3, 38, 40, 42, 52, 54, 58, 67, 69, 70, 72, 75, 80, 84, 85, 113, 116, 177
Underwood, Tom 35
Unger, Robert (journalist) 62, 126
U.S. Army 15, 160, 220, 229, 231
U.S. Attorneys General 7, 8, 9, 11, 13, 55, 70, 107, 116, 117, 142, 190, 195, 202, 203, 235, 243
U.S. Congress: House of Representatives 108; Senate 108, 192, 219, 233, 240
U.S. Department of Justice (DOJ) 7, 9, 11, 55, 123, 138, 142, 149, 181, 191, 192
U.S. Forest Service 40
U.S. Internal Revenue Service 11
U.S. Marshals Service 7, 122, 184
U.S. Merchant Marine 220
U.S. Secret Service 7, 9
U.S. Supreme Court 9, 130, 169, 178, 179, 181, 186, 187, 209, 214, 222, 227
U.S. Treasury Department 7, 39, 91, 116
United States v. Miller (court case) 214
Universal Studios 178
Unsolved Mysteries (TV series) 237
The Untouchables: book 237; TV series 236, 242
Upton, Charles 181
Urban, William 25
Urschel, Charles 68, 69, 73, 74, 76, 77, 79, 96, 109, 139, 147, 150, 167, 178, 196, 213, 222, 224, 232

Valentine, Lewis 198
Vandenbush, Merle 198, 199, 200, 201
Van Ingen, Philip 10
Van Meter, Homer 1, 27, 28, 29, 33, 42, 70, 79, 88, 97, 98, 103, 104, 106, 107, 108, 109, 114, 115, 116, 117, 118, 119, 122, 124, 125, 148, 178, 189, 236, 241, 242
Van Valkenberg, Herbert 75
Vaughn, Norma 1, 67
Vaught, Edward 76, 77
Vetterli, Reed 45, 46, 47, 48, 50, 52, 55, 57, 59, 61, 63, 64, 67, 79, 163, 174, 175, 176, 229
Vidler, William 157, 165
Von Frantzius, Peter 43
von Lengerke, Oswald 43, 226
Voss, Helen (née LaPorte) 104
Voss, Phil 104

Wack, Larry 240
Wade, J.L. 112
Wagner, Eddie 3, 25
Wagner, Howard 118
Wakelin, Joseph 211
Waley, Harmon 166
Waley, Margaret 167, 178
Walker, P.E. 115
Wallace, Edward (Cowboy) 3, 122
Wallace, Jamie 179
Walsh, Gerald 230
Walsh, Thomas 11, 13, 243
Walsh, Walter 145, 153, 206, 230, 235
Walters, Ted 202, 204, 207, 209, 212
Waltz, Milo 211
Wanatka, Emil 103, 104, 106
Wanatka, Nan (née LaPorte) 103, 104
Ward, Alfred 219
Ward, James 25
Warner Brothers 164, 223, 236
Warren, Harry (Ned) 178, 179
Washington Herald 235
Waters, Sally 239
Waterson, Seth 73
Watson, James 58
weapons: Browning Automatic Rifle (BAR) 43; Colt "baby machine gun" 43, 44, 66, 106, 119, 144, 170; Colt Monitor 43, 144; Thompson submachine gun (Tommy gun)

14, 19, 42, 43, 45, 48, 51, 53, 54, 55, 59, 61, 63, 72, 76, 78, 82, 84, 102, 103, 108, 114, 124, 132, 134, 136, 137, 144, 153, 154, 155, 158, 168, 169, 173, 188, 192, 198, 202, 204, 205, 227, 241; Winchester Model 1897 shotgun 46, 62, 63
Weaver, William (Lapland Willie) 2, 157, 180, 187, 189, 195
Webb, Cindy 237
Webb, John 237
Weber, Frank 35
Weeks, Patrick 239
Weiss, William 139, 161, 186
Weissman, William (Solly) 61, 62
Wells, Henry 41
Wesley, Eudy 205, 212
West, Lottie 50, 51, 54, 60, 64, 141, 173, 174, 175, 176
Westberry, Mrs. A.F. 153
Weyerhaeuser, George, Jr. 165, 178, 188, 193, 197
Weyerhaeuser, George, Sr. 165
Whatley, S.J. (Baldy) 2, 158, 161, 211
Wheeler, Chal 179
Wheeler, Edward 100
White, James (Doc) 76, 77, 152, 153
White, Thomas 35
White, Truman 180
White Caps (gang) 29
White Slave Traffic Act (Mann Act) 8
Whitehead, Don (author) 234, 235, 243, 244
Wiard, Seth 171, 172
Wickersham, George 8
Wild, Harry 171
Wilentz, David 150, 151
Wiley, Frank 157, 161, 164, 186
Wiley, Roy 148

Wilkerson, Beatrice 148
Williams, James 157
Williams, Robert 165
Williams, Thomas (Tobe) 164
Williams, Winnie 20
Wilson, Homer 147
Wilson, Roger 161
Winchell, Walter 217, 235, 236
Winstead, Charles 108, 120, 121, 153, 229, 233
The Witness (TV series) 242
Woltz, Grier 120, 153
Woodbury, Willie 153, 154
Woods, Robert 49
Woodson, W.W. 40
Woolverton, Howard 20
World War I 36, 37, 42, 62, 69, 151, 152, 155
World War II 163, 220, 221, 223, 229, 231
Wortman, Nollie (Humpy) 35
Wyman, Alfred 217

Yale, Frankie 24, 43
Yankwich, Leon 217–218
Yeaham, J.A. 142
Young, Henri 212, 219
Young Dillinger (film) 241
Youngblood, Herbert 97
Yulin, Harris (actor) 243
Yurka, Blanche (actor) 213

Zarder, Carl 169
Zarkovich, Martin 119, 120, 231
Zeglen, Michael 225
Zeid, Charles 148
Zumbrunn, W.F. 192
Zwillman, Abner (Longy) 80, 81

www.ingramcontent.com/pod-product-compliance
Ingram Content Group UK Ltd.
Pitfield, Milton Keynes, MK11 3LW, UK
UKHW041929140426
5217IPUK00014B/382